BEHIND THE KAIJU CURTAIN
A JOURNEY ONTO JAPAN'S BIGGEST FILM SETS

NORMAN ENGLAND

Awai Books

BEHIND THE KAIJU CURTAIN

A JOURNEY ONTO JAPAN'S BIGGEST FILM SETS

NORMAN ENGLAND

Book design by Aoi Ota
ISBN: 978-1-937220-10-5

Awai Books

CONTENTS

FOREWORD
By Shusuke Kaneko

I first met Norman prior to the shooting of *Gamera 3: Revenge of Iris* when he was a reporter for *Fangoria* magazine. I'd already heard that my Gamera movies were well received in the United States and other countries. Still, it was my first time to be interviewed by a member of the foreign media in this way. As I talked about myself, I also taught him about Japanese history. We made jokes and, becoming friendly with one another, called each other "war enemies." It fit in with my pet theory that "Japanese monsters (kaiju) are influenced by war."

In 1989, my film *Summer Vacation 1999*, which is unrelated to kaiju, was invited to screen at the Telluride Film Festival in Colorado. The film was also officially selected for MOMA's New Directors/New Films program. Soon after, I directed a segment for *Necronomicon*, a horror anthology film, and for the first time, I worked in Los Angeles. During the production, I stopped by a bookstore and, while browsing through the foreign film section, found a book with an entry on *Summer Vacation 1999*. It was listed with a turkey mark. I understood what this meant and was disappointed to the point that I felt like crying. However, later on, when *Gamera: Guardian of the Universe* received a "thumbs up" from a highly respected film critic in the US, I was giddy with happiness.

Norman's article in *Fangoria* included color photos and was very long and in-depth. I couldn't have been happier. A year later, in 1999, Norman and I traveled to Hollywood together for the international premiere of *Gamera 3* at the Egyptian Theater. When the scene of Shibuya being destroyed came on, I was astonished at how vocal the audience was with its excitement. Quite the opposite, Japanese people are incredibly docile when viewing movies. Norman also took me to the Fantasia Film Festival in Montreal. It was thanks to him that I made friends with a lot of "war enemies."

In return, I took Norman to Tsuburaya Productions monster storage facility, which was within walking distance of my house, and over to Toho Studios where the new Godzilla film, *Godzilla 2000*, was being shot. At the time, I never thought I'd be able to direct a Godzilla movie. Of course, I always wanted to. However, in 2000, the following year, I unexpectedly received a call with the offer to direct a Godzilla film.

My dream had come true. Norman came to the set throughout production and created "The Norman Report" for Toho's website that was read by online fans in Japan. This book includes many stories from this production and this era in general.

Thanks to Norman, I now have many friends in America and, likewise, he made many friends in the Japanese movie industry while covering kaiju movie sets.

This book includes not only the many personal memories we forged together and his coverage of *Godzilla, Mothra and King Ghidorah: Giant Monsters All-Out Attack* (GMK for short), which I directed in 2001. But the book also documents the point of contact I had with American culture. The truth is, America is really the window for cinema if a movie hopes to reach around the world.

In 2000, the Godzilla series wasn't doing well, and Toho was considering terminating the franchise. If GMK had not done well at the box office, we wouldn't have the Godzilla boom we have now. I hope my "war enemies" will be kind enough to allow me this modicum of bragging rights.

FOREWORD
By Ed Godziszewski

As with most kids of my generation, I had a fascination with all things dinosaur. My prized possession was a set of dinosaur figures with which I staged endless pretend battles against a set of army men. In the summer of 1963, as this dinosaur-loving 9-year old sat in the Portage Theater in Chicago watching trailers for next week's movie fare, you can imagine my reaction when a trailer for *King Kong vs. Godzilla* came on the screen…as Godzilla appears, I'm thinking, "Wow! This is the greatest dinosaur I've ever seen!" And when his fins glowed and he shot his atomic breath, little did I realize that I was about to embark on a lifelong journey into the world of Japanese monsters.

My appetite for science fiction and monster cinema remained strong as I grew older. Still, looking back on those days, movies from Japan always held extra appeal to me. I never consciously thought about where they came from, I just knew I enjoyed them. I'd experience an extra rush of excitement whenever Godzilla's name appeared on the marquee or came up in the TV listings. My love for these films and especially the character of Godzilla only increased over time. The look and feel of these films were special, sparking a desire to learn more about them. But in the '60s and '70s, there were virtually no sources of information on Godzilla in the US—if you were lucky, there would be an occasional article in *Famous Monsters* and maybe an isolated photo here and there in books on science fiction film history.

My big break came in *Famous Monsters* number 114, the all-Japanese monster issue in which I found an ad for Greg Shoemaker's seminal fanzine *Japanese Fantasy Film Journal*. At last, a publication dedicated to my favorite films! It was through JFFJ that I was able to build a network of friends around the world who enjoyed this genre as much as I did. This eventually led to some pen pals (yes, people actually used to communicate by writing letters by hand and sending them by mail) located in Japan. And, in turn, this led to my first visit to Japan in the summer of 1979, allowing me to expand my network of friends and realize that there were sources for learning how these films were made. Over the next 20 years, I started researching and writing articles on Japanese SF and began publishing my own fanzine, *Japanese Giants*. Then, in the mid-90s, I authored the privately published book *The Illustrated Encyclopedia of Godzilla*.

Throughout this time, despite my limited success in researching and writing about Godzilla, deep inside I felt I was still coming up short. Learning how these films were made through written sources and the handful of interviews I was lucky enough to conduct, I was still barely scratching the surface. My information was mostly second or third hand and was further filtered through the inherent haze of being translated from another language. And if I learned anything from my dealings with the Japanese, it was that there was a mountain of cultural barriers to climb that made a true understanding of the what's and why's of Japanese film production difficult to penetrate. I often wondered what it would like to be part of one of these productions, to really understand the industry and the nature of the people working on these films, to accumulate anecdotes about the nuances of the set. And I endlessly daydreamed about my innermost secret desire…to actually climb inside a Godzilla suit and experience, even if for just a minute, what it would be like to *be* the King of the Monsters. But I knew that was impossible.

I sorely lacked the necessary language skills, and I certainly didn't have the nerve to abandon my ordinary existence and try such an ambitious plan. Fortunately, there is someone who had not only the skills, ambition, and incredible drive to pull off such a feat, he also the will to share that experience with the world. The book you are now holding in your hands is Norman England's amazing account of achieving everything that I could only dream about.

When I first met Norman at G-Fest 99 in Burbank, I only knew of him from several articles about his experiences in Japan, including his great set report for *Gamera 3*. He was at the convention together with director Shusuke Kaneko, so I have to admit that I was rather intimidated to meet him. He lived in Japan, visited the set, and was friends with the director of one of my favorite films. Even though our meeting was brief, we exchanged information and planned to get together the next time I visited Japan for business. Norman lived in Osaka, where my company was headquartered, so it was an easy plan to make. At the time I had no English-speaking friends in Osaka outside of my company, so I looked forward to taking a break from the usual week of doing business in fractured English. Still, I couldn't help but feel nervous—Norman was a well-known figure in fan circles by now, seemed to be pretty well-connected in the film world, a former New Yorker, and spoke Japanese. Not being much of a conversationalist, I hoped it wouldn't be an awkward meeting. Within 5 minutes of meeting him at Shinsaibashi Station, my fears were put to rest. He was friendly, approachable, and had plenty to say about most any topic—myself being more of a listener than a talker, it was actually an ideal situation. Aside from him wowing me with pictures he took from *Godzilla 2000*, we mostly talked about everything other than Godzilla. It was probably my most relaxed and at-ease time of that trip. After this, we struck up a correspondence by email and our friendship grew.

Not too long afterward, Norman decided to move to Tokyo to be closer to the Japanese film industry. And after the release of *Godzilla vs. Megaguirus*, when Shusuke Kaneko was tapped to direct the next Godzilla film, the stage was set for Norman to do what no outsider, Japanese or not, has ever been able to do—become an insider on a Godzilla production from start to finish. The summer of 2001 was an exciting one for me as well. Daily, Norman kindly sent me detailed reports of his experiences, often accompanied by incredible photos. Indeed, many of those emails have served as the record upon which the GMK portion of this book is based. Those were amazing days as I was able to vicariously experience the production through Norman's insightful eyes. Now, you the reader have the same chance to do so. I am also eternally grateful to him for arranging access to the GMK set for two Saturdays in the month of June 2001, sharing his experience first hand for a couple of days. That time is indelibly etched in my memory.

So, sit back and get ready to enjoy an incredible ride through the world of Japanese film production, narrated with wit and candor by a keen observer, one of the most entertaining yet informative books you will ever read.

ACKNOWLEDGMENTS

Directly and indirectly, a great many people helped to make my experience during the years covered in this book possible. My heartfelt thanks to all of you.

In the West:
Ed Godziszewski, Patrick Galvan, Tony Timpone, Michael Gingold, Steve Ryfle, Bill Gudmunson, Richard Pusateri, George A. Romero, Anthony Ferrante, Matthew Chozick, Mark Schilling, Mark Obert, Bob Johnson, Andre Dubois, Eric Lavoie, Daniel Mann, Rad Silla, Sean Linkenback, Tom & Diane Dougherty, Robert Troch, Buce Robertson.

In the East:
Mitsuo Abe, Nozomu Aida, Hideo Amamoto, Hideaki Anno, Reo Anzai, Kenichi Eguchi, Ayako Fujitani, Kakusei Fujiwara, Toshikazu Fukawa, Kenichi, Hiromi Fukuzawa, Hiroyuki Futami, Michio Hamano, Tomoo Haraguchi, Shinji Higuchi, Hideyuki Honma, Shizue & Hico Horie, Yukijiro Hotaru, Miho Iizuka, Yasuyuki Iizuka, Masato Inatsuki, Midori Inoue, Yoko Itakura, Hideaki Ito, Katsuhiko Ito, Ayumi Kageyama, Shu Kageyama, Yuji & Aya Kaida, Nobuaki Kakuda, Jiro Kaneko, Shusuke Kaneko, Nanako Kaneko, Shizue Kaneko, Suzuyuki & Yurina Kaneko, Mizuki Kanno, Shinsuke Kasai, Yoshiyuki Kasuga, Shingo Katsurayama, Takahiro Kawada, Yuseey Kawakami, Koichi Kawakita, Yuichi Kikuchi, Masahiro Kishimoto, Tsutomu "Tom" Kitagawa, Hisataka Kitaoka, Maki Kobayashi, Masahiro Kobayashi, Tsuyoshi Kobayashi, Katsuya Konno, Yuu Koyama, Katsuhiko Kudo, Makoto Kumazawa, Mitsuyuki & Yuki Kushitani, Ai Maeda, Aki Maeda, Kamiya Makoto, Takahiko "Taki" Mamiya, Shiniichiro Masuda, Hajime Matsumoto, Tomohiro Matsumoto, Takayuki Matsuno, Takashi Matsuo, Izumi Matsushita, Wataru Mimura, Kaho Minami, Kaori Momoi, Kishu Morichi, Hideaki Murakami, Takehiro Murata, Masami Nagasawa, Toshiyuki Nagashima, Takeo Nakahara, Haruo Nakajima, Yukie Nakama, Takayuki Nakashima, Takayuki Nakashima, Shinobu Nakayama, Chiharu Niiyama, Shinji Nishikawa, Takashi Nishina, Takashi Nishina, Masayuki Ochiai, Akira Ohashi, Nobuko Ohmachi, Hidefumi "Jimmy" Ohnishi, Hiroshi Okamoto, Takao Okawara, Chika Okura, Yuki Omori, Rie Ota, Hiroko Otani, Kow Otani, Rosie Otani, Toshimasa Oura, Hariken Ryu, Kaoru Saito, Morihiko Saito, Teiichi Saito, Shiro Sano, Shimako Sato, Daisuke Sato, Yuriko Sato, Kenpachiro Satsuma, Toshifumi Shimizu, Taihei Shimoi, Fuyuki Shinada, Yuri Sugano, Kohei "Thunder" Sugiyama, Kenji Suzuki, Hiromi Suzuki, Kiyotaka Taguchi, Eisho Taira, Isao Takahashi, Kenji Takama, Masaaki Tezuka, Toru Tezuka, Nobuko Tomita, Shogo Tomiyama, Miike Toshio, Masaru Tsuchiya, Akihiro "Tony" Tsujikawa, Norio Tsuruta, Ryudo Uzaki, Shinichi Wakasa, Hiroyuki Watanabe, Akiko Yada, Takuya Yamabe, Senri Yamazaki, Mizuho Yoshida, Tetsuya Yoshida.

Family members and friends:
Carter & Barbara England, Stuart England, Miyako Cojima, David Chess, Billy Flink, David Lachow & any friends lost in time that loved Godzilla with me during our formative years.

NOTES ABOUT STYLE

Movie titles appearing in the text are written first with their international English title, followed by their transliterated Japanese title and Japanese release year in parentheses. This information is included at the first mention. After this, just the international title is used. For example:

> *The War of the Gargantuas* (*Furankenshutain no Kaijū: Sanda tai Gaira*, 1966)
> After this, it becomes: *The War of the Gargantuas*.

When a film is mentioned within a quote, this information is not included. Also, for western films, only the title appears. This formatting applies to the main text and not the book's introduction.

Complex is the long and colorful history of Godzilla titles and the English spellings of Toho's giant monsters. Part of the blame for the inconsistencies can be leveled at Toho Studios for not being particularly hands-on with their films when they were first released in the West. However, the situation was rectified in the 1990s when Toho tried to rein in these inconsistencies by creating an official list of title names and monster name spellings. Do I adhere to this updated list? Yes and no. Why? It's because I spent much of my life calling Godzilla's tenth film *Godzilla's Revenge* and not *All Monsters Attack*. The same goes for certain monster names, such as Gimantis, who nowadays is officially known as Kamacuras. Ultimately, if readers disagree with the use of outdated tiles/names, they are welcome to file it under, "You can't teach an old dog a new trick."

Recurring movie titles in the text are abbreviated. Although the abbreviation is noted when a title first occurs, I've organized them here for quick reference:

G1 - *Gamera: Guardian of the Universe*
G2 - *Gamera 2: Attack of Legion*
G3 - *Gamera 3: Revenge of Iris*
G2000 - *Godzilla 2000*
GXM - *Godzilla vs. Megaguirus*
GMK - *Godzilla, Mothra and King Ghidorah: Giant Monsters All-Out Attack*

Several Japanese words and expressions appear in the text. Some are italicized, some are not. Common words such as "kimono," "kaiju," "otaku," "sushi," etc., receive no italics. Words less common to Japanese non-speakers receive italics.

Japanese names appear in westernized order, with given (first) name first and family (last) name second. In the text (like in real life), I call Japanese by their family name as this is how the Japanese refer to each other. For example, sculptor Hiroshi Sagae is Sagae in the text, which is what I called him in real life. The only time I ever heard him called Hiroshi was by his non-Japanese friends. (I've tried to help some westerners understand this but they seemed unable to get past the thinking that calling someone by their family name is something out of high school gym class.)

Still, there are situations where even the Japanese refer to their fellows by their given names. For example, Isao Takahashi, an art director on the Godzilla series, was known around the set as Isao. GMK lead Chiharu Niiyama was called Chiharu by the upper staff while GXM star Misato Tanaka was called Tanaka. As best as I could figure, this was done when a family name was too ordinary or if their given name somehow fit their personality and status better. A person's full name is given when they first appear in the text. After this, they're referred to either by their given or family name.

Two abbreviations appear frequently in the text: SFX (special effects) & VFX (visual effects). The difference between these two terms escapes a lot of readers. Let me explain: SFX are made and executed on the set. SFX can involve prosthetic makeup, creature suits, miniature explosions, animatronics, and puppetry. VFX can come into play in tandem with SFX but is generally thought of as effects created (or manipulated) outside the set and in post-production. The integration of CGI into live-action shooting is a good example of VFX.

Finally, although I'm not a fan of referring to kaiju as "he" or "she," pronouns such as these are certainly more accessible than the emotionless "it." I refer to every giant monster as "he" except for Mothra, who is regarded here as a "she."

Now, a word about this: The idea of Mothra being female is a Western contrivance. I have yet to see Mothra denoted as female in Japanese print. Decades ago, American fans got it in their heads that Mothra is a "she" and have considered "her" female ever since. While I don't subscribe to this thinking, I decided to go with the female gender for Mothra in the text. I suppose the reason for this is that, as stated above, "it" feels too impersonal (even though Mothra is an insect), and there's something about Mothra that just doesn't feel masculine. I don't think this affects the text either way, but I thought it necessary to mention.

INTRODUCTION

A sweltering noonday sun has the tar in front of Toho Studios' Stage 9 baked to the point it's soft to the touch. As the large steel doors of the special effects stage swing open, a welcome blast of air conditioning gushes out. From within the cavernous interior, crewmembers wheel out a flatbed cart. Bolted to it is a harness jury-rigged from steel pipes, clamps, and chains. Suspended within and propped before me is Godzilla, the King of the Monsters. I run a hand under his jaw and gaze into ghostly white eyes. They stare back at me, an American on the cusp of realizing a childhood dream. Stepping onto the cart, I mimic Yoshida-san, the Godzilla suit actor I've been carefully observing over the past several months of filming.

I grab an overhanging bar and, feet first, hoist my body into the Godzilla suit. The spaces for my legs are tight; I have to fight to get my feet to the bottom. Leaning my torso in, I work my hands into Godzilla's arms. Finally, I place my face against a headrest and my chin on a pad glued to the inside of the throat. Hooks securing Godzilla to the hanger are released. All at once, the suit's weight joins with my own. Stepping forward, we become one. We claw the air wildly. We tilt our head skyward. With all our might, we roar!

Sounds like the daydream of any giant monster fan anywhere, no? In my case, it was as well, but it was a daydream I brought to life through perseverance, hard work, and out-and-out ballsiness. The book you hold is the tale of how I made this—and much more—happen as I traversed the exciting and (literally) explosive landscape of Godzilla and Gamera productions in Japan. But the story starts much earlier and stretches back to when I was a boy and first fell in love with Japan's towering behemoths.

Like most four and five-year-olds, my worldview was limited to my immediate surroundings and what I gleaned off TV. That I shared the Earth with a couple billion people spread across nearly 200 nations was mostly lost on me. Although many of the cartoons I watched at the time—*Tobor The 8th Man*, *Kimba the White Lion*, *Gigantor*—were Japanese creations, the characters' vaguely Caucasian features and the English dubbing masked their origin. However, as live-action productions, Godzilla films were another story. Cities within their celluloid frames were rife with billboards that blazed with unreadable text; countryside villages were dense with porcelain tile-roofed homes; and, of course, the actors themselves were unmistakably Japanese. Not only was there no hiding their origin, but the Japaneseness of these films was as attention-grabbing as the monsters themselves. Through these films I began to realize that a larger world lay beyond the confines of my neighborhood.

When asked about this Japan place, my dad talked about his stint in the US Marines during World War II. Stationed on Midway Island, he was part of the decisive Pacific battle. Years later, when telling him I'd be moving to Japan, the land of his one-time enemy, I wondered what he'd say. True to character, he was supportive, and deep down, I think he enjoyed the irony. Upon hearing the news, he remarked, "If anyone had said in the heat of the Battle of Midway that I'd have a son who'd move to Japan, I'd have told them they were nuts!"

A jazz musician turned college professor, Dad shared an episode with me that took place shortly after WWII: Decked out in his marine uniform, he was lunching with my grandmother and great-grandmother in the restaurant of a popular hotel in Salt Lake City. Adjacent to the restaurant was an area with games, the kind you shoot wood balls into holes. A couple of Japanese boys were playing there, which caused unrest among the white patrons. This prompted callouts to my dad.

"Hey, Marine! What'cha gonna do 'bout them Japs?" a few yelled out.

My dad stood to his imposing 6ft 3in height and responded, "By god, I will do something!" He walked over to the quivering boys, put his arms over their shoulders, and said, "Let's play a game."

Not being of the war generation, I associated Japan with fun. How could I not? The war had been over for twenty years. *Ancient history*! To a boy in Rockland County (a suburb of New York City) in the '60s, Japan was simply a land of giant monsters and cool-looking miniatures. I wasn't alone. Come school Monday I'd be dissecting the weekend's TV viewing of *Destroy All Monsters*, *Son of Godzilla*, or *Rodan! The Flying Monster!* with my closest classmates. We gave these films a level of attention our teachers wished we'd applied to our studies.

But boyhood fancies fade, and my affection for giant monsters waned when I turned to rock and roll in the mid-'70s. My rediscovery of Godzilla came a decade later with the New World Pictures release of *Godzilla 1985* (aka *The Return of Godzilla*). Premiering in Japan a year earlier in '84 under the title *Gojira*, it was the first Godzilla film from Toho Studios in nine years. *Gojira* rekindled Japanese domestic interest in Godzilla, which sparked an avalanche of merchandise: Japanese manufacturers Bandai, Yamakatsu, Takara, Beetland, etc, began producing a wealth of Godzilla toys, figures, trading cards, stickers, magnets, clocks, toilet paper dispensers, you name it; Godzilla started popping up as a product spokesperson (spokesmonster?) in domestic TV commercials and print ads; Japanese publishers flooded the market with books chock full of eye-catching stills from Godzilla films.

Getting hold of Japanese goods at this time was no easy task. I don't mean the stock of cars, TVs, cameras, and countless electronic goods Japan developed to elevate itself out of wartime devastation. I'm talking about the neat stuff: the books, toys, and videos exclusive to Japan. At the time, there were no established importers or vendors that licensed Japanese films, TV shows, and character goods. There was no Media Blasters, no VIZ Media, no Arrow Video, and no Funimation.

Fortunately, I'd moved to nearby New York City, where at sci-fi conventions I could find Japanese pop merchandise brought over by enterprising individuals who'd made the long flight to Japan. They hand-carried VHS tapes, laserdiscs, model kits, and other items back to the US to sell at sizable profits. For those of us thirsting for things Japanese—in my case, things Godzilla—it was the only game in town.

Looking through the Godzilla books I acquired at these conventions, I became fascinated by the behind-the-scenes photos that cropped up throughout them. Before this, I'd never considered what a giant monster production was like. But seeing the sets, the rafters peeking out from the top of photos, the wires running to the various suits, and the crew giant-sized in everyday clothing against miniature buildings or helping suit actors in and out of the monsters set my imagination ablaze. What must it be like to be there, next to the crew, watching Godzilla go through his moves?

From this reawakened curiosity in Godzilla grew a general interest in Japan. I studied the language and read up on its history. The influx of nouveau riche Japanese in New York exposed me to their ways and customs. It was a wonderful time that culminated in my first trip to Japan: three weeks in the fall of '90 spread across Osaka, Kagoshima, Nagoya, and Tokyo. The success of this trip paved the way for my move in '92.

Relocating to Japan (Osaka) was a bold decision. I had little idea what I'd do once getting there. I was a college dropout whose passion had been rock and roll. In fact, until then, my whole adulthood was gambled on "making it" in music. I was playing with a group that had been clawing its way up for years until, out of the blue, our drummer left just as everything was coming together. With the band gone, my tether to the US was severed.

Luckily, my native language is, at this point in history, used for international communication. So, as many Japanese people living abroad support themselves by making sushi, many Americans in Japan earn theirs by teaching English. Finding this type of work was easy enough, but it wasn't what you'd call moving up. After a while, monotony set in; I found myself questioning why I'd given up the exciting life I had in New York City.

Taking action, I started hanging out at what I lovingly referred to as "nerd outlets," places in Osaka that catered to fantastic cinema: hobby shops, movie poster outlets, and film events. Even if my Japanese wasn't up to snuff, I chatted up everyone I met and eventually created my own circle of like-minded pals.

A great passion of mine has long been the films of George Romero, in particular, *Dawn of the Dead* (1979). Through my new-found friends, I came to the attention of Osaka-based game maker Capcom, who flew me to L.A. to cover the production of a Romero-directed TV commercial for their upcoming *Biohazard 2* (aka *Resident Evil 2*) video game. It was a gig that would alter the course of my life.

A chance meeting on the set led to my becoming involved with *Fangoria*, the legendary horror cinema magazine. I was quickly recruited as their Japan correspondent. This led to my coverage of Japanese movie sets, notably the "Millennium Series," the name given to six Godzilla films produced between 1999 and 2004.

Which brings us to this book: my bid to share the exciting and highly personal story of what it took to get myself onto the Godzilla sets and what I experienced once I did. What follows is the first and only detailed description in English of not just life on Japanese giant monster film sets but of life on Japanese film sets in general.

When first conceiving this book I thought to make it a straight "behind the scenes" guide detailing how giant monster films are made in Japan. While not a bad idea, friends I shared correspondence with urged me to find an approach that would take advantage of the personal inroads I'd made with the filmmakers and the hands-on experience I had with the productions. Mulling it over, I began to see that half the story was the journey. Finally, I concluded that a narrative in a diary format would be the best way to share the adventure and convey the daily life of the Japanese film set. In fact, all the entries are culled from emails I wrote at the time—many written on the studio floor during productions—that have been combined with notes I kept and my own recollections of events.

Despite the Godzilla-centric nature of the text, this book is as much about Japan's people as it is about giant monsters. It probably goes without saying that the Japanese interact socially and professionally in ways that are at times baffling to those of us raised in the West. Although I'd been living in Japan several years before setting foot onto one of their productions, I was unprepared for what was to come. I've tried my best to reflect the learning curve I underwent and haven't retrospectively edited out some of my more naïve perceptions and actions. In this way, I believe that my stories and observations, my triumphs and foot-in-the-mouth moments, will unmask the atmosphere of movie sets in Japan, the kind of people who make films in Japan, and the role the culture plays in molding the films themselves.

While many people helped in the creation of this book, no one has been more significant than director Shusuke Kaneko, who befriended me at the start of my reporting career. He repeatedly went out of his way to see that I was treated fairly by the industry and given the set access I sought. Without Kaneko-san's help, neither my journey nor this book would have been possible. I will always be in his debt.

Norman England
Tokyo, 2021

BEHIND THE KAIJU CURTAIN
A JOURNEY ONTO JAPAN'S BIGGEST FILM SETS

ENTRIES
The Beginning

I'm in Los Angeles, neck-deep in the production of *Biohazard 2* (BH2), a TV commercial for the upcoming survival horror zombie game. Inspired by George Romero's living dead trilogy, *Biohazard* (*Resident Evil* in the west) was such a hit that, for its sequel, game maker Capcom has gone the extra mile and hired Romero to direct its TV commercial. My involvement resulted from two pages I wrote on Romero's *Dawn of the Dead* for a laser disc set released in Japan two years ago. Capcom feels they need a "Romero expert" on the shoot, which means I get an all-expenses-paid trip to L.A. and the experience of working side-by-side with Romero.

Lumped in with the Capcom bigwigs, I'm not a moment off the plane before being rushed through an endless string of meet-and-greets, location checks, and production conferences. This culminates in a two-day shoot that—with the first day clocking in at twenty-seven hours—feels more like an experiment in sleep deprivation than a film production.

But who's complaining? The sheer amount of one-on-one time I'm putting in with Romero (top of my "filmmakers I'd most like to hang with" list) is worth the loss of a few nights of sleep. Working with a 1.5-million-dollar budget, Romero describes the thirty-second commercial to me as "the most money I've had on a second-by-second basis." How much of this budget is making it into the production is debatable. Every night, the production elite (with me along for the ride) dine at the fanciest restaurants L.A. has to offer, running up bar tabs as if another go at prohibition is just around the corner.

3

The commercial is being filmed at Lincoln Heights Jail, a former prison that closed decades ago but has since found life as a shooting location for movies, commercials, and music videos. I arrive a little before sunrise on the first night. Burly guys with faded arm tattoos and chronic beer guts are unloading several large production trucks. Cameras, cables, and lights are everywhere.

Romero arrives. We say hello. More precisely, Romero says, "How's it goin', man?" After five years in Japan, it's nice to hear someone call me "man" again. Since the extras are busy being made up as zombies (by Japanese makeup artist Screaming Mad George) and the production staff has its hands full setting up equipment, I ask Romero if it would be all right to do an interview.

We find a couple of canvas chairs to sit on. One is low to the ground. The other has a seat so high you'd have to pull yourself up to sit in it.

Oh, man. Out of professional courtesy, I'm going to have to offer him the tall chair. But at a towering 194cm (6ft 3in), he's already a giant. This will make him tall to the point that I'm going to break my neck looking up at him.

"Look," he says, pointing to the taller seat, "why don't you take this one? I'll take that one."

I laugh. He must be a mind reader.

As the sun sets and a cloudless LA sky fills with stars, I spend a fun hour chatting away with Romero. I ask questions not only about the BH2 production but also personal ones I've had for years about *Dawn of the Dead*. All the while I'm looking down on him as if I were a bird perched on a tree branch.

At last, preparations are done and the commercial is ready to roll. Romero is called to the set. I tag close behind. First

up are interiors of zombies stumbling about the prison halls. A few hours later, the production moves to the front of the jail. A police car is set on fire. Romero calls, "Action!" A dozen zombies grope the air and converge on the entrance now made up to look like the "Raccoon City Police Department," the starting location in the game. The entire time, I'm snapping photos and hanging at Romero's side.

At one point, Romero calls for a stopwatch. No one has one. Thinking quickly, I take off my G-Shock wristwatch and pass it to him.

"Cool, man," Romero responds as I show him how to use its stopwatch feature. And, as if this isn't enough to blow my mind, following one amazingly juicy zombie take, Romero turns to me and asks: "So, Norman... Whada'ya think?" How in the world can I respond? Romero is the master. It would be like John Lennon asking for an assessment of a song he'd just written.

The commercial stars Brad Renfro, a young actor enjoying a streak of popularity in Japan. Before coming out, I watched *The Client* and *The Cure*, his two most popular films. Brad and I forged a bond immediately, our common ground being a love of bands such as The Ramones, Led Zeppelin, and The Clash. During breaks in the shoot, we hum guitar riffs, testing each other's musical knowledge. At the wrap party, Brad is led around to thank the staff. When he gets to me, he stuns the Japanese by throwing his arms around my neck and embracing me firmly. I'm touched. We wish each other well.

During the shoot, I meet Anthony Ferrante, a writer for *Fangoria*, the world's leading horror cinema magazine. He mentions two things: He needs set photos for his article on the Romero commercial, and *Fangoria* is looking for a Japan-based writer. As soon as I get back to Osaka, I plan to contact their office in New York to see if I can land some writing work. After all, I've been reading the magazine since issue #9, and am as up on genre films as anyone. Who knows? It could turn out to be just the thing I've been looking for to bring purpose to my life in Japan.

10 DECEMBER 1997

My wave of articles on the BH2 TV commercial has hit the stands. Of them, my favorite is a six-page piece in a hobby magazine called *Figure-O*[1] (*Figure King*). The *Fangoria* editors have been responsive, too. They published several of my set photos[2] alongside Ferrante's article. One of my shots even became the cover image! I've taken *Fangoria* up on their first assignment and will travel next week to Tokyo to interview a film director named Shusuke Kaneko.

Unsure who Kaneko is, I ask my friend Michio Hamano, a self-confessed movie "otaku" (Japanese term for a fan obsessed to the point their interest supersedes normal life activities). Michio and his brother Akio live in a ratty apartment in North Osaka, the upkeep of which they have forsaken in favor of laser disc and video cassette purchases. Their living room is floor to ceiling with laser discs, videotapes, and theater program books. Against a wall is a large 32-inch monitor that feels more like an altar to cinema than a TV set.

"Don't you know?" Michio responds. "Kaneko's the best director making genre films in Japan today."

I'd seen Kaneko's *Gamera: Guardian of the Universe* (*Gamera: Daikaiju Kūchū Kessen*, 1995) and its sequel *Gamera 2: Advent of Legion* (*Gamera 2: Region Shūrai*, 1996) but that's it. Michio suggests the vampire comedy *My Soul Is Slashed* (*Kami Tsukitai*, 1991) and *Summer Vacation 1999* (*1999 Nen no Natsu Yasumi*, 1988), an odd, fantasy-esque film in which actresses play high school boys.

The Romero interview was the first one I'd done in my life. Even though it went well, I still feel that interviewing is new territory for me. I'm also worried about my Japanese ability. Of course I can speak day-to-day Japanese, but this is an entirely different level. To cover my ass, I plan to go with Nobuko Ohmachi, a woman I befriended at my English teaching day job. A fan of fashion designer Yohji Yamamoto, Nobuko walks around like a lost '80s runway model, dressing in baggy blacks marked by odd folds and sharp cuts. She's friendly, agreeable, and volunteers to be my "gal Friday," helping with translations and whatnot.

Another friend, Reo Anzai, has set up the Kaneko interview with Tsuyoshi Kobayashi, his contact at Daiei, the studio that produces the Gamera franchise. Reo is a guy who's turned being otaku into a business. A notable writer on Japanese heroes, Godzilla, and figure collecting, his work appears in many otaku magazines. Reo is also one of the leaders (if such a word can be used) of Japanese *Star Trek* fandom. We met three years ago and forged a writing partnership. Although we don't always see eye-to-eye, he's been a decent friend. Reo says he has to be there for the Kaneko interview.

---

1 - *Figure-O*, #140, October 1997
2 - *Fangoria* #171, April 1998

"It's my contact. I'm responsible for things going smoothly," Reo insists. I voice my objections, to which he responds to by telling me I need to learn more about "the way things work in Japan."

If you ask me, I just think he wants to meet the director.

16 DECEMBER 1997

Planning to arrive in Tokyo at a reasonable hour, I'm at Shin-Osaka Station, looking to board the 6:18 a.m. Shinkansen (bullet train). Despite the early hour, the station's bustling with businessmen in near-identical dark blue suits. Finding Nobuko amongst the throng is a chore, and we make the train with mere seconds to spare.

Twenty minutes later, as the morning sun breaks over the distant mountain ridges, we glide into Kyoto Station. I spot the five-tier pagoda of Toji temple jutting between some modern buildings. Japan's capital until 1869, Kyoto was spared from air raids during the war by a few level-headed higher-ups in the Truman administration. Because of this, Kyoto retained its centuries-old structures.

A minute later, we're pulling out of Kyoto and speeding through the Japanese countryside, where the morning sun heats the ceramic roofs of rural homes, causing long pillars of white steam to rise like strands of fine silk into the morning sky. Three hours later, we arrive at Tokyo Station.

My first time in Japan's leading city in years, it's as I remember: endless rows of uninspired, shoebox-like buildings, attention-grabbing billboards, and confusing streets that intertwine like spaghetti. After transferring to a local train line, we arrive at Chofu Station. We cab it from here to Nikkatsu, where our interview with director Kaneko is scheduled to start at 12:30 p.m.

One of the oldest studios in Japan, Nikkatsu has a long, rocky history. During the '50s and '60s, it produced many of the nation's highest quality films until the industry crash in the early '70s when foreign films, i.e., Hollywood fare, usurped the domestic market. Following this, Nikkatsu relied on a genre known as "Roman Porno"—exploitation films featuring soft-core sexual situations—to pay the bills.

The road leading into Nikkatsu slopes down to a guard booth. To its left is a large, fading mural depicting the Edo period of Japanese history. If this has anything to do with filmmaking it's lost on me. Beyond this lie the airplane hangar-like sound stages of the studio. After signing in at the booth, we set off in search of the cafeteria, the plan being to meet Reo there.

As we walk the studio grounds, I notice a sound stage that has its large doors swung open. I can't resist the urge to take a peek.

Inside, a model fighter jet hangs by a barely visible wire over a highly detailed miniature village. Arched behind and stretched across most of the back wall is a photorealistic mural of a blue sky dotted with white, wispy clouds. Written on a production plaque at the entrance is the word "Ultraman." Less impressed than me, Nobuko tugs on my sleeve and points to her watch.

Entirely run down, the Nikkatsu cafeteria is little more than a collection of wobbly tables that look as if they haven't been moved since the early '70s.

Deeply wrinkled women, their heads topped with white bonnets, dish out dark brown curry from industrial-sized aluminum pots to a line of tired-looking men. I'm thinking how like the set of a prison film this is when I spot Reo at one of the tables.

"Kobayashi isn't here yet," he says as I sit across from him. "I'm going out to look for him."

No sooner does he leave when director Kaneko walks in.

"That's him!" I say to Nobuko. I run over and catch him with another man, who turns out to be Kobayashi.

Kobayashi speeds off to search for Reo, leaving Nobuko and me alone with Kaneko. Unfortunately, I can't say it goes well. As I'd noticed watching "behind the scenes" Gamera videos, Kaneko often wears a grave, half-interested expression. If this is a result of his position or his personality, I've no idea. I attempt to explain what I hope to achieve in the upcoming interview. Still, no matter how much I speak, he says nothing and simply offers tiny head bobs that come across as mere acknowledgment of having heard what I've said.

Soon, Kobayashi returns with Reo. As he's introduced to Kaneko, Nobuko whispers that I might be talking too much.

Kobayashi leads us to a building where we settle into a windowless meeting room. Wasting no time, I get my cassette recorder running and start the interview with a question about *Necronomicon*, a US horror film Kaneko directed a segment for in '94. I mention that I worked on the BH2 commercial with Screaming Mad George, the LA-based Japanese special makeup artist who also did *Necronomicon*'s makeup effects. I'm betting on this to establish a link between Kaneko and I. It doesn't. He doesn't care one way or the other.

To impress him with my knowledge of kaiju, I mention that my favorite Toho monster film is *The War of the Gargantuas* (*Furankenshutain no kaiju: Sanda tai Gaira*, 1966). Kaneko merely cites it as the film he had in mind when starting the Gamera series. I ask why he chose to become a director. He replies that he simply enjoys film. Given his bland answers, I'm beginning to question if I have what it takes to be an interviewer.

Deciding to try a different approach, I turn away from Kaneko's personal history and instead ask about the movie industry in Japan. Kaneko perks up. He takes care to clarify the difference between moviemaking today and in the '50s, considered to be Japan's golden age of cinema.

"In those days, there was a feudal relationship between director and crew," he explains. "The crew was slave to the will and whim of the director and the cost of labor was cheap. These days, salaries have risen, and the staff has more of a say in things. Today, the director's role is not to dictate but to manage. Many people want to compare then to now, but it's impossible. The systems are entirely different."

When preparing for the interview, I discovered that Kaneko had earned a degree in teaching before seeking work in the film industry. Sure enough, like a teacher, his most enthusiastic responses come when he's imparting knowledge. Thinking quickly, I rephrase my prepared questions to play up their historical connections. For example, rather than ask about his work as an AD (assistant director), I ask him about the studio system at the time. Kaneko tells of a film industry in the '80s struggling to regain a footing and the hardships newcomers such as himself had to endure.

Growing talkative, he returns to a previous question. "Didn't you mention *The War of the Gargantuas*? When I sat down with scriptwriter Kazunori Ito, we both had films we wanted to model Gamera after. Mine was *Gargantuas*, and Ito's was *King Kong vs. Godzilla*. Ito liked the idea of separate monsters brought together. I disagreed as I felt this only augmented the non-reality of the film. It's hard enough for the audience to buy the existence of one monster, let alone two. In the end, however, we went with Ito's approach as this fit with Daiei's wishes."

Kaneko tosses a few stingers the studio's way. "Daiei requested we make Gamera responsive to children like the series was in the '60s. Throughout post-production, they kept reiterating this. It was annoying. I felt it was a naïve approach, as children alienate the adult audience. Ito, too, felt it would be impossible to maintain Gamera as the friend of children, but putting him on good terms with humankind was doable. By creating a high school girl character, I threw Daiei off-balance. They finally came around and saw that our idea worked in the film's favor."

Things are now cooking. Kaneko answers questions fast and furiously. He's laughing and enjoying himself so much that I feel I could ask him for his PIN number and he'd give it to me. At the one-hour mark, Kaneko excuses himself to go to the bathroom. Kobayashi, who has sat quietly in the back, stirs enough to announce that the interview will have to end soon. When Kaneko returns, we jump back in and go at it for another hour.

At one point, Kaneko's expression changes. I turn to catch Kobayashi, his arms up in the air and crossed in an X shape, which is the Japanese way of indicating "no good."

"They've come all the way from Osaka," Kaneko snaps. "I have the time." Kobayashi looks embarrassed.

I eventually run out of pre-written questions. Kaneko seems disappointed. I come up with a few more, but in all honesty, I'm worn out. We've been at it for almost three hours, and the Japanese language doesn't come as easily to me as I'd like. Feeling I've more than enough material for a decent article, I call the interview to an end.

Stepping outside, Kaneko pulls Kobayashi aside and whispers in his ear. A moment later, a surprised Kobayashi says that the director wishes us to join him in the adjacent studio to view scenes from his new film. He calls this request unprecedented.

I'm led into a studio with a large mixing console. Upon seeing Kaneko, the staff stand and bow. Before taking a seat facing a large movie screen on the opposite end of the studio, Kaneko orders them to run a reel. He motions for me to sit in the chair next to him and explains that his new film is called *F* and that today is prep for the sound mix. He shows me a five-minute dance sequence.

Nothing like his Gamera films, *F* is a love story featuring Tetsuya Kumakawa, a renowned ballet dancer. After the lights come up, Kaneko asks what I think. It's the last thing I expected. Moreover, he looks anxious, like my opinion matters. I rattle off a few comments that he seems to take to heart.

Nobuko shifts her eyes to Kobayashi lurking by the door. Taking the hint, I tell Kaneko that we need to get back to

Osaka. As we shake hands, he invites me to the set of the upcoming *Gamera 3*[3] production.

The train ride home gives me time to sort out the day. It went much better than expected. However, Reo gives me a hard time.

"You should have been mindful of Kobayashi," he reprimands me. I'm unsure of his point. "This is Japan. When a representative from an office tells you what to do, you do it."

I counter that Kaneko made the interview go on as long as it did.

"That's because he's a creator," continues Reo. "Creators are pure. It's the job of the office to maintain both their purity and keep the schedule. I'll have to apologize to Kobayashi."

As the nighttime landscape rolls past, I consider Reo's words. It's true, I'm an outsider with much to learn, but his thinking seems excessive. If I'd listened to Reo, I'd have traveled all this way for a brief interview that, at best, would have yielded a collection of shallow remarks. It's at this time I decide that should I continue with this work and ally myself with someone, better the creative people than the office staff.

2 FEBRUARY 1998

Pleased with my Kaneko piece, *Fangoria* quickly assigns another. This time, they've asked I interview the two men synonymous with Godzilla suit acting: Haruo Nakajima and Kenpachiro Satsuma.

Nobuko and I leave for Tokyo on a Sunday, so no swarms of businessmen clamoring for Shinkansen seats. Still, we take the earliest train possible as the first interview is set for 11 a.m.

The three-hour ride offers more than enough time to stretch my legs, have a bite, drink (crappy) coffee, and review the day's questions. The weather is impeccable—blue skies with wispy, pure white clouds—making the view out the window a distraction. Agreeable fishing villages pass by in all-too-quick flashes. Living in Osaka, I don't spend much time in the rural areas, so the Japanese countryside's sights are a welcome part of the Shinkansen experience. But the view I'm anticipating most is the drive-by Mt Fuji, Japan's iconic active volcano, which is briefly visible during the ride's last half-hour. Coming into view, Fuji sits in the not-too-far distance; its snow-capped peak stands tall against a sea-blue sky. I pull out my camera and take a few shots to impress friends back home. Almost immediately, a run of smoke-belching factories cuts into the view. The contrast is a perfect representation of the dichotomy between nature and industry that exists in Japan.

Still, Fuji is just the kick I need to energize me for the interviews ahead. For fans of giant monsters, the world's most symmetrical volcano holds great affection. It was the site of the quintessential kaiju battle. Here, a dozen monsters led by Godzilla took on the three-headed King Ghidorah in *Destroy All Monsters* (*Kaijū sōshingeki*, 1968). Haruo Nakajima, whom I'm on the way to interview, played Godzilla not only in this but in most of the films beginning

---

3 - At this time there was no agreed-upon English title for *Gamera 3*. In fact, when talking to SFX director Shinji Higuchi during production, he asked for my thoughts on using *Gamera 3: Incomplete Battle*, as that was a title they were knocking around. As I didn't know the story then, I wasn't able to offer an opinion.

with the first one in '54—when the suit was so heavy all he could do was drag it a few meters. He continued into the '70s, by which point the suit had become lighter and offered more freedom.

In those later movies, Nakajima played Godzilla with the skill of an experienced circus performer, employing just the right touch to impress and enthuse children worldwide. As Godzilla, he'd raise his arms high in the air before an attack, suggesting the importance of taking on the world with confidence. Even for something as mundane as walking forward, Nakajima would hold Godzilla's elbows up, infusing the suit with a type of kinetic energy. Other times, he'd just claw Godzilla's belly for laughs.

Kenpachiro Satsuma brought a more mature performance to the table in the '80s and '90s. His Godzilla was serious and somber. Pulling his elbows in tight, Satsuma would tunnel his energy into Godzilla's hands. Palms facing out and fingers bent forward, he'd sway Godzilla's paws side-to-side as he stormed through any one of a dozen Japanese cities.

While there have been eight Godzilla actors to date, these two are the ones who define suit acting. Nakajima and Satsuma are as important to kaiju fans as Peter Mayhew and Anthony Daniel are to *Star Wars* fans.

The first interview is with Satsuma. Following his instructions, we take several trains and a bus from Tokyo Station to Seijo, a town on Tokyo's west side. He requested we meet at his dojo. As much as I'm looking forward to meeting the men who climbed into the Godzilla suit, I'm also looking forward to setting foot in a real martial arts dojo.

Stepping off the bus, I crane my neck about. I'm on the lookout for a building large enough to house a room filled with stern-looking men in white *keikogi* (or *gi* in the west) grunting out karate chops before a row of floor-to-ceiling mirrors. You know, like in *The Karate Kid*. But there is nothing remotely resembling this here. We're on the side of a road next to a bridge with a shallow river trickling beneath. The only buildings I can see are off in the distance.

Then, a weird, wobbly structure across the highway comes into view. A shanty of mismatched wood beams, corroded aluminum sheets, and a blue tarp carelessly tossed over the top, the place is so frail in appearance that it looks as if something as innocuous as the backfire from one of the cars whizzing by will cause it to crumble to the ground.

To my surprise, Satsuma emerges from this architectural nightmare. He's waving wildly and has a big grin on his face. Nobuko and I shoot across the street. Extending an oversized, Frankenstein-like hand, Satsuma bids us welcome to his private dojo.

A fence about two and a half meters high surrounds the compound. Yet, the gate leading in is only half that. We have to stoop to get in. Satsuma fastens the gate behind us by hooking a loop of wire over a rusty nail.

The inside is as peculiar as the outside. Mildewed blankets take the place of a lawn and in an open yard are items of dubious origin, including one of those curved mirrors found on Japanese roadsides to help motorists see around tight bends. In the center, a tall wood pole pokes up from the ground.

"I pound my bare fists against it," Satsuma boasts. "Builds stamina." From here, he leads us to a hut off to the right.

Inside, a fire smolders in a recessed

area surrounded by fraying tatami mats. Amateurish drawings of Satsuma in fierce battle poses hang on a wall; beside them are several samurai swords that, on questioning, he admits are replicas. As for Satsuma himself, he's dressed in a torn jacket and wears blue polyurethane jogging pants deeply stained with grease.

After tossing a few sweet potatoes on the coals, Satsuma pulls out some cushions. He drops them near the flames and motions for Nobuko and I to sit. Smoke pours from the fire and quickly envelopes us. Nobuko does her best not to cough as I fight back the tears. To call the scene surreal would be an understatement. I just spent five hours on various modes of transportation and am now sitting around a roadside campfire about to conduct an interview with what looks more like a homeless man than the actor who played Godzilla between 1984 and 1995.

Despite my initial apprehension, the interview turns out to be a blast. Satsuma is accommodating and forthcoming. Best of all, all he wants is to talk about Godzilla.

"Godzilla has had a profound effect on my life," he starts. "I'm proud of having played him and enjoy talking about the experience."

I ask what the most challenging part of portraying Godzilla was.

"People think it's dealing with the weight of the suit. It's not. It's about emoting. This is difficult because Godzilla's face is unchanging. Instead, one must feel with every inch of one's body. Still, just moving the Godzilla suit is a task. For this reason, instead of making the suit match my movements, I made my movements match the suit."

It must look as if I don't understand because Satsuma instantly takes to his feet. He hunches his shoulders and assumes a fierce crouch. Rolling his head, he lets out a deep roar. Shooting out his hands, he claws the empty air.

"*This* is the *Satsuma* Godzilla!" he shouts with pride. His movements are so precise and done with such conviction that I actually see the Godzilla suit around him.

Satsuma volunteers to demonstrate his ability at *Jigen-ryu*, a form of Japanese martial arts that originated around 1600 in Kagoshima, the place of his birth. He brings us back outside, where he grabs a long wood stick from the yard.

"*Jigen-ryu* is an attack and destroy style," he explains. "It is the basis of my Godzilla." Taking a deep breath, he lets out an unexpected, ear-piercing scream. In a flash, he's smacking the stick repeatedly against the pole in the dojo's center. The stick erupts in a spray of splinters that showers both Nobuko and me.

Gathering the wood remains, Satsuma carries the larger pieces back into the hut. After throwing them on the fire, he squats with straightened back before the once again billowing smoke.

"By being Godzilla, my mental prowess has increased," he explains with eyes transfixed on the growing flames. "Small things no longer bother me. Some have played Godzilla and stopped halfway; others have only made it through a single film. They have no claim to say they played Godzilla. It takes at least five films to master the monster."

Although this meeting rates high on my list of weird encounters, and while I could spend the entire day listening to whatever comes out of Satsuma's mouth, it's nearing 2 p.m., the time we're scheduled to meet Nakajima. Fortunately, he lives only a few minutes away.

Satsuma offers to take us to Nakajima. Squeezing sideways, I mind my coat lest it catch on the barbed wire wrapped around the so-called dojo's entrance. Out front, I see another of those bad drawings of Satsuma, which he now tells me he drew himself. I also notice that he doesn't lock the place.

"No need," Satsuma explains. "This is Japan. People do not steal." I have to wonder if there is anything worth stealing.

Walking through the suburban neighborhood, I ask if the local kids ever acknowledge that he played Godzilla.

"Never," he replies, trying his best to act as if my question hasn't hurt his pride.

We aren't twenty meters from where we plan to meet Nakajima when Satsuma announces that this is as far as he'll go and that he has to get back to his workout. I figured he'd want to say hello to Nakajima, but I sense an uneasiness on his part. We say goodbye and I shake those large hands of his once more.

Nobuko calls Nakajima on the phone. Five minutes later, he comes strutting down the road. Like Satsuma, he holds out a hand in welcome; unlike Satsuma, he greets me in English. Switching back to Japanese, Nakajima suggests we go to a nearby café for the interview.

After my experience with Satsuma, I'm ready for more Eastern mysticism channeled through Godzilla. Diving in headfirst, I ask Nakajima to explain his philosophical approach to the inner spirit of Godzilla. Nakajima draws his eyes tight.

"The inner spirit of Godzilla? What are you talking about? I was a stock actor at Toho assigned to the role. When Godzilla came around, there was no precedent, not even the concept of suit acting. How could I see it as anything but a job?"

Looking him over, I wondered why I wasn't more astute. Like most 60-year-old males in Japan, he's balding, is dressed in drab clothes, and wears unfashionable, wire-rim glasses. Nowhere is there anything to suggest that there is something spiritual about him.

However, as the series progressed, didn't a sense of Godzilla, like an extension of himself, develop? Nakajima laughs.

"We were a team. Acting like a prima donna would have been disrespectful to the crew. I was known around the Toho lot for not complaining. I believe this is why I was asked to play Godzilla in the first place. For a film called *Eagle of the Pacific*, I was the first actor set on fire in Japan. Even though I could have, I didn't make much out of it. Ishiro Honda, who also directed the first Godzilla, directed it. I think he remembered this about me when *Gojira* began production."

Nakajima begins to reminisce and talks about his start in the film industry.

"My first film was *Stray Dog* by Akira Kurosawa. He was strict. He asked everyone to be an extension of himself, saying that they should know how he feels. If anyone made a mistake or didn't understand him, he'd tell them to leave the set. I often played a samurai in his films. This is why I liked playing Godzilla. I was always getting killed in samurai films. In Godzilla films, no one ever killed me!"

In total, Nakajima played Godzilla twelve times. Did he have a favorite performance?

"No. They were all great! Godzilla started out very serious, but as the series proceeded it got less so. I liked both the serious and the silly Godzilla as they offered different challenges. In the end, it was all about expressing Godzilla's feelings through body movement. This is what I think is lacking in new Godzilla films. Today it's just about walking from A to B. I don't want to say they don't try their best, but I disagree with what suit actors are doing these days."

Although Nakajima stressed his team player credentials, a strong sense of pride boils under the surface. It shows itself when we talk about Eiji Tsuburaya, the legendary special effects director.

"Tsuburaya didn't speak a lot and was very flexible. He didn't even have anything to say when it came to how to play Godzilla. He just waved a hand and said, 'I leave it up to you.' I went to the zoo to study how animals move, mostly bears. I got a lot of inspiration from bears. So, you see, how to perform Godzilla? That was me! *Me!*"

Near the end of the interview, I pull out my DSC-F1, a camera recently released by Sony that takes digital photos. It's incredible to see pictures right away on the rear screen. I show Nakajima the ones taken on the way over. He can hardly believe he's looking at this morning's sunrise over Kyoto. And the pictures of Mt Fuji stir some sort of national passion in him. Then come the photos of Satsuma's dojo…

Nakajima lets out a sharp laugh. He asks if the swords in the photos are real. I say they aren't.

"Poser!" he scoffs. Then, with one of the most fluid motions I've ever seen, he withdraws an imaginary sword from his side and holds it high in the air. His movements are exact and poetic to the point that I can see a sword waving above his head.

Nakajima purses his lips. He wants to know if Satsuma demonstrated *Jigen-ryu*.

"Did he take wood, and, screaming like an ape, run up to a pole and—*Bam! Bam! Bam!*—bash the hell out of it?" Suddenly, Nakajima's body loses its former grace as he sets out belittling Satsuma's "attack and destroy" style.

Nakajima asks if I'm aware that Satsuma is a stage name. I admit to not knowing this factoid. He then tells the story of when the two of them traveled to America for a Godzilla event.

"Satsuma received a ticket in the name of Kenpachiro Satsuma, as this is what he told the Americans his name is. Unfortunately, his passport bore his real name, causing all sorts of trouble and delays at the airport. When we went to the US a second time, the same thing happened again. When will the guy learn?"

Ultimately, to Nakajima, there is no discussion. He is the one and only Godzilla.

"The new stuff can be labeled Godzilla because that's what Toho wants to call it, but it's just a pale imitation," he insists.

Interestingly enough, Satsuma felt the same way, convinced that he alone understands what it means to play the King of the Monsters. It's clear that these are two incredibly proud men who've both achieved much with the same role. A certain amount of rivalry is natural. To be honest, I'm charmed by both of them.

Nakajima walks us to the bus stop where he mentions that he, legendary actor Toshiro Mifune, and Tsuburaya often sat around drinking whiskey all night long. He then asks if I like whiskey. It isn't until I'm well on the way home that I realize this was his roundabout, Japanese way of inviting me out for a drink.

GAMERA 3: REVENGE OF IRIS

Following up on director Shusuke Kaneko's invitation, I arranged with Daiei Pictures PR man Kobayashi to visit the set of *Gamera 3* (G3) during location shooting at Kyoto Station, the city's recently revamped, one-billion-dollar-plus train depot. Once again, I'll be writing a piece for *Fangoria*. Unlike the previous two articles culled from interviews, this will be a set visit piece. The story will feature quotes from the director, actors, and other staffers, and framed around what I see and experience on the set.

Like Godzilla, Gamera is a Japanese giant monster series I grew up on. The two probably appear identical to the uninitiated: guys in rubbery monster suits tearing through miniature landscapes. To those in the know, however, they're vastly different. Godzilla films had bigger budgets and, for the most part, aimed to be serious sci-fi. Gamera was a lower rent product and was unabashedly aimed at the kiddie market. Kaneko's Gamera series was an attempt to level the field. Each new entry of Kaneko's has seen an increase in maturity. I'm anxious to see what he has in mind for G3.

According to Kobayashi, the staff is working nights in and about the station so as not to disrupt business. I book a room across the street at the Kyoto Tower Hotel. With Nobuko along once again to smooth things over should I fall off the delicate precipice of Japanese protocol, we arrive at the hotel around 10 p.m. I contact Kobayashi following check-in. Out of the blue, he says they're shooting and invites me to the set. He directs me to a nearby pachinko parlor where he says two other reporters will be waiting. Grabbing my camera, notebook, and Nobuko, I rush into the warm Kyoto summer night.

One of the reporters is from *Friday*, a weekly trash publication that could be likened to the *National Enquirer*. The other writer, Takahiko Mamiya, is from the fantasy cinema magazine *Uchusen*. With a shaved head and sympathetic eyes, Mamiya looks more like a Buddhist monk than one of Japan's top writers of the kaiju and hero genres. He introduces himself in flawless English.

"Call me Taki. That's what my American friends use."

Soon, Kobayashi arrives. Wasting no time, he escorts us to the west side of Kyoto Station, where we pass through the dark gate of an employee entrance.

The production is already at work on an unused platform in the station's back. It has a surprisingly small crew. There are maybe thirty people and the most basic of film equipment; unlike the set of *Biohazard 2*, the catering amounts to ice tea and chip-like snacks set atop a wobbly folding table. I spot director Kaneko seated in front of a small, camera-fed monitor. We exchange greetings and I explain the type of articles I plan to write on G3. He gives some non-judgmental head bobs and in stilted English says, "Make yourself at home."

The scene at hand depicts passengers on a train reacting to news that Kyoto is under siege by giant monsters. Bright film lights shine on a motionless train as crew on the opposite platform stand by with water hoses. Kaneko runs through the upcoming shot with Yukijiro Hotaru, an actor who appeared in the previous two Gamera films. For G3, he again plays Tsutomu Osako, a man whose life is continuously disrupted by kaiju. Driven to desperation, his character

has succumbed to homelessness, and, to reflect this, his clothes are torn and stained. As he reviews the scene with Kaneko, Hotaru bustles with playful jokes. He has the usually stoic director in stitches.

The production moves to the inside of the train. Hotaru is seated next to Yuu Koyama, a fresh-faced actor making his film debut. I find a spot near Kaneko and quietly observe him talking to the actors and his ADs. As the scene is shot, an AD reads aloud an announcement explaining that monsters are laying waste to Kyoto. The cast and extras grow panicky. People rush for the doors. Kaneko halts the scene. He makes a few comments and then calls for a reshoot.

After three takes, he lets out a satisfied, "Okay!" Members of the crew echo Kaneko's word. The day's shoot is a wrap. The clock on the platform reads 3:30 a.m.

27 JUNE 1998

I meet with Kobayashi in the early afternoon. We cover my set boundaries and whom I can interview. Overall, he's accommodating and professional. He hands me a set access badge yet fails to understand my "I'm with the band" response.

At 7 p.m., I arrive at an open-air section on the fourth floor of Kyoto Station. The staff is busy setting up equipment and roping off the area. I enter with my pass held out. Nobody bothers to check it. Well, it's not like there are any other non-Japanese on set that need to be kept track of. In fact, many crewmembers greet me with a friendly *ohayo gozaimasu*. Although literally meaning "good morning," it's a phrase used in the workplace no matter the time of day. Sitting alone on a set of steps overlooking Kyoto is director Kaneko. I toss my bag beside him.

"Nice view," I remark.

"Do you know about Kyoto? It's our holy city, which is why you don't see many monster movies set here. There are conservative watchdog groups in Japan that take great delight in condemning and demonstrating against anything they feel disrespects our culture. The story of *Gamera 3* is steeped in mythology, so Kyoto is a natural place to stage the film's final battle. But I have to consider these people's reactions. It's an unnecessary burden."

I wish I could say I'm surprised, but Japan is well-known for nationalists who operate as a cultural police force. For the conservative-leaning government, it's a win-win situation. By allowing these people to do their dirty work, they get the control they want while also boasting that freedom of speech is alive and well in Japan.

At 8 p.m., actresses Shinobu Nakayama and Ayako Fujitani arrive. They bow and exchange the *ohayo gozaimasu* phrase with the staff as they make their way to the actors' waiting area. Trailing behind them are new-to-Gamera series actresses Ai Maeda and Senri Yamazaki, and actor Tooru Tezuka.

Around a hundred onlookers have gathered on the bottom of the stadium-like steps that stretch up a dizzying six floors. Young girls point and wave at Ai, her fame coming from the NHK TV show *Tensai TV Kun* and *Shinsei Toire no Hanako-san*, a summer horror film currently playing in theaters. Ai also has a hardbound photo book out in bookstores alongside one of her younger sister Aki. For a sixteen-year-old, she

seems to be doing well.

With the crew running about and Kaneko engrossed in the first setup, I hit the snack area for coffee. There is none—just harsh, brown *mugi* tea. Chatting nearby are actresses Ayako and Ai. I wonder... Can Ayako speak English? After all, her father is American actor Steven Seagal. Downing my tea, I interrupt their talk.

"Say... You wouldn't happen to speak English, would you?" I ask.

A bright smile spreads across Ayako's face. "Sure do!"

Ayako is friendly and well-spoken for a seventeen-year-old. I learn that she lives in Juso with her mom, which is a bit of a surprise. Juso is not far from my apartment and from the train appears to be little more than a collection of after-hours sex clubs.

As Ayako speaks, I sneak a peek at Ai. She's wide-eyed over her co-star's command of English. Ai is clad in a white, one-piece dress and around her neck hangs a black amulet. Noticing my interest, she takes it off and lets me hold it. It's smooth and shiny and has a bit of weight to it. I'm about to ask its significance when AD Hideaki Murakami yells out Ayako and Ai's names.

"Wish I could speak English, too," Ai confides as she slips the amulet over her head.

In the next scene, the actors watch the ensuing battle between Gamera and Iris, his latest opponent. They're positioned where I sat with Kaneko a few hours earlier. A large cylinder pasted over with strips of gold foil is rotated like a rotisserie on the steps below. This causes sparkles of light to pass over the actors' faces. Off to the side, a pair of men with water hoses stand at the ready. Kaneko calls for action. With the monster battle raging in their imagination, the actors are hosed with ice-cold water.

Once the scene is over, Kaneko checks his playback monitor. Feeling the rain effect lacking, he calls for a retake. In a nearby tent, the makeup staff dries the actors with heaters and blow dryers. Ten minutes later, it's reshot successfully.

At 11:30 p.m., the scenes on the fourth floor are complete. The crew moves their equipment to the first floor, where they're scheduled to work until the station reopens at 5:30 a.m. AD Murakami approaches me. Bowing, he requests that I appear as a runner, one of those stampeding citizens iconic to Japanese giant monster films.

"Kyoto is a tourist destination, and the director feels non-Japanese faces in the crowd will add authenticity." Off to a side Kaneko watches us discreetly.

The ground floor of the station bustles with activity. In addition to the cast and crew, over a hundred extras have joined the production: college students, businessmen and women, gray-haired grannies, housewives, and high school girls in sailor uniforms. They've been hired from local acting agencies and form a comprehensive representation of Japanese society. The night's focus is the main cast gathered around Ai as she leans spaced out against a pillar by the station's entrance. The camera and lights are set while the cast reviews their lines.

Outside, three meters from the entrance, a large, white balloon is released. Part of the lighting rig, it floats to the end of a rope and, swaying gently in the air, gives off a subtle, warm glow.

On the main floor, ADs divide the extras into groups, assigning each a letter from the English alphabet. I get to talking to two people in my group, Yuji and Aya Kaida. Yuji is an artist who creates paintings of kaiju. I've seen his work and think it's spectacular. Devout followers of Japanese special effects films, the couple made the trek from Tokyo to be on hand for the Kyoto Station "running in terror from kaiju" scenes. But tonight is standard fare. Our extra duties are little more than walking across the station floor while the actors exchange dialogue.

When my group is not on call, I stand beside Kaneko. He's staring full-on into a camera-fed monitor. He looks desperate. It's like he's searching for something yet not entirely sure what. Between takes I ask if this is normal. Candidly, he admits it isn't.

"The first two Gamera films came so easily," he laments. "This one... It's killing me."

28 JUNE 1998

The evening gets underway at 8 p.m. with the arrival of the actors. That *ohayo gozaimasu* phrase is passed between crew and cast. Ayako greets me with a cheery "Hi!" Actress Shinobu, whom I have yet to speak to, bows politely my way. Like the night before, the main floor can't be accessed until after the station closes. Shooting on the fourth consists of more monster battle reaction shots.

On a toilet run to the first floor, I bump into Taki, the writer I met Friday night. At the time he let me leaf through proofs of a book he's writing on the production of the US *Godzilla*. With him now is the film's creature designer, Patrick Tatopoulos. In Japan to promote the film, he's in Kyoto to tour the city. It's a thrill to meet the production designer for such films as *Independence Day* and *Dark City*. On the escalator up, Patrick gushes about the amazing time he's having in Japan.

"Such a marvelous country," he says with a French accent. "I've seen so many wonderful sights in Kyoto. It's a magnificent city. And now I get to visit the set of an actual Japanese giant monster film!" Pat wears one of those giddy faces common to first-timers to Japan. On the fourth floor, we slip under the guard ropes, enter the set, and go over to Kaneko's workstation.

Speaking through Taki, Patrick heaps praise on Japanese cinema, dropping names such as Kurosawa and Ozu. Kaneko keeps up his end by singing the merits of Hollywood filmmaking. But with his wife waiting downstairs, Patrick leaves after only a single take.

"That's the legacy directors in Japan have to live up to," Kaneko bemoans after the two have left. "Our past filmmakers had great resources at their disposal and with it made classics. Today we operate in near poverty."

Kobayashi gives the thumbs up to interview Shinobu. I follow him to a quiet section off to the side, where he tells us to wait before speeding off to fetch the actress.

I'm curious about Shinobu. Unlike the other actors, she sits posture perfect in her waiting area, never venturing out and always letting the staff come to her. I don't think I saw her get up for drinks or snacks once. Her mannerisms seem more refined too. She's highly poised and moves with the exacting grace I imagine the kimono-clad women of Japan's royal court did two hundred years ago. It comes as no surprise that she bows slowly and elegantly when Kobayashi introduces us. Shinobu starts the interview with

an explanation of her character: "I'm a bird scientist, an expert. I was in the first Gamera film and was part of the team piecing together the mystery of the Gyaos creatures attacking Japan." Her generic answer tells me that she thinks I haven't seen the first film. I assure her I have.

"Oh, thank you very much," she says and promptly bows with downcast eyes.

Her description of Kaneko's directing method is more insightful and is in keeping with what I've seen.

"He doesn't give much direction or dictate emotions," she reveals. "During the first Gamera, this upset me until I figured him out. You see, he has a vision of the finished film in his mind. If Kaneko thinks a scene falls below his vision then he will give advice. But as long as a scene meets his requirements, he'll let us do what we want."

The interview goes well. Shinobu answers questions with enthusiasm and looks me squarely in the eyes. When it's over, she returns to her chair, places her hands over her knees, adjusts her spine, and resumes that same cultured air she's maintained over the past two nights. I can't fault it, but I do find it aloof. Well, whatever she may be, one thing is sure: she's an extremely attractive woman!

The production stalls over a technical issue. To pass the time, I chat with Ayako by the cooler. I guess since I'm not Japanese, she feels she can unload. Soon she's groaning over the difficulties of being of mixed heritage in Japanese society.

"At school, no one wanted to be my friend because I was of mixed blood. I was lonely most of the time. Then my dad became a movie star and everyone wanted to know me."

I wonder. Could Shinobu's distance be for a similar reason? After all, she's the sister of Miho Nakayama, one of the most popular singers in Japan. It would be like having Cher as a sibling. After a while, you have to question if people are being nice only because of your famous relative.

At that moment, Kaneko moves up quietly beside us. He listens intently, trying his hardest to sort out the meaning of our non-Japanese talk. This is hardly unexpected as Japanese people are fascinated with English. It's compulsory in school, and almost everything—music, movies, TV, advertisements, T-shirt slogans—is given a sprinkling of English to liven things up. Kaneko leans in and adds a few English comments that neither Ayako nor I can figure out.

Bounding over, Ai Maeda carries the video camera used by the cameraman documenting the production. She starts filming us. For fun, I talk into the camera.

"We're here on the set of *Gamera 3* with director Shusuke Kaneko! Mr. Director, I have a very important question, one that has become a burning issue with film fans across the Japanese nation—neigh, across the very globe itself!" Ai whip pans to Kaneko. "Could you, please," I ask, "tell us—your audience—just what is your favorite color?" Kaneko strokes his chin. He turns to the camera.

"Black," he answers deadpan.

We laugh loudly.

With a booming voice, Murakami announces that the tech problem is resolved. Without hesitation, everyone reverts to work mode and dashes to their posts. It's then I notice PR man Kobayashi off to the side. He'd been watching my exchange with the cast and Kaneko. He doesn't appear happy.

Once the station has closed, everything is hauled down to the main floor. Like the night before, a hundred extras stand in wait. Unlike last night, when the extras played people calmly going about their business, tonight is for a panic-stricken citizenry to run past the camera.

Kaneko is sitting alone in front of his monitor and paging through the film's script. My maiden flight in a giant monster film, this seems like the perfect opportunity to get first-hand advice from the premier kaiju film director on how to run from skyscraper-sized creatures.

With a serious tone, I ask how one tackles the task of being a runner in a Japanese monster film. Is there a particular pose you assume or a mindset you should have? How should you hold your arms? Up and out? In close tight? Should I scream? Kaneko's eyes tighten.

"Well..." he begins. "You take a foot and place it in front of the other. You repeat this over and over, faster and faster, until your body has built up enough speed to go from one side of the station to the other."

I'm confused. What can that mean? Aware I don't get it, Kaneko simplifies it for me.

"Just run," he says, punctuating the advice with a smile.

With scenes of people running from kaiju such an ingrained part of the Japanese giant monster genre, I'd assumed it was handled with a special approach or method. I suppose "just run" is all it really amounts to.

For the past three nights, Nobuko has been helping with interviews and keeping an eye on me, which is great of her as I tend to let my emotions get the better of me. This has worked out well until her mother calls. She's upset at her for being away several days in a row.

In a near-panic, Nobuko announces she has to leave. As much as I'd like to express surprise at an over 30-year-old woman having to answer to her mom like this, I can't. In Osaka, nearly all of my unmarried friends live at home—even those in their forties. It's just one of many differences between Japan and the US. Nobuko gives a hurried bow to Kaneko and Kobayashi and rushes to catch the last train to Osaka.

I return from seeing her off just as the crew is sitting down to eat dinner. They form a line in front of a table from which one of the crew is passing out *roke-ben* (the *roke* is a Japanization of the English word "location" and the *ben* comes from *bento*, the Japanese word for "boxed lunch").

Hungry myself, I go to get my food when... *Shit!* It's in Nobuko's backpack! I look around for an alternative, but the station is closed and all the restaurants are shut tight. Sliding up beside an eating Kaneko, I ask where he got his food.

"It's provided by the studio," he says. I ask if he knows of any open stores in the area. "How would I know? I'm from Tokyo. Why?" I explain the situation. "No problem," he responds. "We have plenty of *bento*."

Walking me to the food station, he removes a *roke-ben* from the stack and hands it to me. Just as I have a hold of its plastic edges, a loud "STOP!" echoes throughout the empty station. It's Kobayashi. He's rushing over with his arms above his head in that damn X position.

"Norman! Those are crew only!" He's insanely furious. I release my hold on it. Kaneko furrows his brow.

"Look, his assistant left with his dinner," he explains. "I told him it would be alright."

Kobayashi doesn't balk. "It's crew food!" he screams.

Ignoring him, Kaneko thrusts the *bento* into my chest. "Take it!" Waving a hand in the air, he calls over one of the PAs and orders her to give me a can of tea. I refuse, but he won't hear of it.

Kobayashi is clearly pissed. His eyes burn into me like hot needles, and his expression reads an unmistakable, "You made me look like an ass in front of the director." I guess I did, but, *screw you*, it's your own fault. Besides, it can't be more than a measly 500 yen (about $5) meal—get over it, *man*!

Food in hand, I sit with Kaneko. And not a moment too soon! I'm hungry to the point I'm ready to faint. I eagerly pop the lid off. However, I'm underwhelmed by what I see. In the sectioned off parts of the *bento*, I find lumpy rice, oily chicken nuggets, a clump of shredded cabbage topped by a small tomato, and several strands of spaghetti with sauce that turns out to be ketchup.

"Daiei is not known for providing the best *bento*," Kaneko says with his mouth half full. All that trouble for this? I'm sure I won't hear the end of it from Reo.

After the meal, Kaneko falls asleep in his director's chair. Clutching a towel, Ayako creeps up on him. In one swift move, she tosses it over his head and dashes away. Kaneko stirs and yanks it away. With Ayako talking in an unnaturally gleeful tone to the other actors, it's not hard to deduce the culprit. Pulling the towel back over his head, Kaneko returns to his nap. Ayako and the cast burst out laughing.

Finally, it's time to film the running scenes. Once again, the cast gathers around Ai at the station's entrance. The ADs place the groups of extras about the station. Mine is dumped on the second floor. We're told to run down and go out of the main exit. There are two paths before me: the escalator or the stairs. I pick the stairs. It has to be safer than running down an escalator. Still, thick electrical cables and large film lamps mark the way.

Everyone in my group braces for the first take. An AD taps the shoulders of the first few people in line. They sprint away. My shoulder is tapped. I shoot over the cables, under the lamps, and down the stairs. From the corner of an eye I make out Ai running up the escalator. Hot on her heels are Shinobu and Ayako. Kaneko yells "cut" just as I make it past the camera lens.

Kaneko calls for another take. Once again, we extras speed for the station's entrance, while the cast heads for the spot up on the fourth floor. I run down the stairs, hit the floor, and zoom to the entrance. That's when I see Shinobu. Focused on her performance, she doesn't notice that our trajectory is aligned. With me moving too fast to stop—that's that—we collide!

A loud "cut!" roars from Kaneko's megaphone. The smoke clears. All eyes are on me as I stand with my arms clasped tightly around the lead actress. Embarrassed, Shinobu's face is a deep scarlet.

I brace myself for a scolding—instead, a wave of laughter echoes throughout the station. The crew is in stitches. I release the actress, and we apologize to each other with unending bows. I look around for Kaneko, hoping I haven't pissed him off. He gives me the thumbs up.

By 3:30 a.m., I'm beat. Like the other groups, mine sits huddled on the station floor hoping that the evening will end soon. But sitting only invites sleep. Picking myself up, I leap around, announcing to my fellow runners that this is how Mikhail Baryshnikov would flee from a giant monster. Next, hunching over and flicking my thumbs off my nose, I air punch while shuffling forward, demonstrating how Rocky Marciano would hightail it from a kaiju attack. Bent ever so slightly ahead, I fast-walk with a determined, unstoppable look on my face. You know, how a T-1000 would dash away. Unlike the other groups sitting quietly, everyone in mine is laughing loudly.

"You guys! In the back!" yells an AD from the balcony. We're thrown to the farthest point possible for the last shot. (I find out later we were put here because my group was deemed the liveliest and runners in the distance are needed for speed.) Placed at intervals of three meters across the station floor, we wait for "action."

This is it! I think as I begin my final run; this is my contribution, as small as it is, to Kaneko's masterful Gamera series! I run like never before. Dashing wildly, I make it past the camera as cut is called. From his megaphone, Kaneko lets out, "Okay!" Everyone cheers.

It's now 4 a.m. *Bentos* are passed around to the extras. I grab one, half-expecting Kobayashi to come screaming out of a shadow. After eating, I find Kaneko. He looks fatigued but manages a smile. I thank him for the past three days. We shake hands, and he asks when we'll meet again.

"In Tokyo," I reply. "I'll be at the studio for the second half of my G3 reporting."

He bobs his head in that fact-absorbing, non-judgmental way of his.

As blue seeps into the morning sky

and the chirp of birds flying down from the surrounding Kyoto mountains fill the early air, I'm on the platform waiting for the first train to pull in and take me back to Osaka. Although every muscle in my body aches, my head is spinning with the thoughts, images, and conversations from the past several days. My first step into the world of Japanese filmmaking went well, better than I'd imagined.

Yet the real target looms ahead. Watching people stand in front of a camera delivering lines is fine, but more than anything I want to witness the art of suitmation, the process by which men in monster costumes beat each other senseless within a miniature city. My goal is not only to see but also to learn how these monster clashes—as famous the world over as Mt. Fuji, geisha, sushi, or any of the many things typically associated with Japan—are put together.

If the past few days are any indication, it's an adventure to look forward to.

31 JULY 1998

With Nobuko in tow, I'm headed for Daiei in Tokyo for the second half of my G3 coverage. I stare bleary-eyed at the first Shinkansen as it pulls into Shin-Osaka Station. Twenty minutes after leaving Osaka, we pass through Kyoto Station. I spot the open plaza on the fourth floor where the Gamera crew worked a month earlier.

As with most film studios in Japan, Daiei is not located within Tokyo proper, the land being cost prohibitive for the amount of space required. Instead, it's in a rural outskirt called Chofu (not far from Nikkatsu). Like Nikkatsu, Daiei resembles a stretch of warehouses. If not for the studio logo

pasted atop the stages I would have mistaken them as such.

Kobayashi greets us at the studio gate with a welcoming *ohayo gozaimasu*. Thankfully, I don't sense any of the bad feelings we shared at Kyoto Station. He leads us onto the lot and over to a large sound stage. Asking us to wait, he disappears inside. We stand beside an aluminum shack that has "Gamera Staff" written on the door. Peeking in, I find director Shusuke Kaneko and actress Ayako Fujitani watching unedited scenes from G3. Spotting me, Ayako waves frantically.

Kaneko steps outside and lets me know he's made time for our interview.

"I am ready for your tough questions," he says with a smile.

I pull out a scrapbook of photos I took at last month's shoot, a present for the director. Within it, I announce, is the ultimate Kaneko photo.

"I'm confident this picture will become synonymous with the face of the modern Japanese film director," I say.

I open to the page with the photo, remove it, and hand it over to Kaneko. Eagerly he pulls it to his face as Ayako peeks over his shoulder. It's a photo of Kaneko with the towel Ayako tossed over his head. The two explode with laughter.

Kobayashi returns. His brow tightens as he tries to make sense of our chumminess. Business-like, he announces that the interview with actress Ai Maeda will begin once she finishes with costume change. Pointing at Stage 5 (S5), he suggests we look over the live-action set. Kaneko and Ayako return to the trailer.

A large structure flush with the ceiling fills most of sound stage 5. Carved from Styrofoam, it looks like a massive lump of white coal held together by wire, glue, wood, and nails. Filming, Kobayashi explains, is being done within. He motions to a ladder that leads into the structure's entrance. Taking a deep breath, I put a foot on the first rung and wobble up as carefully as possible.

Unlike the exterior, the interior is black and rock-like, and the ground is covered with dirt. It's almost pitch black inside. I put a hand against a wall for guidance. Soon, the tunnel opens to a dimly lit cavern. Moist roots hang from the ceiling. Against the back are several props that look like dinosaur eggs; the center one is the size of a small man. They're riddled with thick veins and covered with slime.

"This," Kobayashi states, "is where Ai will perform today."

I take a step forward, mindful of a spot in the center covered by a sheet of paper with the simple word *ana* (hole) written in *kanji*. The drop is at least four meters.

Next, Kobayashi takes us to the special effects stage. It's near deserted. Today, SFX director Shinji Higuchi and his crew are working at neighboring Nikkatsu.

In a corner is the Gamera suit. It stands upright in a metal support frame. Its posture is fierce; its details are intensely realistic. Despite a lack of movement, Gamera looks as if he's about to shake off the frame's steel cables and fly off.

Propped in another rig is Iris, Gamera's latest foe. Iris has an unusual look for a giant monster. Traditionally, kaiju features have been soft-ish, probably due to the material available to suit makers in the '50s and '60s. Iris's face comes to a sharp point and there are a dozen spike-like projectiles jutting off its back. The long orange tentacles of the suit lie neatly at its feet.

Near the center of the sound stage is a miniature of Kyoto Station. But at ten meters in length it's hard to call it a miniature. Its detail is astonishing. As on the real station, steel window panes crisscross the front. All the signs adorning the actual location are reproduced accurately within. I find the stairs where I did my running scene. And there is the spot I smashed into Shinobu! It's so eerily real that I feel powerful, god-like. No wonder kaiju are always knocking buildings down. It's irresistible!

Resting on a collection of wood tables, the station miniature is surrounded by photos of the actual location. Taped to them are color charts with lines pointing from various shades to sections of the station. Inside, several men glue pieces to the walls. Kobayashi explains that the station is ninety percent complete.

Kobayashi walks us back to S5. Mentioning that Ai will film a scene later covered in goo and wearing disheveled clothes, he asks that I not take photos of her full body. We enter a building beside S5, place our shoes in a cubbyhole rack, and go to a room where Ai is waiting.

To get permission for the interviews, I had to agree to several of Kobayashi's requests. Paramount is the amount of time I take. He was very insistent on this over the phone. No doubt he wants to avoid a repeat of my hours-long interview with Kaneko.

Hoping to impress him with my newfound team player ability, I begin the interview promptly. Ai is responsive and sharp. She sets in explaining how she never had any interest in the genre: "The boys at school were always talking about Godzilla and Ultraman. It was all guys in funny suits to me. This production has shown me that many special people are involved in the creation of these films."

Ai also shares her point of view on the shoot at Kyoto Station last month.

"Maybe you couldn't tell, but I was upset because Kaneko filmed the last scenes first. Everything has been so mixed up with this film, which is difficult for an actor."

With that, we hit the ten-minute mark—the limit allotted by Kobayashi. I end the interview and thank her for her time.

"That's it?" asks a confused-looking Ai.

I glance at Kobayashi, who does his best to avoid eye contact. He merely raises a hand and nudges it forward, a signal that I may continue. Honestly, I only prepared a few questions as he was so adamant about keeping things within ten minutes. Thinking quickly, I come up with a few impromptu questions that stretch the talk out another ten minutes. I finish by taking a few headshots of Ai, who carefully conceals her disheveled high school uniform with a red pullover.

After saying goodbye, Ai walks to the adjacent room and sits in front of a small TV to watch a daytime drama. Seeing this annoys me. Kobayashi was so steadfast about the time limit, yet there she is, vegged out in front of the boob tube. Considering this and how eager she was to talk during the interview, I can't find much to support Kobayashi's stringent time limit.

Sure, you can argue that it's his job to manage time and that he couldn't know beforehand how free she'd be when we got together. I can argue in return that he should know it was a possibility and could have said something like, "If she's busy, I can only guarantee ten minutes, otherwise twenty or thirty minutes." Really, sitting down to conduct a ten-minute interview with the lead of a film is like asking someone to compare the filmmaking styles of Yasujiro Ozu to Akira Kurosawa in twenty-five words or less. Can't be done.

A minute up the road, the Daiei "executive lunch room" is a medium-sized room with a wide-screen TV surrounded by plush couches. As if on guard duty, a human-sized statue of Daimajin (a warrior character from a trilogy of films Daiei released in '66 that looks something like the Golem in the 1920 German film) stands beside the entrance. Kobayashi has made the room available for my Kaneko and Ayako interviews. First up is director Kaneko.

From the start, Kaneko is open and freely admits his dilemma with *Gamera 3*.

"My vision for this film is not as developed as it was for the first two. It's because we've lost luxuries afforded early entries of a film series. For example, in the first Gamera I built the film around the premise of what if giant monsters were real. It was enough to show people's reactions to the monsters. We did the same thing in the second but expanded it to what if we were attacked by a creature from space. But now, with giant monsters firmly established, we can't get away with simply showing them. To hold the interest of the audience, we have to integrate them with the human characters in a way not done before."

Elaborating on this, Kaneko describes Gamera's character arc. "In the first film he's a hero, but in the second we wonder whose hero he is. When he fought against Gyaos we assumed he was protecting us. What if that was just how we interpreted his actions? Now, in *Gamera 3*, we aim to expose the truth of Gamera's action."

As Kaneko speaks, it feels like more than just material for my article. It's a way to see firsthand how films, even seemingly silly ones (after all, Gamera is just an oversized turtle), are treated seriously by those in charge of bringing them to the screen. I know I'm here to work, but it's no crime to admit that it's great fun to listen to Kaneko.

Next is the interview with Ayako Fujitani. I'll be using her quotes in the main *Fangoria* piece and a new sister publication called *Sci-Fi Teen*. Kobayashi says he has business elsewhere and leaves Nobuko and me alone with Ayako. This, too, is baffling. Why so strict with Ai, yet so lenient with Ayako?

Sitting down with the young actress, I start the interview. However, Ayako is tense and not forthcoming. I suspect this might be her first interview in English. A few jokes and some silliness balancing magazines on the Daimajin statue's head puts her at ease, yet she still isn't coming out with anything noteworthy. Although I must say her ability to answer "yes" or "no" to questions beginning with "how" and "why" is fairly impressive.

Being new to this work, I'm unsure how far I can push. Still, I think I might be able to get away with being a bit demanding. Turning off my tape recorder, I lean in and tell her point-blank that she has to try harder, that if she doesn't start answering questions properly I'll be forced to cancel the piece.

Ayako is stunned; Nobuko looks at me as if I'd committed professional suicide. I turn my tape machine back on and—lo and behold—Ayako opens up! I guess all she needed was a slight kick in the pants.

My favorite of Ayako's stories is the one about her Gamera audition.

"I met Kaneko at a film festival in Osaka," she explains. "Two weeks later, I got a call from Daiei. He asked them

to contact me about auditioning. I agreed even though I'd never done any real acting, and to be honest, I didn't even know what acting meant. I came to Tokyo, went to the audition, and was told to read lines. I tried, but I was too nervous and ran out in the middle. I was sure I didn't have the part. However, Daiei called to tell me I'd won the role. When I met Kaneko the next time, I asked why he chose me. He kept insisting I *was* the character; I *was* the part. Truthfully, it was kind of creepy."

The interview done, we walk over to S5 where Kobayashi said I could catch some of the shooting of the night's live-action sequence. Ayako seems happy to have the interview behind her, and I impress upon her that after getting over the opening bump, she came out with interesting insight into who she is as a person and an actress. This seems to please her and she begins to chat happily about small stuff until we meet up with Kobayashi in front of the sound stage.

Within the cave set, the crew is minutes away from shooting. In full work mode, Kaneko sits nestled behind his monitor. Jammed inside the largest egg and covered with icky goo is Ai. A deep blue light illuminates her from below. She looks uncomfortable. The crew hushes. Kaneko calls for action. Ai tilts her head side to side as the camera pulls in slowly. The scene is shot several times. I leave before the last take.

2 AUGUST 1998

Kobayashi calls at 9 a.m. to say that everything is a go for today. I dress and shoot out of the hotel. Here it is! The long-anticipated day—the day I watch the filming of Japanese giant monsters! Though the train can't move fast enough for my taste, it gives me a chance to reflect on the work that SFX director Shinji Higuchi has contributed to the Gamera series: His incredible attention to detail, the dynamic angles he chooses for the monster battles, and the smooth, realistic integration of his effects with Kaneko's live-action footage that has earned him the unofficial title of leader of modern Japanese special effects.

Unlike the day before, when the effects stage was void of human activity, it's bustling this morning. Dozens of people are engaged in various tasks: attending to the monster suits, the cameras, the lights, the pyrotechnics, and the miniatures. Some staffers are even in the rafters high above doing god knows what.

Today, Kobayashi has to be on-location outside of Tokyo with Kaneko and his crew. He's turned me over to a subordinate, Masaru Tsuchiya. Younger and hipper looking than Kobayashi, Tsuchiya is decked out in a snazzy leopard fur patterned shirt. Positioning me in the center of the large sound stage, he calls for attention. The crew assembles around. Tsuchiya announces who I am, that I'm here doing a story for *Fangoria*, and to help my newsgathering in every way possible. The staff gives a low bow and a loud *yoroshiku onegaishimasu*. In return, I bow and repeat the same, honorific phrase that has no equivalent in English but, in this case, means something like, "please honor my request."

Tsuchiya brings me to a row of tables covered by drawings, American action figures, and stacks of production papers. Hunched over with pen in hand and sketching a Gyaos is special effects director Higuchi. He wears small, wire-rimmed glasses; his long hair is collected

in a ponytail, and tufts of unkempt facial hair root from the lower half of his face. He certainly looks the role of the rebel filmmaker. I spend a few minutes discussing my article and thank him for agreeing to an interview during an obviously busy time.

"No trouble at all," Higuchi insists. "Make the most of your day here."

A couple of men wheel the Gamera suit over to a platform in the center of the stage. They unfasten the suit from a portable support frame and, grabbing thin steel cables running from the ceiling, attach them to metal eye loops in the shoulders. Once secure, they hoist Gamera onto the platform, where they position him in a corner. Higuchi steps up, cups a hand over an eye, and scrutinizes the monster turtle. After deciding on the camera placement, he gives orders to the staff.

Tsuchiya introduces me to the men playing the kaiju. Inside Gamera is Hirofumi Fukuzawa; Akira Ohashi is Iris. Since the scene is nowhere near ready, I interview both men separately.

Both show the same passion and drive I found in Nakajima and Satsuma. Ohashi cites Satsuma as his hero.

"Playing kaiju is hard psychically and mentally," Ohashi explains. "Even though he was past his prime when he got Godzilla, Satsuma energized the role and redefined what it means to be a suit actor. He moved the Godzilla suit with vigor, bringing it to life, and giving it vitality. I model myself after him."

Ohashi came to the studio to find there were no scenes for him today. He doesn't seem perturbed. "It's not unusual to have no idea what will be filmed until that morning." Instead of returning home, he remains to help Fukuzawa with his suit acting duties. "I know what it takes to play Gamera," he adds. "After all, I was Gamera in the last film!"

During our interview last year, original Godzilla suit actor Nakajima said he went to zoos and studied bears to prepare for Godzilla. In his approach to playing Gamera, Fukuzawa claims a similar method but one with a modern twist.

"Higuchi lent me videos of animals, ones with reptiles, bears, and jaguars. I studied many animals to prepare. Bears are best in terms of balance and grace. I also watched *Jurassic Park* to get a feel for the proportions of the dinosaurs to their environment."

What advice does Fukuzawa have for would-be suit actors? "You need to understand the concept of atmosphere, and you need vast amounts of mental stamina. If you have this, you can overcome a lack of physical strength. As long as you're in good health and really want to, anyone can be a suit actor. Though not an easy job, it's enjoyable, and I get to experience a different challenge every day. Beats a desk job any day of the week!"

Fukuzawa is called to the stage, ending our interview after fifteen minutes. With him half in the Gamera suit, Higuchi explains the scene. Today, Gamera is to be delivered a seemingly fatal blow to the chest. Fukuzawa pays close attention as Higuchi thrusts an imaginary spike into Gamera's abdomen. Fukuzawa shakes the suit. Higuchi excitedly agrees with the movement.

With the intent of the scene settled, a long spike is brought over. It's worked into a pre-drilled hole in Gamera's stomach plate. Two men carefully push

it through until it emerges on the other side. As they do this, Fukuzawa works his body around the spike. A staff member slips on a detached Gamera arm and moves to the side opposite the camera. Gripping the projectile, he tugs at it while Fukuzawa yells and thrashes about. Guided by radio control, the animatronic head of Gamera shoots into the air. Its mouth opens, simulating agony.

Following the walkthrough, Higuchi calls for a dry run. For the take, Gamera will spew green blood; for now, water is used. Several men ram the spike into Gamera. The crewmember wearing the free-floating arm grabs the projectile. Fukuzawa roars horribly as water discharges from the wound. The rehearsal goes well, and Higuchi orders lunch break, which means our interview is about to begin.

Back in the meeting room, I wait for Higuchi. He comes late, complaining that today's scene is not materializing as envisioned. As is customary in Japan, I reciprocate with an apology of my own, insisting that disturbing him is discourteous at such a crucial time. We talk for the next hour. Higuchi is honest, open, and frank.

"When I got the offer to do Gamera," he begins, "I asked Daiei if they would let me approach the effects as I wished. They said okay. But it turned out that what they wanted was for me to do things how they wanted. We had many fights. So, in the first Gamera, my work was compromised. Japanese companies are very set in their ways. It's difficult to get them to do things differently. When I saw the American *Godzilla*, I was impressed how much they could alter Godzilla. Man, I envy the person who persuaded Toho to let them do that! But with each film, I've been able to wrest more and more control, and I feel *Gamera 3* will offer visuals of the level I wanted from the start."

Higuchi makes a few interesting cultural observations when asked to compare the Japanese SFX industry to that in the USA:

"Let me use the automobile industry as an example," he says. "In Japan, our approach to SFX is like how the Italians make Ferraris. Each of our shots is done to order. The American way is like Detroit: many people producing many cuts using an assembly line method. This gives a uniform quality, and if somebody gets sick or dies, the industry is unaffected. In Japan, there are very few people who do the work we do. And because it's handcrafted, the quality varies.

"I can put it another way if you wish," he continues. "Technically speaking, Japan made the best fighter planes during the war, but they could only be flown after intense training. The Americans made the Mustang. It wasn't as good, but it was easy to fly. Ultimately, the Mustang was the more successful fighter jet."

Near the end of our talk, we touch on the core of Higuchi's SFX philosophy.

"My approach is to add as much detail as possible to the background. This creates an impression within the audience's mind, helping them believe they're really watching giant monsters fighting. Although some fans will disagree, just being fun is not enough, especially when trying to appeal to the general audience. It's like having two monsters fight on a dusty field. Only the most hardcore fans can enjoy this. The illusion is created by the world around the monsters, not by the monsters themselves."

An hour later, we're back in the studio.

With Gamera in place and the angle Higuchi wishes to film established, large lights with colored gels taped to their fronts are hauled around the suit. The lighting director and his crew spend the next hour putting up "flags" (black squares that remove flares from the camera lens). During this time, Higuchi runs between answering crew questions to reviewing scenes shot by the live-action staff.

Some of the crew not directly involved with the setup sit on the sidelines. Partially hidden behind stacked boxes, they smoke cigarettes and relax on tatami mats. I spy both Fukuzawa and Ohashi taking catnaps.

To add to the decidedly Japanese aura, *enka* music pours from an old radio next to a section of the studio used by the art staff. *Enka* is best described as sentimental, melancholy music that features high-pitched female vocals, koto picking, slightly corny guitar strumming, and the most basic drumming possible. The contrast between the music and the scruffy, long-haired crew would be like going to a house party in the roughest section of East Orange, New Jersey to find everyone partying to Lawrence Welk.

At last, the scene is ready. Green, soupy "blood" is poured into a compressed air pump. Plastic sheets are draped over everything. Those closest to Gamera don raincoats. Fukuzawa climbs into the back of the suit and is sealed within. The air conditioner is shut off, casting the studio in an eerie silence. Higuchi makes a few last-minute checks before settling into a seat snug between the camera and a video monitor. As a last touch, dry ice mist is poured around Gamera. Finally, Higuchi yells, "Action!"

Several men drive the spike into Gamera's chest. The muffled scream of Fukuzawa erupts from within while the man controlling Gamera's detached arm reaches around to grab hold of the projectile. Green blood shoots everywhere as several large bangs, reminiscent of car backfire, pop from pyrotechnics wired into the suit.

The scene ends when Higuchi bellows, "Cut!" Fukuzawa is quickly removed from the suit. Higuchi reviews the shot on a monitor and, smiling, calls it a take.

Behind schedule, the crew prepares to move over to Nikkatsu, where they will capture an outdoor scene, a leftover from the previous day. Higuchi calls it a neat one of Gyaos being blown to smithereens. As much as I want to go, I have to catch the last Shinkansen back to Osaka. I thank Higuchi for the day on the set.

Before leaving for Osaka, I circle the stage one last time: The elaborate monster suits, the platform being cleared of lights and cleaned of kaiju blood, and the gigantic Kyoto Station miniature with model makers huddled around and within gluing piece after piece to it. In another week this meticulously crafted model will be no more, lost in an explosion I'd give anything to see.

26 FEBRUARY 1999

With the imminent release of G3, Daiei has set up a promotional event at Kyoto Station, which I catch wind of from Reo. A phone call to Kobayashi gets me the low down: A buffet followed by a screening of G3 at a theater within the station. Attending will be director Kaneko and actresses Ai Maeda and

Shinobu Nakayama. I balk when he mentions the price—an unbelievable ¥25,000 per person (which in today's dollars would be equal to $340)! To his credit, Kobayashi says he'll give me press passes.

Nobuko and I meet Kobayashi in Kyoto Station. He leads us to a fancy banquet room. In no time, a hundred or so people filter inside. Although there are children and, oddly enough, seniors, most are guys in their late 30s. Many wear suits, giving the affair an unwelcome formality. I mean, it's a party commemorating a giant monster movie! Why dress as if you're going to a shareholders meeting? To be fair, Nobuko points out that it being a Friday night, they might be coming directly from work.

At 7 p.m., an emcee takes to a podium on a small stage at the end of the room. She bows politely and in honorific Japanese welcomes all to the event. She signals that we're now free to eat and drink. Up to this point, everyone has been hungrily eyeing the food and beverages.

A person in a Gamera event suit shuffles out from a side door. Accompanied by a man from the Japan Rail (JR) office, Gamera makes his way from table to table. While the children are content to pose like wooden soldiers beside the fierce-looking suit for photos, older fans manhandle it remorselessly. One guy even takes its claws to engage in a mock battle, stopping only when the JR man intervenes. I can just imagine the "take this job and shove it" expression on the face of the person within the suit.

I find Yuji and Aya Kaida. I haven't seen them since the G3 shoot last summer. Kaida is a tough one to figure. He doesn't say much, leaving that to his ardent wife. They've already seen G3.

While liking it, Aya says they feel the first is still the best. She then begins a highly detailed explanation as to why. Listening to her dissect the film, you'd have thought David Hume had risen from the grave and issued a new treatise on the human condition.

Finally, it's time for the event's highlight: the visitation by Shusuke Kaneko, Shinobu Nakayama, and Ai Maeda. A rope is strung in front of the stage, creating a one-meter gap between it and the audience. The emcee asks for quiet and for all to sit on the floor. A couple of guys don't move quickly enough and a furious Kobayashi dashes over, yelling that everyone had better obey or the stars will not appear. Once satisfied, he raises his arms to form an O, a signal Japanese people use to mean "okay." The lights dim. From a side door, Kaneko and the two Gamera actresses walk in. The audience claps wildly.

For forty minutes, the emcee solicits comments from each guest. Starting with Kaneko, she has him describe his vision of the Gamera series and what he hoped to accomplish with each film. Kaneko is confident, alert, and his humor playful and witty. The highly refined Shinobu reiterates each question with perfect enunciation before taking an affected pause before answering. Unlike the others, Ai is the most regular, speaking as if she were just hanging out. Listening to her mumble into the mike, I wonder if she even takes the event seriously.

Throughout the show, the fans sit huddled together. Many have their hands wrapped tightly around their knees. They stare up at the stage with transfixed smiles, hanging on every utterance with an intensity one would expect to find at cult meetings. After this, the audience stands and engages in a session of "rock paper scissors." The winners are handed a few prizes and get to shake hands with the guests of honor. From here, we're led to the movie theater for a sneak preview of G3.

At the theater door, bags of Gamera goodies are handed out: Gamera and Iris key chains, a 12-piece Gamera jigsaw puzzle, and limited edition promotional cards. The Gamera guests take to the stage at the base of the movie screen. Director Kaneko expresses his pleasure at seeing the completed film within the shooting location. Shinobu again demonstrates that she could be a spokeswoman for a chain of charm schools. And Ai, well, she just seems to want to get out of here. Flowers are brought out, and each receives a bouquet of their own.

The film plays. After the end credits roll and the lights come on, the event ends. I'm stunned. This is it? This is the extent of interaction with the audience? And for ¥25,000, no less!

I grew up on events such as this in New York City and spent many hours talking one-on-one with my media heroes. Such as in 1975 at one of the first *Star Trek* cons when I puzzled Isaac Asimov by asking him to sign a copy of *The Making of Star Trek*.

"You want me to sign a book I didn't write?" Asimov responded. "*Ah!* What the hell!" he said before kindly scribbling his name inside.

Or sitting around with comic book legends Stan Lee and Jack Kirby at the sparsely attended Marvel Comic Con in 1976, free to ask the sort of inane questions their work brewed in the mind of this geeky teenager. I'd even cut school to make the show. An amused Stan Lee offered to write me a school absence note, jotting on a piece of paper, "Please excuse Norm's school absence, 'twas for a worthy cause!"

I realize that comparing cultures only leads to endless arguments, but I can't help feeling that both the audience and the guests at today's show got clipped. Here, there was zero audience interaction. Just a paid emcee reading predetermined queries and responding to answers with a dubious wide-eyed expression and an equally suspect, "Is that right? *Wow!*" How can this be satisfying to anyone?

I catch up with Kaneko in a café in the station for coffee the next morning. I tell him my feelings about the previous night. He bobs his head, mulling my words over. Then, in an unexpected turn, he agrees with me.

"No doubt about it. It was an entirely bizarre affair."

GODZILLA 2000

Back on assignment for *Fangoria*, I'm heading to Tokyo to visit Toho Studios and the mother of all Japanese fantasy film franchises: Godzilla! To say I'm excited would be an understatement. Don't get me wrong, the Gamera set was incredible. But Gamera isn't in the same league as Godzilla. Comparing the two is like comparing *Buck Rogers in the 20th Century*, the late '70s TV show featuring that Twiki robotic thing, to the superlative *Star Trek* series. As good and as fun as Gamera may be, Godzilla is, after all, the King of the Monsters!

Toho's new film comes after a five-year Godzilla hiatus. Between now and their last run of Godzilla films, Toho licensed the rights to Sony Pictures, which made a US version titled, simply enough, *Godzilla*. Helmed by *Independence Day* director Roland Emmerich, *Godzilla* opened in Japan this past July. Like my friend Reo, the Japanese press was careful not to come out with criticism guns fully loaded. Instead, they let elaborate audience survey charts and low attendance statistics do the dirty work.

However, *Godzilla* was cited on morning TV talk shows as an example of western failure to grasp Japanese culture. Don't take this to mean they felt insulted. On the contrary, the film's critical failure allowed them to paint Japanese culture as unfathomable to everyone but the Japanese people, stroking viewers' egos and allowing them to feel "unique." Still, they weren't wrong to point out that Godzilla's personality was entirely out of line. Rather than a raging force with a never-back-down personality, Godzilla was a towering lizard that scampers about, lays eggs, and, worst of all, hightails it from the military when attacked.

Upon learning that Toho is gearing up for a new production, I contact their PR department and arrange a set visit. The preliminary information is sparse. All they will say is that the film is titled *Godzilla 2000: Millennium*[4] (G2000) and that it will usher in a new round of films to be dubbed the "Millennium Series."

Unfortunately, my visit comes during *bon* (sometimes written as *obon*), a holiday period when Japanese return to their hometowns to pay respect to deceased relatives. A peak travel season, *bon* means Shinkansen tickets are pricey. Fortunately, I worked out with Kaneko to stay at his home, which is located near Toho Studios. So, at least there's no hotel fee to cover. In keeping with *bon*, Kaneko's wife and kids are staying with her parents down in Kyushu. This means it's just the two of us, for this first night at least. Nobuko arrives tomorrow to help with the interviews.

I get to Kaneko's at 10 a.m. It isn't any great "long time no see" reunion since both of us were in L.A. not three weeks ago as guests at G-Fest, a convention for western kaiju fanatics.

Over coffee, we recall the trip's memorable moments, such as visiting the home of Forrest J. Ackerman, founder of the magazine *Famous Monsters of Filmland*. It was a pure delight to listen to the aged writer/editor tell first-hand stories of Boris Karloff and Bela Lugosi. His home, called the Ackermansion, overflows with books, art, and rare movie memorabilia, such as dinosaur models used in the original *King Kong*, Lugosi's ring from *Dracula*, and even a creature from *The Outer Limits*.

The trip's highlight was a screening of *Gamera 3* at the Egyptian theater on Hollywood Boulevard. Before the show, Kaneko, Nobuko, and I did a Q/A in front of the packed theater. Afterward, Kaneko signed autographs and mingled with fans. Unlike the Kyoto Station event and its stilted, funeral home-like air, the friendliness of this one pleased Kaneko much more.

"So, what do you want to do today?" Kaneko asks when the coffee runs out. "Would you like to go to the Godzilla set?" This is unexpected. Officially, my visit begins tomorrow.

"We can do that?" I ask.

His smile indicates we can.

Outside, the sky over Setagaya is overcast, and rain feels like a distinct possibility. I'm expecting Kaneko to drive. He points to a pair of bicycles.

"This one's mine, you take my wife's." It turns out he doesn't know how to drive.

The suburban roads are thin, winding, and lined with rows of western-styled, upper-middle-class homes. Unsure where we're going, I ride closely behind Kaneko. Ten minutes later, we arrive at Tsuburaya Productions, the production house founded by SFX director Eiji Tsuburaya.

Credited with popularizing the "man in the suit" style that defines Japanese fantasy films, Tsuburaya oversaw the special effects on the Godzilla series from the first film in 1954 until his death in 1970. But, as a pioneering special effects artist, there was more to Tsuburaya than just Godzilla. Whenever a film needed any visual trickery, such as New York being hit by a meteorite in *Battle in Outer Space* (*Uchū Daisensō, 1959*), a volcanic eruption in *The Three Treasures, Nippon Tanjō, 1959*), or a plane crash in Frank Sinatra's *None but*

---

4 - The film would be retitled *Godzilla 2000* for its US release.

the Brave, Tsuburaya was there to make it happen. He even put together the famous Toho logo seen at the top of all their motion pictures.

Godzilla aside, Tsuburaya's most significant contribution to Japanese popular culture was Ultraman, a superhero clad in red and silver who battles invaders from space and defends Japan from alien subjugation. Ultraman seemed to come out of nowhere when it premiered in the mid-'60s and took the nation by storm, eventually spawning dozens of spin-offs and inspiring other hero shows of its kind.

Despite its success, Tsuburaya Productions is little more than a parking lot and a few prefab one and two-story buildings. Large statues of Ultraman from various points in his history stand along the front. After parking our bikes, Kaneko snaps a few shots of me striking goofy poses with the statues before going in. Like at Nikkatsu, people bow upon seeing Kaneko.

Kaneko leads me to a building in the back and up a rusty set of stairs. Here, he shows me a storage room overflowing with kaiju costumes. Like row after row of suits at a dry cleaner, they hang tightly together from the low ceiling. On the floor near the door, a stack of rubbery Ultraman suits lie slumped over each other. Two men sit with folded legs. One paints detail to a chest plate while his partner uses chopsticks to force white hair into a monster costume.

"These aren't for TV use," Kaneko explains. "They're for events and promotional shows."

Back on our bikes, we continue. Almost immediately the sound stages of Toho break over the tops of the surrounding homes.

"Tsuburaya picked that spot because, back then, they had a close working relationship with Toho," Kaneko says as we coast down a long slope.

I feel my heart pound the closer we get. All those films I watched as a kid, all those Godzilla, Rodan, and Mothra adventures that filled hour after hour of my time and imagination. And now, here I am—about to visit the location where those wonderful images originated. And doing so on the bicycle of the wife of a Gamera director!

We glide up to a white and blue office building with the words Toho Studios strung along the front. Kaneko dips an ID card into a box at an unmanned guard booth. The gate beside it buzzes open. We walk our bikes in and park between Stages 1 (S1) and 2 (S2).

"These two were the first stages built and date back to the early '30s when the studio was called PCL (Photo Chemical Lab)," Kaneko explains as he leads me around to the back of S1.

I go to open the studio door when Kaneko holds out a hand.

"Hold on," he says and points at a spinning red lamp like the kind you see atop fire engines. "A take is in progress." A moment later, the lamp goes off. He motions for me to enter.

Inside it's cool, near frigid. In the center of the stage is the crew, which number around thirty-five men and women. Although smaller than the stages at Daiei, this one has a higher ceiling. Three of the walls are covered from floor to ceiling by a massive blue screen. However, the real attention grabber is the rooftop mock-up of a Tokyo high-rise sitting square in S1's center. Kaneko points to a man seated on a small, wooden box a few meters away.

"That's Takao Okawara, the director," he

whispers. "He directed *Godzilla vs. Mothra*. Did I tell you I tried to get that gig?"

Dressed in light browns and wearing a tan fishing vest, Okawara strokes a graying beard as he leafs through a large 3-ring binder. Looking up, he calls for action. Standing on the lip of the rooftop set is a collection of five or six actors. They peer out with focused eyes, grimacing over the camera and into one of the blue screens, which I imagine will be replaced in post-production with shots of Godzilla stomping through Tokyo. Suddenly, a large, cannon-shaped wind machine whips air mercilessly over them. They cower and fight against the strong wind.

When the take is complete, we walk to a spot with several rows of folding chairs. Here and there, men in military uniforms are napping.

"Wait here a sec," Kaneko says. He walks over to the crew, who bow and look genuinely surprised to see him. I occupy myself with a copy of the script I find on a chair, careful not to wake the catnapping extras.

Kaneko returns with Naomi Nishida, G2000's female lead. A fashion model turned actress, she appeared in Kaneko's *School Ghost Stories 3* (*Gakkō no kaidan 3*, 1997). Shaking my hand wildly, Naomi explains she can't speak a word of English.

Two more actors join us, Takehiro Murata and Shiro Sano. Murata has appeared in a couple of Godzilla films, but G2000 marks his graduation to lead. Sano starred in Kaneko's *It's a Summer Vacation Everyday* (*Mainichi ga natsuyasumi*, 1994).

For some reason, Kaneko feels the need to tell them I'm crashing at his place while his family is away.

"And what kind of trouble are you guys planning?" Naomi asks in jest.

Shiro Sano is well known for his love and knowledge of Japanese SFX films. He seeks to engage me in a chat about kaiju movies of the 1960s, the genre's acknowledged peak.

"Tell me your favorite Toho kaiju film," he asks point-blank. "There can be but one answer," he adds, turning up the heat.

"*The War of the Gargantuas...?*" I respond.

Sano takes my hand and pumps it up and down. I seem to have passed some sort of otaku initiation.

Shooting returns to the rooftop. Military extras gather underneath tents surrounding map-covered boards. The cast stares at a blank computer screen while Sano dispenses difficult, jargon-laden dialogue. Kaneko points his nose at two crewmembers turning hand-cranked fans and whispers that Toho is the only studio in Japan still using these. As is often the case in Japan, one finds a mix of old and new technologies coexisting side by side.

Kaneko wants to show me the "big pool." Built in 1960, it has appeared in nearly all Toho monster films since. The scene in which Godzilla and crustacean sea monster Ebirah volley a boulder? The opening to *The War of the Gargantuas* when suit actor Nakajima (as the green gargantuan) wrestles an octopus? Godzilla and King Kong tumbling together down the hillside beneath Atami Castle in *King Kong vs. Godzilla* (*Kingu Kongu tai Gojira*, 1962)? Jets bombarding Mothra as it enters Tokyo Bay in *Mothra* (*Mosura*, 1961)? That great shot of Godzilla rising out of the water before it blasts a ship to smithereens in *Ghidorah, the Three-Headed Monster* (*San Daikaijū: Chikyū*

Saidai no Kessen, 1964)? All these and more were realized in the big pool.

Along the way, we pass sound stages of varying sizes, and buildings with words such as wardrobe, makeup, and props stenciled on their doors; I even spot a barbershop. There seems to be a little of everything and I'm struck by how much more spacious Toho is compared to Nikkatsu and Daiei.

"In the Japanese film industry," Kaneko notes, "it doesn't get bigger than Toho."

We cross a small bridge. Orange carp laze within the shallow waters below. On the other side sit Toho's two largest sound stages, S8 and S9. We take a right at S9 and go up a short incline. There, at the top, is the big pool—and in front of it, the special effects crew of G2000.

Although big, the big pool isn't quite as big as the name implies.

"It's been reduced in size a few times," Kaneko reveals. "The cost of filling it with water is high, and many shots can be done today with computers."

Anchored to the tar before it is a large crane. At its top is a gearbox, which hangs high above the pool. From it runs a thick steel cable that goes down to... *Holy crap!* It's connected right to the back of Godzilla! I rush to the edge of the pool.

There he is all right. Godzilla—the ultimate badass kaiju. Half-in and half-out of the water, with a tough as nails "don't tread on me" expression plastered across his reptilian face, Godzilla awaits his cue. Action called, Godzilla claws at the air as he makes his way to the camera.

I'm awe-struck. Make no doubt about it, Godzilla is one of those ultimate creations—a superlative—a pinnacle conception born from the desperation of women and men wishing to birth a metaphor out of the madness of the atomic bombings that abruptly ended Japan's last war and ushered humankind into the age of nuclear fear.

Should Godzilla's awesomeness be lost on you, let me put it this way: If Godzilla were a Greek god, he'd be Zeus. If Godzilla were a baseball team, he'd be the '27 Yankees. If Godzilla were a woman, he'd be Marilyn Monroe. If Godzilla were an electric guitar, he'd be a '57 Les Paul. If Godzilla were a scream, he'd emanate from the mouth of Fay Wray. In the face of such eminence, I can only stand there gaping at, not more than five meters off, the King of the Monsters as he makes his way through the waters of the legendary big pool.

Several men surround Godzilla once the take is complete. They pop the back fins off. In a movement resembling a backward caesarean operation, a man is pulled from the suit. Watching him emerge and catching the flinty look on the suit actor's face, I wonder what it must be like to be *in* Godzilla. To *be* Godzilla. How must the world appear through those tiny peepholes punched in the neck?

Kaneko calls me over to a makeshift tent where the upper staff is at work. He introduces me to effects director Kenji Suzuki. G2000 marks Suzuki's second go at overseeing special effects on a Toho production. His first was last year's *Rebirth of Mothra III* (*Mosura 3 Kingu Gidora raishū*, 1998). I saw that in the theater. As much as I'd like to, I cannot comment on it because I fell asleep around the halfway mark.

Suzuki walks us to props lying by the pool. The largest is the broken-off front-half of a fishing trawler. "We shot this for a sequence in which Godzilla bites it in half," Suzuki tells us. There are also two UFO props. One is metallic blue with jagged marks on its side. The other is encased in what looks like rock.

The sky, which had been a deep gray all day, finally gives in—a loud thunderclap cracks over the area. A second later, rain pelts down. The crew hauls Godzilla out of the pool and wraps him in cellophane and blue tarp. Other crewmembers scramble to cover equipment. Kaneko and I make a beeline for S9.

With the storm raging outside and the air of dimly lit stage S9 damp and musty, it feels as if we've found shelter in a subterranean cavern.

"This is where Toho shoots their effects scenes," Kaneko says, spinning a hand in the air. "So much has happened inside here that I don't even know where to begin."

If this moment is any indication, it is, as he implies, a room of film legends. Even now, taking up most of its interior, S9 is host to a sprawling miniature of Shinjuku, one of Tokyo's central business districts. Countless knee, waist, and forehead-high buildings fill the stage. Many show strong attention to detail. The signboards of well-known companies sit atop the rooftops of several of the larger buildings. Apartment balconies are accurate down to tiny laundry, with rooms impressively furnished with miniature beds, tables, and TVs. Some go so far as to have still pictures glued to their pinkie nail-sized screens.

Off to the side and suspended in a metal frame is the Godzilla suit. Another one?

"There are always multiple suits," Kaneko points out.

Attending Godzilla is Shinichi Wakasa, a short man with an intense grin. Wakasa is head of Monsters Inc., a modeling, special makeup, and monster suit company he founded in the '80s. Wakasa has been involved in the creation of countless monsters for countless movies and TV shows. He even made suits for Kaneko's *Gamera 2*. I have a ton of questions that I do my best to hold off on until our scheduled interview the next day.

However, I have to bring up Godzilla's color. He's green. Wakasa lets out a laugh that echoes loudly throughout S9. Those who know Godzilla in passing believe him to be chameleon green. Those who know better, know him to be gray.

"It's the same in Japan," Wakasa says. "When I built the suit, I figured to go with it. If people think Godzilla is green, let's make him green and put an end to the argument!"

The suit is colorful in other ways too, with the tips of the back fins a metallic red and purple. Moreover, they're wild and jut out like insane icicles.

With permission, I touch the suit. Some parts are soft like a ripe avocado; others are hard, like plaster. The mouth is wide, which Wakasa says was inspired by a king cobra. Taken as a whole, the suit is surprisingly small. In fact, I'm taller than Godzilla! Wakasa takes a few photos of Kaneko and me standing beside Godzilla. By this time the rain has let up. Not wishing to push our luck, we get on our bikes and hightail it home.

After a late lunch, we get on the train and go over to Shimokitazawa, a town a few stops away on the Odakyu train line. Waiting for us at the station is Ayako Fujitani. It's the first time seeing her since our interview at Daiei last year. She looks great, which Kaneko and I waste no time pointing out. Aya (as called by friends) is hardly pleased.

"What's with you guys? Can't you see

I've been up for the past twenty-five hours straight? I look like hell!"

Aya's t-shirt catches my attention. It reads in Japanese, "Feel depressed about your life."

I'm given a tour of the area. It's thick with second-hand stores selling clothes, magazines, CDs, and books. There are also lots of quaint knick-knack shops, trendy hair salons, and sneaker outlets—lots of sneaker outlets. Aya explains that Shimokitazawa's real appeal lies in its many small performance theaters, music clubs, and that it's home to a vibrant artistic community.

From what I see, Shimokita (the shortened version of the town's name) is as close to beatnik as one will find in Japan, and is a bit like my digs back on St. Mark's Place in New York City. It's certainly more appealing than my current pad in Osaka. I live in Nishinariku, the domicile of Osaka's homeless.

"If I lived here, I think I'd be a hell of a lot happier than in Osaka," I announce.

Aya labels my growing affection for the area "cute."

Kaneko leads the way to a hobby shop on the south side of the station. He thinks I'll be interested in the toys, forgetting I told him that I've long since abandoned collecting. We poke around US action figures and chuckle over the heavily discounted prices on US *Godzilla* toys.

"Mr. Kaneko, *Gamera 3* is a masterpiece!"

We turn to find three young men bowing so far over I think their noses are going to touch their knees. Kaneko responds with a couple of head pecks and a few *domo*s (thanks). All at once, each of them thrusts out a G3 action figure.

"Please honor us with your autographs!" they say in unison.

Stepping outside, Kaneko and Aya scribble their names on the figures' tags. Aya seems embarrassed. That Kaneko is taking pictures with a pocket camera as she signs them probably isn't helping.

Kaneko takes us to a small restaurant for dinner. Aya and I blab away much of the night. I'm discovering that there is a lot to her. She has an intense nihilistic streak and a sharp, critical mind. In Japan, these are considered off-putting traits; I find them refreshing.

Aya talks a lot about her mother and their strained relationship. Kaneko adds that to get her out of her situation at home, Aya moved in with his family for a year during the shooting of the first Gamera. Aya adds that she considers Kaneko her Japanese dad.

At 11 p.m., we call it a night. Aya is off to meet friends and is planning to "drink all night."

Kaneko and I train it back to his home. In his den, he shows off *My Lost Domestic Popular Songs* (*Ushinawareta Kayokyaku*), a recently published book he wrote on Japanese pop music of the '60s and '70s. A massive fan of Japanese idols, he pulls out a collection of vintage singles he bought as "research."

I laugh. "No excuses! You got them because you wanted them!"

Kaneko blushes. "You are exactly right!"

We spend the night drinking beer and geeking out to laser discs of Pink Lady, the iconic Japanese girl group from the '70s, and Chisato Moritaka, a pop singer from the '80s with legs that seem to go on forever.

14 AUGUST 1999

Kaneko somehow manages to get one of his daughter's plastic-wrapped Pokémon jelly bread packets caught in the toaster. As we down our morning coffee, it starts belching foul-smelling smoke until releasing an electrical *poof*. We look at each other dumbfounded as flames spring from its back grill. Kaneko manages to unplug it while I take care of the fire with a cup of water. Burning to death from a kid's snack is not how I want to start my first official day on the set of Godzilla!

The rain is still coming down, leaving us no choice but to cab it to Toho. We find Nobuko waiting at the guard booth out front. Buzzed in, we go to the on-lot publicity office in a small building tucked behind the guard booth. Inside are two men from Toho's PR department, Masaki Nakayama and his boss Suzuki. Both are surprised to see Kaneko. To be honest, I'm unsure why he's tagged along.

In the back corner of the room is what looks like a walk-in closet, only there's a combination lock embedded in one door. Suzuki struggles with it before stepping in. He emerges with press information. I'm more interested in why they feel the need to keep press kits in a safe.

"That?" Suzuki asks. "Long ago, this was the payroll office. It was used to hold cash."

Suzuki's knowledge of Godzilla is impressive. Over the years, I've met Godzilla fans who can rattle off the most inane facts or argue the merits of a 3-toed Godzilla over a 4-toed one, but it's different coming from him. He speaks with zero passion. Godzilla facts flow out of him like production statistics from a floor manager at a Honda car plant. In a way, I guess they are as such to him. Godzilla is just his job.

I can't say director Okawara looks thrilled to be interviewed. This comes through in the reply to my very first question. "We're having a lot of trouble, but despite disturbances, we're managing to keep up with the schedule." I do my best not to smirk. This is a Japanese communication technique where one drops a hint and expects the listener to piece together the intention. Out of respect, I keep our talk focused, which is just as well. Okawara comes across much like Suzuki: A guy whose job is Godzilla, nothing more, nothing less.

However, impassioned or not, as the director of three previous Godzilla films—including *Godzilla vs. Mothra* (*Gojira vs Mosura*, 1992), the most successful of the Heisei series[5]— Okawara does have legitimate claim to the monster.

"To me, Godzilla is a rough and wild character," he insists. "I never think Godzilla fights for justice or favors children. The US version was conceived by Americans pursuing the reality of dinosaurs, not kaiju. Our Godzilla is fundamentally different. It's entertainment with metaphorical overtones concerning war and atomic weaponry."

Okawara touches on the difficulties of working with a long-running character. "In the past, a director could start off showing Godzilla little by little, part by part, building until we see the full power of Godzilla. We can't do this anymore as people know the outcome before the first frame. It's not like this just for Godzilla. All established series suffer the same fate. All we can do is try our best to come up with new ways to introduce Godzilla and maintain his

---

5 - Heisei series is the name given to Godzilla films shot between 1984 and 1995. The name derives from the Heisei era, the reign of Emperor Akihito, which ran between 1989 and 2019.

character throughout the film."

Okawara's struggle is easy to see when you consider that Godzilla has been in twenty three movies to date. It must be difficult to come up with new things for a fan base expecting both the familiar and the new while also trying to appeal to non-fans. He offers a solution: "One way to skirt this is through an original enemy, which is why we came up with the film's alien threat."

Okawara started his Godzilla tenure with *The Return of Godzilla* (*Gojira*, 1984) as an AD. "I didn't raise my hand for the position, I was assigned to Godzilla. Looking back, it was exciting to work on such a historical series. But everybody took it too seriously. I think we should have been more relaxed and concentrated on making it more entertaining." Looking at the solemn look on Okawara's face now, I wonder if he isn't guilty of the same thing.

Animated, talkative, and bursting with jokes, the actors are a lot more fun. Their answers surprise me, too. For example, I thought it unique to giant monster films that an actor plays opposite an unseen creature. Takehiro Murata insists working with monsters isn't much different from working with humans.

"It doesn't matter that I'm acting off kaiju I can't see; I often work off people who aren't there. Maybe for a close-up or if the other actor is off that day and a stand-in is used. What are they thinking? Why are they doing what it is they are doing? I have to imagine them there and imagine their feelings. Like today, I'm looking out over the city and must 'see' Godzilla like I'd 'see' any actor not there. The only difference is that I have to consider why he wants to crush the building I'm inside!"

Naomi Nishida got her part in G2000 through an audition and admits to surprise when reading the script the first time. "I thought I'd been cast in a small role," she says, "but found I had a major part!"

Naomi has her own thoughts about the kaiju acting process. "We've spent a lot of time in front of blue and green screens, which take twice as long to shoot as normal shots. I think it's easier in a regular drama to imagine the finished film because you can relate it to real life. I'm having trouble imagining how Godzilla will look in the final film."

Kaneko brought his family's mini-DV camera. During my interview with Naomi, he films us. It's annoying—*I'm working*! Still, it keeps Naomi in high spirits, and turning the camera's way, she continually makes that ridiculous peace sign the Japanese people are so fond of.

Actor Shiro Sano does nothing to hide his love of Godzilla. His first words are, "I love Godzilla." He's so "up," I fear his head's going to pop. He goes on and on about his favorite kaiju films, which is fun to listen to but probably not relevant to my articles. Still, it's interesting to hear what he's doing as winks to fellow fans.

"There's a scene where I'm explaining something to a group of people," Sano details. "Suddenly, I notice my tie is sticking out of my jacket. Do you know what this is from?" I shrug. "It's Takashi Shimura from the very first Godzilla film!" Now, why didn't I know this?

However, one actor keeps his distance. During camera setups, Hiroshi Abe takes a spot on the opposite side of the room, opting not to socialize. His character is the film's bad guy. Maybe he feels the need to maintain a wall between himself and the others to stay in character. It's an odd contrast to the chummy relations the rest of the cast share. In any case, he refuses to be interviewed.

After the interviews, publicist Nakayama says the next scene features thirty or so extras. Is it possible? *Could I...?* He looks me over. "It's set in a business section of Shinjuku, and since you aren't in a suit, it probably won't work." Not only am I not in a suit, but I'm in a yellow, Hawaiian *Star Wars* shirt spotted with Storm Troopers. Considering the offer, it's probably the worst wardrobe choice I could have made this morning.

"What if my character is some totally lost tourist?" I posit. Nakayama says he'll ask.

He walks over to Okawara, who looks up from his binder, listens to Nakayama, and then glances my way. With no change in expression, he nods and then drops his head back into his notes. Nakayama turns to me, smiles, and holds his arms up in an O shape.

The extras gather in the Toho cafeteria. I'm surprised to find a few familiar faces. One is a man I met in Kyoto during the G3 shoot; another was at the G3 screening in L.A. Both are kaiju otaku in their early 40s. One of the film's producers comes in and with the help of Wataru Mimura, the film's scriptwriter, explains the scene to us.

"Thanks for coming out in such awful weather," he begins. "The scene is set in Shinjuku, where a large UFO is descending on a building. Just run as if your life depends on it. Think you can handle it?"

The crowd lets out a collective, "*Hai!*" We're led through the rain to nearby S5.

In the center of S5 is a knee-high ramp with a green screen stretched tight behind. Off to the side, director Okawara is seated in front of a small monitor on which the shape of a UFO has been drawn in marker. We're positioned to run up the ramp, cross it, and then go down and off at the opposite end. I get in the middle of the line, figuring they won't use either the top or end of the take in the final edit. On "action," we run across the ramp, screaming, looking over our shoulders, and doing our best to act scared. We do this several times.

I return to S9 to catch a simple shot of Godzilla's face caught in the headlights of a car. Positioned in front of a black curtain, Godzilla is having white smoke fanned behind him by a couple of crewmembers. When the shot is ready, the room goes quiet. Action is called.

Godzilla bends forward and the beams catch him in the eyes; he tilts his head skyward in reaction; a man operating a remote control unit hits a switch and Godzilla's mouth opens. With mist obscuring the stage and the room being pitch-black, scale is difficult to judge. For all I can tell, Godzilla really is a towering beast a kilometer away!

In between takes, actress Naomi Nishida, her shooting done for the day, slips up beside me. "Is that, Godzilla?" she whispers. "He's so...small!"

She admits it's her first time to visit the effects set. At that moment, Godzilla takes a step forward. Naomi jumps and lets out a loud yelp. She had no idea Godzilla was a man in a suit.

My interview with Godzilla suit actor Tsutomu Kitagawa is next. Kitagawa is the first man who grew up with Godzilla to play Godzilla.

"Godzilla was born in '54; I was born in '57," he says. "When little, I saw a scene where Godzilla rises from behind a mountain. Whenever traveling with my family, I'd point to a mountain and ask my mom, 'Is Godzilla going to show up?' We filmed a scene similar to this the other day. I was thrilled beyond words!"

Kitagawa explains how he got the coveted role of Godzilla. "Most of my experience comes from my *sentai* work, where I do live-action battle shows for children at amusement parks. Last year, director Suzuki and suit maker Wakasa hired me to play Grand Ghidorah in *Mothra 3*. I guess they liked me because they asked me to do Godzilla this year. I thought it wouldn't be so hard, but it's tougher than I expected. The first time I wore the Godzilla suit, it was so heavy that I thought I was going to die!"

Next, I meet with Shinichi Wakasa. He's pleased that *Fangoria* is paying attention to his work. "First, I must explain," Wakasa begins. "I'm not a suit maker. I'm a creature creator." I'm not sure of the difference, but fair enough, I think.

"Until now, all Godzilla suits have been made in-house," he continues. "I head my own company. We're the first company not owned by Toho to make Godzilla. It's a great honor as it's the top job in this field." He's right. It would be like a tailor entrusted with the Superman outfit.

Wakasa then details the evolution of the suit. "The new design is inspired by a silhouette of Godzilla drawn by artist Shinji Nishikawa. Everyone thought the long fins on the illustration's back were cool-looking. One of the goals of this Godzilla is to make him more violent and aggressive. We feel the new back fin design exemplifies this. My Godzilla is the Godzilla of the 21st century!"

Effects director Suzuki concurs. "We're calling this Godzilla the "Millennium Godzilla." Together with Okawara, producer Shogo Tomiyama, and Wakasa, we've decided on making something unlike anything seen before."

Since the last Godzilla entry, *Godzilla vs. Destoroyah* (*Gojira vs Desutoroia*, 1995), computer-generated imagery has begun to replace traditional effects, such as miniatures, matte paintings, creatures, and, in some cases, the actors themselves. I question Suzuki on the growing dependency on CG within the film industry.

"It's a mixed bag. Maybe it will replace suit acting in the future, but I don't think this will happen anytime soon. The thing with CG is that everything is predicted beforehand. When shooting with suits, you never know for certain how it's going to turn out. Sometimes things don't go as planned, but other times they exceed your expectations. It's in this unpredictable realm that the charm of Godzilla exists."

After the interview, Nobuko and I return to Kaneko's. The director takes us to a nearby restaurant for yakiniku, beef cut thin and cooked on a hot plate in front of you. Kaneko and I enter into our usual talk about movies, women, politics, and Russian literature. But one point stands out. Kaneko says he's confident that Toho will offer him the job of Godzilla director.

If so, I can't wait. Then I'll really be able to raise hell on set!

6 NOVEMBER 1999

Traveling to Tokyo on a Saturday is much less the hassle—many empty seats on the Shinkansen. Outside, the

Japanese fall has reached its zenith. The bright morning sun shimmers off the orange and yellow leaves of trees speeding past. Between this and my excitement over today's trip to the premiere of *Godzilla 2000* at the Tokyo International Film Festival (TIFF), I find it impossible to nap.

I signal the woman carting concessions through the aisle for a cup of coffee. She bows before placing the paper cup on my tray as if it were made of fine china. Like something out of an old World's Fair pamphlet, her uniform appears as if it hasn't seen a fashion change since the mid-'60s. She asks if I require "fresh," a small packet of creamer. Unfortunately, due to Japanese pronunciation, "fresh" sounds more like "flesh."

I've arranged to meet Kaneko in Shibuya in front of Hachiko, a statue of a dog he said acts as the area's meetup spot. Sure enough, dozens of people stand around the metal statue, dividing their time between straining their necks in the air looking for friends and bowing to them in greeting.

Kaneko is punctual. With the screening at 3:30 p.m., we have a few hours to kill. "Anywhere you want to go, anything you want to do?"

One of my favorite scenes in *Gamera 3* is the Shibuya battle between Gamera and Gyaos. I ask if he wouldn't mind giving me a tour of the scene's locations. "You're kidding, right?" he says, but points the way nonetheless.

We walk over to Parco, a department store. Reluctantly, Kaneko shows me where falling debris crushed bystanders. He points out the spot where a couple on a date noticed an explosion in the sky that turned out to be the flaming remains of a Gyaos killed by Gamera. I

ask if they were hired actors. "Just two people I picked out of the extras on hand that day."

He leads me to where a "scout" (parasitical young men who pretend to be from talent agencies but seek women to work at "hostess bars" and, in some cases, to appear in pornography) tries to lure a woman into a con. "We had the camera here, in the road," Kaneko explains as he steps into the street. "Right here!" A car speeds around him, barely missing his hip.

Despite his initial apprehension of the "G3 Shibuya Tour," Kaneko is now highly animated. After excitedly showing where actor Hotaru sold used magazines on the street, he points up a road.

"The NHK offices are up there by Yoyogi Park. We shot the scene with Hotaru and a group of homeless men there. I'll show you where the flaming Gyaos carcass pulverized them!"

Checking my watch, I see it's nearing the time I have to meet a few friends at Hachiko. Kaneko looks disappointed.

Waiting at Hachiko is Hiroshi Sagae. A model/prop maker, Sagae was part of the G3 art department; his built-from-scratch model work is often featured in model magazines such as *Hobby Japan* and *Hyper Hobby*. Sagae's style is distinct; it's as if his sculpts are crafted from wispy, three-dimensional brush strokes. With him is Hisataka Kitaoka, a stunt actor Kaneko and I met in LA this summer. Soon, the four of us are pushing our way through the Shibuya crowd and up to Bunkamura, a cultural center with a concert hall, a theater, and a museum, that is the location of this year's TIFF.

A long line stretches outside of Orchard Hall, Bunkamura's 2,150-seat concert hall. Kaneko's wife calls and he excuses himself. Sagae and Kitaoka take a place in line. Promised a ticket from PR man Suzuki, I break through the crowd and make for the front of the hall. There, Suzuki has me sign one of several open books on a pair of tables. He gives me a press pass and lets me in.

In the lobby, I exchange a head tip greeting with Shinji Higuchi before bumping into Godzilla suit maker Wakasa. He mentions his trip to AFFE (Asian Fantasy Film Expo), a film event in New Jersey he guested at. "I had a great time! So many Godzilla freaks!" As usual, Wakasa punctuates his sentences with long, loud laughs.

Standing nearby is Taki, the writer I met on the G3 set. He says he's now writing for *Televi-Kun*, a monthly hero magazine published by Shogakukan. Like Wakasa, he's back from AFFE.

Gamera series AD Murakami is here too. He recently married a woman from the Japanese Self Defense Force he met during the production of *Gamera 2,* where she worked as a military advisor. I'm not surprised. Murakami keeps his hair closely cropped and the order-driven style of his I saw during G3's production struck me as a bit military-like.

I also bump into the Kaidas, Aya and Yuji. A rarity in a fandom dominated by middle-aged men and young boys, Aya bubbles with anticipation over the new Godzilla film. She says she's looking forward to the scenes from the day they visited shooting at Toho. As usual, Yuji just smiles, adding little. This is fine. Aya has enough exuberance for the two of them.

The inside of the hall is large. It even has a multi-tiered balcony. Both sides are lined with TV cameras that point at the stage. Once the doors open, people flow in en masse. But where is Kaneko? I call his cell phone. He says his family just arrived and I should come to the lobby. This makes me antsy. Seats are filling fast. Everyone has their quibble; mine is seeing a film from a bad seat.

Working against the incoming crowd, I rush to the lobby. Kaneko's there with his wife and kids. He holds out his tickets. Third-tier seats. *You're kidding?* No way am I sitting where the screen will appear no larger than a postage stamp. Cursing silently, I race back to the main floor. By sheer luck I snag a seat front and center.

Waiting in front of the stage with cameras at the ready is a mass of reporters. Getting out my own, I push my way in and take a spot. With ten minutes until show time, I use the moment to take the scene in:

Orchard Hall is buzzing. What can only be described as Godzilla diehards take up most of the first-floor seats; it's as if every other person is a nerdy-looking, over-30 male. The balconies are crowded too. The din of excited chatter is enormous. I don't know why this surprises me. For the Japanese, Godzilla is their *Star Trek*, *Star Wars*, and *Planet of the Apes* all rolled into one. Tonight's film also marks the return of Godzilla to Japanese shores. For domestic fantastic cinema, this is as good as it gets.

The show begins when two women take to the podium—an emcee and her English translator. (English is provided because TIFF is, after all, an "international" film festival.) Following a brief welcome, they call the G2000 actors, director, producer, and effects director to the stage. The applause is thunderous, and the guests are cast in the near-unending light of camera flashes.

One by one, each step up to a mike to share a thought or two about the film. Finally, the true star of the evening is summoned: Godzilla! From the right side of the stage, a Godzilla event suit shuffles out. Cameras flash rapidly, giving his movements an odd strobe effect. Next, the actors and staff pose with Godzilla. Then, at last, it's showtime! The lights dim, and *Godzilla 2000* begins.

My heart beats wildly when my scene comes on screen. Will I make the cut? The UFO descends around Shinjuku and… *Wow*! There I am! Well, sort of. I'm basically just a yellow blur. Still, I can tell it's me. This is in contrast to G3, where I'm just a small dot running out of Kyoto station.

Unfortunately, I can't say I enjoy the film. I find the pacing odd, the effects uneven, and the music inappropriate. Even the audience is unusually harsh. For example, when the alien nemesis, an improbable looking squid-like creature, makes its first appearance, there is an eruption of laughter at the unimpressive CGI.

These thoughts—how much I disliked the film—are foremost in my mind when stepping out of Orchard Hall. As bad timing would have it, this is when producer Tomiyama calls my name. "What did you think of the film?" he asks proudly.

"Yeah…" I begin as I attempt to come up with some kind of response. "I guess… it was… You know… Okay…?"

The instant this escapes from my mouth is the instant I wish there was a device that would let me redo the previous five seconds of my life. Tomiyama looks at me bewildered before thanking me for attending the screening and walking off.

Later on I mention this foot-in-mouth episode to Kaneko. He offers advice: "I often go to screenings in which the filmmakers are in attendance. You must find something about their film that you can compliment when they corner you after the show. But one thing, do *not* compliment the cinematography. That's code for *I hated the film.*"

Although the overall response to the film was lukewarm, the scene outside the hall is alive with flashbulbs and excited fans. Autograph hunters, their pens and pads high in the air, surround the film's staffers. Answering a reporter's questions, SFX director Kenji Suzuki's face is caught in a TV camera's harsh light. Nearby, the actors stand in a line fielding reporters' questions.

I meet up with Kaneko. Together with his family, Murakami, and Kenji Takama (cameraman for many Kaneko films), we go for Italian in a restaurant on Bunkamura's top floor. None of us are impressed with the film. Over dinner, we tear into G2000 like sharks into a stray tuna.

After a while, I begin to feel bad. Bringing the talk to a halt, I suggest we each find one positive thing to say about the movie. The group goes dead silent.

Finally, Kaneko mentions a particularly good shot. Everyone shakes their head in agreement. Takama points out that the lighting in one scene was quite superior.

"That's all fine," I say, "but that's not exactly what I mean. Something like the direction, a performance, the music…"

Silence. No one can identify anything but little moments here and there. In fact, a livid Murakami jumps to his feet and, overcome with emotion, yells out, "The movie sucked!"

By contrast, Kaneko's seven-year-old son Suzuyuki (often called Suzu for short) cannot contain himself. He goes on and on about Orga (Godzilla's foe) and his battle with Godzilla, and how cool it was when the fighter jets took on Godzilla at the beach.

In a way, his opinion might be more of an indication that the problem is not in the film but in how we've changed since giant monsters first enamored us as children. And more to home, I perceive something deeper going on. It's not so much that the movie "sucked" but that G3, an arguably better-made film, didn't receive half the attention this new Godzilla film is receiving.

After dinner and after his wife and kids have gone home, Kaneko, Takama, Murakami and I go to a party given by TIFF. It's a new thing for me, and I meet many filmmakers and film festival people from around the world. At 10 p.m., Kaneko and I cab it back to his home where we sit up discussing the latest Godzilla film and what steps Toho ought to take to reinvent the kaiju genre.

Kaneko still holds out hope that Toho will "pass him the megaphone" and give him the chance to direct a Godzilla film.

16 FEBRUARY 2000

I'm heading to Tokyo for another round of interviews for *Fangoria*. Tony Timpone, the editor, has been mulling over the idea of an issue dedicated to the gaining-in-popularity Japanese horror movie boom. The issue, he envisions, will focus on the films born in the wake of the domestic and international film festival hit *The Ring* (*Ringu*, 1998). He's affectionately calling it the "Norman issue."[6]

I spend my first afternoon with director Masayuki Ochiai discussing *The Hypnotist* (*Saimin*, 1999), which is being released soon on DVD in the US. I also meet with Norio Tsuruta, director of *Ring 0: Birthday* (*Ringu Zero: Bāsudei*,

2000), the third film in the *Ring* series. I guess it's the third. There seem to be other connected films, like *Spiral*, and a TV series.

A self-professed horror fan, Tsuruta is insanely happy to find his work spotlighted in *Fangoria*. I find it peculiar that he's insistent on my labeling him "the John Carpenter of Japan." I like Carpenter as much as the next guy, but it doesn't tell me anything more than the fact that Tsuruta is a fan of Carpenter. It's about as revealing as calling Björn Ulvaeus the Sonny Bono of Sweden.

Kaneko has been kindly putting me up in his house, letting me take over his son's room. As Suzu is not yet nine, his bed is small. Sleeping in it is like sleeping in a suitcase. More enjoyable are the mornings. As the children play with kaiju toys (Suzuyuki) and Barbie (Yurina, their younger daughter) in front of the TV, Kaneko's wife, Nanako, makes us huge, wonderful breakfasts.

One night, during family dinner, we were playing, "If dad makes a Godzilla film, which monster should he revive?" Nanako suggested the shaggy dog-like King Caesar, a monster based on Okinawan myth. I put forth my favorite, Gimantis (aka Kamacuras).

Immediately Suzuyuki chimed in, "Yes, Gimantis! Dad, bring back Gimantis!" Kaneko looked at us disbelievingly.

"Are you two serious? That's not kaiju—it's just a praying mantis with a hormone dysfunction!"

Ignoring him, Suzu and I broke into a chant of "*Gimantis! Gimantis! Gimantis!*"

This time out, however, I'm staying at an apartment Kaneko shares in Shimokitazawa with three other directors who live outside Tokyo. They split the rent and arrange with each other when one plans to use it. For Kaneko, it's a get-away for writing.

A small, '60s era-built, five-floor walk-up, the room has straw-woven tatami mats and a Japanese style squat toilet. I'm thrilled over the tatami, which gives off a pleasant aroma, but the toilet, which I refer to as "the hole," is a source of anxiety. Made of porcelain, it has a splash guard at its front, which is actually its back. Like most non-Japanese, I make the mistake of facing the door. Fortunately, I have a good friend in Kaneko, who gives me a lesson in toilet etiquette a few days after I move in.

As expected of a place shared by four men, no one has bothered cleaning beyond the basic act of picking up. Everything is coated with a thin layer of dust. There is also paint peeling off the walls and a few of the windows have long cracks running through them. Then there's the room's water heater, which looks like it was installed around the release of the first Godzilla film. Like a wild, out-of-control tumor, it juts out of the wall by the front door to the point you have to work yourself around it just to get into the place. Worse, when water passes through, it rattles as if someone is banging it with a rock.

Other than these quibbles, it's a great pad with a superb view overlooking hundreds of porcelain-roofed homes. And just in case I forget I'm living in one of the world's great metropolises, the skyscraper district of Shinjuku looms in the near distance. It's the type of view I always imagined I'd have if I lived in Japan.

Kaneko promises that I'm welcome to use it free of charge when the others aren't around.

2 APRIL 2000

I'm in Tokyo for the wrap party of *Crossfire*[7], a sci-fi action film Kaneko directed for Toho that I covered for *Fangoria* last February. Kaneko was kind enough to give me a brief, on-screen cameo where I turn to face the camera and look surprised.

After dropping my bags in the room, I leave to meet up with the director at Toho. I'm excited because this is my first time walking around the studio lot unescorted. I spot a small warehouse beside a sound stage and, seeing no one around, stick my head in. It's old and musty and full of props. Most everything is wrapped in plastic sheets yellowed by grease, dust, and age. Dozens of military airplane models hang from the ceiling, and clamped to the walls are prop knives and swords. I even spy the green and white Mothra Leo from *Rebirth of Mothra II* (*Mosura 2 kaitei no daikessen*, 1997)

Resuming my trek to find Kaneko, I pass a few people who tip their heads in greeting. Trying to look like I belong, I return the gesture. The truth is, I'm lost. I ask the next person I see where the production offices are. He points at the stage where I did my running scene in G2000.

"Go past 5 and take a left," he says. "It's there on the right."

His directions lead me to a two-story building with a large plaque out front listing the week's bookings for Toho's various stages. I walk into a hall and spot a room with the word *Crossfire* on the door. I push it open slowly hoping I have the right place. There, in front of a small TV, is Kaneko.

The production room is not what I was expecting. It's just a rectangular box with a

---

7 - The international title would later become *Pyrokinesis*.

door on one end and a couple of windows on the other. The walls are a chaotic mess of production designs, photos (location shots and goofy crew photos), and documents. A whiteboard jotted over with notes and the film's remaining task list covers half of the left wall.

Kaneko waves me over. With him are ADs Nozomu Aida and Murakami. Kaneko pops a VHS cassette into a player to run a few scenes from *Crossfire*. He shows me my scene. It's brief but thrilling to watch. After this, he turns on a baseball game and the two of us drink beer while watching the Yomiuri Giants kick ass.

On the way out I notice a sign on the frosted glass window of the production room next door that says "Godzilla."

"Wanna pop in?" Kaneko asks.

We knock and step in. The layout is the same as the *Crossfire* room except the walls are covered with drawings of Godzilla, a monster I can't identify, location photos, and diagrams of miniature sets. Stacked in a corner are several boxes of beer: gifts given from production well-wishers. Having interrupted a staff meeting, we find all eyes turned our direction. However, seeing it's Kaneko, everyone stands and bows. Kaneko raises a hand to one of the men.

"This is Tezuka," he explains. "He's directing the new Godzilla."

Masaaki Tezuka is somewhat stocky, which is unusual; most people in the film world in Japan tend to be on the lanky side. Also in the room is SFX director Suzuki, who remembers me from last year. As Kaneko explains to Tezuka what I do, I pull out a copy of *Fangoria* with my G2000 article and pass a copy to Suzuki. He and Tezuka flip through the issue, bow my way, and promise their full support. I bow in response, adding a

yoroshiku onegaishimasu to the mix.

Back outside, Kaneko hails a cab; we ride into central Tokyo.

The party is in the banquet room of a hotel in Iidabashi. About a hundred and fifty people connected to *Crossfire* wait as one of the producers takes to a podium. He asks everyone to hold their drink up (limited to beer, whiskey & water, oolong tea, and orange juice). A unified *kanpai* (cheers) resounds as a toast is made. With this, the night is underway.

I fill a plate from a buffet in the center of the room. Pulling up beside me is Wakasa, who created a series of burn effects for the movie.

"Have you heard about the new Godzilla film?" he asks. I mention I met director Tezuka today. "I'm making the suits again. It's gonna be the best Godzilla film ever! Can you keep this under your hat? The secret kaiju in the film is Megaguirus!"

Mega-what?

Wakasa laughs loud, attracting the attention of everyone around us. "It's a minor creature from the movie *Rodan*. In the new film it goes through several stages of development. It's less kaiju and more creature! When you write about it, be sure to emphasize it's a creature! You got it? A *creature!*"

I've noticed a peculiar insistence by Wakasa to have his work described in western terms. Given his heroes are men like Dick Smith, Rick Baker, and Stan Winston, all top Hollywood special make-up effects creators, it's no surprise he wishes himself cast in the same league.

I spot lead actress Akiko Yada. She has a trendy cashmere shawl draped over her shoulders. I thank her for the interview at the restaurant shoot last February. It's also my first time to speak to co-star

Kaori Momoi beyond the simple greeting we exchanged during shooting. An award winning actress who has worked with Akira Kurosawa and Yoji Yamada, she tells me that she lived in London when she was 12. This explains why her English is near flawless.

I also introduce myself to actress Masami Nagasawa. Just thirteen-years-old, she's the winner of the latest Toho Cinderella Audition, a talent search the studio does every few years. Masami beat out 35,153 girls for the win. We talk for a bit. I'll be damned if I can find her different from any other Japanese female teen.

"The truth is, there was no part for her in the film," Kaneko reveals when we meet for beer refills. "Toho ordered me to use her. She has no experience and directing her was a pain in the ass. Truthfully, most of these Cinderella girls go nowhere."

Kaneko is called onto a platform in front of a *kin byobu*, a gold-colored folding screen. He gives a speech about the production and thanks the staff and Toho. He speaks of traveling to L.A. for the screening of *Gamera 3* and his impressions of western fans. He explains how he was taken by their passion for movies and how they integrate cinema into their lives. Following Kaneko, the main cast steps up and each one offers a few words of thanks and praise for the production.

Once over, about thirty of us head over to the after-party at a local karaoke. It's interesting how the room divides itself. Kaneko sits in the back center seat with the main cast gathered around him. At the table to his right are the producers and production people. At another table are the technicians, pyrotechnic staff, special makeup artists, lighting crew, etc.

I note that the further down one is on the production food chain, the further away they sit from the director. As I don't care about such stuff, I plant myself between the director (Kaneko) and the film's star (Akiko Yada).

Almost immediately the room fills with smoke, most of it coming from the rugged-looking technicians. Nearly everyone is drinking hard, particularly Kaori Momoi, who hoots and hollers as she does. She appears to be having the best time out of everyone.

Momoi is soon standing in front of a large Karaoke TV singing a duet with boom operator Eisho Taira. Male lead Hideaki Ito gets up and walks out of the room. A moment later, female screams fill the air. Ito spied a group of young girls in the room next to ours. As a prank, he walked in on their party, causing them to shriek and swoon.

The party ends at a little past 11 p.m. People filter out; some head for yet a third party. Kaneko and I train it back to our respective homes in Setagaya. I return to Osaka the next day.

GODZILLA VS. MEGAGUIRUS

8 JULY 2000

Godzilla X Megaguirus[8] (GXM) is currently shooting. As anticipated, I've been given the assignment from *Fangoria* to scribe a report covering its behind the scenes activities. I arrange with publicist Suzuki for both a set visit and a round of interviews. He mentions that the crew is currently shooting in Osaka and, coincidentally, not more than ten minutes from where I live.

"Just show up at the set," Suzuki says. "It'll be fine. You don't need any special permission."

10 JULY 2000

It's 1:30 p.m. and I'm in Nishi Umeda at the Osaka International Convention Center, a large, modern complex overlooking the Dojima River. The Godzilla crew is working in a spacious area at the center's entrance. Children carrying colorful balloons and escorted by their moms parade in front of the camera; above them, a large banner announcing "Clean Energy Factory" flaps in the humid air.

With no contact name and unsure what protocol is expected, I'm concerned about how to approach the set. Do I walk over, waving my hands high in the air, drawing undue attention, or meekly slip in through the back of the production and hope no one notices? *Keigo* (respectful language) and its proper application worry me to no end. Figuring it's sink or swim, I decide to play the naïve foreigner card and approach director Tezuka directly.

"Norman, what are you doing here?" Tezuka asks, glancing up from a heavily notated script.

Oh great, I *have* exceeded my bounds.

---

8 - The international title would later become *Godzilla vs. Megaguirus*.

Anxiously, I explain the set visits, the interviews, the article, and assure him I have permission to be here from the office at Toho.

"No. I mean, what are you doing *here*? In Osaka?"

I point down the road. "I live that-a-way."

Tezuka breaks into a smile. "And you're only just coming to the set now?"

Across the way, a half-dozen people from the local press surround a PR man from the Toho office. Dressed in a 3-piece suit, he fields questions about the film and the production. As my priority is less the PR side and more the filmmaking effort, I opt to stay with the crew, watching as Tezuka preps a shot of a reporter.

For me, the shoot is the thing. Even seemingly mundane ones like this I find more interesting and relevant than PR facts, such as when the film will open, how many theaters it will play, and the variety of promotional stunts planned. Besides, with my article aimed at the western market, domestic release points are irrelevant.

After dinner, the production moves to the other side of the river. There, the camera is aimed at the Dojima Bridge. Large movie lights cast its looped arches in a subtle, greenish hue, causing the structure to pop out against the early evening sky.

"Looks sweet, doesn't it?" Leaning against a wall running the length of the river is an elderly, near-skeleton of a man. He puffs away on a cigarette with the passion of a baby on its mother's nipple. "Where're you from?" he asks with eyes focused on the shimmering bridge.

"An American magazine called *Fangoria*," I reply. "We cover horror mostly, but get away with Godzilla because it's a monster." I mention this since people often think Godzilla belongs in *Starlog* (Fango's sci-fi counterpart), not that I expect an elderly Japanese man to know this or even care.

From his jacket, he pulls out a business card: *Kishu Morichi—Producer*. The font is different from other Toho ones I've received—more elegant. I suppose it means he's someone important. I pass him my own card. Morichi glances it over before dropping it in a side pocket.

"Osaka's a great locale," he insists. "We always get fantastic meals here." He's referring to Osaka's reputation as the pinnacle of Japanese food culture, which is itself considered one of the world's pinnacle food cultures.

After agreeing with him, I make a joke request about a few eyesores in Osaka that, if it's okay with Toho, I'd like to see Godzilla trample. As I run down the list, the old man roars with laughter.

Once the bridge's establishing shot has been captured, the crew moves onto the bridge itself. Three soldiers carrying formidable-looking bazookas are set to dash across. One is a woman with a lovely face and large, dark eyes. I can't recall ever having seen a female soldier in Japan and set in taking photos of this rarity. For some reason, she appears ill at ease with each shot I snap. *Whatever.* As an extra, she should be happy for the attention.

Standing beside her is a man in a business suit. Jacket off, his shirt is stained with sweat. Between takes, he dotes her with attention and even takes to rubbing her shoulders. *That's odd.* From what I've seen, extras fend for themselves, even the female ones. I go over to Tezuka to see if he can unravel the mystery of these two.

"What's up with that extra and that

guy?" Tezuka doesn't follow. "Them." I toss a thumb over my shoulder.

"Them? You mean, *that* woman?" I roll my eyes, letting him know he's hit the target dead on. "That's no extra!" he exclaims. "That's Misato Tanaka, the star of the film. Didn't you know this?"

One self-inflicted head slap later, I explain my set faux pas. After his laughter subsides, Tezuka walks me over and explains to Tanaka and her manager that I'm a US reporter covering the film. With a bow, he requests their cooperation. An intro from the director seems to be the magic charm. They wave off any notion I may have overstepped my boundaries.

The production moves back to the Convention Center, where it sets up at the base of a ramp leading into a parking lot. Waiting in full army regalia is Toshiyuki Nagashima, an actor I met during *Crossfire*.

Just before the first take, the crew lays white mist across the area. Tezuka starts things off by having Tanaka aim a bazooka over the camera lens. On cue, she heaves the heavy-looking weapon onto a shoulder and tightens her face. Rushing to her side, Nagashima orders her to leave before Godzilla attacks. It appears to be a scene with great dramatic tension—or at least the kind of over-the-top dramatic tension common to kaiju films.

Nagashima's shots are completed within an hour. In no time he's out of his fatigues and back in street clothes. I'm standing against a lighting scaffold when he asks why I've come all the way to Osaka. Like everyone, Nagashima is surprised to learn I live here, which, despite what Morichi said earlier, makes me wonder the reputation Osaka has around Japan.

26 JULY 2000

Today marks the start of my apartment share in Tokyo. I step out of the overly air-conditioned Shinkansen and onto the platform of Tokyo Station. It's so fricking hot out that I feel like I've been slapped in the face with a hot frying pan. Dragging my large suitcase over the cancerous glut of staircases strewn throughout the city only exacerbates the heat.

Finally, I get to Shimokitazawa Station, wheel my stuff to my new place, and struggle with the five-floor walk-up. But my enthusiasm is not diminished. I plop my suitcase on the kitchen floor, rush to the balcony, slide the glass doors open, and let the wide view of Tokyo welcome me.

While I don't consider myself a Japanophile—which at its worst denotes foreigners with an unfounded kinship to things Japanese—I enjoy the serendipity of the situation. It's as if one moment I'm a boy of eight sitting in a theater in New York enchanted by the miniature cities in *Destroy All Monsters* and the next I'm sucked into the screen and dropped into the very same city.

After a day of unpacking and cleaning, I travel to Kaneko's station, where I meet up with him, Nanako, and their children. They treat me to a fantastic meal of yakiniku. Nanako says the kids are excited to have me around. Is that why they bounce ceaselessly up and down in their seats and vie for my attention? It's the sort of family moment I haven't had in a long time.

27 JULY 2000

I tag behind Kaneko as he leads me to Shinjuku, onto the Yamanote train line, to Ebisu Station, and finally to

Yebisu Garden Place. We're here for the premiere of *Shiki-jitsu* (*Ritual*), a film starring Ayako Fujitani and Shunji Iwai. As a run of moving sidewalks carries us to the station's exit, Kaneko's face turns crimson red.

"I don't believe it!" he blurts, and points his nose at a man zipping past. "It's Nanri!"

I remember Nanri from the G3 shoot in Kyoto. He was one of the producers. Shaking his head, Kaneko explains the situation between himself, Nanri, and a director named Hideaki Anno.

According to Kaneko, Anno, creator of the popular *Evangelion* anime series, was hired to direct a documentary on the production of G3. Considered a visionary, he was expected to do something cool and edgy.

"When I saw the rough cut, I was shocked," Kaneko complains. "Rather than make a film about the creation of G3, Anno made one about what he perceived to be the rivalry between the live-action and special effects sets. I asked him and Nanri to drop it. They promised they would, but they didn't." It's then I find out that Anno directed *Shiki-jitsu* and that Nanri produced it.

"It's a safe bet," I posit, "Anno will be here tonight." Kaneko's fists tighten as the sidewalk ends.

Shiki-jitsu is based on *Touhimu* (*Flee-dream*), a novel by Ayako. As the film unfolds, I'm surprised to find, among other things, it lays bare the state of Aya's relationship with her mom, who was once caught up in a bigamy case with estranged husband Steven Seagal. It seems the famous action icon remarried an actress without bothering to file for divorce from Aya's mom.

The film over, Kaneko and I join the after-screening crowd in the lobby. He introduces me to two directors. One is Shimako Sato, known for the film *Eko Eko Azarak: Wizard of Darkness* (1995) and the opening movie sequence in the *Resident Evil* video games. The other is Takashi Yamazaki, director of *Juvenile* (*Jubunairu*, 2000), a science fiction film produced and released by Toho that opened two weeks ago. It turns out they live together in Shimokita, making us neighbors.

Shimako grabs the arm of a man making his way between the various groups throughout the lobby. He's unusually tall, has scraggly facial hair, and a belly that protrudes like on one of those Buddha statues sold in Asian gift shops.

"Kaneko, have you met director Anno?" she asks. The two men look at each other. Kaneko's face goes red and Anno tenses up.

"Yes, I have," Kaneko says curtly. "Actually, I don't like this guy."

Shimako chirps out a nervous laugh. "You're joking, right?"

Anno pulls his arms taut against his body and bows. "I am very sorry," he says.

"I'm not kidding," Kaneko insists, ignoring Anno's apology. "I *really* don't like this guy."

Despite Anno bending at a nearly 90-degree angle, Kaneko waves a judgmental finger at him. "Can you tell me why you lied about the G3 video?"

It's at this point that Aya breaks out in tears. Grabbing Kaneko's arm, I plead for him to stop. He looks at Aya, whose head is buried in Shimako's shoulder. Feeling the point made, he lightens up.

"Okay," he says. "Let's get dinner."

As we leave, Anno maintains his bow Kaneko's way.

Over at the Sapporo Beer Station, we put the incident behind us, filling up on large glasses of ice-cold beer and various small dishes in an eating style the Japanese call *izakaya*.

Shimako is somewhat hard-edged. She demonstrates an unusually strong will that I attribute to Carlos Castaneda, a writer she boasts as an influence on her life-outlook. I'm impressed. I've never met a Japanese person familiar with Castaneda. She also speaks terrific English, having studied filmmaking in London.

Quite the reverse, inspired by *Star Wars* and *Close Encounters* as a child, Yamazaki is the typical film-geek-turned professional. The two of us toss science fiction titles back and forth, soliciting opinions as we gauge each other's sensibilities.

On the way back to Ebisu Station, I lend Aya a sympathetic ear.

"I was unsure about inviting you guys," she admits. "But Kaneko's like a dad to me. And Anno's a good friend, too. Why can't everyone just get along?"

Kaneko and I travel back home to Setagaya together, me getting off at Shimokita, and him traveling on to his stop.

My first full day in Tokyo, I wonder if every day will be like this.

28 JULY 2000

My GXM set visit begins today! I arrive at Toho a little before 11 a.m. and meet Kaneko in front of the fountain—only it's not a fountain.

"There's a circular set of seats out front with a Godzilla plaque in the center that was a fountain for decades," he explained on the train last night. "Even though it changed a year or so ago, everyone still calls it the fountain."

Sure enough, I find him sitting there reading a book. He holds it up. "English history. It has interesting parallels to Japanese history."

We walk the five meters to the PR office where Suzuki is waiting. As we set the ground rules for my set visit—whom to interview, when to interview, when Toho would like the article to run, photo usage, etc.—a bus pulls into the lot and parks beside the fountain.

A woman in a tan jumpsuit leaps out. Patched to one of her shoulders is an insignia for "G-Force," a fictional division of the United Nations seen in the '90s Godzilla films. Following her is a long line of kids, adults, elderly, and otaku-looking guys—*a lot* of otaku-looking guys. With great theatrics, the woman holds her hands in the air and shouts, "Welcome to Toho Studios!"

Kaneko and I turn to Suzuki, who merely shrugs. "This is producer Tomiyama's latest brainstorm: a Universal Studios-like tour of Toho," he explains.

After the tour wanders off, Kaneko and I stop in S1, where GXM's live-action crew is filming a scene of soldiers aiming bazookas at a large blue screen. We park ourselves in folding chairs. Director Tezuka brings a dish of candy. He bows and offers us each a piece. I ask what will be superimposed on the blue screen.

"It's part of the opening scene in Osaka," Tezuka explains. "We're going to drop in Godzilla smashing a building." For the next shot, the actors are strapped to harnesses. With the camera rolling, they are pulled violently through the air.

Back outside, we head to S5, the final stop on Tomiyama's "Toho Studio Tour." At the entrance stands an animatronic

Godzilla and behind it is a Styrofoam cave opening. Colored lights strobe across thick mist as Akira Ifukube's famous Godzilla theme thumps from speakers hidden in the rafters. Every now and then, a low-fi recording of the kaiju king's trademark roar overpowers the music. The whole thing feels tacky, and goofing around, we pretend to be scared by the animatronic Godzilla, scurrying into the cave like frightened children.

Photos and posters detailing Godzilla's nearly 50-year history line the walls. At the end, large, garish Godzilla and Mechagodzilla heads confront us. Standing beside them is Hariken "Hurricane" Ryu, a storyboard artist and suit actor in such films as *Godzilla vs. King Ghidorah* (*Gojira tai Kingu Gidora*, 1991) and *Godzilla vs. Destoroyah*.

Ryu tells us he's been hired to perform stunts for the tour. He adds that it's been designed by Koichi Kawakita, the Toho effects director best known for his work on Godzilla films shot between 1989 and 1995. Next to the exit are tables covered with leftover G2000 theater-exclusive items: notebooks, medallions, pens, etc.[9]

Kaneko and I walk to the far end of Toho and step into S9, where a sprawling miniature set takes up much of the studio floor. Buildings, many taller than us, are positioned around an open field littered with debris. Windows, walls, roofs, support beams, and jagged bits of crushed building cover the stage. Off to a side is a tiny parking lot stocked with cars and buses. It's detailed down to fences, lampposts, and shrubbery. Behind this is a miniature construction site. It, too, has been given an impressive amount of attention. I spot a crane, a digger, and a

shed with tiny sewer pipes. The detail is mesmerizing and I'm drawn into it in the way a child is drawn into the front window of F.A.O. Schwartz.

I'm interrupted by kaiju suit maker Wakasa yelling, "Let's Fango!" It's baffling that people still remember this silly '80s *Fangoria* catchphrase. He scurries over and, pulling me from Kaneko, leads me around the set.

"A beauty, isn't she?" By the pride in his voice, it sounds more like he's telling than asking. A moment later, leading me by the sleeve again, he takes me to where his staff maintains the various monster suits.

"We slightly redesigned Godzilla," Wakasa says as he points to a Godzilla suit hanging in a metal pushcart. "Feel the arms! See how thin they are?"

It's true. Touching the suit reveals it to be almost paper-thin in parts, although the chest and legs remain heavily padded.

"And it's tough, too. I use only the best latex. US-made. The same stuff Rick Baker uses."

Various versions of Godzilla's latest foe reside at Wakasa's station. "It starts out as an egg," he explains. "It then becomes a larva called Meganulon." He points to what looks like a giant, mutant ant with large green and black eyes. Like Godzilla, it's suspended in a support rig. Next, he pulls a dragonfly-like creature out from a box. "This is Meganula, the next stage. Megaguirus, the big one on the set, is the final, adult stage."

Although they look like insects, it's hard to call them such. They're spiky, toothy, and purple-tinged. "That's because," Wakasa reminds me, "they're creatures. Be sure to refer to them as such when you write about the production,

---

9 - The tour would soon be canceled by the head office. I believe over insurance concerns, but don't quote me on it.

okay? *Creatures*! Got it?" I assure him I will not call them anything but.

Wakasa's name rings out. Director Suzuki is calling him to the stage. Before rushing off, he gives me permission to take photos and hit his staff up with questions.

After conferring with Wakasa, Suzuki explains the upcoming shot to Kaneko and me. "It's a tough one," he admits. "We have to fly Megaguirus down a wire and get its tail right into Godzilla's mouth."

Making small talk, I tell Suzuki how impressed I am by the set.

"Do you know where this is?" he asks. I don't. "It's Odaiba, an artificial island in Tokyo Bay." I point out a futuristic-looking building of unusual design near the back.

"*Oh*, that," he huffs. "It's supposed to be the Fuji TV building. We wanted to destroy it, but Fuji TV wouldn't hear of it." I'm surprised to hear this. It was my understanding that Godzilla destroying your office or home is an honor.

"Most companies are happy to see their buildings demolished by Godzilla," Suzuki continues. "But some feel it might hurt their image or bring bad luck. For the Fuji building we couldn't perfectly reproduce it and were forced to alter it into a suggestive likeness."

The crew wheels the Godzilla suit over. One man carries just the fins. Off to a side, Godzilla actor Kitagawa does stretching exercises. Suspended in the air by thin steel wires is the final version of Megaguirus. It's flown to a spot a few meters from the edge of the set. Wakasa's crew tends to it, searching for areas that might need touching up and double-checking that the remote controller is functioning correctly. Signaling himself ready, Kitagawa is helped into Godzilla.

He works his feet in, then his arms, and finally his head. Lastly, the suit team attaches the fins.

Suzuki calls for a test. Megaguirus is released. Building up speed, it zooms down a nearly invisible cable. Instead of hitting Godzilla in the mouth, it catches him between the eyes.

"Cut!" screams Suzuki. The staff gathers to figure out where adjustments need to be made.

Kaneko and I use the downtime to take a breather. We find seats on dusty folding chairs in the back of S9. From here, we can see the whole of the Godzilla production.

"It's hard to believe that just six months ago this was the set of *Crossfire*," I say.

"That's the thing about filmmaking," Kaneko remarks. "It gets so larger than life and you find yourself so deep inside a production that it can feel as if the end will never come. But it does. It always does. Even the good ones—the ones you don't want to see end—end."

Looking at the set of GXM, it certainly seems to be a huge production. At least fifty people are running this way and that, doing jobs I'm only beginning to understand. Somehow, when taken as a whole, it comes across much like the floor of a factory.

"Everything you see here is directly connected to the '54 original *Gojira*," Kaneko adds. "Some of the staff are only a generation away from those who originated the techniques being used now."

I climb onto a platform that offers a better view of the action. After snapping a few shots, I notice everyone is looking at me. Worse, they're frowning. It must have been repositioned while I was with Kaneko because, turning around, I'm eye-to-eye with the flying version of Megaguirus.

"You should not stand there," someone near the edge of the stage says in English. I catch the eye of the man speaking. *Crap!* Not only am I being reprimanded, but by producer Tomiyama. Cursing under my breath, I jump down and walk over to apologize.

He shakes his head. "It's fine," he assures me.

With me out of the way, action is called. Megaguirus sails down the wire and, as planned, catches Godzilla right in the mouth. After reviewing the shot, Suzuki approves it. Following this, an AD announces dinner break.

"I have to talk with Tomiyama about something," Kaneko says ominously. The two leave together.

Once the sun has sunk behind S9 and the sky sufficiently darkened, Tezuka and his staff gather on the right side of the big pool. Suspended by a crane, a collection of broken concrete slabs hang eerily twenty feet in the air.

"This is a continuation of the scene in Osaka," Tezuka tells me. "We're going to squash Nagashima with that rubble up there!" Tezuka calls for action. Actors Nagashima and Tanaka dash past the camera. Satisfied with the take, Tezuka bellows, "Okay!" An AD calls Nagashima to the center of the production and announces that the actor's work on the film is complete. Tezuka walks over with a large bouquet of ornately wrapped flowers. Taking them, Nagashima bows as the staff applauds.

The final shot of the night is the concrete crashing down. Stunt doubles are called in. I'm surprised to find that Tanaka's is not only a man but Ohashi, the suit actor who donned the Iris suit in G3.

"This isn't my first time playing a

woman," Ohashi admits. "I'm rather small, so I do stunts as a woman all the time."

With everything in place, Tezuka scales a ladder and balances himself beside the camera crane. On his command, the hovering rocks are released. They fall through the air—large, broken concrete slabs—and smash about the stuntmen, who leap for cover. The pieces hit the ground and bounce harmlessly away. Although looking incredibly heavy, they are actually made of lightweight material. Tezuka yells "Cut" through a megaphone.

The stuntmen stand and brush the dust off their uniforms. With that, the day is called a wrap.

30 JULY 2000

The shots for today are close-ups of Godzilla taking Megaguirus's stinger in the abdomen. With no need for miniatures in the frame, Godzilla stands on a couple of pushed-together platforms.

The staff wheels over a crane that has a detached Megaguirus tail clamped to its tip. It's crimson red with rows of spikes painted a bright banana yellow. Wakasa puffs madly on a cigarette while directing the positioning of the monsters. Spotting me, he waves a hand. "See this? I made it strictly for close-ups. Nice, isn't it?"

It *is* nice. I run my fingers along a ridge of stingers. The detail is incredible; the colors are vivid.

"Push on the stinger tip," Wakasa orders. It must be set on a spring because it sinks into the tail. "It's the ol' collapsing knife effect," he adds.

Suzuki calls for rehearsal. A crewman swings the stinger into Godzilla's belly. Gripping it with both sets of claws, Godzilla thrashes it about and then wrenches it out. Kitagawa pops his head out of the Godzilla suit and Suzuki offers the actor feedback.

Feeling daring, I climb onto the stage during a prep to test my set boundaries. I take a few close-up shots of Godzilla. For the first take, I crouch down with the crew around the film camera. I'm expecting to be told to stand off to the side, but no one seems to mind. My heart pumps wildly. It's exciting being in the trenches so close to the Godzilla suit during an actual take. Looking up at the King of the Monsters as he struggles with the stinger, I can hear Kitagawa's muffled screams filtering from the suit.

4 AUGUST 2000

Nobuko has come to assist me with the day's interviews. At Toho, we check in with Suzuki in the PR room before joining the Godzilla staff around the big pool.

It's muggy and blistering hot out; the type of day that can turn plastic toy dinosaurs into puddles of green goo. Wakasa calls me over. He looks like hell. His hair is greasy and clings to the sweat dotting his brow.

"The heat is murder," he complains. "Everyone is tense. Nothing would make me happier than to blow up the pool right here and now!"

The edge of the pool is being made to look like a beach. Crewmembers shovel and pat dirt around Styrofoam rocks painted brown. A huge green screen covers the wall behind the pool. I ask SFX director Suzuki why they don't just use a mural as they have in the past.

"Take a look at it," he says pointing to an exposed edge. "It's faded and needs a paint job. Besides, with a green

screen, we aren't locked into a single background. We can decide that during post-production."

In the Godzilla suit, Kitagawa is guided by two crewmembers into the water and positioned to face the shore. A large, noisy fan starts up, causing the water to swirl aggressively. Standing in the pool in rubber fishing overalls and out of camera range, a crewman holds a 3-foot wood beam across the water top. He bobs it up and down, chopping the water into small waves.

"It makes the water look more realistic," continuity person (a job called "scripter" in Japan) Junko Kawashima tells me. "This way the waves look proportionally correct against Godzilla."

As the scene is shot, the wave chopper comes under the ire of one of the ADs. "Come on you lazy son of a bitch!" he yells, hands cupped around his mouth to cut over the din of the fan. "Make them waves! Harder! More power! This is for *Godzilla*!!!" His friendly chiding causes the crew to break into uncontrolled laughter.

Following the take, lunch is called. PR man Suzuki gives us vouchers for a meal at the Toho cafeteria. I grab a tray and stand in line with the grimy Godzilla crew.

A half-hour later, I'm at the door of the PR room thanking Suzuki for lunch when another bus from the Toho Studio Tours parks in front of the fountain. Stepping from it is a fresh load of sightseers. Surprisingly, there are white people in the group: a middle-aged woman, a college-aged boy in a *Godzilla vs. Megalon* (*Gojira tai Megaro*, 1973) t-shirt, and a teen woman. Spotting me, they break from the group.

"Are you Norman England?" the college boy asks. "I read your articles all the time!" The look on Suzuki's face is priceless as I pose for photos with them.

The shoot at the pool continues with Godzilla making a few more advances onto shore. This goes on until director Suzuki is happy. Kitagawa is removed from the Godzilla suit. Two guys from Wakasa's crew come over carrying hacksaws. Right away, they start sawing into Godzilla's legs, cutting deep until they have broken through to the yellow foam under the green skin. I turn to Wakasa for an explanation.

"That was the last shot showing the water suit in its entirety. The only scenes left are from the waist up. As the suit absorbs a lot of water, it makes it easier for Kitagawa to move and will speed things up."

With that, the legs separate from the suit. A staffer carries the amputated feet to the side of the pool and squeezes the water out of them.

I have an interview scheduled with Shinji Higuchi to cover his new film *Sakuya: Yokaiden*[10]. I thank the Godzilla staff and zip out of Toho. A half-hour later I meet up with model maker Sagae at Meidaimae Station, where we have dinner with Higuchi, conducting the interview as we eat. Once again, Higuchi is in full-on artist mode; I hate to admit it, but I have trouble following his Japanese. Luckily Nobuko is here to keep the ball rolling.

After dinner we go to Motor/lieZ, Higuchi's office, where he shows off an import DVD of *Galaxy Quest*. With the film unreleased in Japan, he's intensely curious to understand the story. Popping it into a DVD player, Higuchi asks if I'll translate. I do the best I can, which must be good enough because Higuchi gives off deep, booming laughs throughout the entire thing.

5 AUGUST 2000

Before heading to Toho, I go to the offices of Asmik Ace, a film distribution company. I'm doing a Fango piece on the latest movie in the Ring series, *Ring 0: Birthday*. Asmik set up an interview for me with its star, Yukie Nakama. I spend an enjoyable hour with the actress talking about her role as Sadako.

I'd mentioned the interview to Kaneko and he told me that she had a small part in G3. Kaneko added that, as a popular idol, her presence had all the guys on the crew "very animated." It's understandable. Yukie is a beautiful young woman. Once done, Nobuko and I hightail it over to Toho.

Suzuki kindly lets me take over the PR office for my interviews. First up is Wakasa. As I've come to expect, he's upbeat, confident, and elated to be interviewed by the foreign press. I begin with a question about changes in this year's Godzilla design.

"The decision came early to keep the same look as last year," Wakasa explains. "Although I didn't make any major modifications, I did alter the color. Remember when I said I wanted Godzilla green? I was disappointed to see how gray it looked on film. This year I've used a more vivid color. I want the green to leap off the screen!"

I'm curious how last year's production and this one stack up against one another. As he thinks, Wakasa pulls over an ashtray and lights a cigarette.

"If I compare the pressure this year to last, rating last year a 100, this year would be a 5. For one thing, I didn't have to create Godzilla from scratch. Most of

---

10 - Although never properly released in the West, the film is known internationally as *Sakuya: Slayer of Demons*.

my effort has gone into improving things. For example, I cut a third of the weight and made it more flexible."

But the holy grail of information comes from asking just how Godzilla suits are made. Wakasa lets out a long, loud cackle of a laugh.

"To explain that would take a while. Tell you what, after the production is over, how about stopping by my studio? I'll give you a lesson in how to build Godzilla." Now we're talking! I tell him I'm going to hold him to it.

Following Wakasa, Suzuki brings in lead actress Misato Tanaka. Throughout the shoot, she's been dressed in an unflattering military outfit with her hair bundled up and shoved under either a pilot cap or a field helmet. Today is my first time seeing her out of costume. She wears form-fitting blue jeans and her thick, black hair runs over her shoulders and down her back. As she glides in with the relaxed poise of a professional model, I'm awestruck by her beauty. I start by asking the 24-year-old Tanaka how she got the starring gig.

"Beats me," she admits. "I've never had a part like this before. Kiriko Tsujimori, my character, is tough and uncompromising. All my roles have been timid women trying to overcome personal hardship."

Suzuki steps in: "Director Tezuka wanted a Toho actress to play Kiriko, not someone from outside the studio. Of all our stable actresses, he felt she was best for the part." From the look on Tanaka's face, I'm guessing she's hearing this for the first time.

Looking at Godzilla fandom and the disproportional boy/girl ratio, it's safe to label them "guy flicks."

"That's not entirely true," Tanaka insists. "My parents took me to see Godzilla movies when I was a girl. I loved them! I didn't find him scary or villainous—just the opposite! Godzilla is cool. I take my part very seriously. For example, there's a scene where I ride on Godzilla. After I was cast, I went to see the Godzilla suit. I walked up to it and touched the spot I'd be clinging to—just the spot—imagining myself holding on for dear life. In movies of this nature, an actor has to work hard to connect with the unreal world in which their character lives."

Tanaka, a Special Jury Prize winner at the Toho Cinderella contest in '96, describes the shoot as, "very physical. Remember in Osaka when I had to throw that missile launcher over my shoulder? The guys in the crew were handling it like it was nothing, so I figured it was light. It wasn't. I thought it was going to break my back when I first picked it up!"

Following this is my interview with first time Godzilla director Masaaki Tezuka. A warm, ear-to-ear grin on his face, Tezuka comes into the sunny PR room with a bundle of paperwork under his arms: a copy of the GXM script, storyboards, and other papers overwritten with notes and impromptu drawings. He holds out a hand. We shake as he thanks me for taking the time to visit the set.

"Maybe it should be me thanking you for your time," I say pointing to his workload.

At 44, Tezuka is probably a first-generation kaiju fan; he's the right age. My suspicion is confirmed when I ask him to describe his relationship with the giant monster.

"In the 1960s, nothing was more important to me than Godzilla. The first one I saw was *King Kong vs. Godzilla*. I remember it vividly. The theater was packed and I couldn't get a seat. I watched it standing and could only see the screen by peeking through the spaces between the adults. But that was enough to blow me away. Godzilla was everything—terrifying, fierce, and indestructible. Unfortunately, children today don't know Godzilla the way I did then. This makes me sad. One of my motivations is to make Godzilla exciting for kids today. They're the ones who'll carry the dream."

Questioning Tezuka's background, I learn he worked as an AD for G2000 director Okawara on several Godzilla films in the 1990s.

"It no doubt helped me land my current position, but it has come back to haunt me. I was constantly passing Okawara ideas because I figured I'd never direct Godzilla. Now that I am, I'm kicking myself for giving away too many of the concepts I've had since I was young."

With so many Godzilla films—twenty four to date—I'm interested in what new things Tezuka plans to bring to the franchise.

"Early on in the film's development I thought it would be great to have physical contact between humans and Godzilla. We created a scene where Tanaka rides on Godzilla. I had the art staff build a full-scale section of Godzilla's side that we shot Tanaka clinging to. While it's been done in other giant monster films, such as in the Gamera series and in *Orochi, the Eight-Headed Dragon*, it's never been attempted in a Godzilla movie."

A staple of Japanese giant monster films is the hordes of extras fleeing for their lives. As I asked Kaneko during G3's production, I ask Tezuka if he has tips for would-be runner extras.

"It's important not to laugh. We ask extras to keep their mouths shut when running. This makes it less likely for them to laugh or smile. Still, when we were shooting at Odaiba, a lot of people kept laughing. I don't blame them. It's absurd to run back and forth on a hot, muggy day from a giant monster you can't see."

Tezuka has to return to the production, and we end things after an hour. Following this is my meeting with SFX director Suzuki, my last interview of the day. I go to S1 to wait for him to finish with the day's shoot. Nowhere near as exciting as yesterday, the SFX set is in the midst of green screen photography.

Hanging by wires in front of one of those unnaturally pure green screens is the model of the "Griffon." It's a craft piloted by the "G-Graspers," a branch of the military tasked with ridding Japan of Godzilla. In a quiet corner of the stage, Suzuki holds a Styrofoam version of the ship at arm's length and moves it about, making jet plane sounds while visualizing how the model will appear on film. After this, he works with the crew in plotting the camera movement.

Seeing as Suzuki won't be done for a while, I pop in next door to S2, where, coincidentally, the live-action crew is shooting close-up shots of the cockpit of the Griffon. Misato Tanaka, fresh off our interview and back in military uniform, is strapped within a full-scale mock-up of the ship's cockpit. Seeing me, she waves from her seat in the blue and white craft. I think I'm falling in love with this work...

Several hours later, the SFX crew has wrapped; I can interview Suzuki in the PR room. This being his second Godzilla production, I'm interested to hear him compare the two.

"When we made G2000," Suzuki begins, "Toho hadn't made a Godzilla film in five years. Everyone was out of practice. For this reason, we felt it best to take it straight-ahead, meaning a film that wouldn't push the Godzilla envelope too hard. If you look carefully, you'll see that Godzilla's personality is kept at arm's length. This time, however, we're doing things no one's done before. For example, when Godzilla is surprised, his eyes open and shut rapidly. We're infusing him with personality traits. I hope that this and other touches—touches I consider manga-influenced—will win over today's younger audience members."

This time out, Godzilla's nemesis is the flying Megaguirus. "Nothing's harder than dealing with airborne kaiju," Suzuki insists. "Although just flying around doesn't pose too big of a challenge, pitting it in a fight against Godzilla while flying is. For Godzilla, we have Kitagawa inside the suit where he can emote; however, no one can fit into Megaguirus when it's in the air. I'm planning to add CG effects to the wings during post-pro. I'm after those quick, jarring motions dragonflies have and want it to pop around Godzilla. I imagine Megaguirus to be like a ninja."

The successful creation of Megaguirus was paramount to Suzuki. "It took almost three months to come up with a design I was happy with. Not just the main, final version, but all the various stages. The design had to consider how it will look on its own and how it will appear when in the frame with Godzilla. The two kaiju must complement each other while also looking capable of ousting the other. The final Megaguirus underwent a lot of changes. I ordered five sculptures based on the design until I was happy."

Although I'd like to go longer, I keep Suzuki's interview at an hour. After seeing him off, I thank the PR staff for their help. Lots of bowing and handshakes. With

the weight of the interviews behind me, I breathe easier and take a leisurely stroll through the early evening ambiance of Toho. I nod to a few familiar faces as they make their way between the various stages, and at the gate I thank the guards.

5 OCTOBER 2000

I arrived in Tokyo in the morning and am now having coffee with Kaneko at the Starbucks in Shimokita. The rumor mill has been running wild and I've decided to confront him about his next film gig, which onliners are saying will be Godzilla. We get seats with a nice view of a rug shop dressed up to resemble a quaint English teahouse.

I ask what's new. Kaneko covers family stuff, day trips, and other things with the kids. That didn't work, so I nudge closer to the subject by asking what's new in the movie world. He goes over a few films he saw, and we waste a bit of time praising/condemning recent movies. Taking a step closer, I ask what professional plans he has on the horizon. He mentions a couple of pet projects, complaining how nothing is concrete. This is getting nowhere. I guess I have to go the direct route.

"Isn't there something you want to tell me?" I ask, abandoning tact. Kaneko looks at me blankly. "You know, isn't there something *big* coming up?" He still appears to have no idea what I'm talking about. "Look!" I say in a near bark. "I know you got the job directing the next Godzilla movie, tell me already!"

He tries, but can't hold back a smile. "Yes...Toho has asked me to direct the next Godzilla film."

This is great news—for both of us. I've been looking for a way out of Osaka. Nishinari, the ward I've been living in is nothing to write home about. (To be honest, I don't. I send my family photos of my previous apartment.) While void of dilapidated and abandoned buildings, Nishinari is downscale enough to be considered a slum. Homeless abound, and many are drunk to the point that on more than one occasion I've had to drag inebriated men passed out on the road to the safety of the sidewalk.

"If that's the case," I say point-blank, "I want to get out of Osaka and live in Shimokita permanently. I want to go to the Godzilla set every day and follow its creation from pre to post-production. I want to see everything, experience everything, take pictures of everything—I want to write about it like no one ever has." It's a bold request; too bold, I worry.

Judging from the look of zero surprise on his face, there's no question he was expecting this. Still, never one to blurt out a reply, Kaneko sits back and runs my proposal through his mind. The minutes tick by. We drink our coffee in silence.

Finally, he looks my way. Shaking his head up and down, he says, "I think that will be fine."

My excitement cannot be overstated. My life has always revolved around fantasy-driven pop culture. Real life has never stacked up against the imaginative situations in genre works and I've gravitated to them from the moment I became a conscious member of the human race.

This development...it's kind of cool. I mean, here I am, a guy who was hanging Godzilla posters on the wall of his Manhattan office not ten years ago. Me...no one in particular...just a fan. Yet, someone who—by sheer force of audacious will—has talked the most celebrated living director of giant monsters into giving him the keys to the upcoming Godzilla production.

I guess my thoughts had overtaken me because Kaneko is just sitting there watching me think. Snapping out of it, I try to come up with something appropriate to say, something to let him know how important this is to me, and how grateful I am. Try as I might, I can't find anything notable to say and simply come out with a weak-sounding, "Thank you."

He looks at me and smiles. Perhaps "thank you" is all that can be said.

With the cat out of the bag, Kaneko tells me producer Tomiyama asked him to direct a while back and he's been struggling to come up with a story ever since.

"My first idea was to bring back Gimantis," he explains. "You know it?"

I give him a hard time for forgetting the chorus of his son and me begging him to use that particular monster.

"Toho didn't like that idea," he admits. "Then I had one for three god-like monsters, each representing the various earthly elements. Toho liked this, but not my choice of monsters and have forced me to use ones of their choosing. It's ridiculous. For example, I have Mothra, a bug, representing water.

"It was a shock when they told me this," he adds. "I sat in the Toho office for fifteen minutes without saying a word as I ran it through my head whether I could or couldn't make an interesting film that meets their demands. In the end, I said I could."

We go back to my place to watch a subbed copy of *Crossfire*. Kaneko wants me to check the English, while I want him to explain certain moments in the film: why he shot them the way he did and what he feels works and doesn't work.

Later, after seeing him off at the station, I bump into Ayako, who, judging by her colorful hippie clothes, looks as if she just stepped off the set of *Laugh-In*. Last time I met Ayako I gave her a collection of my poetry.

"Read your stuff—It's good! I hadn't realized you'd lost your mind."

7 OCTOBER 2000

I spent yesterday at director and makeup artist Tomoo Haraguchi's home in Shibuya conducting a Fango interview for his *Sakuya: Yokaiden* movie. I went with Sagae, who worked on the SFX set of the film. Haraguchi is a fan of *yokai* and his living room is filled with nearly every creature built for the film, including bakeneko, a supernatural cat. The thing is huge! By my best guess, it's over 210 centimeters (seven feet) tall!

While the interview with Haraguchi went well, I feel I'm short on quotes from Higuchi, who handled the film's special effects. Fearing I might have trouble with Higuchi's Japanese, I call Ayako to see if she'll help with a follow-up interview. More than happy to, she asks if it's okay to invite some people along to make a party out of it.

I meet Ayako at Shimokitazawa Station and we travel to Shibuya, where we connect with her friends. Haraguchi, who I just saw yesterday, is among them; we tip our heads in greeting. Ayako introduces me to her brother Kentaro. Like Ayako, his Japanese features dominate his western ones. He shakes my hand. "What's up, man?" He sounds like a California surfer.

Ayako introduces me to Yuriko, the only other woman in the group. She says she manages the Shinjuku club Loft Plus

One. Also joining us is director Hideaki Anno. *Ugh*, I hope doesn't remember me from the premiere of *Shiki-jitsu* last July.

We go into a slightly rundown *izakaya*, order beers and snacks, and get the party going. As we eat and drink, I question Higuchi over *Sakuya* specifics. As I had most of what I need from the previous talk, we're done in twenty minutes. Now I can focus on having a good time. But right away, Haraguchi starts in on me.

"The first time I met this guy I was like, 'I know him!'" he says loudly. Haraguchi stands and points at me. "You're into *Dawn of the Dead*, right? You think I don't watch TV? This freakin' guy! He was a guest on *Nandemo Kanteidan* as a *Dawn of the Dead* collector!"

A wildly popular TV show, *Nandemo Kanteidan* focuses on people and their collections, the more bizarre the better. I was featured twice a few years back and people still haven't forgotten. Despite the level of renown at our table, everyone is impressed.

Yuriko pulls out oil absorbent paper and presses it to her nose. Grabbing the pack from her, Higuchi proposes that we have a "nose oil competition." We each press a sheet against our nose. On the count of three, we pull it off. Higuchi's turns out to have the most oil, with Anno a close second.

"No! I don't want to be the oil paper nose champion!" he cries out.

As is often the case, the men steer the conversation to my relationship with Japanese women. It's a subject Japanese men never tire of, and the level of misconception is great. Invariably, they're under the delusion that non-Japanese men need only to look at a Japanese woman and, faster than you can say, "life should be this easy," they're in a hotel screwing like rabbits.

Higuchi asks if I have any photos of girls I'm interested in. I happened to have one in my wallet and pass it to him. His eyes ignite. He smashes a fist against the table.

"I quit being an effects director!" he screams. "I never meet pretty girls! There are no pretty girls in the SFX business!"

Everyone breaks up laughing. Even Anno, who has spent most of the evening staring into space while stroking the stubble on his face, let's out a laugh.

3 NOVEMBER 2000

I'm back in Tokyo, this time for the premiere of GXM at the Tokyo International Film Festival, held once again at Bunkamura Hall in Shibuya. A long line stretches from the hall's entrance and down the street. It's composed almost exclusively of guys between the ages of 30 and 50, or what I call "the kaiju generation."

Like last year, Suzuki hands me a press pass and lets me in early. In the lobby, the cast and staff of the film have gathered for a pre-show photo op. I take some pictures and then enter the hall.

I grab a fifth row/center seat that promises a perfect view of the film. A second later, the audience is let in, setting off a mad scramble. I toss my jacket over my seat before working my way against the incoming mass. Back in the lobby, I meet up with Kaneko, where well-wishers constantly interrupt us to congratulate him on getting the Godzilla gig. I can't help thinking that this has to be the world's worst kept secret. I feel sorry for him. Unable to admit to it for professional reasons, he's forced to respond with denials and I-don't-know-what-you're-talking-about looks.

The pre-show entertainment is a rehash of last year's: the same two women host, one speaking Japanese, the other translating. I'm sure the ten non-Japanese people in the audience are grateful for the English. Not too sure about the other 2,140 Japanese. I feel this is a case where English is more for the Japanese as it gives the event that all-important international feel.

Decked out in suits and gowns, the main cast and staff of GXM take to the stage. I join a squash of reporters squatting at its front. One at a time starting with producer Tomiyama, each staffer/actor steps up to the mike to offer a tidbit of praise for the production. The comments are gushy and complimentary to the point of being completely unmemorable.

Following the last speech, a Godzilla event suit parades onto the stage. *The crowd applauds enthusiastically.* Godzilla rolls his body and claws the air. *The crowd cheers!* Opening his mouth, Godzilla lets out a spray of white mist. *The crowd goes apeshit!* From the opposite side of the stage steps a Megaguirus event suit. The two grapple to the delight of the audience. Then, the lights dim. It's showtime…

It's thrilling to see the scenes I was on hand for during shooting. The Osaka bridge scene is right at the top of the film, and the shots of Godzilla stepping from the big pool are part of a wonderful sequence where the radioactive behemoth sets foot on an island in the South Pacific and battles a swarm of angry Meganula.

While Japanese audiences are noted for being docile throughout movie screenings, one moment in the film brought the house down. During the scene when people are saved from a flooded Shibuya, one of the rescue boats carries several *gyaru*. A transliteration of the English word "gal," *gyaru* are young, fashion-conscious women noted for bleached or dyed hair, tanned skin, painted fingernails, colorful outfits, and chirpy, shallow personalities. When a boat debarks after rescuing the *gyaru*, every single person in Orchard Hall lets out a loud laugh, myself included.

Following the screening, the lobby is buzzing with activity. I find the Kaidas. Aya is thrilled with the film. "That opening scene in the B/W flashbacks was simply amazing. And that battle on the island with the Meganula showed just the right kaiju sensibility." On these points, I'm in agreement with her.

I see Higuchi. He shakes his head up and down. "Yes... It was a strong entry. How I wish I could direct a Godzilla film."

Wakasa is in the crowd too. I can't remember seeing anyone more proud of themselves.

"Was that or was that not the finest Godzilla film you have ever seen?" he asks. I know better than to disagree.

While the show is similar to last year's, the notable difference is that there is less pomp to the proceedings. The audience, too, is more relaxed. No longer is there the pressure of having to compete with a big-budgeted US production. Tonight, Godzilla is back to its top-dog domestic status, right where the Japanese fans like it.

Following this, I have dinner with Kaneko and his family at the Italian place upstairs. We have a fun time going over the film's good and bad points. All in all, while no one thinks it was a great film, we agree that it's a far better entry than last year's.

7 NOVEMBER 2000

The story I pitched to *The Japan Times* has been given the green light. I meet Ayako Fujitani in a café in Shimokita to cover her film *Shiki-jitsu*, which co-won "Best Artistic Contribution Award" at the Tokyo International Film Festival. She arrives looking adorable in leather boots and a one-piece brown sweater that ends halfway between her waist and knees. Despite it being on the cold side, we sit outside and drink Coronas. Soon, we have a blissful afternoon buzz going. The interview goes well, and once over, we meet Kaneko for a late lunch. With him is his younger brother Jiro, who I'm told is a scriptwriter.

Later that night, back home and bored, I call Shimako Sato to see if she feels like hanging out. A half-hour later, she's leading me down a rat hole alleyway in Shimokita and up a set of stairs to a small bar.

"The guy running the place is a movie freak," Shimako explains. "He's got his bar decorated from floor to ceiling with movie posters. I think you'll dig it."

I know the type of bar she refers to. Small and niche, they're run by guys the patrons call "master" who arrange their places like altars to their interests. I remember one in Osaka dedicated to The Rolling Stones. The tiny, 8-seat bar played nothing but Stones music.

Right away, we hit the saké. On a whim, Shimako calls Higuchi. "I'm out with Norman. We want to do something!" She cups the receiver. "He says he's doing a plastic modeling event at Loft Plus One."

Unexpectedly, she throws the phone my way. I put my ear to it to hear not Higuchi's voice but that of a Japanese woman's.

"Hello? This is Ayako Fujitani."

I laugh. "Ayako Fuji...who the hell is that?"

"Norman, is that you?"

Shimako and I catch a cab outside. "Let's raise hell," she says as we head for Shinjuku.

Loft Plus One is in the basement of a building in Kabukicho, Shinjuku's notorious watering hole/red-light district. This being Japan, the area co-exists with game centers, McDonald's, and a square of legit movie theaters. It's common to see smiling families walking under illuminated posters of half-nude women offering "oil massages" and the euphemistically termed "lip service."

The two of us are already smashed when we hit Loft, putting us at odds with the focused, you-can-hear-a-pin-drop ambiance of an event that turns out to be a room full of nerdy guys silently gluing and painting models of jets, castles, and Transformer-like robots. On the left side of Loft is a small stage where Higuchi and Sagae are running the evening. Higuchi works on a model of Himeji Castle, a location in the James Bond film *You Only Live Twice*, while Sagae is putting together a jet model.

As no one has noted our arrival, I yell out, "I'll fuck anything that moves!" I don't know if anyone will recognize the *Blue Velvet* line, but it has the desired effect: Everyone peeks up from their kits. Shimako and me stagger on to the stage, where Sagae introduces us.

Once he's done, Shimako grabs the mike. "Gentlemen, my partner Norman and I will combine our considerable skills and construct one of these here model thingies!"

Diplomatically, Higuchi motions to an empty space beside him. Shimako and I squeeze in and rummage through unbuilt kits Sagae has slid our way. We pull out an unidentifiable robot model.

But drunk as we are, it's impossible to focus. The pieces look the same and the glue seems to gush all over the place—and I can't keep my eyes off of Higuchi's model of Himeji Castle.

"Say, isn't that the secret ninja training camp?" I ask, hoping he gets the reference. In the end, given our inebriated state, we don't last ten minutes.

"Where the fuck is Aya?" I ask. Higuchi looks over his glasses and nudges his head toward a door off to the side.

In Loft's VIP room, Shimako and I find Ayako sitting alone holding a mixed drink the color of a Smurf. It attractively offsets her tomato red dress and chocolate brown cowboy boots. This being more to our liking, we order drinks: Shimako/vodka, Ayako and me/tequila. That the two of them speak English is a godsend, and I enjoy the rare opportunity to make jokes and off-the-wall observations in my native language. However, the conversation takes a strange turn.

"Did you ever notice," Shimako asks Ayako, "that Norman curses a lot?"

"It's because he's a New Yorker," Ayako posits. "They're pretty rude. And did you ever notice that half the time he's like a brain-dead bull, focusing only on what he wants and not giving in until he gets it?"

"Hold on!" I protest. "This is unfair! You two sound like a pair of man-hating lesbians condemning a guy for having moderate obsession issues."

Shimako turns to Ayako. "Lesbians? Oh, that sounds nice. I'd *love* to have an affair with Aya." The three of us start laughing wildly.

A knock sounds. The door creaks open and two men walk in. "Please excuse us," one says. Both carry their shoulders hunched and their heads tilted downward, a signal they've come with a request.

The older of the two explains that he's a budding talent agent and would be honored to run potential actresses past Shimako. Pulling out a portfolio with photos of young girls, he passes it to her. Right away Shimako blasts out comments, brutally criticizing the way a photo is shot or how a girl holds her face. To each comment, the man nods his head, adding, "Thank you very much."

Later, the three of us, with Higuchi and Sagae in tow, go out for ramen. As we slurp our steamy noodles, I spy over at Ayako and Shimako laughing it up several stools away. By the time we finish eating, the sun has risen.

16 DECEMBER 2000

Although Kaneko said the next Godzilla film would be announced on the 16th—the opening day of GXM—so far, nothing.

"The whole thing's up in the air," he complains over the phone. "The Toho heads have decided to commit only if the current film lives up to box-office expectations." I sense the frustration in his tone.

With my buddies Michio and Akio, Mitsuyuki Kushitani and his wife Yuki, and Nobuko, we travel to Umeda for the opening of GXM. Following it, we enjoy our traditional, after-viewing coffee in a café in Umeda. I'm hardly surprised to find that no one cared for the film. Mostly, though, I feel bad for Akio. He was so put off by *Godzilla vs. Destoroyah* that he vowed never to see another Godzilla film. He even refused to join us last year for G2000. It was at our behest that he came tonight. After a prolonged period of giving icy stares while we talked about the film, Akio bursts into a tirade of insults, completely destroying any claim of Japanese being soft-spoken.

I understand his points: low production values, hammy acting, disjointed visual style, and childish rather than childlike approach. He goes on to say that although SFX techniques have improved since the so-called golden era ('50s~'60s) of Japanese films, it's come at the cost of a diminished level of grandeur.

He's quick to point out that he loved Kaneko's Gamera films and that the issue is not handmade visual effects but the philosophy behind their implementation.

"If they have to change anything, it's those unbelievable mecha-tanks and jets," he insists. "That stuff only flies with kids and otaku."

We all agree with him. Moreover, it shows how high expectations are for Kaneko's Godzilla film. If it happens, that is.

23 JANUARY 2001

Jiro and I have started a website on Kaneko's films and career. Jiro is handling the Japanese, me the English. I'm no expert in web design but I try my best to make a logo, a front page, and a photo gallery featuring shots I took on the G3 and *Crossfire* sets. I decide to call it the "Shusuke Kaneko Information Website" for lack of a better idea. We got it up the other day and, for something made by a couple of guys who don't know what they're doing, I think it looks pretty good.

Kaneko is happy with it and says he's keen on having me report on the Godzilla production in real time, updating it with events as they happen, something never done on a Godzilla film before—or any film in Japan for that matter. He thinks this will make it easier to sell Toho on my set presence rather than my eventual

Fangoria article, which, although planned at a lengthy five pages, isn't enough to justify my being on set near daily.

The thing I'm waiting for is permission to up the official announcement of Kaneko being offered the Godzilla job. He finally calls to say, "Run the story!" I go to bed excited over what the response will be from the western online Godzilla community.

However, in the morning, I find the announcement gone. It turns out Kaneko meant, "Run it next week after the official press announcement." I'm not sure where the mix-up came from but he assures me it's not my fault.

14 FEBRUARY 2001

My Tokyo move is ten days off. As these are my last, great days in Osaka, I'm going to restaurants every night and enjoying all the meals the city's famous for. It's hard to decide which to make my last: okonomiyaki at a place in America-mura that also serves mouthwatering gesso-butter (fried squid legs marinated in butter) or okonomiyaki at a place in Umeda I go to whenever I see a new movie. Wherever I decide, it looks like I'll end things with okonomiyaki.

Now that GXM is over and word is out that another Godzilla film is underway, foreign kaiju fans are posting unfounded rumors and massively self-important opinions on how the new Godzilla film should be handled. The most vocal have unrealistic, dare I say, pathetic views. One suggestion is for Toho to start a series of films with each centering on one of their stock of monsters. The guy suggesting it even calls the studio "stupid" not to follow his advice. Do I

really need to get online to tell him that not only is there not enough audience to make such a thing economically viable, there isn't enough staff in Japan to make films of such quantity? There's also the usual discussion of which monster(s) should fight against Godzilla.

Skimming the remarks, it's clear most fans seek a rehash of the past and to recapture some feeling they had when young and seeing Godzilla for the first time. I find this thinking unrealistic. A film coming from a franchise with a history might conjure up its creators' original spirit and intent, but there is no way an adult in the audience will feel the way they did when they were five.

Another common thread concerns getting a name Hollywood actor (or Steven Spielberg to direct). Actor Nick Adams is used as a model. Adams was part of the new wave of young Hollywood actors in the '50s. By the time he began appearing in Toho films in the '60s, he was having trouble securing work in L.A. While the reason for his premature death at 36 remains a matter of speculation, one claim is that he was distraught over slumming it in Japanese monster films. So, given the history between Hollywood and Japanese giant monsters, to expect Hollywood actors (or Spielberg) to take part in a Toho Godzilla film is unrealistic to say the least.

On top of moving, I have to redo my visa. Fortunately, Kaneko has agreed to be my guarantor, ensuring that I can stay in Japan legally and headache-free for the time being. I feel bad having to make him come up with personal documents, a financial disclosure, and a letter stating his responsibility for my actions while preparing for what is basically the biggest film of his career. In exchange, I've agreed to teach his children English.

GODZILLA, MOTHRA AND KING GHIDORAH: GIANT MONSTERS ALL-OUT ATTACK
Pre-Production

Hungover, I'm riding the Shinkansen to my new life in Tokyo. As the train glides out of Shin-Osaka station, Umeda's buildings stand across the bay like tombstones. Although my nine years in Osaka had many enjoyable episodes, sadly, it never found its core. In New York, that core was my band. Life revolved around gigs and the goal of "making it." It was only when the band broke up and my core lost that I felt empowered to move to Japan. This was fine for a while, but once the sheen of living in Japan wore off it was back to simple day-to-day living.

As the Japanese countryside zips past and the Kansai region recedes, I wonder if I'll find my core in Tokyo. Perhaps in my friendship with Kaneko? Godzilla? Whatever it is, I'm optimistic.

5 MARCH 2001

How an apartment this small can take this long to clean is beyond me. Still, after removing the dust and grime of a place shared by four middle-aged men, it's wiped down, set up, and ready to go!

It's an absolute joy to wake in Shimokita. Every winding street, every dingy alleyway, every café, bar, and restaurant holds my interest. And the convenience of the area can't be understated. Two train lines converge on Shimokita, making a trip to madhouse Shinjuku a painless eight-minute ride, or trendy Shibuya in half that. Best of all, Toho is a single, five-minute express stop away via the Odakyu line.

Speaking of which, Toho is being vague regarding my coverage of Kaneko's Godzilla. There's a publicity guy I haven't met telling me over the phone that the only reason he's letting me on set to begin with is that I'm friends with the director. He doesn't sound at all happy. When I ask permission to attend the press junket tomorrow, he describes it as "unimportant" and "not worth the time."

Tonight, Kaneko, Murakami, and a few others working on Godzilla come to Shimokita for dinner. Kaneko has the film's script and storyboards under an arm. It's my first time to see the title: *Godzilla, Mothra, King Ghidorah: Daikaiju Soukougeki.*

"That's quite the mouthful," I remark.

"We're calling it GMK for short," Kaneko says. "It stands for Godzilla, Mothra, and King Ghidorah."

I leaf through the storyboards. One series of drawings shows a bedridden girl in a hospital room that gets smashed to bits by Godzilla's tail.

"What happens to the girl?" I ask.

Kaneko smiles. "She dies."

In another sequence, a man stands at a urinal. The room shakes and he looks out the window to see Godzilla's giant foot come down on him.

"I guess he dies, too," I remark.

Kaneko smiles again.

I flip through a few pages until I find a drawing of Godzilla. Rather than a fierce, irradiated dinosaur, he looks like a big, wet rat with jagged teeth.

"Godzilla's tough to draw," Kaneko admits.

I ask if Wakasa is building the new Godzilla.

"I've asked Fuyuki Shinada, a different suit maker. Wakasa's work always has a touch of cuteness, which I don't want in Godzilla. I requested he make Baragon, but he didn't take well to that. 'It's Godzilla or nothing!' he said. I'm afraid it may have hurt our working relationship."

I'm disappointed because with Wakasa out, I have to start all over with a whole new suit maker.

"Shinada said he's going to have a maquette of the new Godzilla ready for tomorrow's junket," Kaneko continues. "So far, I've only seen drawings."

I then explain how Toho has been non-committal about my joining the junket.

"You're kidding," he says. Taking a bottle of saké, he fills my small, porcelain cup. "To the future," Kaneko adds as we bump our drinks together.

6 MARCH 2001

Last night I returned home to find an 11th hour invite from the Toho PR department to today's press junket. They'd requested I arrive at 1 p.m. So, here I am, a half-hour early, and near the Toho office in Yurakucho watching a father and son pose for pictures in front of the meter-tall Godzilla statue that stands in a small park in the area.

Erected in 1995 to commemorate the "death" of the King of the Monsters in that year's *Godzilla vs. Destoroyah*, the statue is a kind of poor man's destination for fans. They gather to snap photos— grinning wildly around it while making V hand signs. The sculpture incorporates features of various versions of Godzilla from over the years. But, by being on the smaller size, that Godzilla is a towering behemoth is lost. It's unfortunate since Godzilla is, depending on which film you watch, anywhere from 50 to 100 meters tall.

Spread across a floor of one of several buildings Toho owns in the area, the PR department is an assembly of desks grouped into rectangular blocks and peopled by dozens of men and women. Colorful PR material hangs from the ceiling, and large cardboard displays lie stacked in cluttered piles along the walls. Leafing through press kits for upcoming films, I pass the time. However, when 1 p.m. rolls by, rather than reporters arriving, I see them emerging from a side conference room with the words "Kaneko" and "Godzilla" on their lips.

Suspecting the worst, I seek out Suzuki. He matter-of-factly informs me that the conference started at 11 a.m. and has just ended. Without waiting for my reaction, he turns me over to an underling. *This guy?* I remember him. I met him on my last night on the *Crossfire* set. He was always telling me "don't move" or "don't look at that," but when asked what I could do and look at, he'd go blank and run to Suzuki for an answer. Even Kaneko complained about him, labeling him "the staffer who doesn't get it."

Taking printed information from a plastic folder, he hands me generic press info, adding he'll translate a few quotes from the junket into English and email them to me. I can't say I'm worked up over this as I've yet to hear him utter a single word of English.

Thinking me pacified, he waits for my thanks. Instead, I pull out a notebook and ask permission to run some information on the production past him. I mention a few actors that have been cast. His face turns chalk white and he rips the notebook from my hand.

"How do you know this?" he shouts. "This is secret information!"

"Which is why," I respond, "I requested to be at the press junket. It would have let me know what information is and isn't permissible to print at this point."

Regaining his senses, he hands my notebook back.

"Well, is the Godzilla maquette around at least?" I ask, trying to make the most of my trip here.

"No. It isn't," he replies.

At that moment, a smiling Kaneko walks out of the junket room. "Wanna see the Godzilla maquette?" he asks.

I look at the underling—he's staring at his feet.

In the conference room, Kaneko has someone run a teaser announcement of the new Godzilla film. It's a speedy, thirty-second piece featuring shots of Godzilla from previous films with Kaneko's name superimposed over the images. Kaneko beams with pride. He then points to a table off to the side where the Godzilla maquette sits. Claws extended and mouth open in a toothy, primordial roar, Godzilla is fierce-looking—dare I say, insanely fierce-looking.

Trying to make up for my missing the junket, Kaneko's gives me interview time. He takes the maquette and sets it on a table in one of several cubbyholes by the entrance. With Godzilla positioned between us, I ask him to explain the difference between Gamera and Godzilla.

"Gamera is Shintaro Katsu and Godzilla is Toshiro Mifune," he offers, comparing the monsters to two of Japan's most legendary actors. "Whereas Gamera is a masochist, Godzilla is a sadist. In Gamera films, he always gets wounded in the middle but comes back to claim victory. On the other hand, Godzilla attacks and attacks and never lets up; from start to finish, he pounds away strong and cruel, always taking the direct path to what he wants. Although recent directors often ignore it, Godzilla's brutality was established in the first film. They would rather the audience sympathize with Godzilla. I feel this is a mistake. Godzilla should kill as many people as possible. He must be feared."

I ask Kaneko for his basic concept of Godzilla. "I see him as a ghost, one influenced by the spirits of the victims of World War 2. When I say victims, I mean those who suffered: Japanese, Chinese, British, and American. Godzilla is the manifestation of their pain and anguish; he's the embodiment of their wrath. In a way, Godzilla can be viewed as a spiritual monster that conventional weapons cannot kill.

"One nagging question kaiju fans have is why giant monsters keep attacking Japan. In GMK, I plan to suggest it's because Japanese have forgotten the sins of their fathers and that affluence and luxury have made them complacent. Godzilla doesn't like this. He's angry at the Japanese people and wants to smash them! Unfortunately, as much as I'd like, I can't come out and say this directly. There are zealots here who will make a stink if they believe I'm bashing the nation. I'll have to say these things in a roundabout way."

I take out my camera to get shots of Kaneko with the Godzilla maquette. The moment I do, the underling rushes over.

"No photos!" he yells.

"Suzuki said it's okay. Go check," I reply.

During the wait, Kaneko and I exchange greetings with director Tezuka, who has come to inspect the box art for the upcoming GXM DVD and VHS releases. The underling returns with the non-shocking news that it's fine for me to photograph Kaneko sitting beside the Godzilla maquette.

Before leaving for a production meeting, Kaneko calls Shinada. After giving him the lowdown on me, he hands the phone over. Shinada is friendly and thanks me for taking interest in his work. I arrange to visit his workshop next Monday.

12 MARCH 2001

I'm on the Sobu train line heading to Shin-Koiwa Station to visit Vi-Shop, where the new Godzilla suit is being built. First, I stop off at the Mr. Donuts in front of the station. Kaneko mentioned it's good manners to bring *sashi-ire* (a gift), usually a snack, when trying to ingratiate yourself or seek a favor. I figure a box of donuts is a small price to pay to see the birth of Godzilla.

I bus it from Shin-Koiwa and, fifteen minutes later, step off in front of a well-landscaped park with a stream running along one side. Surrounding the park are upscale suburban homes.

I call Shinada from my cell phone. As I wait, out-of-season snow begins to fall. A minute later, a man sporting a thick black beard wearing a red flannel shirt comes bounding over. His hand is outstretched from halfway down the block.

"I'm Shinada," he says as he pumps my hand. "Thanks for coming all this way." I notice his glasses are smudged with oily fingerprints, and I catch a peculiar odor coming off him.

With the snowfall growing heavier, Shinada quickly leads the way, apologizing several times for taking up my time. Opening the door of his workshop, he welcomes me to the incredible sight of Godzilla sectioned off and spread throughout the room.

The smell on Shinada turns out to be clay. He and his staff of eight must be working with a ton of it to shape and mold the King of the Monsters. I pass Shinada the doughnuts, and he holds them up. In unison, the staff lets out a loud *arigatou gozaimasu*! Shinada tells me to make myself at home and gives me permission to take photos and to ask questions.

The shop isn't as big as expected: Four car lengths wide and two deep, by my best guess. However, its potential has been maxed out. There are shelves against every wall, and a makeshift rack covered with boxes divides the room in half. Creatures from past productions dot the shelves. Among them is the head of the Godzillasaurus from *Godzilla vs. King Ghidorah*.

The staff doesn't seem to mind the tight proximity. They sit focused on sculpting duties, silently pulling molding tools through wet, gray clay as they form Godzilla's various body parts. On a table by the door rests the front half of Godzilla's body, and on the adjacent table lies his back. Working at a bench, a man carves Godzilla's hands starting just after the elbows. Squatting nearby, another staffer shapes Godzilla's feet from the knees down. However, the real attention-grabber is Godzilla's head. Raised high on a table, it sits propped up by braces running right into his neck and chin.

While the body parts are obvious, there's one I can't figure out. It's a flat, one-meter by one-meter square the texture of Godzilla's hide.

Shinada peeks up from his work. "That's spare skin," he says. "If the suit rips, gets a hole, or incurs damage, we can use it as patch material."

Tacked to a nearby post are photos of Godzilla from *Mothra vs. Godzilla* (*Mosura tai Gojira*, 1964). Looking back at the head, it dawns on me why this new one is so familiar-looking. It's a reworking of the '64 Godzilla.

Shinada, who has taken up duties on the head from a younger staff member, comments on the photo. "It's my favorite Godzilla suit. Kaneko wants the GMK Godzilla to echo both this and the original '54 suit."

Sure enough, hanging beside it is the famous shot of the '54 Godzilla walking through Tokyo Bay. Next to this is one of a man at work on the original Godzilla suit. "That's Teizo Toshimitsu," Shinada continues. "All suit makers in Japan owe him a debt of gratitude."

I mention how the suit appears different from the maquette at the press conference, and Shinada details its modifications.

"See the curve behind the head? I've straightened it to lessen the dinosaur look. The bulk under the jaw has been trimmed, too. This gives it a more classic look. Kaneko and I have an idea about the color. I'm going to paint it in a way that will make it appear black and white on screen. The inside of the mouth will be very dark too. And the eyes will be gray-white balls."

Across the room and sculpting Godzilla's hands is Takuya Yamabe.

"Check out the thumbs," he says. "See how long the nails are? My concept is that Godzilla uses these as weapons. He can jab them into an opponent." Putting his tools down, Yamabe stands and hunches his shoulders in a Godzilla-like stance. Extending an arm quickly, he pokes me square in the chest with his thumb. "If I were Godzilla, you'd be dead!" He laughs as he returns to his sculpting duties. I'm left rubbing my chest and scratching my head.

Stashed behind some clutter is a crude, foam version of King Ghidorah, the three-headed monster. Its heads are held atop plastic coil tubes by gaffer's tape. Shinada pushes boxes aside and pulls it out.

"This is a test," he explains. "I had the notion that as this version of Ghidorah is basically a hatchling, it has stumpy, undeveloped necks. Since they don't have to be long, the actor in the suit can control the side heads with his own arms."

Shinada sticks his hands in and moves them about. While not as dynamic as the long neck version of Ghidorah, it's a creative solution.

"With his arms raised up," I observe, "don't you think the actor will get tired quickly?"

Shinada furrows his brow. "I hadn't thought of that," he admits.

As for Baragon, Shinada says he farmed out its construction to Kaimai Pro, another suit making company. "I wanted to build it myself, but there's just not enough time," he laments.

After a few hours, I decide to leave. But first I stand in a corner and take it all in one last time: the light snow through the open door (to keep the shop ventilated), the pungent smell of clay, a barely audible, low-fidelity radio playing domestic pop music, and the staffers quietly working on Godzilla body parts. It's enchanting to see a sci-fi icon synonymous with destruction coming to life under such a serene suburban setting.

I thank Shinada and his staff for allowing me to intrude on their work. Everyone lines up at the door and, with deep bows, utters the *yoroshiku onegaishimasu* phrase as I leave.

14 MARCH 2001

Jiro calls on the phone. He's upset. The Toho PR office made him remove the

stock photos of Ghidorah, Mothra, and Baragon from Kaneko's website, claiming they weren't properly licensed. *Huh*? They'd given me those shots at the press conference and told me to use them on the website. I hadn't even asked for them! Now they want Jiro to work out a licensing deal for images appearing on the site. Jiro added that he spoke to producer Tomiyama, who promises to straighten things out for us.

3 APRIL 2001

It's that time of year when cherry trees dominate life in Japan and Kaneko has invited me to tonight's cherry blossom viewing party at Toho Studios. I arrive in the late afternoon and head for the Godzilla staff room.

I hadn't realized it but the stream dividing the studio is lined with cherry trees. At the peak of bloom, they explode with a force of pink I've never encountered. Remarkable is how the fallen petals have formed a solid silky blanket that completely covers the stream's surface. The studio grounds are no different. Petals tumble through the air like snowflakes in a blizzard. People walk past with velvety leaves stuck to their clothes and caught in their hair. Pink is so rampant that, quite frankly, I feel as if I've arrived at the home of an eleven-year-old girl suffering from a bad case of Hello Kitty-itis.

The Godzilla production has expanded since my last visit and now occupies three production rooms. There's the original one for *Kaneko-gumi* (Team Kaneko), one for *Kamiya-gumi* (Team Kamiya) named after SFX director Makoto Kamiya), and one for the art staff. I find Kaneko reviewing documents in his production room.

"You're early," he says without even a hello. "I have a meeting to go to. Wait here."

Alone in the production room of the new Godzilla film, how can I not poke around? Pinned to the walls are wonderful production paintings of submarines, shrines, and giant monsters. One particularly nifty painting depicts the monsters lined up, their sizes compared to those of Tokyo Tower and Landmark Tower (Japan's tallest building). Amidst the clutter in the room is a plastic binder filled with actor profiles. I flip through to see if I recognize any faces. Lastly, I make myself at home with a large pile of fresh storyboards. It's like getting a sneak peek at the film before a single frame has been shot.

One of the tenets of Japanese culture is the idea that good and evil are subjective. A person may be hailed a hero on one side, while on the other they're condemned as a villain. The concept that good and bad exist independent of man's perception is not the drawn-in-sand line it is in western storytelling.

Looking through the storyboards and seeing this duality at play sheds light on something Kaneko said recently during a recent dinner: "In GMK, King Ghidorah, Mothra, and Baragon were enemies of the Japanese people in the ancient past. At some point they were defeated and their human victors entombed them. However, these monsters have returned to fight against Godzilla. Nothing has changed in their relationship to man except now they're fighting a foe out to do man harm. For this reason, we perceive these kaiju as protectors, but they're as much protectors as is a boy playing on a riverbank who inadvertently redirects a flow of water that saves an anthill from washing away."

Throughout the storyboards are instances of the so-called good kaiju indiscriminately killing bystanders, with the human casualties being of absolutely no consequence. We're like bugs at a picnic swatted away if we intrude or left alone if we don't.

Just when I make it to the end of the storyboards, Kaneko returns. Of all people, Kobayashi, the Daiei publicist, is with him. He's astonished to see me.

"Norman, are you…staff?" he asks nervously. After all, if I were actively involved in the production it would mean he screwed up in his treatment of me during the G3 shoot.

To put the past to rest, I insist I'm not and attempt to engage him in friendly chit-chat. Relieved, Kobayashi says he's come to entice Kaneko into directing another Gamera movie. I ask about *Daimajin*, a '60s trilogy whose remake has been on the rumor mill for the past decade.

"I wouldn't hold your breath over that one," he admits. "Unless it's thought to have wide appeal, period pieces are just too costly. If we were to, it would have to be set in modern times."

We say goodbye to Kobayashi at the studio gate.

"You handled that well," Kaneko says as we move on to the party. "It's important for Japanese people to have no negative feelings in relationships. Even if you're in the right, they won't work with you if they feel discomfort."

The night air is cool, crisp, and comfortable. People are walking out of the studio offices and, like us, heading over to a large parking lot behind S10. Along the way we bump into Hideyuki

Honma, a producer I met on *Crossfire.*

"He's a producer on GMK as well," Kaneko says. "As the budget is three times that of *Crossfire*, the pressure is on!"

Honma laughs nervously.

We arrive at the party. Makeshift tents stand in the center of the parking area. Squid legs, yaki-soba, and other Japanese dishes are being cooked in the open air. Here and there are large, plastic garbage cans filled with ice and water and stocked with cans of beer, soft drinks, and brown tea.

"Everything's on Toho," Kaneko says. "Dig in!"

I get in a food line with Kaneko's family, who arrived a few minutes ahead of us. I had my first English lesson with the kids the other day. I ask if they've done their homework; they yell "no" in unison. I'm left with no choice but to chase them mercilessly around the area, threatening to devour them as punishment.

Everyone who's anyone at Toho is here. I spend a few minutes shooting the breeze with producer Tomiyama. Politely, he thanks me for my *Fangoria* articles on Toho productions. I also chat with Shinada. He can't stop thanking me for going to his workshop and insists I come for another visit to see where things stand with the Godzilla suit. In anticipation of seeing him tonight, I printed out photos as a gift. He's overjoyed to a point I find awkward.

Standing off to a side is SFX director Kawakita. He and Kaneko are in discussion and I ease myself into the conversation. As we chat, Kaneko's son stares up at Kawakita with worship-filled eyes Finally, Kaneko turns to him. "What's up?"

"I can't believe it," Suzuyuki says. "It's

him. The *real* Kawakita!"

We break out laughing.

When the party ends a few hours later, Kaneko invites me to join him, Jiro, and some GMK staff at a nearby restaurant for more food and drink. In an *izakaya* in front of Seijogakuen-Mae Station (Seijo, for short), we start with a round of beer.

My curiosity over GMK remains unabated. I hit Kaneko up for new information, this time for his thoughts on how he wants Godzilla's radioactive beam to appear in the film.

"I haven't decided," he admits. "I know I don't want it to be a thin ray like a '50s Buck Rogers gun. I'm thinking of something wild, like a powerful force that devastates everything it strikes."

After I vow secrecy, Kaneko confides that the latest cast addition is Hideyo Amamoto. I'm overjoyed. Amamoto is a veteran actor who appeared in several Toho kaiju films during the Showa[11] era. Since moving to Japan, I've enjoyed spotting Godzilla actors on TV and Amamoto has always been a favorite to catch. Not only because of his connection to kaiju film history but because of his blatant disrespect for authority. If asked something dopey on a noisy, primetime celebrity gathering, Amamoto will mumble the Japanese equivalent of "WTF" under his breath before coming out with a response so off-kilter the other guests can only respond with nervous giggles.

Kaneko tells me that Amamoto has led a rebellious life that began when he was conscripted into the military at 19 and sent to fight on the Chinese front.

"He's one of the few people in Japan who'll just come out and say, 'I hate

---

11 - The Showa series is the stretch of Godzilla films shot between 1954 and 1975. The name derives from the Showa era, the reign of Emperor Hirohito between 1926 and 1989.

Japan' without softening it by saying nice things first[12]," Kaneko remarks. "He also refuses to appear in films that praise the Japanese military. Today, he lives rent-free in a small room above a Jonathan's restaurant in Tokyo."

While things between Kaneko and me are good, I notice how testy he gets when in filmmaker mode. For example, Jiro and I were joking that, as the guys doing his website, we should be featured in a scene, like the boyfriends of Ai and Aki Maeda when they put in a scheduled cameo as the "Mothra girls." I couldn't figure out if Kaneko was going to yell or cry tears of frustration.

The thing is, Kaneko can't take kidding at this phase of the production, friendly or otherwise. He sometimes falls deep into thought or gets strict over something minor. In fact, Kaneko started complaining to me about the online postings of a Godzilla fan going by the handle "Gojira Ningen #1."

"This loser won't shut up about how the director of Gamera should not be allowed to direct Godzilla," he bemoans.

Now it's my turn to get annoyed. "The people online...*screw 'em*," I tell him. "I'm sure most mean well, but some of them fixate on nonsense, and their writing is nothing more than the musings of the obsessed."

Kaneko looks at me with interest.

"What they're after is to show off their knowledge," I continue. "They want the world to know that their fervor is second to none; their sole purpose is establishing their superiority. Engaging them is futile. If it's not this it'll be something else."

I make him promise to stop reading the web boards.

13 APRIL 2001

I meet Sagae at Seijo Station at 1 p.m., and we walk over to Toho. He's scheduled to talk with Toshio Miike, the art director on GMK. I've come along because, although I met Miike on the GXM set last year, Sagae wants to reintroduce us. With Miike one of the main guys on the SFX set, Sagae feels this will help smooth out my time during shooting.

Until now, I've taken a bus. Sagae tells me that's unnecessary and shows me how to reach the studio by foot. It's a nice walk down a long, straight road that passes a stock of affluent looking homes.

The production room for the GMK art department is a few doors down from Kaneko's. It's slightly larger than his, yet just as cluttered—more so, if that's possible. The walls are a mass of drawings, photos, and material samples. Four men are in the room, each one hunched at a desk, toiling over an illustration, diagram, or diorama.

Sagae will be building various miniatures throughout the production, including a model of Godzilla's heart. He pulls up a chair beside Miike's desk to talk details but first he calls me over to explain that I'll be on set near daily doing coverage for Kaneko's website and *Fangoria*.

Friendly and professional, Miike thanks me for my time and interest, but he does give a warning. "If I come across as distant or even mean during the production, don't take it personally. When working, I tend to focus solely on the job." With that, he gives me a firm handshake.

---

12 This is a Japanese technique when wanting to criticize something and not be accused of being one-sided or not considering other people's feelings.

"Let me take you around," Sagae offers after finishing conferring with Miike. In a corner is Yoshiyuki Kasuga. Sagae describes him as the best draftsman of military equipment in the business. Sure enough, he's at work on a detailed schematic of an atomic submarine. Kasuga's hair is long, which he keeps tied in a ponytail that juts out from under a snug-fitting baseball cap. Across from him is Masato Inatsuki, a hip-looking guy who gives me a friendly, "Welcome aboard!"

"You've come all the way from America to be on this set?" questions the man at the desk next to Miike's.

"No...that is...I, uh, live here," I say, unsure what to make of his sarcastic tone.

"Being born here," he continues, "we have no choice but to work here. You, however... Why anyone would voluntarily move to a pitiful country like Japan is beyond me."

Now, I'm really confused.

"*Oh*," interjects Sagae. "This is Isao Takahashi, GMK's second art director. You'll get used to him." Without looking up, everyone snickers from behind their desks.

Before leaving, Isao asks me to pose with a foam mock-up of Baragon hanging from the wall. "We're getting photos of everyone on the staff with it," he explains. Sure enough, taped to a whiteboard in the middle of the room are almost two dozen photos of people hugging the foam Baragon.

On the way back to the station, Sagae clues me in on Isao. "He's been working on Godzilla since *The Return of Godzilla*. He's seen it all and can come across as a little gruff. But he's a good guy, and I can tell he likes you. If he didn't, he wouldn't have asked to take your photo. It's his way of saying he approves of you."

20 APRIL 2001

The Godzilla suit test was yesterday, but I was unable to attend. As I plan to be on set as much as possible, I need to double down on work and save money before shooting starts. I've arranged with the school where I teach to put in two or three days a week during the months of production. Kaneko's helping by shouldering most of my rent; even so, I have to cover 40,000 yen ($325) a month, plus utilities. Not sure how I'll survive...

Kaneko calls tonight to share his enthusiasm over the suit test. "It's huge—really huge! The suit is still unpainted. It's white, like a ghost, and very haunting. The suit actor gave it a real workout so we could see what sort of limitations there are to its movements. After that, the actor gave us his feedback."

Once off the phone, I immediately call Shinada. He says it's okay if I visit tomorrow to catch up on the progress with the Godzilla suit.

21 APRIL 2001

Even if I didn't know the way to Shinada's, I could have found it by the smell. The moment I step off the bus, I'm hit with the overpowering odor of chemicals that grows steadily the closer I get to Vi-shop. Unsure what to expect, I carefully slide open the workshop's frosted glass door. Rather than the quiet serenity of artisans molding clay parts, it's a madhouse of men banging, spraying, and gluing as they work on various monster suits. Shinada shakes my hand and thanks me for coming.

Shinada has a boyish quality about him. It might be because of how he talks through gritted teeth, or maybe it's how he avoids eye contact much of the time. Mostly, I feel, it comes from the gleam he gets in his eyes when talking about giant monsters and the childhood hobby he's turned into a profession.

"And thank you for the photos," he says. "If you don't mind, would you take more today?" Like I need to be asked?

Space in the workshop is limited but Shinada clears off a table stacked with Godzilla fins for my computer. He then leads me to a man sculpting Mothra. It's in pieces. Shinada has him put it together so I can take photos.

"Do you think those came out well?" he asks nervously. I find it charming how he's more worried about the pictures than me.

In a corner, a man works on one of Ghidorah's heads. The sculpt is big, roughly half the size of his body, and Ghidorah's eyes are shut as though the monster has fallen asleep. Shinada confirms this; the prop will be used in a scene where Ghidorah is discovered in suspended animation under the ice. I ask about the main Ghidorah suit.

"It won't be needed until over a month into the shoot," he explains. "We'll start building it soon. The scene with the giant head is scheduled early on, so we have to ready it now."

But the main sight is the Godzilla suit. Massive, it hangs in a metal rack in the middle of the shop. Taller than everyone in the room, Godzilla's head sticks through the rack with the lower jaw resting on its top beam. Staffers, sealing seams and patching gaps, glue pieces of latex about it. The chemical smell is intense and makes my head swim. I wonder if the people working aren't a little high off the fumes.

I ask Shinada about a man in blue and white sweats sitting off to the side. Slapping a hand against his head, Shinada rushes over to introduce me to Mizuho Yoshida, the man selected to perform Godzilla.

Yoshida is a little taller than me, meaning he's a lot taller than previous Godzilla actor Kitagawa. Personality-wise, he's friendly right out of the gate. Yoshida shakes my hand enthusiastically when Shinada tells him I'll be joining them for the production.

Yoshida and I get to talking. Mostly unmemorable, getting-to-know-each-other small talk. Where do you live? How do you know Shinada? Of course, we eventually get to Godzilla. How can you not talk about Godzilla with Godzilla? One thing I like is how he doesn't come out with dour comments about the great honor it is to play Godzilla. Rather, the constantly smiling Yoshida strikes me as a personable guy who's worked hard in his field, proven his qualifications, and been rewarded with the task of performing in the Godzilla suit. I ask how he got the part.

"Shinada called me on the phone one day," Yoshida recalls. "He didn't reveal the name of the project, just that there was a special effects film that needs a tall guy to play a kaiju. I worked with Shinada when I played Legion in *Gamera 2*. Seriously, I wasn't excited about doing another kaiju movie because I figured it would be a low-budget indie film. When he told me it was Godzilla, I accepted the role without hesitation."

There comes a bang on the front door. Two men enter carrying a bright red costume. It's the floppy-eared, dog-faced kaiju Baragon. Everyone stops work and gathers around. Shinada steps forward to inspect the suit. After shifting Baragon around and looking it over from several angles, he unexpectedly hoists the empty suit above his head. All at once, he lets out a deep growl. The staff roars with approval. Shinada is recreating the famous moment in *Frankenstein Conquers the World* (*Furankenshutain tai Baragon*, 1965) when the Frankenstein kaiju held Baragon in a similar pose.

The Baragon suit is still in the process of construction. It's legs and arms are not yet attached, and the horn, head spikes, and teeth all share an identical yellow color. What stands out most about it is how minuscule it is. I ask Shinada who can fit into such a small space.

"We've hired a twenty-one-year-old woman to play Baragon," he says.

"She must be tiny," I remark.

"She's no giant."

As Shinada talks things over with Tetsuya Yoshida, the man in charge of Baragon's construction, I take a free-floating Baragon arm lying off to the side and force my hand inside. It's lined with a silk-like fabric and there is what feels like a glove where the paw is. Lifting my hand, I claw at the air with three thick nails. It's my first time to wear a suit (okay, just an arm). I try to imagine it on stage in less than a month battling Godzilla.

Although Baragon is far from complete, two of SFX director Kamiya's ADs have come to take pictures, the reason why the suit has been brought over from Kaimai Pro.

One of the ADs, Kiyotaka Taguchi, is in his early twenties. "I've been a kaiju fan for as long as I can remember," he says. "I'm excited to work on GMK because I loved Kaneko's Gamera trilogy."

The other AD, Hiroshi Okamoto,

seems less passionate. "I got into film through *Star Wars*. I'm neither here nor there when it comes to kaiju."

After Yoshida has left with Baragon, Shinada calls me over. "Well, what do you think?" he asks as he waves a hand up and down in front of the Godzilla suit.

This is when it hits me: Godzilla is being born before me. In an abstract way, Shinada's shop is a weird kind of monster womb. Near speechless, I can only come out with an uninspired "Looks good." I know it sounds silly, but I'm so moved I think I might cry. While the suit is still on the shabby side, there's no mistaking: This is the one, the only, Godzilla, King of the Monsters!

24 APRIL 2001

I'm at my local Starbucks writing brief profiles of the people working on GMK for Kaneko's website—nothing fancy, just a paragraph for each to put a human face on the production. Most fans tend to focus solely on the top tier: director, producer, writer, and actors. Once shooting begins and I meet more staff, I hope to give a face to those neglected by the press, the ones with less glamorous titles yet without whom the film couldn't be made.

With that said, there remain several upper-tier crewmembers I haven't met. One name stands out—Kow Otani—the man slated to score GMK.

Otani has been one of Kaneko's main composers since *Yamadamura Waltz* (1988). His music and orchestration are topnotch, as demonstrated by his lush soundtracks for the Gamera series and *Crossfire*. It's said that he's the worthy successor to Akira Ifukube, the man who wrote the score for the original *Gojira* and many other Toho science fiction films.

At this moment, a man sitting at one of Starbucks' two outdoor tables catches my eye. Dressed in black, his hair is slicked over and he has a biker magazine propped in front of him. Maybe it's because of the mag, but his beard and mustache bring to mind Tom Savini from the George Romero film *Knightriders*. However, the more I look, the more I feel there's something familiar about him. That's when it hits me. Stepping outside, I approach him.

"Excuse me," I say, "you wouldn't happen to be Kow Otani?"

He looks up from the magazine. "Yes, that's me."

The serendipity of the moment is not lost on Otani as I explain my connection to GMK. In fact, of all things, it turns out that he lives just down the road and frequents the same Starbucks as me.

Joining him with my coffee, Otani shows me the magazine he's reading. He flips to a page showing himself beside a Harley.

"This is my bike," he boasts. "I ride whenever I get the chance."

Soon his wife, Rosie, joins us. From Okinawa, Rosie speaks native-level English. She explains that the Otani family has lived in Shimokita for more than a hundred years and that Otani's parents ran a dance studio in town for decades. Before we part, they invite me over for a visit to their home.

Forgoing contemplating the odds of what has just occurred, I simply take this as a positive sign. I wonder if turning 42 today has anything to do with it?

26 APRIL 2001

Today is the camera test for the Godzilla suit. Several two-foot-high platforms have been wheeled out of S9 and pushed together in front of the big pool. SFX director Kamiya and his staff have a 35mm camera and several movie lights aimed at the stage. By 10:30 a.m. things are ready to roll. But where's Godzilla? The suit has yet to arrive from Vi-shop. Glancing nervously at his watch, Shinada makes a call.

"The guys are stuck in traffic," he announces apologetically.

A few minutes later—and to Shinada's relief—a white van pulls up. Jutting from its back is the head of Godzilla, which must have freaked out any tailgaters on the ride over.

The suit staffers untie the costume and hoist it onto the platforms. Suit actor Yoshida, who has spent the wait warming up, looks eager to get inside. I don't know if it's meant as a joke, but he's wearing a t-shirt with the logo from the US *Godzilla*.

After Yoshida has squeezed into the suit, Kamiya hops on stage. "For the first shot, let's get you roaring," he says. "Put your hands near your chest and lift your head like this." Demonstrating, Kamiya tips his head back, claws at the air, and howls loudly. Climbing down, Kamiya gets behind the camera and calls for action.

Leaning back, Yoshida points Godzilla's head into the air and, via a remote control operated by Yamabe, Godzilla's mouth opens wide. From deep within the suit comes Yoshida's muffled roar.

As the test continues, I acclimate myself to the look of the suit. It's a lot different from the last two. For one thing, Godzilla's feet are huge, and they have a heel or lift under them. Godzilla's neck is thicker than expected, and sometimes the head weighs weirdly into it. The hips are extremely broad, too, and the belly juts out in an unflattering way. I also notice gaps between the seams, and that there are still unpainted spots here and there around the suit. Shinada admits that more work needs to be done and that he and his team will be at it until the very moment the first frame is shot.

Despite this, when flipping through the photos on my camera's monitor, I notice from certain angles the suit looks ferocious; in some, I'd go so far as to say Godzilla looks entirely badass! I mention my discovery to Kamiya.

"That's the point of what we're doing today," he says matter-of-factly. "The purpose of the camera test is to see how the suit looks on screen, what color it appears, and to find its best angles."

The test lasts two hours. From foot pounding to hip pivoting, from tail whipping to arm thrashing, Godzilla is given such a workout that I don't think there's a position or move Kamiya hasn't made Yoshida go through. Satisfied, the crew wraps for lunch.

Several hours later, a dozen of us gather beside a nearby storage shed. Its work done for the day, the Godzilla suit stands in a metal cart just inside the shed. At its feet rests the Baragon suit. Two men from Vi-shop pick it up and carry it outside.

Baragon is still far from finished. It's unpainted with yellow glue stains running along the seams. Sewn into the spaces between the back plates of the neck is a soft, silky material, and both the teeth and horn between Baragon's eyes look like they were attached this morning.

Joining the test is Baragon suit actor Rie Ota. Shinada was right. She *is* short.

Already in one of those silk-like body outfits suit actors wear to protect their skin, she stands poised and confident.

Getting into the Baragon suit is unlike any entry process I've seen to date. Typically, an actor gets in feet first, entering the costume as if it were a pair of pants. Then, in the way a doctor dons a surgeon's smock, they work both arms in through the back. In Baragon's case, the suit is placed belly down on the ground. Following this, suit maker Yoshida and another staffer pry open a long, slit-like opening running down the back. This gives Ota the space needed to work herself in. She wiggles her legs and arms simultaneously until she's in place. After giving her okay, the costume is shut behind her.

Everyone steps back to give Ota room, yet she does nothing. For what seems an eternity, Baragon lies unmoving. Suddenly, a limb twitches. Then another. Finally, as if the spark of life has entered the suit, she pulls the front off the ground, lifting the back higher and higher until the suit is up on its knees. As Ota prepares to give the suit a workout, the sun sets. A soft, amber glow illuminates the area. It plays well against the reddish-brown of Baragon's skin. Ota gives a few twists and turns, causing the chatter between the staff to grow in excitement. Scanning their faces, I can see that everyone is impressed.

Beside me is Isao, the sarcastic art director I met the other day; he's taking photos with a small digital camera.

"I've been working on these films so long I hardly care about Godzilla anymore," he divulges. "But Baragon! It's been over thirty years since we made a film with Baragon. This is why I'm excited about this production!"

I've decided that Shinada is otaku. What I mean is that most otaku are shy at first, but once the engine of their obsession revs, a geekish drive takes over. In Shinada's case, he started out nervously explaining various aspects of the suit to Kamiya. Now that his enthusiasm has kicked in, he's discussing its details with confidence. As Kamiya gives feedback, Shinada makes notes directly onto Baragon with a black magic marker.

Although she isn't complaining, Ota seems to be in discomfort. For one thing, for her to wear the suit properly, she has to prop herself up on the tips of her fingers and toes. Shinada comes up with the idea of putting tennis balls in the gloves that would rest in her palms and help cushion the weight.

A staff member guides Ota, who now stands upright, back a few feet. Shinada asks her to jump over to him. Up and down, as if she has springs on her feet, Ota bounds across the asphalt. Shinada catches her as she smashes into his shoulder. This is done a few times. For the final test, AD Yuichi Kikuchi grabs hold of Baragon's tail. As the monster tries to scamper away on all fours, he holds it steady by the tail. Worried it might tear, Kamiya asks suit maker Yoshida if doing this is okay. He assures him the tail was designed to be manhandled in this way.

Once the Baragon suit test is over, I collect my things and head over to Kaneko's house for an English lesson with his kids. After the day's excitement, I'm in a great mood and feel like treating myself to a cab. Unfortunately, my finances don't care about my emotional state and I've no option but to walk. On the way, I pass the café where I did my interview with Godzilla suit actor Nakajima for *Fangoria* back in 1998. I hadn't realized how close he lives to Toho.

28 APRIL 2001

I stop by Toho to go over the shooting schedule and to see how things are progressing. Kaneko tells me that the live-action "crank in" (Japanese term for first day of shooting) is set for 11 May and that the SFX crew will start a few days after this.

Before leaving, I walk over to S9 to see how set construction is going. The art department is slicing up large blocks of Styrofoam with knives and cutters that they then glue together to form mountains. Unpainted, they're bright white and look much like the snow-covered mountains of Antarctica; it brings to mind the snow set in *King Kong Escapes* (*Kingu Kongu no gyakushu*, 1967). I ask a staff member what they will eventually be.

"Do you know Hakone? It's a tourist destination with forests, hot springs, and a great view of Mt. Fuji. After we get these shaped, we'll paint them brown and put foliage on them, turning them into the mountains of Hakone."

1 MAY 2001

I finished a "meet the staff" section for Kaneko's website. Digging through the reactions on the online discussion boards, I'm relieved that the usual slew of preproduction fan jitters appears to be quelled. For the moment, that is. Fans always find a way to see the worst in things.

2 MAY 2001

I'm over at Starbucks, hanging with Otani. He has the sort of easy-going personality you find with people who've spent a lifetime closely associated with music. He's very open about his work, too. As we sit outside and drink our morning coffee, he talks freely about his upcoming Godzilla assignment.

"I want to do something original," he says. "I'm not interested in using any previous music associated with Godzilla. However, I'm afraid Toho might request I rework some Ifukube scores."

I tell him about a recent chat I had with Kaneko concerning the film's soundtrack. Kaneko, too, is unsure whether to use any classic themes. Otani and I agree that unless a full orchestra is employed, it's a good idea to avoid updating Ifukube's work, à la those tinny rock versions that marred the soundtrack of *Godzilla vs. Biollante* (*Gojira tai Biorante*, 1989).

"That's the thing," Otani says. "I don't want to be in a position where I have to update his music simply for the sake of updating it. His work is best left untouched." With that, we make a toast with our coffees to the greatness that is Ifukube.

Feeling bold, I suggest that should he want inspiration, he should give the Italian group Goblin a listen. It's a prog-rock band that has done numerous scores for horror films, including *Suspiria* and *Dawn of the Dead*. Otani admits to not being familiar with their music. I promise to make an MD of their best pieces for him.

7 MAY 2001

Today is one of those days where I wish I could go back and do everything differently. I'm unhappy to report that I was the victim of theft.

It happened on the Yamanote train line. With much to catch up on with GMK, I put my bag in the rack above and sit to write in my journal. When I got up at Sugamo Station, I discovered my bag was gone! Someone must have snatched it in the crush of passengers exiting at Ikebukuro, the previous station. This is a real disaster. Inside my bag was my digital camera, cell phone, and wallet.

With no money and thus no means to get anywhere, I had to go to the station office at Sugamo. There, I was greeted with frowns and disinterest from the station staff. I might be imagining things, but the JR guys appeared more concerned with their reputation being tarnished than my plight. Not one of them asked if I was okay or if I'd been hurt. Obviously obeying protocol, they simply gave me a train ticket to get to the closest police station.

I can't say it was much better there. The police showed hardly a modicum of concern and bluntly said I'd never see my stuff again. Fortunately, the company I teach English for said they'll advance me 30,000 yen ($240). With another "free" train pass, I rode to the office and picked up the money.

As if being the victim of a robbery isn't enough, the way some people try to comfort me is entirely out of line. I keep getting reassured that it was probably a Chinese person who stole my bag. Man, I try to imagine the backlash I'd get in New York if I was to accuse a minority of this crime without the culprit on hand to back up the claim.

Of all the crummy timing. GMK starts shooting Friday and here I am without a camera. Replacing it will cost at least 100,000 yen ($800).

8 MAY 2001

I'm over at Otani's. Kow and Rosie are supportive. They offer to lend me their camera, and Rosie says I can use her cell phone. Of course I refuse. Still, their kindness is touching and helps to calm my stress. The camera offer is one I'd have taken were it not a simple point-and-shoot. There's no way I'd get any useful photos with it given how subtly lit movie sets are.

9 MAY 2001

Ed Godziszewski, a friend in the US, has offered to buy me a new camera.

"This is the first time a non-Japanese has been allowed on the set of a Godzilla film from start to finish," he writes in an email. "There's no way I'm going to let you be without a camera!"

Ed is transferring money to my account, but it will take at least a week to clear. In the meantime, I'll use Sagae's camera, which is a step up from the Otanis'. Although the cost of film and developing is astronomical, I also have my 35mm film cameras. So, with a little help from friends, I think I'll be fine for the start of the shoot.

10 MAY 2001

Today is the *Oharai* for GMK. This is a purification ritual in which a Shinto priest blesses something, in this case, the film production. It's done to ward off evil and mischievous spirits.

I've found two Shinto shrines at Toho. One is tucked away in the bushes between S8 and S9. The other is larger and located on the east end of the studio near the PR office. Today's *Oharai* is held in front of the larger shrine, where the parking lot in front of S1 offers enough room for the entire staff to gather.

Conspicuously absent from the ceremony is SFX director Kamiya. "He said he feels religious ceremonies don't have a place on film sets and has opted not to come," Kaneko reports afterward.

Kaneko's feelings on the matter are more diplomatic. "*Oharai* doesn't bother me. I participate because it's a tradition. If anything were to happen during the production, the staff would say it happened because an *Oharai* wasn't performed."

GODZILLA, MOTHRA AND KING GHIDORAH: GIANT MONSTERS ALL-OUT ATTACK
Production

I arrive at Toho's back entrance at 8:30 a.m. and flash the guards my studio pass. Inside the small sentry box are two uniformed men: one in his late 50s, the other a 20-something. I hold up a box of Mr. Donuts I bought near the station.

"I'll be coming to the production off and on." I say as I pass them the box. They're delighted. After all, who doesn't love Mr. Donuts?

In high spirits and pleased with how everything has worked out, I tip my head to everyone I see as I make my way across the studio lot. When I get to S1, I find its large doors are swung open wide.

Leaning against one is director Kaneko. With exaggerated hand sweeps, he beckons me inside. "Welcome to Studio 1 and to…*Godzilla*."

It takes a moment for my eyes to adjust to the dimly lit interior. When they do, I see it's some type of subterranean cavern. Stalactites drip from the ceiling, and the floor is a hardened mass of molten rock. Over fifty staffers are rushing about, moving lights, setting up camera equipment, laying cables, and touching up the set.

I have my cameras and laptop computer with me. But with so much going on, I'm unsure where to set up. Kaneko points to an unused table near Teiichi Saito, the soundman. "Why not set up over here?"

Seated in a folding chair is actor Yukijiro Hotaru. A little dirt here, some dust in the hair there, a bit of blood at the corner of the mouth…a woman is applying makeup to his face.

"You remember Norman?" Kaneko asks Hotaru.

"From the shoot at Kyoto Station, right?" he replies. I'm flattered he remembers. I use the opportunity to gather comments from Hotaru.

"There are two things I've wanted in my acting career," Hotaru reveals. "To be in a Kurosawa film and a Godzilla film. As Kurosawa is no longer with us, that's impossible. But Godzilla...I've arrived! In today's scene, I'll be discovering the slumbering body of King Ghidorah. It's got a couple of physical moments. I hope I can handle it."

Kaneko raises a reassuring hand. "You'll be fine. You've been through worse, right?" The two men share a laugh.

The cave set is massive and stretches from the floor to the rafters. Its base juts out across the floor of S1 and takes up most of the available space; the staff has only a small area in front from which to work. Complicating things are the many well-wishers who've come to see the production off. I spy SFX director Kawakita talking to Kaneko. Walking through the doors is director Tezuka; he's got a case of beer for the crew. Kenji Takama, the cinematographer on *Crossfire*, has stopped by as well. Like odd men out, several of the top brass from Toho are lined up against a back wall, decked out in expensive-looking suits.

Producer Tomiyama is on hand, of course. As the lighting crew prepares the first shot, he talks things over with Kaneko and Hotaru, checking their moods and making sure nothing is amiss. Then, spotting me, he walks over.

"How are you today, Norman?" he asks politely.

"Fine," I say. I'm not sure I like being singled out this way.

"The director tells me you'll be joining the production often. I'd like to take this moment to make sure that you know the set dos and don'ts. First off, we're here to make a movie; nothing must get in the way of that goal. What the crew does takes priority. Even though you're here to get a story, please remember you won't be able to see everything. Do you understand?"

Tomiyama's talk turns out to be mostly common sense things. It's annoying to listen to, but I can't fault him for it. His priority is the production. His responsibility is that things go smoothly. I am, after all, an anomaly in the equation. After Tomiyama splits, I mention our "rap" to Kaneko.

"Don't mind," he says. "I trust you. You'll be fine."

With the scene's lighting finally worked out, AD Aida calls Hotaru to the front of the stage. "Everyone, let me introduce actor Yukijiro Hotaru," he announces. "He will be playing the part of the suicidal businessman. A round of applause, please."

The staff and set visitors clap loudly as Hotaru bows deeply.

The first take is a master shot of Hotaru falling into the cave. Mitsuo Abe, the film's action director, reviews the how-to's of tumbling down the cave wall with the actor. Hotaru is energetic and appears ready for anything. A 3-camera shoot, when each camera is up to speed, their operator yells out, "A, okay!" "B, okay!" "C, okay!" With cameras rolling, Kaneko calls, "Action!"

There is a rumble of rocks from the top of the set. Dust and stone pushed by out-of-sight crewmembers pummel down followed by Hotaru. He flips over himself the length of the cave set.

The moment after Kaneko calls cut, Hotaru springs up to show he's uninjured. The crew applauds. The next shots are of Hotaru sitting up and noting that he shares the cave with a gigantic sleeping monster. The main camera is positioned before Hotaru and tilted up to hide that he's lying on a wood table covered by a blanket.

After lunch are green screen shots. Hotaru is positioned in front of a crude drawing of Ghidorah's head. In charge of this is Hajime Matsumoto, a VFX (visual effects) supervisor who did a similar job on Kaneko's Gamera trilogy.

"My job," Matsumoto explains, "is to oversee the compositing and integration of the film's various elements. This means I'll be going between the live-action and the effects set often. I'm the guy who has to make sure the footage matches up."

The day is called a wrap at 6 p.m. "There are a few shots still needed at the head of this scene," Kaneko divulges. "Where Hotaru falls into the cave. But we won't shoot those for another month." Kaneko waves to his brother Jiro. "How about we go to the restaurant across the street for a beer?" Jiro and I give the thumbs up.

The area surrounding Toho is residential, so it's no surprise to find the restaurant empty. We walk down to the basement dining area where a corner bar is decorated with gaudy plastic flowers. Kaneko and Jiro take seats while I walk behind the bar.

"Your credit's fine, Mr. Torrance," I say to the men. They stare at me blankly. "You know...the bar scene in *The Shining*!"

Sitting with them, I ask Kaneko to compare the first day of GMK to G3. "*Gamera 3*'s first scene was in a museum with Ayako and Shinobu," Kaneko explains. "That didn't go well. They aren't the best actresses." The three of us roar with laughter as a waiter brings us beers.

"Seriously, though," he continues. "I picked this scene with Hotaru for the first day because he has the energy I want to start things off with. Today went well, and I feel it's a good sign for things to come."

"To the road ahead," I say. With that, we knock our glasses together and toast to the coming shoot.

12 MAY 2001

I make it to Toho at 8:30 a.m. The crew is already setting up the camera and rigging lights around the cave interior. At 9 a.m., Kaneko walks in with Hideyo Amamoto.

Having grown up on a diet of Toho monster movies, I recognize the actor right away. Amamoto's role as the diabolical Dr. Who in *King Kong Escapes* made a sizable impact on me as a boy; I also loved him as the toymaker in *Godzilla's Revenge* (*Gojira-Minira-Gabara: oru kaiju daishingeki*, 1969). Seeing him now at the doorway of S1—the bright sunlight from outdoors shining around his body—I'm awestruck. It's this moment when the Godzilla I grew up on and the Godzilla of now have come together.

While the makeup woman checks Amamoto's face and adjusts his collar, he unconsciously shifts his jaw back and forth. He looks around S1 without focusing on anything in particular. That is until he sees me. Breaking away from makeup, he walks over.

"Where're you from?" Amamoto asks point-blank. "*Ah*," he grunts with disappointment upon hearing I'm American. "I was hoping it was Spain." Kaneko jumps in to explain that Amamoto is a fan of Spanish culture.

"I go as often as I can," Amamoto

elaborates. "See these pouches?" He points to two odd bags hanging from his hips. "I bought them there. They're my contribution to my character."

I walk with them to the cave set to find it's been altered from the day before. "It's now the opposite side of the cave," Kaneko explains. He has Amamoto stand on the edge of the rocky set. "It's an SFX shot," Kaneko adds. "He'll be looking out over the sleeping body of Ghidorah."

Relatively simple, Amamoto just has to stand and stare out. It's done in one take. After Kaneko calls cut, two ADS help the aged actor off the stage. He walks over to where I have my computer set up.

"I want to show you something," he says. From a pouch, he pulls out a travel guide to Spain. "Ever been here?"

I mentioned the three months I spent near Barcelona in the summer of '70 with my family when my dad was on sabbatical from teaching.

"The Franco years," he replies. "Awful time for the Spanish people." From the other pouch, he pulls out a pack of cigarettes. "I got these in Spain, too. Smell 'em." They have a sickly sweet odor that I don't care for. Amamoto is called back on stage.

During lunch yesterday, I hung around S1 to take photos of the emptied set. By the time I got to the cafeteria all the good food was gone. Not wanting a repeat of this, I'm first in line today. After loading my tray, I take a seat in the cafeteria. As I don't know anyone that well and feel self-conscious as the only non-Japanese, I sit apart from the rest of the staff. I'm cool with this. I have a pen out and am ready to jot the morning's events into my GMK diary. However, just as I touch pen to paper, a figure appears over me.

"You mind?" It's Amamoto! He's in his GMK outfit and clutching a tray. Without missing a beat, I push my notebook away and make room. He mumbles something and sits down.

"Tell me more about the time your family visited Spain," he requests.

I talk about Cambrils, a fishing village my family rented a home in, and the time beggars chased my brother and me through the cobblestone streets one night. As I speak, I see from the edges of my eyes that everyone in the cafeteria is staring at us: the eccentric, legendary actor and the peculiar foreigner. Honestly, I'm trying to stay out of the spotlight. This isn't helping!

My memories launch Amamoto into a disjointed recollection of his own. "Nothing like the old days," he says somewhat disgruntled. He rotates a finger over his head without looking where he's pointing. "Thirty years ago, the cafeteria was across the way and was much bigger. It would fill up with a lot more people than you see here. A *lot* more. See there? That's where I saw Kurosawa for the last time... I was in *Yojimbo*, you know. You liked *King Kong Escapes*? They stuck those damned eyebrows on me and put white powder in my hair. It was a load of hogwash!"

Mentioning that I thought he and the beautiful actress Mie Hama made a striking pair in the film, I try to lighten his mood. He glares at me.

From time to time, staff members interrupt us to bow in front of Amamoto and show their respect. Amamoto either flat out ignores them or makes the slightest acknowledging hand gesture.

Back in S1, Kaneko orders the staff to set up light shafts to beam behind Amamoto. When the lighting is ready, the actor heads for the stage. Unexpectedly, he comes to a halt. There, on an unused platform, is the Ghidorah toy Kaneko has been using to illustrate what his character sees embedded in the ice. Amamoto glances my way. Cracking a toothy smile, he lifts the figure, places it on his head, and gives a wink. It takes all my strength not to laugh aloud.

As live-action shooting is still a ways off, I zip over to S9 to check on the SFX staff's progress. I notice a makeshift shed on the far right side of the big pool that must have been erected over the past week. Curious, I poke my head inside. There, I find two smock-clad men constructing miniature buildings. I introduce myself, exchange a few *yoroshiku onegaishimasu*, and take photos.

With the first day of SFX shooting less than a week off, S9 is in full prep mode. The previously white Styrofoam mountains are now painted in earth tones. Several art staffers are fastening pieces from real trees to them, ones I'm told come from bushes around the studio. Some of the work is less meticulous than expected. I mean, one of the crew is simply ramming branches into a mountain side with a staple gun.

One mountain dominates the set. Like a dividing wall, it cuts S9 in half while nearly touching the maze of rafters hanging just below the ceiling. Two guys on ladders work tiny homes into spots along its front. Perched atop a Styrofoam mountain across from it is the miniature of a resort with a parking lot beside it.

"This area is based on Owakudani," assistant art director Inatsuki informs me. "There are sulfur pits all over the place due to an active volcano. However, the first scenes will be of Godzilla in a valley taking hits from fighter jets. After that, we'll redress it and start in on the Owakudani Baragon/Godzilla battle."

Back in S1, the scenes with Amamoto continue. SFX director Kamiya has come in with Matsumoto to consult with Kaneko. Over the director's monitor, Matsumoto places a sheet of paper onto which Kaneko draws a sketch of Ghidorah's head. "This is where I want Ghidorah to appear," he tells them. The three discuss how best to accomplish the effect, with Matsumoto saying what can or can't be done. They'll be a while, so I decide to take the plunge and journey up into the rafters of S1, a catwalk grid strung above the studio floor.

I find a set of stairs in a corner and follow it up. To my surprise, I discover that the rafters are free floating and hang from the ceiling by some of the thickest rope I've ever seen. Great, I think as I step out onto them, this will do wonders for my fear of heights...

If dust could talk, the rafters would be a cacophony of set tales. There must be an inch of grime and goo clinging to the ropes. And the smell. Like the worst mildewed attic aroma you've ever had the displeasure of inhaling, the stink is intense.

After the day is wrapped, I pack my stuff and head to the production room. I want to say so long to Kaneko before leaving. I find him on a computer looking troubled.

"Fans," he says harshly. "Somehow, someone got a hold of the movie's poster and uploaded it. One guy says it lacks passion."

Sitting next to him is Miho Iizuka, the movie's continuity person. "Don't ask me," she says with a shrug. "I don't know why anyone would care that much."

Suddenly, Jiro rushes into the room. He

insists we follow him. Leading Kaneko and me, he takes us to the PR building in front of S1.

Seated at the conference desk are Matsumoto and ADs Murakami and Toshifumi Shimizu. They hold dilapidated scrapbooks with still photo contact sheets taped one to a page.

"You gotta check these out," says an excited Shimizu. Jiro points at the safe in the back corner. Its thick steel door is wide open. "Grab one and dig in," he adds.

I stick my head in to find row after row of similar-looking books. I pick one and open it. Inside are hundreds of contact sheets from *The War of the Gargantuas*. Barely hanging in place, they were put in with scotch tape that has long since dried and yellowed.

For the next hour, the five of us pour through every still taken during the Showa Godzilla series, noisily pointing out the ones that catch our eyes. At one point, Matsumoto starts laughing. He's found old shots of Amamoto in leotards and a Tudor ruff collar around his neck.

"We should print it out and hang it on his dressing room door," I say.

"Do that and he'll walk off the set," Kaneko warns.

Fascinating is how Kaneko and the others look at the photos. Although making a Godzilla film at Toho, they're a generation removed from the one that originated the series. Like the rest of us, they can only look at photos, read interviews, and maybe meet surviving staffers to get a sense of what was going on back during the golden age of kaiju.

Finally, we put the books down. "I'm completely stuffed!" Matsumoto announces as he rests his hands on his belly.

13 MAY 2001

It's 8:45 a.m. and the crew is readying the day's first shot: an ancient-looking statue falling onto a sheet of ice. An hour and a half later, the take is still not complete. The statue keeps falling and—despite being made of solid stone—rolling away. Kaneko wants it to hit with a stationary thud. Also, the surface of the ice (in reality a thick sheet of plastic) keeps shaking from the impact. A bunch of guys get under and secure it with poles and clamps. Visible in the shot, too, are the legs of Amamoto. Only they aren't Amamoto's. They're Aida's. He's in the actor's outfit.

The real Amamoto shows up at 10:15 in a knitted skullcap. He strikes me as looking feeble today. Well, he is 75 years old after all, and I'm sure those sickly sweet cigarettes he smokes aren't helping him maintain a youthful vigor. He gives me a "good morning" without removing the cigarette from his mouth and sits with me to wait for the statue shot to finish. Finally, at 10:45, it's in the can.

Many types make up the Toho staff, but one man in particular stands out. He looks oldish, but his hair is a deep, unnatural black (probably dyed) that he wears in a tight, yakuza-style punch perm. Large pilot glasses tinted yellow, the kind that went out of fashion thirty years ago, cover much of his face. I've no idea what he does as I haven't actually seen him do anything. The best I can figure is that he's a litmus test for the staff's effort. Every day he's either yelling out, "*dame, dame, dame!*" ("No good, no good, no good!") or "*ii ne*" ("Very nice").

I asked Kaneko, and he told me he heard that he is, or was, a member of the lighting staff. He also tells me the man's name: Futami.

On the first day of the shoot, Futami came up to me to tell me that my red sunglasses are cool. I tried to respond, but he just snorted and walked on. Yesterday, even though I said *ohayo gozaimasu* to him, he flat out ignored me. Later in the day, he saw that the table I used for my computer was taken away and that I was struggling to type atop a small opera box. All at once, he ordered the staff to wheel over a metal cart and told me to work on it. I don't know how to describe this behavior other than to label it wholly Japanese: Ignoring me directly yet ultimately taking care of me from afar. After he saw I was happy with the cart, he gave me a big smile and then peered over my shoulder at my writing.

"Can you really read this gobbledygook?" Futami asked.

"Do you mean English?"

"I'll have you know," he insisted, "I'm completely fluent in English."

I was thinking he was serious until I saw Saito, the soundman, cracking up.

Kaneko and crew are still busy setting up the cave. I pull up next to Kaneko. "You should use more blue lighting," I suggest.

"You think so?" Kaneko responds.

"Might give it a more dream-like quality," I add. "Surrealism never hurt Bunuel, you know."

This perks Kaneko's ears. He likes talking about film and seems to enjoy my analogies. For example, I told Kaneko I wasn't planning on coming in today because I had a lot of housework to deal with. Yet, when waking up, I felt a physical, overwhelming desire to be here.

"Being on a movie set is like having sex," I tell him. "Being on a Kaneko movie set is like having sex with a beautiful woman."

Kaneko starts laughing and shares my simile with the crew. Well, I can't say I'm proud of this one, but everyone appears tickled by it.

A Sunday, the cafeteria is closed. A takeout menu is passed around. Flat broke and unsure if Toho's paying, I order the cheapest thing. When it comes, I sit outside against the wall of S1 and make the most of the meager portion, cursing myself out under my breath because Toho *was* buying. When I'm about finished, Masahiro Kishimoto, the live-action cameraman, comes over. In his hands is a white t-shirt wrapped in plastic.

"Want this? It's a GXM t-shirt given to extras following a running scene last year"

I'm surprised and thank him for it.

"If you ask me," he adds as he passes it my way, "it's pretty ugly."

Lunch lasts an hour, and I spend the latter half in the staff room. I talk to Kaneko about the sudden passing of writer Douglas Adams. From the original radio series to the book series, *Hitchhikers Guide to the Galaxy* has been one of my favorite fiction pieces. Kaneko is only vaguely aware of him.

PR man Shinichiro Masuda steps into the room.

"There you are," he says looking my way. "The effects set starts up Thursday. I assume you want to be there for that." I shake my head yes. "You can take all the photos you like, but there will be others taking photos too. One is our staff photographer. The rest are from publishing houses making GMK books. Also, we plan to premiere the first shots of Godzilla on the 27th. They'll be in the weekly magazine *Friday*." Masuda makes me promise not to upload any photos of Godzilla until after the 27th.

S1 is ready for the "Amamoto awakening Ghidorah" scene. The actor stands near the edge of the cave with the camera three and a half meters in front of him. A large wood board covered by dirt and rocks is hoisted into the air. When Kaneko calls for action, two staffers on step ladders shake the board, causing dirt to fall between the actor and the camera. Amamoto raises his arms theatrically.

Kaneko's unsatisfied with how the dirt fell and asks for a retake. During the time the board is lowered and re-covered, I sit with Amamoto.

"You like Spanish folk songs?"

I admit to not knowing a single one. Staring intensely into my eyes, he sings a ballad that I guess is supposed to be in Spanish. When he finishes, Kaneko joins us.

"Did you know that Norman spent a summer in Spain when he was a boy?"

Amamoto's eyes widened. "Yes, I know!" he exclaims. "He gets it!"

Actually, I don't, but what the hell. He's happy thinking I do.

The next take goes better. Again, Amamoto raises his arms as dirt and rock crash before him. This time, the whole thing has more life to it. It actually looks like he's summoning the gods. Once all the dirt has exited the board, Kaneko calls cut.

S1 is now filled with a thick cloud of gray dust. The studio doors are opened to air out the stage. The last shot of the day, Amamoto can leave. The crew gives him a round of applause as he departs.

I have to return Sagae's camera and leave it for him in the art department staff room. I speed back to S1 to see if

Kaneko has time to grab a beer. He's busy talking with Matsumoto about how the composite of Amamoto's death scene will be handled. For the hell of it, I climb up onto the cave set and stand in the same spot as Amamoto. Raising my arms, I reenact his death to see what it was like from his viewpoint. Kaneko sees me and points. He and Matsumoto start to laugh.

"Hey!" I yell. "Can't a guy have some fun around here?"

16 MAY 2001

As much as it annoys me, I go to Akihabara to buy a new camera. I must have walked around for hours trying to find the best deal, but the price is the same no matter where I go. I do find a used one, but it's only 10% cheaper, not much of an incentive to go used. I also get a 64MB memory stick. Test shots seem fine. I guess it's safe to say I'm ready for the first day of SFX shooting tomorrow.

17 MAY 2001

Out of bed at 6:30 a.m., I shower and pack my things: VAIO laptop and three cameras (the Sony F505v I bought yesterday, a smaller, older Sony DSC-F3, and my antique Nikon FE, a 35mm film camera from 1978). I wouldn't call this setup anything to drool over, but it's not bad for an amateur.

Under clear skies, I arrive at Toho and head straight for the PR room. Including me, there are eight reporters from various publications. Masuda covers production points: the actors, the shooting schedule, the currently permissible information to publish, and the plan Toho has to handle publicity until the premiere this December. He also mentions press restrictions, such as where to stand and whom to speak to. The talk takes a half-hour, and, frankly, I'm a bit fidgety. I just want to get over to S9 already!

As if reading my mind, Masuda ends the briefing with a much welcome, "Is everyone ready to go to 9?"

On the way, we pass S1. A hardhat construction crew is pulverizing the Ghidorah cave set. That's that, I think, as a digger truck smashes into a row of stalagmites.

Masuda leans over. "Don't worry," he says. "The press restrictions don't apply to you." That's a relief.

Things are hectic in S9. Stagehands run about: some lug cables, some wheel lights, others do mundane things such as spray water onto the set's miniature mountains. Yoshida is standing on the side of the stage, preparing himself to become Godzilla. He rolls his head, hunches his shoulders, and holds his hands close to his body like tiny T-rex arms.

SFX director Kamiya calls for Godzilla. The suit crew wheels over the steel contraption housing the suit. With their help, a beaming Yoshida hops in through the opening in its back. The first shot is Godzilla walking through a valley as he fends off fighter jets. Raising his head (controlled offstage by Yamabe), Godzilla claws the air. Kamiya cries out, "Okay!" And with that, the first shot is in the can!

Masuda calls me over. "Norman, there's someone I'd like you to meet." He leads me to where an older man is seated on some opera boxes. "This is Takashi Nakao. He's the Toho set photographer for the special effects team." Masuda explains who I am to Nakao and asks

him to look after me when he can't be on set. Nakao straightens out his baseball cap and shakes my hand.

Even though it's my third Godzilla set, it's new territory for me. I was little more than a spectator the previous two times. I still am, but I've evolved into something else. What this is, I've no idea. The thing is, I hardly have a clue as to what my boundaries are. The stage where Godzilla performs is on a collection of pushed-together platforms. Crew jump on and off freely. Am I allowed up there, too? If I climb up, will I be yelled at and subsequently banned from the set? Should I chance finding out? I'd rather stand in a corner and watch the production from afar than get thrown out for being brazen on the first day of shooting.

Watching people come and go on the stage, I conclude that there isn't anyone checking who does and doesn't have permission to be up there. *Screw it!* I put a foot to the stage and hoist myself up. I walk over to Godzilla and start taking photos. No one says a thing or even seems to care.

Eventually, my camera's memory sticks fill up. Crap, I have to dump the data into my computer. Now here's a thing I hadn't thought of: Where do I set up camp? S9 may be enormous, but with close to a hundred people here, every inch of the studio is in use. I find an outlet between some shelves beside the art department and plug my computer in. No sooner do I than art director Miike tells me it's probably not a good idea, which is Japanese for, "Don't plug your freaking computer in there!" Unfortunately, this catches the attention of producer Tomiyama.

"Norman," he calmly begins. "Thank

you for joining us again today, the first day of the special effects shoot. I see you're looking for a place to put your equipment. Regrettably, every part of S9 is utilized to realize the latest entry in the Godzilla franchise. We at Toho are grateful for your interest and commitment to the project and the publicity your work will generate for the movie. However, you'll have to be more careful as to how you integrate yourself with the crew. Tell you what, I'll see to it that you can set your computer up in the PR room. How's that sound?"

My ears are bleeding. I don't even know what to make of Tomiyama's verbose lecture. What he suggests isn't a bad idea, but the PR room is on the far end of the studio; it's over a ten-minute walk there and back. This isn't counting the ten minutes it takes to copy the photos into my computer. I'm thinking that's got to be a lost half an hour each run, and judging by how fast I'm filling up cards, I'll lose a lot of set time.

"*Wow!*" I respond. "That's great! I'll talk to Masuda and get on this right away!"

Tomiyama smiles, tips his head, and then moves his attention elsewhere. Luckily, the battery in my computer is full, so I don't need to plug it in yet. Ducking behind the big pool, I empty my memory sticks before returning to S9 for another go.

The finished Baragon suit has been brought to the studio for inspection. Kamiya and a few higher-ranking SFX staffers gather around. After Ota dons the suit, suit maker Yoshida uses a remote control device to make the ears move, the mouth open and—as a bonus—the horn glow like the one on the original Baragon suit.

"This isn't anything I asked for," a surprised Kamiya remarks.

Yoshida looks disappointed. "I did it just in case you wanted it," he replies.

Once the inspection is over, everyone returns to the set. I sit with Ota and make small talk. I ask about her suit experience.

"It's my first time," she admits. "To be honest, it's my first time to be on a movie set. I've only ever done character appearances at department stores."

Despite a lack of experience, she seems willing to do whatever it takes and comes across as eager to please. I can relate. Everyone has to start somewhere, myself included.

During the time Kamiya looked over Baragon, the Godzilla suit was rigged with explosives. Yoshida is sealed inside Godzilla. Walking across the stage, he looks upwards and claws the air. "*BANG! BANG! BANG!*" It's Kamiya. He's mimicking the sound of the blasts to show when he wants them to detonate. The director makes some adjustments and the scene is ready to shoot.

Looking around the stage, I'm unsure where to get the shot. It seems there are two choices: one is a "making of" photo that includes stage and crew, the other is a shot taken directly in the world of Godzilla (i.e., a picture with no crew or stage visible). Yeah, I want one in the world of Godzilla…but where to take it? I then notice all the still photographers are huddled in the same general area. I walk over and, well, it does seem to be the best angle to capture Godzilla in his environment. Maybe I should keep an eye on these guys. They obviously have experience.

Kamiya calls for a take. Miniature trees are set on fire. Godzilla takes a few steps, looks up, and *BANG-BANG-BANG!*

Holy shit! I was *not* expecting the sound

to be so jarring. They weren't even pleasant sounding. In the movies, explosions are deep and powerful; these were like the pop of cheap firecrackers, only at about a hundred times the volume.

As the crew extinguishes the trees, I check the photo I took. It's a total blur, the result of jerking when the charges went off. Befuddled, I ask Nakao to show me his shot. It's rock-solid; you can even see the blast coming off the suit. I ask how he does it.

"I don't do anything. You just get used to it. In another day or two, you won't even notice the noise."

I get to talking to second art director Isao. Like the first time we met, he eyes me with friendly suspicion. Though "suspicion" might be too strong a word. It's more like he's sizing me up in order to come out with a chiding remark.

"Norman," he starts in. "You need a nickname."

I do?

"What do people call you?"

"Just Norman. I did once tell a friend in New York that if I had to choose a Japanese name it'd be Maki Goro, the reporter in *Son of Godzilla*."

"That's it!" Isao yells. "Like him, you're a reporter that's pushed your way in. I'm calling you Goro-chan!"

So, now I've got a nickname. I hope it doesn't catch on.

Shinada is working on one of the Godzilla suits for the photoshoot with *Friday* magazine. Despite the pressures of the first day, he's as friendly as always. I ask about Godzilla's eyes. They'd been all-white when I saw the suit last. Now they're dark around the edges with veins that hint at pupils.

"Ah, you're observant," Shinada notes.

"Ultimately, we decided against all white because in Japan this indicates blindness and the producers don't want backlash from visually impaired groups."

The next shot exemplifies the differences between recent and previous kaiju SFX styles. For this, Godzilla will walk by a highway overpass with the monster seen from the structure's underside.

In the so-called old days ('50s~mid-'90s), massive sets were built and used like real locations. Nowadays, they're erected directly in front of the camera. So, rather than the art staff building a complete highway and letting the director choose where to set the camera, just the overpass parts the camera will pick up are erected.

Nakao leans in close to me just before Kamiya calls for a take. "Back in the day it was easier to get shots in the world of the kaiju," he says. "With this method, it's almost impossible since it's designed solely for the movie camera."

The day comes to an end at 9:30 p.m.

18 MAY 2001

The morning continues with Godzilla engaging a squadron of fighter jets. Explosives are again affixed to Godzilla's body. When set off, the charges cause me to jerk my camera. The playback screen reveals another annoying collection of dreadful blurs. They do four takes right up until lunch. All my photos suck! Will I ever acquire a steady hand like Nakao?

Between shots, Nakao calls me over to his space in S9. He's brought over a couple of photo books of Toho films to show me.

"Most of these shots are mine," he says with pride. He flips through to a section on *King Kong vs. Godzilla*. "I did stills on this one."

I'm impressed. I can't calculate how many hours I've spent looking at photos from this film. I flip through to *King Kong Escapes*.

"Those are mine too," he adds. "Back then, when productions were longer, we'd have entire mornings just for stills. I could set things how I liked and would go wild. No one makes that kind of time for stills anymore."

I have lunch in the cafeteria and share a table with SFX director Kawakita, GMK SFX director Kamiya, suit actors Hurricane Ryu and Yoshida, and model maker Sagae. Everyone is in a playful mood. Kawakita gets to teasing Kamiya about attaining the title of director, which probably has something to do with Kamiya being one of his ADs years ago.

At times attention turns my way. I'm asked how I know Godzilla films, which ones I like, and what I think of the US version. Kawakita, probably feeling I've usurped his dominance at the table, interrupts to let loose remarks I suppose would be considered racist were this America. Fortunately, Sagae quickly works to smooth things out. Despite Kawakita's rudeness, everyone else at the table is respectful and merely curious about my being here.

Me? Sitting here with the movers and shakers of Godzilla at Toho Studios is an incredible experience. Of course, I keep how mind-blowing it is tucked out of sight. I figure it's best to act casual and to add to the upbeat air, even if I do have to take a bit of crap from Kawakita.

Now that the jet fighter scene is done, the first real SFX money shot of the production is in preparation. The storyboards reveal it to be Godzilla stepping on and crushing a *ryokan*, a type of Japanese inn. Yamabe wheels in a large Godzilla foot[13]. Right away, crewmembers hoist it onto a bare stage and attach it to a glide plate at the top of a steel rig. Five crewmen grab hold of a rope connected to the plate. Pulling the rope lifts the foot up, releasing it brings it crashing down. At the moment the foot hits the stage, another staffer pushes a metal bar that knocks the foot forward. The upshot is that when the crew's actions are coordinated, this creates the illusion of Godzilla's foot stepping down and moving forward.

After working out the timing between the guys on the rope and the guy at the bar, a paper version of the *ryokan* is placed on the stage. On Kamiya's command, they heave the rope back in unison. The foot goes up and—on release of the rope and push of the bar—it comes down and squashes the stand-in perfectly.

"I think we're good to go," Kamiya says.

The foot is tied off in the air and the space below is turned over to Miike and his art staff. After laying out a dirt base, the real *ryokan* model is brought over. It's highly detailed with a porcelain tiled roof, TV antennas, air conditioners, and is even topped with a solar panel. The art crew goes to work dressing the area around it. In the meanwhile, Kamiya concerns himself with the camera and its setup. This continues until Miike calls the night a wrap at 9 p.m.

19 MAY 2001

As dreaded, I'm stuck setting up my computer in the PR room per Tomiyama's

13 - A left over prop, the large Godzilla foot was originally built for *The Return of Godzilla*.

orders. Feeling sorry for me, Masuda lends me a bicycle, which helps cut down on the trip between the PR room and S9. While setting my computer up on the coffee table, Masuda walks over. "Norman, I have a request from Tomiyama."

Oh, Jesus, I think. What now? But before he can continue, Tomiyama himself steps in.

"*Ah*, there you are," Tomiyama says.

I smile nervously.

"Everyone's doing something for Godzilla. I was thinking about what you can do. Well, I've come up with the idea that you write a series of reports for Toho's Godzilla website. Since we're in the Internet era, it might be good to take advantage of this and do something not done before on a Godzilla production. We can call it the 'Norman Report.' How does this sound?"

I'm shocked. I was bracing myself to be thrown out. Instead, I'm asked to do official writing.

"*Hmm*… Sounds good," I say, playing it cool. "I can do that."

Tomiyama and I shake on it.

After Tomiyama leaves, Masuda confides in me. "This will make it easier for you to move around the studio. Don't screw it up."

For some reason we both grow silent. Then, as if on cue, we start laughing. I like Masuda.

Following lunch, I wander over to the big pool to watch the suit actors train. Action director Abe is putting Ota through the paces. He has her scampering across mats stretched across the tar pavement. After a bit, Abe has her put on Baragon's paws—just the paws. She runs back and forth until he feels she's ready to try it in the suit. He has her get into the full costume except for the head. I'd laugh at the sight of her tiny head jutting disproportionately from Baragon's neck if it wasn't apparent that Ota is in discomfort from the workout's intensity.

Assisting them are Godzilla and Ghidorah suit actors Yoshida and Ohashi. They help Ota in and out of the suit and offer advice where they can. When it's Abe's turn to work with Ota, the veteran suit actors do calisthenics in front of the pool.

There's another man with them who I haven't seen before. "My name's Sasaki," he says. "I'm the stunt double for Rie."

A stunt double for a suit actor?

"There are a few shots, such as when Baragon leaps at Godzilla, that she isn't trained for. I'll handle those. But it's a secret. Promise you won't tell anyone?"

The "foot smashing the *ryokan*" shot was scheduled for 10 a.m.; it's now 4 p.m. and the crew is still in prep mode. It's the art staff; they've been relentlessly pouring detail into it for hours.

I climb up on stage and let my eyes roll over the meticulous work: a washing machine, some bicycles, a stone path, potted plants, a couple of rowboats with fishing gear, and two smaller yet equally detailed homes around back.

"The detail isn't there to wow you," Miike insists when noticing my interest. "It's there to convince you." Miike adds that the house is built at 1:12 scale.

I take a few close-up shots of the set and the staff working, mindful of the large Godzilla foot dangling overhead. I know it's secured, but it certainly looks like it could come smashing down any second.

Things get feverish around 5:30 p.m. when Kamiya announces it's time to film. The art staff steps out of the way to make room for the lighting crew. They'd worked around the art staff throughout the day but need full access for final tweaking.

At 5:50 p.m., as rehearsed the night before, several of the crew take hold of the long rope connected to Godzilla's foot. They pull until it's taut. The foot is then released from its lock. It's now held in place solely by the men's strength. Staffer Akihiro Tsujikawa (Tony as he's known on set), readies himself at the bar that'll move the foot forward. With the scene set in the rain, art staffers spray water and wet the model.

I get in a huddle with the still cameramen. Kamiya calls action. The foot comes down and, with a loud crash, flattens the house. A split-second later, it picks up to reveal the remains of the once intricately constructed miniature.

Kamiya asks for playback. We gather around his monitor. The shot is run several times. Heads shake up and down. It appears to have gone well. Kamiya calls, "Okay!" Not like there's a choice. It was a "get it right the first time" kind of take. The *ryokan* is now as flat as Wile E. Coyote following a boulder launch gone wrong.

With the shot over, the art staff starts to clean the remains of the house, shoveling it like trash into garbage bags.

20 MAY 2001

I'm at the Starbucks in Shimokita catching up on set notes. Otani spots me through the large front window and comes in.

"If possible," he asks, "can you print out some photos of Godzilla and the other monsters? It'll give me something to work with until the film is edited." I ask for a week or two since I don't have any good monster shots yet.

"By the way, Norman," he adds. "You're looking a bit thin."

After he leaves, I feel my jaw. It does feel bony. I wonder if I might be pushing myself too hard. I order a Cinnamon Roll to help fatten up.

24 MAY 2001

By coincidence, I exit the station at the same time as Kawakita. As usual, he forgets my name and greets me with a painful slap on the back. It's annoying but hardly worth making a stink about. Kawakita is what you'd call *oyaji* in Japanese: Older guys who try to be cool but aren't. They make jokes that no one gets, and, because of Japan's age-hierarchy, they tend to be on the arrogant side. You could say that *oyaji* have a license to be foolish.

On the way, Kawakita explains he's directing a TV commercial about "unbreakable homes." In it, he explains, Godzilla will step on a house but finds he is unable to crush it.

"Pretty good advertising catch, no?" he asks. I gotta admit, it is kinda cute.

Finally, the Hakone set is complete and the Baragon vs. Godzilla battle can commence. The mountain wall splitting S9 down the middle is impressive. It brims with all sorts of neat detail: pipes, walking paths, those mesh nets Japanese place around falling rock areas to hold them in place, and even a few shacks here and there. It's also rigged to emit steam from various cracks in the mountainside.

Colorwise, the wall is mostly brown with gray rock and stone, but there are also strips of greenery running across two levels at the top. Art staffer Thunder (a nickname given to Kohei Sugiyama because he shares a family name with pro wrestler "Thunder" Sugiyama) is up near the top with a spray bottle in hand. He's wetting down the branches to keep them from drying out.

The rest of the set is made up of smaller Styrofoam hills stapled over with greenery. Unlike the tall mountain, these are movable and can be arranged to suit the shot. There is also a collection of trees bolted to long wood planks. These come in handy to fill in gaps between the mountains should they appear. On the back wall encircling the set is the painting of a blue sky with clouds and mountains.

Even though people scurry around with great urgency, the set's mood is one of focus; some are even enjoying themselves: Off to the side, Godzilla suit actor Yoshida shares laughs with Yamabe. Even the ordinarily serious-looking Miike is smiling as he watches his art crew prep the first shot. If anyone looks uncomfortable, it's Ota. She wears a grim expression that I attribute to pre-shoot jitters. After all, it is her first day. Well, I do like the *Akira* t-shirt she wore to the set this morning…

At a little before 10 a.m., AD Okamoto calls Ota up onto the main stage. Asking for everyone's attention, he introduces the actress.

"This is Rie Ota. She will be performing from today as *daikaiju* Baragon."

The staff applauds; she bows in response. The *yoroshiku onegaishimasu* phrase fills the room. Once this is done, director Kamiya wastes no time. He hops onto the stage.

"This is how I want you to behave when you see Godzilla come around the mountain bend." Kamiya squats and growls loudly. Ota watches carefully.

"Okay, let's shoot this!" Kamiya yells in a deep voice.

Ota has on a silky silver-white leotard. After she's slipped on a matching headpiece, suit maker Yoshida tops it off with a fiberglass helmet. Three of the crew pry the back of the Baragon suit open. Ota slips in legs first. After some effort, they're in place. She then works her arms in. Finally, she places her head inside. After this, Yoshida "zips" the suit's back via a series of hard plastic snaps hidden deep in the spine. Yoshida asks Ota if she's okay. From deep within Baragon comes a muffled "*hai!*" The entire process takes nearly five minutes.

The first shot is Godzilla appearing from around the side of the mountain as Baragon scampers up in challenge. Kamiya calls for a rehearsal. Yoshida is helped into the Godzilla suit. AD Okamoto takes a position beside Godzilla, with AD Kikuchi standing next to Baragon. As it's near impossible to hear within the suits, the ADs repeat messages from the director to the actors. In turn, they relay responses back to the director.

Once rehearsal is under way, the various crewmembers focus on their responsibilities. Lighting chief Saito yells orders to his assistants in the rafters to adjust overhanging lamps. Saito himself moves a few floor lights hooked to a steel scaffolding. Miike has his hands full with a pair of radio-controlled helicopters. One of the blades has started behaving erratically; he's up on a ladder dealing with its internal mechanics.

After a few more run-throughs to work out the kinks, Kamiya calls for a take. Smoke is laid around the set to add air density. The director yells for action and the monsters start their face-off. Crewmembers crouching out of camera view spray compressed air onto triangular trays holding fine, gray "dust" that billows around the monsters' feet. This gives the illusion they're churning up the mountain's base. After Kamiya yells cut, everyone gathers around his monitor to review the take. Satisfied, he yells, "Okay!"

After lunch, Nakao asks if I'd like to check out his studio. I follow him around to the back of the big pool. I thought it would simply be a storage spot for his equipment; it turns out to be a bona fide studio.

"In addition to my work at Toho, I also shoot photos for families in the neighborhood," he says. Sure enough, there are framed photos on the walls of smiling children wearing kimono. Next to these are posters for Fuji and Kodak film, the kind you see in camera shops across Japan.

"I like the family stuff because it's so different from the SFX set. In the old days, I used to take all the children's photos when they came to visit Toho."

On the way back to S9, I bump into Tomiyama.

"Norman," he starts. "Were you able to finish the piece for the Toho website?"

I race into S9, grab a printout from my bag, and race back. He reads it in front of me. As he does, his face perks up. He smiles and even laughs at several passages.

"Thank you," he says. "I'll have Masuda put it up on the website as soon as possible."

The afternoon is focused on Godzilla. Shots include a close-up of him roaring, turning the mountain bend, and finally, one where rocks roll down the mountainside behind Godzilla.

I get in close for the rock-dropping scene. A staffer on the first tier of the mountain shakes dirt off a wood board. A rock bounces and lands directly on my foot. *Ow!* I thought it'd be fake, like in the Amamoto cave scene, but they're using real rocks! That hurt!

25 MAY 2001

The morning shots are of Baragon boring into the ground. Several men aid Ota into her kaiju suit. Once locked within, she's helped up onto a platform with a wooden runway that slopes to the floor below. It's covered with soft mats and has six cowbell-shaped canisters packed with dirt and explosives bolted to each side. The plan is for the canisters to shoot dirt in her wake as she moves down the slope. This will give the illusion that Baragon is throwing off earth as he digs into the ground.

During rehearsal, Ota scampers down. Kamiya yells out, "*Bam! Bam! Bam!*" to show when he wants the explosions to go off. After reaching the bottom, Ota is helped out of the suit. She takes a seat off stage and waits for the crew to make adjustments.

Kamiya feels the canisters won't produce enough dirt to sell the effect. He has crewmembers fill a bucket with soil and place it at the slope's base. A hose from a compressed air canister is fit to its bottom.

Kamiya yells for action. Ota works her way down the runway with Baragon's red tail swinging freely behind her. Suddenly, the charges in the canisters go off. They blast dirt high into the air. Some of it lands on my head. Kamiya checks the playback. He calls the shot a keeper.

Before lunch, I stop by the big pool. A truck is unloading equipment. Futami is here. He's in blue shorts with his shirt off "supervising" the load out. When a large fan is roughly unloaded from the truck, he belts out a critical "*dame, dame, dame!*" When placed gently on the pavement, he christens it "*ii ne.*" I say hello to him but he ignores me.

Godzilla reacting to Baragon digging underground is on the agenda after lunch. The model of a highway rest stop is set in front of the camera. As soon as it's in place, the art staff gets to work. Miike sits behind the camera. After looking through the viewfinder, he tells his art team where to make adjustments.

"We're never 100% sure how it's going to look until we check through the lens," explains Miike. "The fine-tuning comes after the basic parts are laid before the camera. It takes a lot of back and forthing to get it to look right."

The cowbells are filled with dirt, wood chips, and pine needles, and are laid across the floor. Once again, they're wired with charges. The Godzilla suit is wheeled over and hoisted onto the stage. Lifting it takes several men. Unified "heave-hos" fill the air.

Kaneko stops by the effects set. The crew bows as he makes his way around. Kamiya explains to him how the day is progressing and where they are in the shot list. Kaneko looks through the storyboards and offers a few comments. Once done, the director approaches me.

"We're going to Yokohama to shoot scenes at the Bay Bridge," he says. "Chiharu Niiyama, the film's lead, will be there. Wanna come?" It's a hard choice, but it sounds like a good chance to reconnect with the live-action crew and to meet the star. I grab my things and run over to the fountain, where the buses for the live-action crew are waiting to depart.

We arrive at Yokohama Bay Bridge just before 5 p.m. Kaneko and some of the staff gather in the parking lot. They page through the latest issue of *Friday*, which features a photo layout of Chiharu posing with the Godzilla, Ghidorah, and Baragon suits. Peeking over Kaneko's shoulder, I see it's a twist on the "damsel in distress" theme. Rather than the traditional "screaming girl," Chiharu is laughing wildly. It's as if she's in control of the monsters and not the other way around.

Before the gear is unloaded, dinner is called. Not like I expect another *Gamera 3* incident, but the truth is, I'm flat broke. With my already part-time teaching work whittled down by two-thirds, I have to watch my expenses. I'm relieved when I'm told it's okay to grab a *bento*.

Set meals in Japan always come down to a choice of two food types, and crewmembers line up in front of a pair of tables with the *bentos* stacked neatly on top. Today's selection is fish or chicken. I go for the chicken.

After dinner, the equipment is hauled up to a pedestrian walkway that stretches across the bridge's underbelly and ends under the first tower. Kaneko, DP Kishimoto, and VFX supervisor Matsumoto walk its length to talk out the scene. Once the camera angles are decided, the crew lays out tracking and rigs the lighting. On hand are leads Chiharu Niiyama and Masahiro Kobayashi.

Chiharu wears a mustard-colored shirt and tan pants. Her clothes are stained and her face has bruises compliments of makeup woman Izumi Matsushita. When she starts wrapping a bandage around Chiharu's head, Kaneko approaches.

"I'd like it to unravel a bit as she runs down the walkway," he says. Crewmembers surround Chiharu. They try to work out Kaneko's request.

"We still have time as we have to wait for the sun to set," Kaneko tells me. "When time permits, like now, it's always good to add details that might seem unimportant but contribute to the film's look and feel."

Just before 8 p.m. Chiharu and Kobayashi run down a portion of the walkway. As planned, the bandage on Chiharu's head unfurls. After Kaneko approves the shot, the crew moves to a circular observation deck/lounge/gift shop area at the walkway's end.

The night sky is exceptionally clear. The whole of Yokohama sparkles in colored streaks against the dark water of the bay. I point out the Ferris wheel featured in *Godzilla vs. Mothra* to Matsumoto as he was on Kawakita's staff for the film. He growls.

"Tell me," I ask. "Have you ever worked on a film and afterward thought, 'Boy, that was great!'?" Matsumoto thinks about it. "No!" he barks. We laugh. Although said in jest, I wonder how much truth there is to his answer.

The final shot of the night is Chiharu looking over the bay to where Godzilla battles King Ghidorah. Turning around, she gives a rousing speech about the ensuing fight and the fate of the nation. Considering how focused Chiharu is, I don't think it's the right time for self-introductions. I spend the rest of the

night on the sidelines, happy to watch a pivotal scene being shot.

The day is wrapped at 9 p.m. We pull back into Toho at 11:30 p.m.

26 MAY 2001

Making it to S9 a little after 9 a.m., I'm confronted by a Godzilla with a large piece of yellow foam covering half its head.

"I had to do an emergency repair this morning," Shinada explains. "I used a lot of epoxy; the foam helps to distribute the pressure evenly." I don't want to sound disrespectful, but Godzilla looks entirely un-ferocious with its head in what appears to be a bonnet. "Yeah, he does look ridiculous," Shinada admits.

Godzilla reacting to Baragon digging underground continues. The scene calls for the earth to loosen under Godzilla, who loses balance, staggers, and then topples over. While Kamiya maps out the camera angles, Yoshida is helped into the suit. After locking him in, the suit team crouches out of sight, ready to catch him when he falls, goofy foam bonnet and all.

The dry run goes as expected: A feel in the dark. Once over, the discussion begins. Kamiya bats ideas around with the various department heads on how to best pull off the shot. At 10:50 a.m. Shinada removes the bandages from Godzilla's head for the second test run.

Satisfied with the test, Kamiya calls for a take. However, the moment before the camera rolls, he stops the shoot. "Get me more detail in the foreground!"

Art staffers Hidefumi "Jimmy" Ohnishi, Thunder, and Yuri rush over with miniature trees and other odds and ends. They frantically work them into the landscape in front of the camera. In the meanwhile, Yoshida has slipped half out of the suit for a breather. An AD fans him with an *uchiwa* (Japanese style fan). Once satisfied with the additional detail, Kamiya resumes the shoot.

Charges connected to buckets of dirt are tripped. Soil shoots around Godzilla, who claws the air before plummeting from a moderately high fall off the stage. Dust and smoke are everywhere. As it clears, Yoshida emerges from the suit. "Need me to do that again?" he asks.

As of yesterday, the first "Norman Report" is up on the Toho website. This seems to be good for my relationship with the production. Some of the staff approach to say they enjoyed it. A crewmember who hasn't said a word to me tells me he thinks my photo running with it is "funny." I'm unsure of what that means but I'm happy he's finally talking to me.

Another writer has begun coming to the set, a chubby guy named Morihiko Saito from *Uchusen*, a popular science fiction and fantasy magazine. He seems nice enough, but right away a weird dynamic erupts between us. For example, several times while chatting with staffers, I spot him nearby pretending to be looking at something when he's obviously listening in. He's also asking what I've seen so far and who I'm friendly with. Maybe I'm making too much out of it but the rush he seems in to figure out my status on the set strikes me as irrelevant.

I spend time today testing my boundaries within S9. My first target is Vi-shop. I want to see how they react if I just plop myself carefree in their area. Casually,

I sit next to a couple of guys changing batteries on remote control units. Not only do they not bite, they smile and ask how I'm doing. Feeling as if I've tamed the suit crew, I poke around their space. Although only up for a few weeks, it looks as if it's been around for years. Paint splotches cover their long, wood, work table, and where there isn't a paint stain, there's a knife gash.

Not in use today, all three Baragon suits are at rest in steel pushcarts on a side of Vi-shop. I run a hand over one. Baragon's latex skin has a familiar, rubbery feel. It's akin to the Don Post masks I'd buy as a boy. One of the staff pulls a suit over and begins patching a small tear under its arm. Making small talk, he asks who my favorite kaiju is in the Godzilla universe.

"Gimantis," I answer without hesitation.

"Me too!" he says with a laugh.

I've been familiarizing myself with the Godzilla suit. Much of the time it's just in its cart unattended. I know it sounds silly, but I've been putting in one-on-one time with Godzilla. Pretending he's alive, I'll pull up a chair for small chats. That the suit is realistic looking makes it easy.

However, during lunch yesterday, I was taking photos with Godzilla. Just when I'd worked an arm in his mouth for a silly shot of being bitten, I looked up to see Kamiya a few meters off staring at me blankly. Engaging him in a chat about '50s sci-fi movies, I managed to play it down. Still, it was a good reminder not to let myself get too carried away.

Back on set, I wander through the spaces between the hills; they're a maze of detached mounds stapled over with tree branches resting atop opera boxes. I get to the Godzilla suit, where a crewmember has attached "piano wire" from the ceiling down to the tail. He gives it a few test tugs and sways it about. Art staffer Yuri then paints the wire with a small brush from atop a ladder. I'd expect her to use black, but she's giving it a whitish tint. She says this will blend it into the backdrop painting better.

The next shot is another angle of Godzilla breaking through ground weakened by Baragon's subterranean tunneling. I decide to take it in from the trenches. Getting on my hands and knees, I crawl next to the suit crew hiding under one of the hilltops. Before a take, several of the staff spray smoke around the set. Smelling like a bag of garbage that's been sitting out for a week, it covers me completely. The others don't seem to mind; getting covered with crummy smelling smoke appears to be just a part of the kaiju workload.

Kamiya calls action; the cowbell canisters blast out dirt. Large clumps of brown soil rain around the set. Godzilla smashes with a hard, startling thud onto the mat beside me. The crew springs to action. They have Yoshida out of the suit in a flash. Afterward, I walk over to Kamiya's station with Yoshida.

"Did you really watch from under the stage?" Yoshida asks. "You're nuts!"

The scene is played back on Kamiya's monitor. About twenty of us crowd around. As the ground blasts around him, Godzilla claws the air and falls to the side. The staff lets out an approving, "Ohhhh…"

Saito is back at it. He's asking I show him photos from yesterday's Yokohama shoot and wants to know what I saw and whom I talked to. More than wanting, it's like he's demanding. He's also made a lame attempt at being my buddy by offering copies of videotapes in his collection. He's even handed me passes to a movie theater in Shinjuku.

This is the downside of the Japanese gift-giving tradition. While used to honor someone or to show heartfelt thanks, it's also used to indebt yourself. I also wonder if this ticket-giving isn't some strategy to keep me off the set. Well, he can give me all the crap he wants, but it's his call, not mine. And I certainly don't feel I owe him anything in return.

28 MAY 2001

I plan to spend the day catching up on the next "Norman Report" and updating Kaneko's website. Now, I'm at the Shimokita Starbucks, where composer Otani joins me for coffee. As promised, I've printed out shots of Godzilla.

"I'm getting an Ifukube vibe off of these," Otani says as he thumbs through them. "But I can't succumb to that. I have to do my own thing."

He asks my impressions of the set and how the performances are developing. I tell him some of the things Kaneko said about Godzilla's personality. As I do, Otani jots notes into a small pad of paper.

31 MAY 2001

Both crews are working at Toho today: Live-action in S1 and SFX in S9. As it will take hours for the SFX crew to get to their first shot, I opt to start the day with the live-action unit.

Housed in the center of S1 is a reproduction of the Sky Lounge observation deck under the Yokohama Bay Bridge. I'm astonished at its faithfulness to the real location. The walls are the same exact shade of blue, working vending machines stand in the same spots, and there are identical tourism posters on the walls. But my attention is drawn to the bolted-to-the-floor binoculars, which I find to be non-working on closer inspection.

Kaneko walks over. "Pretty nice, no? Toho has a reputation for making the most accurate sets in Japan."

First up is a low angle tracking shot of actors Chiharu and Kobayashi dashing onto the observation deck. It's run through several times. Kaneko is specific about where he wants his actors caught in the camera frame. In fact, Kaneko is specific about everything. For example, when Chiharu leans against the window, Kaneko tells her how and where he wants her left hand to rest and exactly how co-star Kobayashi should position himself beside her.

I still have yet to communicate directly with Chiharu. I keep expecting Kaneko to introduce us, but he hasn't made the effort. I guess it's up to me to make the first move.

"Shusuke…" I say as he scribbles notes into the margin of his script. "Chiharu. Me. Introduction." He closes the script, and we go in search of the film's star.

We find her in a quiet side hall of the deck set, where Futami is lecturing her. He's telling her how she's entering into a long line of Godzilla heroines, what a great honor it is, etc. etc. etc. From the sidelines, Kaneko and I try not to snicker. Chiharu looks around to see if anyone is witnessing her "Futami moment." She catches our eyes. Kaneko uses the opening to wedge himself into their talk.

"Excuse me, I'd like to introduce you to Norman," he says. Futami frowns and walks away.

I sit on the floor beside Chiharu. "Are you okay?" I ask, pointing to the white bandage on her head and the dirt smudges on her face. "Looks like you took a nasty bang."

Her eyes widen. "No! No! This is just my character! I'm fine. Really, I…" Realizing I'm teasing, she looks at Kaneko.

"As I said," says Kaneko dryly, "I'd like to introduce you to Norman."

Back in S9, Baragon is barking at Godzilla from atop a parking lot with Godzilla roaring back from the ravine below. Being a wide shot, a good deal of the set is visible, meaning a good deal of extra prep time is necessary. Complicating matters are two model helicopters that hover over the action. The copters—one military and one from a news station—are suspended by nylon thread. They hang from opposite ends of a wood stick attached to a long steel pole. The steel pole connects to a system of wheels and pulleys that when switched on make the stick rotate and the helicopters circle the kaiju battlefield below.

Things are hectic. Kamiya is blocking off a shot with Satoshi Murakawa, the director of photography for SFX. At the same time, Murakawa's assistants run light meters over every object within the shot. Lighting director Saito is yelling to his staff in the rafters, telling them which lights to move, where to aim them, and what gels to cover over them. The art staff is split between the overhanging helicopters and dressing the set. Some shuffle through plastic boxes filled with model cars; they pick the ones they like and place them in the parking lot beside

Baragon. Yuri and Kasuga check the greenery around the mountain and spray water onto branches while also looking for gaps that might need filling in.

Ota is up on the parking lot. Kamiya has asked her to run through a practice without the Baragon suit. Once the staff clears the area, she gets on all fours, lifts her head, and lets out a high-pitched howl.

A few minutes before 3 p.m., all is ready. Kamiya calls for action. Now in the suit, Ota's muffled barks compete with those of Yoshida's. Godzilla raises a foot and turns to face Baragon; his tail moves about, compliments of piano wire and a staffer pulling with all his might. Above them fly the helicopters. It looks incredible. It's hard not to just put down my camera and take it in distraction-free.

With the next SFX shot a while off, I hightail it back to S1. Just when I arrive, Futami zips past on a bicycle. Seated on the rack above the back tire is Chiharu. She's laughing wildly. They disembark in front of S1. Futami looks pleased as punch at having given the lead actress a lift to the ladies' room.

The live-action crew has reached the point in the story where the force of Godzilla's blast against the Yokohama Bay Bridge has tossed Chiharu out of a broken window pane. Saving her from plunging into the water is actor Kobayashi; he's to catch her in mid-air. The crew struggles to figure out how to make the shot look convincing.

Standing in for Kobayashi, AD Aida leans out one of the broken windows and extends a hand. Cameraman Kishimoto sits on the bare floor of S1 and peers through his viewfinder searching for the best angle; Kaneko leans over his

shoulder to explain what he wants to see in the frame.

Soon, things are decided and the actors are called over. Chiharu is seated on a pair of opera boxes beside Kishimoto. He has the camera aimed right up her arm at Kobayashi, who leans out the window.

Kaneko calls for a rehearsal. As intensely as he can, Kobayashi yells to Chiharu. "Hang on! I'll save...!"

Before he can finish his lines, a grinning Chiharu interrupts the shot. "Kobayashi... Uh, you're hurting my hand."

Kobayashi's eyes widen. "Sorry!" he exclaims. Chiharu rubs her hand and laughs it off along with the rest of the crew.

Masuda calls me to the PR room. There, he points to a rack of windbreakers. On the backs are prints of Godzilla and the Toho logo. "Pick one," he says. They come in a variety of colors. And when I say "variety," I mean a rainbow of bizarre shades.

"Let's see, I'm not a florist, so I'll pass on the moss green one. The yellow one looks too much like raincoats Japanese school kids wear. I guess whoever decided on pink was drunk at the time..." I hate to be finicky, but... "No black?"

"What's with you and black?" he sighs.

I settle on a gold one. I figure if I'm going to go all out, a gold Godzilla jacket is the only course of action.

Looking like Elvis were he a Godzilla fan, I proudly strut back into S1 in my shiny-as-sin gold crew jacket. Sitting with Chiharu in front of his monitor is Kaneko. Like some sort of cosmic coincidence, he's wearing the exact same gold jacket!

Playing it cool, I slip up next to them. "Now, this is one director with stunningly good taste in clothing," I say coolly.

Chiharu looks at my jacket and then at Kaneko's. She explodes with laughter.

1 JUNE 2001

Morning shots are of Baragon climbing onto the parking lot as he retreats from Godzilla. A crane shot, cameraman Murakawa is up in the air with assistant Yoko Itakura seated beside him. I say "seated," but that's only if you consider two opera boxes strapped together a seat. It looks precarious to me. They ride up and down, far over my head, rehearsing the shot while Kamiya works with Ota on how to crawl over the ridge.

With time before the take, I zip over to S2. The art staff has just taken over the stage and is preparing it for upcoming underwater scenes. Miike and his crew are carving blocks of Styrofoam into mountains and organizing them onto a platform.

Back in S9, the first take of Baragon isn't to Kamiya's liking. He walks over to Ota still in the Baragon suit. "Can you hear me?" A muffled *hai* filters out. "Please exaggerate your movements when coming over the ridge," he requests. It takes two takes until he's pleased.

A half-hour later, Shinada and his crew wheel in a not-quite-finished King Ghidorah suit. It's fiercely gold with large, open seams where the necks connect to the body, and there are gaps under the chin through which the inner mechanics are visible. Despite this, it looks great. Most striking is the mass of scales covering it. There must be a thousand of them. And not all are the same size. The ones around Ghidorah's belly are

the largest, about three inches in length, with the sizes tapering off as you move around the body. Those by the heads are the smallest. There, they're fingernail size. Shinada tells me each were glued on by hand.

"It's going to be painted and toned down to look less plasticky," Shinada assures me.

Word spreads about Ghidorah arriving and the crew gathers around the Vi-shop area. Kamiya and Ghidorah actor Ohashi listen on as Shinada covers points about the suit and what work is left to do on it.

As they talk, Yoshida bobs two of Ghidorah's heads in his hands. "I'm so going to kick your ass," he jokes aloud.

Ohashi slips into a black bodysuit. With the help of Shinada, he enters Ghidorah through its back. After resting his head under the middle head, he puts his arms into the right and left heads of the suit. Kamiya stares blankly as Ohashi wiggles them about. If I had to make a guess, I'd say that Kamiya is not sold on the idea of arms operating the heads.

The afternoon sees the complicated effect of Baragon falling from the sky and smashing into a helicopter. The crew has taken an empty Baragon suit and hung it upside down from the rafters. Once it's tied off, the various stations go to work. The camera crew picks their position, which is the cue for the art staff to dress the space in front of the camera. Their job is to blend four opera boxes into the landscape that the pyrotechnic crew is wiring with explosives. Charges are also set on Baragon's back.

It takes about an hour until the first shot is ready: a basic, SFX guide shot. AD Taguchi holds out a wood beam with a Styrofoam helicopter stuck on an end. This marks the spot where a model helicopter will be composited in during post-production.

Once everything is ready, Murakawa calls out "speed" to indicate the camera has achieved its high frame rate. A woman on the crew cries out, "1, 2, 3!" On 3, Baragon is released. The suit speeds to the floor. Upon reaching the halfway point, the charges on Baragon go off. A ball of orange fire ripples around the suit. A second later, it hits the studio floor with a hard thud; charges in the ground ignite, releasing a plume of smoke and dirt.

Kamiya calls cut. Swiftly, men with fire extinguishers race over to put out the fire on Baragon's back. Kamiya reviews the footage. He's not pleased with the timing of the blasts and calls for a reshoot. Working quickly, it takes the staff a scant fifteen minutes to reset things. It's run again. Once more, Kamiya is not happy. The staff sets up for a third try.

The issue isn't so much technical as it is human. The two sets of explosions, triggered by hand, have to go off at just the right moment. Bear in mind that monster footage is shot at a high frame rate to create the ponderous, weighty look associated with giant creatures. While it might seem in the finished film that it could be handled with relative ease, in reality, it takes the suit a little over a second to go from the rafters to the floor. Both explosions must go off at the precise millisecond.

Fortunately, things go well the third time around. After running the take several times on his monitor, a satisfied Kamiya calls out, "Okay!"

Shinada and one of his crew wheel the Ghidorah suit outdoors and park it a few feet from the entrance of S9. Ten minutes later, Kaneko comes to inspect it. As he looks it over, Shinada explains how the heads will be articulated, how Ohashi will fit into it, and where wires will attach to the wings and body. Kaneko asks for a demonstration. Ohashi climbs into Ghidorah. After a few minutes of studying him operating it, Kaneko is all smiles.

As Shinada's crew carries the suit back into S9, it leaves a trail of scales on the pavement. "Yes," Shinada admits after I point this out. "We're going to spend a lot of time re-gluing them during shooting."

A little before dark the live-action crew preps the big pool for a scene of degenerate kids and their attempt to drown a dog. Two ADs in rubber overalls help the actors onto a rowboat docked at the pool's edge. Once everyone is aboard, they guide the boat into the pool's middle.

With the crew caught up in technical concerns, I tap Kaneko on the shoulder. His attention mine, I pat an envelope sticking from my shirt pocket. Understanding, he gets up from his director's chair and we walk to a quiet spot a few meters from the crew. I hand him the envelope. As he counts my share of this month's rent, we start giggling. With the way we're creeping around, it looks like we're engaged in an illicit deal.

When the camera rolls, two actors stand holding a box with the dog (a stuffed animal). They go to toss it overboard. Compressed air is pumped through tubes under the water that froth large, white bubbles around the boat. Out of the camera's view, the ADs rock the boat to and fro. With a nod at each other, they capsize it, sending the actors into the drink. Kaneko yells cut.

While it's warm enough out, it's not yet summer. The actors holler from the cold water. The crew has prepared a set of chairs around heaters and a pile of towels and blankets for the actors, who dry off once director Kaneko gives the scene his approval.

2 JUNE 2001

My friend Ed Godziszewski is in Japan on business, and today being a Saturday means he doesn't have any meetings to attend. I've been writing to Ed daily, keeping him up-to-date with the production. Naturally, he's eager to come for a set visit. I checked with Masuda and he said it was okay to bring him along. Meeting up at Seijo Station, Ed and I grab a quick breakfast before walking over to Toho. Along the way, I give him a crash course in set dos and don'ts.

The morning starts in S7, where Kaneko and staff are shooting a scene in a police visitation room. Kaneko calls for rehearsal. Actors Chiharu, Kobayashi, and Takashi Matsuo step in to speak with Amamoto. During the dry run, Amamoto raises a hand and touches the glass panel separating him from his visitors. Chiharu responds by touching her side of the window. Kaneko rushes over and puts his face close to the glass to see how their hands line up. He tells cameraman Kishimoto how he wants it captured. While he does, Amamoto catches my eye and gives a wink.

Watching Amamoto work is a joy. He is without question the most experienced actor I've ever seen. It comes through in how he relates to the set. When a camera assistant holds a meter to his face, it's as if it doesn't exist. When Izumi sets his hair, you'd think there was only the tiniest insect buzzing around him. It's not that he's nasty or prima donna-like,

just that decades of film and TV work have produced a man unconcerned with the profession's trivialities.

In this regard, I guess you'll have to label me green. Every bit of the filmmaking process fascinates me. All the lights, the mysterious boxes of equipment, the weather-worn cables, even Izumi's makeup kit with its brushes, creams, and knickknacks holds my attention. Perhaps after a lifetime like Amamoto's I'll feel differently.

After lunch, we go back to a deserted S7. Ed wants to see the rafters. However, the moment we reach the top, Amamoto walks into the studio. We dash down to talk to him. Despite his disappointed to learn that Ed isn't from Spain, he's friendly and warm. Hearing that Ed is from Chicago, Amamoto shares what he knows about American gangsters. I feel sorry for Ed. He's mentioned how it bugs him that Japanese associate Chicago with gangsters. But, hell, this is Amamoto. He could talk about cookie recipes and we'd be happy.

Over in S9, Yoshida is snapping the Godzilla suit to the side and coordinating his movements with a staffer who tugs at the wire attached to its tail. In the scene, Godzilla swats Baragon away. Baragon is not present, however, and will be superimposed in during post-production.

Murakawa sets the camera low to the ground and aims it between a detached mountain ridge and a clump of greenery that art staffer Yuri prunes quietly. As she does, Kasuga sprays touch-up splotches of brown to the mountain. Jimmy stands on a ladder off to the side, where he readies a miniature helicopter. When the preparations are done, Kamiya screams for action. Less than a word, his command to start has evolved into a loud grunt. Yoshida spins to the side while the man working the tail wire yanks down with all his might.

Next is Baragon scampering up the mountain. Hot on his tail is Godzilla. In terms of chronology, this shot is before those from the day before.

"Shots are organized by what sections of the set they utilize and the angle in which they're shot," explains Miike. "We decide in advance where the basic camera setups will be. We group similar ones together, so we don't have to redo the set each time."

A wood ramp pre-dressed to look like a section of the mountain is brought out and attached to the rock wall base. Quickly, the art staff works to blend it into the mountainside. Where the ramp meets the studio floor, they lay out a large, brown burlap tarp pre-covered with gravel. This, too, is blended in with the rest of the mountain.

A run-through has Godzilla coming in from stage right. Yoshida leans down to muster his strength, stands back erect, then shoots his atomic beam at Baragon.

At 4 p.m., the Baragon/Godzilla shot is set to go. On the studio floor with its back open and its arms and legs spread eagle, the empty Baragon suit is laid out like a split pig. Ota snaps on her helmet before wiggling in. Across from her, Yoshida grabs the overhead bars of the Godzilla cart and, lifting himself up, sinks his feet into Godzilla. After working his arms and head in, staffers secure the back fins. Like a boxer going through warm-ups before a match, he gives the suit a workout, tilting it up and down and moving the arms about.

A canister of chemicals is placed to the side and set on fire: it's all that's left of the crashed helicopter. Kamiya calls for action. A crewmember with a scooper blows compressed air across the top sending gray dirt out and around Baragon's feet. As an effect, it adds a nice touch. However, the compressed air makes an annoying high-pitched hiss whenever a blast is released.

4 JUNE 2001

Stepping out from Seijo Station, I bump into Godzilla actor Yoshida. He's on his way home. "There's nothing on the schedule for me today," he says.

"They couldn't have told you that last night?" I ask.

"Things change on the spot. It's safer to come in than to take the day off, go somewhere, and then get a call telling me to hightail it into the studio."

I go over to Nakao's station to drop my stuff off and say good morning. Unlike other departments, he's a crew of one. Always friendly, he seems to welcome the company. Best of all, he doesn't engage in that friendly set chiding that gets tiring after a while. He also doesn't tease me about my less-than-perfect Japanese.

Nakao likes to ask me everyday things, too, such as about my family, where I've been in the world, or what I like to do. As we talk now, I remember dropping a memory stick in S9 yesterday. A high-capacity, 128MB card, it cost a whopping 8,000 yen ($65). Gotta find it!

Excusing myself, I hightail it to the set. The thing is, it's the size of my pinkie, making it the proverbial needle in a haystack. I start crawling around the dusty studio floor.

"Lose a contact?" Thunder asks when I emerge from under a platform. By sheer luck, I find it on the roof of a miniature building against a far wall. I'm the first to admit that I've got an awful habit of putting stuff down and forgetting it. I wonder if it got caught in any shots...

For the day's shot, Baragon will scamper up the mountainside as Godzilla's ray just misses him. Earlier, the staff laid steps into a mountainside stuffed with explosives that they now dress with dirt and rock. As Ota can't possibly scale the mountain wall on her own, steel cables have been attached to the suit to help her along.

The shot is ready to test a little past 2. One of the crew pulls on the cable attached to her back, nudging Baragon upwards. Ota moves the suit's paws as if she were climbing. Kamiya cries *Bam! Bam! Bam!* to indicate where he wants the blasts. The test over, Ota is helped out of the suit. Everything is then given a final check through.

I decide to watch the take from one of the lighting scaffoldings. Utilizing the monkey bar skills I honed as a boy, I climb to the top and find a nice, clear view. At 2:30, Kamiya lets out a loud, "Action!" An instant later, half the mountainside erupts in a deafening explosion. Dirt and rock shoot in every direction. Even way up here, I'm plastered.

7 JUNE 2001

I arrive at S9 to find the Baragon suit at the mountain base surrounded by a half-dozen staffers. With the red kaiju lifeless on his back and the staff standing around stern-faced, the scene seems more like the aftermath of a hit-and-run than a giant monster film shoot.

The plan is to have rubble from yesterday's explosion fall on Baragon's head. After rehearsal, Shinada's team gets to touching up the suit. In the shot, Baragon will be on his back; as his underbelly has been scraping the stage since shooting began, the stomach area is lined with scratches and tears.

At 10:40 a.m., all is ready. Ota, in a new pink bodysuit, enters Baragon. The suit is flipped over. Dirt and debris are laid on and around Ota. Kamiya orders filming. Two crewmen atop the ridge shake dirt down onto Baragon, who claws the air wildly. Kamiya calls cut. As usual, the take doesn't meet his expectations. He orders more detail into the set. Jimmy and other art staffers place additional pieces of rubble and broken building sections around Baragon. The retake goes well.

After lunch, the staff shoots a close-up of Baragon's face. Rather than Ota, AD Kikuchi slips on the top half of a different Baragon suit and positions himself against the base of the mountain. Murakawa has the camera on a tripod extended as high as it will go and angles it down on Baragon. For the shot, Baragon lifts its head, looks at the camera and, under the guidance of remote control, flips its ears out.

We gather around Kamiya's monitor to watch playback. The consensus is that Baragon's close-up is "cute," which Kamiya confirms with an "Okay!"

The next shot up is the explosive death of Baragon, a setup guaranteed to take several hours. I split my time between talking to Nakao and taking pictures of the crew at work.

Nakao, like many of the older staff, comes across at first as somewhat nondescript.

But dig a little and you find a fascinating person within. He doesn't always respond well to direct questions, but given the chance, he comes out with bits of intriguing information. For example, we went to the cafeteria for lunch today and he told me about the old food system.

"As hard as it might be to believe, and despite there being two cafeterias at the time, the food was even worse in the old days!" he explains over a lunch of fried fish atop shredded cabbage. "There were so many people working at Toho that it was all they could do just to feed us. There was never any choice on the menu. You accepted what they dished out."

He points out the window to the space before S1 and S2. "During lunchtime, that whole area was wall-to-wall with people. By comparison, it's a ghost town today."

That's when Nakao drops a bombshell. "It's still a secret, but I'm retiring after this production. I'm also shooting fewer stills than before. I guess when it comes to GMK, you'll have the biggest photo collection."

Generally speaking, I feel I've found my place within the production. It seems everyone is comfortable with my presence. If they aren't, they aren't saying anything because, when you get down to it, my being here isn't that big of a deal.

Up until figuring this out, I'd been holding back a bit. However, watching Nakao and the guest photographers, I've figured out the policy: If you've managed to pass through the studio gatekeepers, and as long as you're not annoying anyone, then all is good. Even Nakao said I need to be bolder in my determination to get shots. As I've discovered, the rule is that if you can wedge yourself into a spot by the stage, it's fair game. With that said, Nakao, being the Toho still

cameraman, gets priority. After him, it's a free for all. Of course no one is selfish. If one of us photographers finds a good angle, we alert the others. Sometimes we pick different locations from which to purposely make our photos dissimilar.

Only Nakao comes every day. At max there are six of us taking stills at a time. This is not counting Saito, who sometimes tries to buddy-buddy up with us but is utterly clueless on how to tuck one's body into as compact a space as possible when in the photographers' huddle. This means no knees or elbows jutting out, your camera is raised up and down, not swung from the hip where it can get in the way of the other cameramen, or worse, the crew. Besides, his camera is the lamest piece of pocket shit there is, which I find an insult to the production. My cameras might not be top of the line, but they're at least in the semi-pro range.

Although there is a slight rivalry between the cameramen, we also share great camaraderie. After a take, we often gather around Nakao's desk to talk shop.

"I wish they'd have blown that last take so I could have gotten one more chance at it," says Yasuyuki Iizuka from publisher Asahi Sonorama. I'm relieved to hear this. I often feel the same way, secretly hoping the crew will screw a take so I can get it from another angle or just get one more shot at it.

One of the still cameramen is Yussey Kawakami. Working for publisher Shogakukan, he's a veteran still photographer of Godzilla, Ultraman and other shows and films of this type. He's the only one amongst us with an assistant, a woman in her 20s named Chika Okura. With Ultraman now shooting at Nikkatsu, the two alternate between the sets, Chika coming on less critical days or assisting

Kawakami when there's a major effect here on Godzilla. Chika's sociable and we've struck up a set-friendship, chatting around Nakao's desk or by the big pool during setup waits. One of the things I like about her is the zero interest she has in Godzilla. For example, I showed her a printout of a Godzilla shot I'd taken and asked her how cool she thought it was.

"You're kidding, right? It's just a puppet."

Work on the next shot is progressing slowly. Yoshida is sticking out of the back of the Godzilla suit while a staffer next to him waves a fan to keep a breeze rolling over him. On Yoshida's face is a wide, brimming smile.

To describe Yoshida as simply a hard worker would be a disservice. He's not only channeling every ounce of effort into his performance but is enjoying the hell out of it. When not playing Godzilla, he's talking to someone about an upcoming shot, or he's off on the sidelines striking Godzilla stances and growling about the stage. Like now: Half in the suit, he has his hands raised and his fingers spread like claws. After growling and snapping his head around, Yoshida turns to me. "Watch! I'm going to blast the hell out of Baragon!"

With Baragon on his back stage left and Godzilla shooting his beam stage right , it means the art staff has their work cut out dressing a wider than normal set. Miike is in serious-mode and has his crew pulling sections of terrain around to build up the landscape in front of the camera. Part of the work goes into hiding set seams, such as the studio floor and a wood panel in front of Baragon laid out with explosives. Rather than a perfectly aimed, square-to-the-chest hit, the plan is for Godzilla's beam to sweep up to Baragon. The panels' explosives will go off one by one a fraction of a second before the primary blast on the Baragon suit. Due to the number of explosives involved, Ota will not perform within the suit.

The pyro guys are out in full force, wiring the Baragon suit over with dozens of squibs. Osamu Kume, the head of Toho's pyrotechnic department, supervises his crew. VFX supervisor Matsumoto is here today to work with Kamiya on the shot. We share a chat about Kume, one of Toho's last remaining old-timers.

"The truth is," says Matsumoto, "explosions like this are dangerous. If it were anyone but Kume at the helm, I'd step out of the building in fear and wait for it to be over."

Two hours after starting, Miike and crew have the art direction under control. When seen from above, the space between the camera and the monsters looks like a mass of haphazardly laid out platforms; a peek through the camera viewfinder tells a different story. There, every detail, every bush, and every miniature line up perfectly.

One touch I like is a tiny construction shed with a digger out front that Miike has placed in the shot's lower right. "It's the little things that bring life to the landscape," Miike notes.

As the art staff gets to the final touches, the Baragon suit crew is finishing painting the squibs to match the red of the suit.

At 5 p.m. the shot is nearly ready to go. I'd eyed out an excellent spot to take stills from, but I find Nakao sitting there when I go to reclaim it. Oh well, it's his show. I snuggle up next to him.

"It's a tough one," Nakao admits. "Everything is precisely lined up with the film camera, making it impossible to get a good still shot."

He's right. I look in my viewfinder and can't quite find an angle that shows both Godzilla and Baragon while also hiding the undressed sections of the set. There is either a piece of wood exposed or you can see the studio floor. Reluctantly, I opt to do a "making of" style photo.

With the shot featuring explosions, a switch box is necessary. An ancient-looking thing, the one used by the pyrotechnic staff is called a *shamisen*. It works via a metal rod pulled across a long row of thick wires strung like teeth along the top. Cables from one side are attached directly to the explosives on the set. The metal rod completes an electric circuit that detonates the charges. I suppose the *shamisen* name comes from its slight resemblance to the Japanese stringed instrument of the same name.

At 5:15 p.m., Yoshida is locked in the Godzilla suit. A bluish light is cast against Godzilla's fins. Kamiya calls for action. Dust is blown around Godzilla's feet. Godzilla extends his arms to the sides and leans forward. Off-screen, Yamabe hits the switch on the remote controller to make Godzilla's mouth open. The suit has also been outfit with a movable fin plate. Yamabe hits another switch causing the fins to spread apart. On cue, the rod is slid across the *shamisen*. With that, the area around Baragon erupts in a deafening roar. A fireball the size of a car billows into the air.

I can hardly believe the size of the explosion! It's massive! I look up from my camera to see an inky black cloud of smoke dissipating into the rafters. Crewmembers with fire extinguishers rush over to the Baragon suit. They spray it down and put out the fire raging across it.

I eagerly review the shot on the back of my camera, which unfortunately has no rapid shutter feature. With only one chance to get it right, I have to do my best to time explosion shots. I look at it. A bit premature but at least I no longer jitter like at the beginning of the shoot. Nakao leans over.

"See," he says with a smile. "You're getting the hang of it."

8 JUNE 2001

My first stop of the day is S7, where Kaneko's crew is working on a scene in which Baragon rescues Amamoto from jail.

The jail cell set has been ingenuously designed to break apart. A walk around reveals it to be like a large 3D jigsaw puzzle. Above the stage, loose slabs of "jail" (good ol' Styrofoam) hang, rigged to fall when the walls cave in.

Inside the jail, Kaneko works with Amamoto and two actors sharing the cell with him. Script open, Kaneko explains the details of the scene. As he talks, Amamoto stares out at nothing in particular. Moving outside the cell, Kaneko peers through the bars as the actors do a dry run. Satisfied, he calls for a take.

The actors react to the giant eye of Baragon (to be superimposed in later) peering in through the jail window. They fall to the back of the cell, yell for help, and turn their backs to the bars. With that, the set comes crashing down! The walls tumble in and ceiling pieces smash around the actors' feet. Dust clouds billow everywhere.

The crew is electrified by how well it

went. Except for Amamoto. He's sitting on the floor as calm as a napping kitten. An AD helps him up, and he walks to the stage doors and steps outside. The rest of us gather around Kaneko's monitor to review the shot.

While the crew cleans up, I step outside with Kaneko, Tomiyama, and actor caretaker Shiro Kido. We join Amamoto on folding chairs. After a few minutes, I ask Amamoto if I can take his photo. He shakes his head "yes" and, without a word, stands against a nearby wall. I snap a few until noticing the expression on his face—it's like he just finished sucking a basket full of lemons.

"Amamoto-*san*," I say. "Do you think you could, perhaps, you know…*smile*?"

He mumbles something inaudible, but complying, opens his mouth. Just that. It appears his idea of a smile is to release his lower jaw bone and let it hang free. His eyes still hold that penetrating Amamoto sting. Figuring this is the most he's going to give, I don't press it.

Kaneko has been watching us and has that "take a photo of me with the actor" look on his face.

"Hey, director," I say, taking the hint. "How about a shot of the two of you?" Amamoto walks back and sits next to Kaneko. I snap a few of them together. Kaneko looks happy and—*wow*—Amamoto has brightened up. He even laughs when Kaneko apologizes for not having any scenes in the film set in Spain.

Feeling it's now or never, I ask Amamoto if I can have a photo taken with him too. I hand my camera to Kaneko, who snaps two shots of us standing side by side. I'm astonished when I review them. Amamoto has an honest-to-god smile on his face! I thank him. He responds with a grunt.

Sitting with Amamoto, out of the blue, he asks if my dad was in the war. I tell him that he was in the Battle of Midway. Amamoto starts mumbling something; I ask what's on his mind.

"The war," he says. "I'm angry at the Americans." I assure him that's understandable given incidents such as Hiroshima and Nagasaki. "No! That's not what I mean. I'm angry that MacArthur let the emperor live! It was our chance to rid ourselves of this damned emperor system!"

Following lunch, I zip over to the Toho screening room. Junko, the continuity person for the SFX crew, has allowed me to sit in on dailies. This is a pretty big deal and is one customarily reserved only for staff. Even Kaneko doesn't let me sit in on the live-action dailies.

While a treat to see raw, unedited Godzilla footage, it gets tedious at times. The shots tend to go on forever. I begin to doze off. This sleepy feeling is compounded by the theater. It's too damn comfortable! Compared to conditions in S9, the on-lot theater's cushiony seats are like cottony puffs of heaven-sent silk. It's not just me. Many of the staffers snooze off the moment their rears hit a seat.

Throughout rushes, Junko reads notes aloud, explaining why something was re-shot or makes a technical comment. Competing with her are the snores of staffers who've succumbed to the comfort of the theater.

The main shot on today's agenda is a POV of Godzilla from a helicopter. Yoshida is already zipped into the suit and waits for Tony to wire up his tail.

"Say…you wouldn't mind if I gave that a tug?" I ask after he's secured it. There's time to kill as the camera crew is still far from ready. Tony smiles and hands me the cable.

I pull up and down and make the tail sway around. It's got weight to it but not enough to be considered heavy.

"Yoshida," Tony yells. "You're under Norman's control!"

Yoshida's distinct laugh filters out of the suit. As if reading my mind, Yoshida starts thrashing around. I spend a couple of minutes getting a feel for the job of tail operator, tugging at the wire, and trying to match the tail movement with that of the actor's. It's not as easy as it looks.

9 JUNE 2001

Carpenters from Toho's prop department are working in front of the big pool building consoles for the upcoming "mission control" scenes. At this point, they're just wood cases with blank spaces into which monitors, buttons, and switches will be added. Twenty freshly painted stations, they sit drying in the sun.

On the floor of the shed in the back corner of the pool area is a miniature of Yokohama's Landmark Tower. Beside it is a hospital. Both will appear as featured buildings: Landmark Tower to be leveled by Godzilla's atomic breath, the hospital to be done in by Godzilla's tail. At the moment, both are shells, details to be added over the next week or so. The serene, focused atmosphere of the shed's modeling crew reminds me of the first day I visited Vi-shop when Godzilla was being rendered in clay.

Inside S9, Godzilla is set for a medium close-up. The art staff lugs movable mountain sections into position behind Godzilla as Yoshida is fit into the suit. A simple shot, it's an insert for when Baragon lunges at Godzilla from a perch atop the ridge.

The camera, taking the POV of Baragon, is set on rails and glides quickly toward Godzilla. The plan is for Yoshida to whip the suit to the side while AD Yoshida (yeah, quite a few Yoshidas) tosses Godzilla's tail into the air. No matter how many times it's shot, AD Yoshida gets into the frame.

"To hell with it," Kamiya finally says. "No one other than otaku fans will notice; if they do, it'll give them hours of joy to have found something as mundane as this." The staff breaks up laughing.

The next scenes are additional close-ups of Godzilla and Baragon. Godzilla is walked to a platform sandwiched between two sheets of Styrofoam dressed to look like mountainsides. Between them is Baragon. A rehearsal is called, and the two monsters roar at each other. The scene is fierce, but Yoshida and Ota's voices, muted by their suits, add a comic touch to the moment.

At 5 p.m., the Ghidorah suit is back for another round of inspection. Shinada and his staff piece it together and prop it up by a steel cable hanging from the ceiling. While still that outlandish gold color, it's a lot more complete than before. Of note are its fully extended, rigid wings.

Kamiya requests a demonstration. Ohashi hops in and works his hands into the side heads. Growling and flailing his arms, he walks across the floor in front of the suit station. While no one looks unhappy with the suit's performance, no one is overly ecstatic. The method of using arms to control the heads is only mildly convincing. As Ohashi slips out of the suit, Kamiya looks on with a "how am I going to make this work?" expression.

The final shot of the night is another angle of the kaiju posturing just before battle, this time it's an over-the-Godzilla-shoulder shot of Baragon yipping after having emerged from an underground tunnel. During the Ghidorah suit inspection, the art staff built a rocky hole covered with moss and grass. Ota pulls herself onto the ridge. With suit maker Yoshida and AD Yoshida prying open its sides, she maneuvers herself inside. Yoshida, already in Godzilla, waits to begin.

Rehearsal is called. Ota arches her back and growls at Godzilla. The size difference between the two monsters is striking; it's like one of those clips in *America's Funniest Home Videos* where a kitten takes on a Great Dane.

Kamiya makes a few adjustments to Ota's movements and then calls for action. As a continuation of Baragon emerging from underground, dirt is pumped out of the hole behind Ota. Kamiya approves it after the second take. The night's last action is to move the Baragon suit up onto the parking lot in preparation for tomorrow morning.

14 JUNE 2001

With most of the Godzilla/Baragon battle in the can, the SFX crew has moved to the smaller S2 to lens the film's underwater scenes. Two miniature submersibles have been built for the film; only one is used in the first shot. The model hangs above a large whiteboard, suspended by wires attached to its balance points.

As the crew prepares the first shot, I walk around the model (called the Satsuma, named after the region in Japan, *not* the former Godzilla suit actor) to inspect it. My favorite part is a light dish under the front nose. It shines bright enough to make me see spots.

To create an underwater setting, S2 is filled with paraffin fog. At its thickest, it's difficult to see anything but what is immediately in front of you. Most crewmembers wear heavy-duty masks with double filters on the sides. Even the camera is wrapped in protective sheets. Director Kamiya has come dressed for the occasion. Wearing a hood, goggles, and an industrial filter mask, he looks like an alien from a low budget sci-fi film.

I have to assume the fog is not something you want to ingest for any prolonged period. Unfortunately, I'm ill-prepared. In a feeble attempt to protect myself, I take one of the cup masks at the snack table. I hate these things because they fog up my glasses and leave a ring around my face. Besides, they never seem to fit properly. There's a small strip of aluminum at the top you're supposed to contour around your nose, but it never works right. After a while, it feels like someone is jabbing pins in the sides of my nose.

Having reached my fog tolerance level, I take a breather and stop in at the art production room. Isao is painting a large model tank in the middle of the room. I'm treated to one of his sarcastic looks as he feigns surprise that I didn't pass out from the fog in S2. Miike, on the other hand, doesn't seem to notice I've dropped by. As is often the case, he's engrossed in notes and diagrams. His desk needs one of those "Do not disturb: Genius at work" signs above it.

Lungs cleared, I'm back in S2. None of the still cameramen have come today. It's just Nakao and me. In all honesty, the scenes are not that dynamic. I'm here because I want to see all I can; Nakao because it's his job. For me, it's worthwhile if only to see the intensity and effort being put into something you would consider a cakewalk compared to the kaiju battle scenes.

At 2, the art staff moves several charcoal-colored mountains behind a pair of hanging submersibles. Some of the mountains are set atop opera boxes, others onto rolling carts. More of that awful, foul-smelling fog is blown around.

After staffers have evened the smoke out with hand fans, Kamiya calls for action. The subs move about via pulleys and wires, rising and falling until a staffer sends out a burst of dirt via compressed air. One of the subs spins off to the side.

The room is dead quiet except for the clicking of Nakao's and my camera. Playfully, we both vie for the same angle and nudge each other with our elbows. Once done, the doors to the studio are opened wide and the room is aired out.

Ghidorah and Godzilla are wheeled into S2 at 3:15. Tomorrow begins their underwater fight. The finished Ghidorah looks fantastic! The scales—now a gold bullion color—hang like intricately woven chain mail. There's also a tinge of flat black around each, which must've taken a hell of a long time to apply. In addition to the wheeled cart used to move the three-headed kaiju, three wood beams have been nailed into an opera box. When the suit is at rest, Ghidorah's heads are placed on the top of each beam. This not only secures them when not in use, but also helps prevent damage to the necks.

AD Okamoto calls suit actor Ohashi to the middle of the room. "Everyone, let's welcome Akira Ohashi. He will be portraying Ghidorah." The staff lets out a round of applause.

Once Kamiya finishes giving preliminary instructions to the suit actors, the monsters are put into their mid-conflict battle positions. Godzilla has Ghidorah's side heads locked under his arms. To position Ghidorah better, it's decided to have Ghidorah up on a platform and to leave Godzilla on the studio floor. Kamiya runs an eye over the two monsters, sizing up the suits and how they will interplay during the actual shooting.

I stay until 4:30. My lungs can't take any more. I'd hate to pass out and prove Isao right.

15 JUNE 2001

Ghidorah actor Ohashi is in a black jumpsuit. He seems eager to climb inside the suit. I ask how he feels. "Never better. I'm all set to take on Godzilla."

Yoshida, doing stretches nearby, chimes in. "Over my dead body!"

With setup moving at a snail's pace, I zip over to the big pool. Kaneko and the live-action staff are working on the scene at the film's end when Godzilla rises out of Yokohama Bay. Unfortunately, it's raining. I dash under a makeshift tent next to the pool where actors Chiharu and Kobayashi sit in front of Sterno fueled heaters. Seeing me half-wet, Chiharu grabs a chair and sets it before the stove.

"Don't catch a cold, Norman!" she says, concerned. As I dry off, I ask about the day's agenda.

"We have the unenviable task of getting into the pool," Kobayashi explains. Across the way, the staff is suspending a massive plastic sheet over the pool to prevent rain from interfering with the scene.

Two ADs escort Chiharu and Kobayashi to the set. Holding umbrellas over their heads, they walk them to a rowboat in the pool. After some struggle, they're over the edge and in the boat.

On the pool's right are several large tetrahedrons, which the ADs guide the boat toward. Someone must have said something funny because Chiharu is in stitches throughout the entire four-meter ride. Hopping off, the actors position themselves against the tetrahedrons.

In the scene, Godzilla is to rise up in front of the pair, causing water to splash about. Before shooting, the actors have to be wet down. An AD runs a hose over them. When hit, Kobayashi manages to maintain his cool. Not so for Chiharu. The second the ice-cold water touches her body, she lets loose a high-pitched shrill. This is followed, naturally, by an uncontrollable laughing fit. After wringing out her hair, Chiharu notices I'm taking photos. Smiling widely, she holds up a peace sign.

On my way back to S2, Aida calls me over. "We need English labels on the drill missile and the large version of the Satsuma submersible. Would you mind writing something that looks like proper English?"

I'm glad he asked. It shows they care enough to get it right. I used to get annoyed at my friend Reo over this. He'd never run English past me before publishing articles; his reasoning was that Japanese don't care since English is thought of as a design. If it's just a design, then draw squiggles, don't open yourself to ridicule using a language a fifth of the world speaks.

"It'll be my pleasure," I tell Aida.

"Great," he responds. "Do you think we can have something within the hour?"

As I break away from Aida, worried what I'll come up with on such short notice, I see a couple of guys lugging a large, army-green missile launcher model into the production offices. I follow them to the art department's staff room, where they set it on a table.

Taking its remote, Isao makes the double-barreled missile turret rise and shift back and forth. "Take a good look," he insists. "We're going to blow the crap out of it during the shoot."

Back in S2, Ghidorah clings to Godzilla's back as Godzilla wrestles with Ghidorah's side heads. Once again, the Godzilla suit is on a bare stage with Ghidorah on a platform behind him. One of my suspicions about the Ghidorah suit is confirmed. The scales covering Ghidorah's body are shedding like crazy. They litter the stage and floors. Shinada will have his work cut out keeping those things attached.

The amount of fog in the studio is back to brutal levels. It's so thick I feel like I've stepped into the world of *The Slime People*. As I've no idea where to buy a decent mask, I still rely on the studio's. I'm using two now: one of the flat ones under one of the cup ones. I've got a towel over my head too because after an hour the fog turns hair rock hard.

I see Isao walking through a thick cloud of smoke. He's not wearing a mask of any kind. "Shouldn't you be covering your face?" I suggest politely.

"I've been working on Godzilla for twenty years," he says proudly. "At this point, it doesn't matter if I wear one or not."

Inatsuki overhears the comment. "Any brain cells Isao had were fried long ago," he adds.

With a Ghidorah head puppet over his arm, Kikuchi is atop a ladder behind Godzilla; squatting out of sight below and ready to spin the wheeled platform Godzilla stands on is Tony. As an effect, I don't think it gets more analog than this.

The smoke in the room is playing havoc with my camera's autofocus. Whenever I push the shutter, the lens spins around, unable to locate a focal point. The camera has an autofocus assistant, but this shines a red spot on the subject. I can just imagine the tar and feathering I'd get if I ruined a take. I mention this to still cameraman Iizuka.

"See this?" He says, pointing to the top of his camera. "I keep the flash covered with tape. It's already set to off, but the crew doesn't know this. When I started out, I noticed they'd look at me wondering if my flash was really off or not. I tape it over for them. When they see it like this, it's one less thing for them to worry about."

Shinada's brought Mothra in for inspection. On the left side of S2 he unboxes the suit. Well, I guess suit isn't the right word since it's too small for anyone to fit into. It's more an automaton with motors.

Although Mothra looks like Mothra, it also doesn't look like any Mothra I've seen before. For one thing, it has two feathers jutting from the top of its head, antennas, I guess. Plus, the abdomen is wasp-like rather than moth-like. It reminds me of something I can't quite finger. I ask VFX supervisor Matsumoto. Without missing a beat, he says, "*The Zanti Misfits.*"

The sides of Mothra's face differ from each other. One side has long strands of white hair while the other is covered with tight white curls.

"Kamiya will decide today which look he likes better," Shinada explains. "By the way, want to see the eyes light up?" Flipping a switch on a control box running from Mothra's back, they shine a bright purple.

A Saturday, the cafeteria is closed. The only place open is the poorly stocked convenience store on the corner, which the staff affectionately calls the "*inconvenience store.*" The moment AD Okamoto calls lunch, I hightail it over, scoring a salad consisting of a single piece of lettuce, a few shreds of onion, twenty kernels of corn, and some tuna that wouldn't fill a thimble. And people wonder why the Japanese are so thin.

After lunch, the stunt crew brings in a large green mat and places it behind Ghidorah. With a "heave-ho," they hoist the three-headed monster onto opera boxes in front of the mat. Following this, Godzilla is brought over. Long fluorescent lights are fit between the ridges of the back fins. The first time testing them, the crew laughs at the glow it forms around Godzilla. I think it looks cool, but Kamiya feels it makes Godzilla look like something out of *Ultraman*. The crew wraps the fluorescents with gels to reduce their "hero" effect.

Action called, Godzilla turns on his hip to face Ghidorah. He shoots his beam (to be added in post), knocking Ghidorah backward. Precariously positioned atop the opera boxes, Ohashi simply lets gravity lead the way, and Ghidorah crashes onto the mat!

At 2:30, the pyrotechnic staff wires Ghidorah with squibs. For the shot—a reversal of the previous one—Godzilla stands on the studio floor. Ghidorah is up on the edge of a half-meter high platform covered by tarps made to look like seabed. Cameraman Murakawa has decided to shoot handheld and, after wrapping the camera in plastic, takes a position to Godzilla's left. Kamiya calls for action. A moment later, a blinding explosion rips across Ghidorah's chest.

Kaneko is off today and has taken his family to see *The Mummy Returns*. On the way home, he stops by the studio with his family to pick me up; he's asked me to join them for dinner. Kaneko's kids come into S2 and Suzuyuki looks like his head is going to explode when he sees the Godzilla suit. I take a few shots of him and Yurina standing beside it.

As much as I want to stay on the set, I join the Kanekos. We drive to a restaurant near their home. After a few beers, Kaneko starts complaining about mundane stuff, such as staff and studio incompetence. Then it's my turn. After listening to me whine about not having any photos of Chiharu without dirt and bandages, he invites me to the shoot next Sunday.

"It's in an office," Kaneko explains. "No dirt. You can take all the photos of a clean Chiharu your little heart desires." I roll my eyes at his sarcastic tone.

21 JUNE 2001

This morning, still cameraman Nakao said it'd be no trouble to keep my equipment at his station. This is terrific news. It's been a real pain running between S9 and the PR room to transfer photos from my camera to my computer. He's even brought a folding table from home and set it up next to his desk for me.

While waiting for the crew to prep the first shot, Nakao and I settle into one of our morning chats. He shows me photos of his sister and how she married one of Japan's top actors. I tell him about my mom being a dancer in Hollywood films such as *Oklahoma* and *You're Never Too Young* when that Saito guy comes over and interrupts us.

"Hey, wanna check out my photos from the day you weren't here?"

The day I wasn't here…? I look at Nakao. He shifts his head to hide his smirk. With little choice, I look through Saito's shots. They're fuzzy and off-center. "Oh, and I had this *totally* interesting talk with Niiyama-san," he boasts.

Saito goes on to tell me about a press screening of *A.I.* he caught a few nights ago that had a satellite hookup with director Spielberg. I'm made to suffer through another collection of unclear photos, this time ones of Spielberg's face on a projection screen.

"Congratulations," I say, passing the shots back. Puzzled, he asks what I mean by that. Rather than explain, I excuse myself to go to the bathroom but instead step into S8 next door.

In S8, Kaneko's crew is in front of the kitchen of the *ryokan* inn, a full-sized interior of the miniature Godzilla's foot crushed last month in S9. The kitchen stands on a platform suspended upon dozens of heavy-duty springs. Seeing me, Kaneko calls me over.

"Norman, this is the actress for the scene. Her name is Hiromi Suzuki. She was in *Crossfire* too."

Suzuki is wearing a *yukata* and really looks the part of *okami*, the term for a *ryokan*'s proprietress. Playfully, she brings the tips of her hands together and gives a bow with downcast eyes, just the kind you'd get when visiting inns of this type.

The scene itself is simple: Suzuki is to walk into the kitchen when, unexpectedly, the place rattles around, the result of Godzilla's heavy footsteps. When action is called, the ADs shake the set. Dishes and bowls crash and smash as she falls screaming to the floor. Unhappy with something, Kaneko asks for a reshoot. The staff spends the next ten minutes sweeping up and replacing the dishware on the shelves. The second take meets with his approval.

The next shot features Yukijiro Hotaru finishing his fall into Ghidorah's cave. The continuation of a scene shot on location, it's to be lensed across from the kitchen set in a precarious-looking, four-meter-tall T-shaped contraption. Stepping into S8 and seeing the odd-looking thing, Hotaru lets out a loud, "*Wow!*"

While the crew prepares, Kaneko, Hotaru, and I sit for coffee on a foldout bench. After they reminisce over the Gamera trilogy, I join the conversation by mentioning I was in *Stacy*, a zombie film that Hotaru was also in. He admits to not having seen it. I tell him he made a wise choice.

An AD interrupts to say they're ready. I follow them up a set of stairs to the structure's top: a large, flat platform covered with leaves and dirt; it's dressed to match the actual forest location. There's even a fake tree in the center with a branch for Hotaru to hang himself from. The plan is for Hotaru to balance himself on a rock and throw his necktie over the branch. After this, the area around him will collapse, plunging him into Ghidorah's cave. It sounds dangerous but Hotaru doesn't

seem worried. He inspects the tree and listens to Kaneko describe the scene's setting. Meanwhile, ADs spread leaves on the ground as men from the tech staff inspect Hotaru's safety harness. All is ready a half-hour later.

Deciding to catch the take from the rafters, I zip down, rush across the studio floor, and dash up the stairs to the ceiling's catwalk. Scurrying across the creaky wood walkways, I make it to a spot right above Hotaru. I have company: live-action still cameraman Katsuhiko Kudo and Chika. Also present are several large movie lights; they give off tremendous amounts of heat. Soon, our foreheads are beaded with sweat.

Not a meter below is cameraman Kishimoto, who must have zero fear of heights. He's calmly planted in the tiny seat of a crane with the camera aimed straight down on Hotaru.

It's time to roll, yet I still can't figure out how to photograph it. No matter where I stand, Kishimoto is in the way. Feeling brave, I grip the railing and lean out as far as I can. Hot and sweaty, and at least eight meters over the studio floor, I want this over with as fast as possible.

Finally, Hotaru steps up to the necktie hanging from the branch. Kaneko yells, "Action!" The space around Hotaru's feet drops out with a roar, sucking him down into a large black pit. A few moments later, once the shot is over, the safety cables lift him back up and place him next to the crew atop the contraption. Grey from dust and dirt, Hotaru is all smiles. The staff applauds.

Over in S9, the SFX team is busy with the destruction of Landmark Tower, one of the film's money shots. I've been poking my head in and out all day, watching the art staff carve break lines into the clay walls within the hollow model. Seeing me, Isao climbs down off the scaffolding next to the tower. After a few expected sarcastic remarks, he answers why they cut lines into the model.

"If we don't," he explains, "the miniature will break away consistent with its actual size. Cutting break lines forces it to come apart in smaller chunks, adding to the illusion of it being bigger than it is."

As luck would have it, the art staff just finished; they're now moments away from blowing up the model. For the shot, the camera crew rented a high-speed camera that runs at a whopping 360 frames per second.

After picking a good spot to photograph from, I check my camera settings. *What the hell?!?* My memory card only has space for three more photos! In a panic, I rush to my computer and start uploading its contents. But, it's going to take ten minutes to empty out. At the halfway point, I hear Kamiya call for ready. *Screw it!* I rip the card out and rush to the set, manually deleting photos one by one.

I get to the spot I'd staked out to find Miike. He's got his own camera out and at the ready. I've about five seconds until Kamiya calls action. With no choice, I lift my camera over Miike's head and hope for the best. With that, Kamiya screams, "Action!"

In a flash, a blinding blast erupts around the miniature. The entire top of the building is sent flying. Scraps hail down throughout S9. The explosion was so loud that my ears ring. My photos? Yeah, they all look like utter *shit*.

The Kaneko crew will end the night with the full-scale Satsuma submersible as it skims the water of the big pool. *Whatever!* I'm so pissed over the crummy photos

I took of Landmark Tower that I head home in a huff.

Thirty minutes later, I get to my apartment, reach for my keys, and— *WTF*? I suddenly remember that I'd put them in a bag I keep in S9. I've no choice but to *go back to Toho*!

During the time I was gone, the lighting crew went to work on the Satsuma. I have to say, seeing it floating in the middle of the pool with colored gels subtly bouncing across its gray surface calms me considerably. I decide to stay.

To prepare the pool for the shoot, the three wave-makers on the left side— essentially large motors connected to steel plates—are turned on. They slosh the water back and forth. Loud as hell, they piss off a family of ducks living under the pool, who squawk back in anger once the machines are shut off.

I join Matsumoto at the edge of the pool. "Looks nice," he says.

"The thing I like most," I add, "is the water. It's like water from a Tsuburaya film of the '60s. All the scene needs is a giant water snake, like in *King Kong Escapes*."

With that, Matsumoto starts humming the film's theme.

Kaneko joins us. "*King Kong Escapes*?" he asks.

I have to wonder just how otaku the three of us really are.

22 JUNE 2001

The Satsuma sub is still in the pool this morning. Only, now it's covered by nesting birds. Wanting to take photos of the labels I wrote, I scare them away— don't want revolting dung all over my *incredible* work! I stand on the edge of the pool, aim my camera, and... *What?*

They left an "of" off the English in one of the sentences! Just as I'm in the middle of a facepalm, Shinada comes over to gaze at the sub.

"The full-scale model is wonderful looking," he says. "Kaneko told me how moved he was when first seeing it."

On a whim, I jump on top and pop open the hatch. Raising my hands in the air, I yell down to Shinada. "That's it! I'm heading back to America! Wait a second! This thing! It has no motor! *No...!* I'm stuck at Toho Studios *forever*!" Shinada laughs wildly.

I pop my head into S8. The Toho carpenters are busy constructing the military command center. At one end is the frame of a gigantic monitor; cables hang over its lower edge. Lined up in the middle of the stage are the consoles I saw drying in the sun last week. They're being fit with TVs and electronic buttons.

Back in S9, I sit with Nakao. We're both annoyed at Saito. Actually, I'm the annoyed one; Nakao is merely amused. He admits to getting a kick out of my complaints and wants to know what he did this time to piss me off.

"For starters," I begin, "I was shooting the breeze with art staffer Yuri over something unimportant, like where to buy cheap bicycles in Tokyo. Saito brazenly interrupted us to say to her, 'I took a perfect photo of you last week that I'll give you later as a present.' For one thing, that can't possibly be true. The guy's incapable of taking 'a perfect photo.'" Nakao explodes with laughter.

"Seriously," I continue, "the same thing happened when he saw me talking to Kaneko yesterday. He rushed over and cut into our conversation like we weren't having one. Even Kaneko gave me a 'huh'

look. Worse, during shooting, I notice he hangs back, waiting for me to get close to the set. Once I've tested the waters and shown that the staff won't make a fuss about my being there, he slides up with his Instamatic camera and literally holds it above my head." Nakao is in tears over my rant.

I forgot to mention, but Shinada came in today with his arm in a sling. "I was doing some cutting and wasn't focused," he admits. "I pulled when I should have pushed and drove a knife into my hand." Between him and Kamiya with his foot in a sling (I also forgot to mention that Kamiya injured his leg, which then became infected from neglect), this place is starting to look like a hospital outpatient ward.

The first shot of the day is Godzilla walking past a window that will integrate with live-action footage of a panicked woman in a hospital bed. In the sequence, Godzilla will veer away at the last moment, leaving her relieved. This relief is short-lived as Godzilla's tail returns to smash into the hospital a second later, killing her.

Godzilla rests empty in his cart as staffers position three buildings nearby. One of them is the specially prepared hospital; the others are generic stock buildings. A staffer draws a chalk line directly onto S9's concrete floor from the camera to Godzilla, the path Yoshida will take. Once Kamiya gives the line his approval, the chalk is replaced by gaffer tape. Yoshida is helped into the suit and, after Kamiya calls action, he walks the line—and, the shot is in the can!

Before Yoshida steps out of the suit, a staffer asks if he can take a photo with his son and Godzilla. The boy, around five years old, seems pleased as punch to be meeting Godzilla. However, the closer he gets to the monster, the uneasier he grows. Yoshida hams it up by clawing at the air, which does little to calm the boy's escalating nerves. Standing next to Godzilla, the dad picks up his son for a pose. That's when it happens! The kid explodes into a river of tears and wails out a sonic boom of panicked screams. The roar of laughter this produces from the crew is intense. Once at a safe distance from Godzilla, the boy calms down. Wiping the tears away, he says, "I liked Mothra better."

Following lunch, the staff heads to the screening room for rushes of the Landmark Tower destruction. PAs have the job of taking headcount. Today, a guy who started a week ago and so far only tasked with sweeping the floor of S9 is given the assignment.

"I want everyone to know I just turned 20," he announces from a corner next to the movie screen.

The room is silent.

"*Uh…*" he says, turning beet red. "I've no idea why I said that."

Everyone breaks into laughter.

Fifteen minutes later, we're filing back into S9. Judging by the faces of the staff, the Landmark explosion wasn't a success. The issue appears to be a time lag between the blast and the fire coming out of the structure. I talk to Isao.

"It just didn't come out well. Not like when the UFO landed on a building in *Godzilla 2000*. That went perfectly." I ask why that went well and this didn't. "Who knows? It's just the nature of the beast."

The next shot is a POV of Godzilla's tail smashing into the hospital. In this, the tail will strike right in front of the lens.

The staff nails together a sturdy plywood box that they place around the camera. A window-shaped square for the lens is cut out in its center.

For the shot, the suit's tail isn't used. In its place, a standalone tail with a wood handle jutting from an end is brought out. A crewmember picks up the tail and, like a baseball player stepping up to bat, swings it in preparation. A few test passes are made with the staffer gliding the tail slowly at the cutout square.

Kamiya calls for a take. Pulling the tail back, the staffer lets go and swings hard. It strikes with a loud slap. Playback shows it was a little off. After a few tries, Kamiya calls, "Okay!" Now, the staff moves onto the last shot of the night, the destruction of the hospital.

The same crewmember will swing the tail against the hospital. With this being a "get it right the first time" type of take, precautions are made to ensure he doesn't miss the mark. Rather than swing freely, a wood platform is set in front of the hospital. The tail will slide across it, launch briefly into the air, and strike in a predetermined spot.

After double-checking everything, the staffer wraps a towel around his head and begins doing body stretches. Slowly sliding the tail back and forth across the table, he tests it out. When ready, he gives Kamiya the thumbs up. After Murakawa announces camera speed, Kamiya yells for action.

With all his might, he sends the tail sailing across the table; after clearing it, the tail takes to the air. *Bam!* It smacks hard against the hospital's side! Building shrapnel flies from the contact spot. The roof cracks and tilts down. Everything is going without a hitch when the roof stops dead still.

I look around. It's as if a cold wind has blown through S9. Lots of long faces. The staff gathers to inspect Godzilla's tail lodged in the hospital. The plan had been for the hospital's roof to break apart completely and for the tail to pull out. For some reason, the roof fell half-way and trapped the tail. Now, a workaround has to be found.

Kamiya's solution is to change the camera angle and pull the tail out, letting the roof fall down around it. Others offer their solution. Whatever they're planning, it looks like it will add hours to the evening. I ask Nakao for his opinion.

"They won't finish until midnight for sure," he insists.

Leaving my computer and camera behind, I head for home.

23 JUNE 2001

Ota is upright in the Baragon suit with Godzilla suit actor Yoshida helping her waddle over to the miniature of a mountain-side tunnel. Today's shot calls for Baragon to burst through the tunnel's left side and peer out its entrance. This will be intercut with live-action scenes of a truck and a motorcycle gang.

Two cameras are aimed at the tunnel entrance. During the dry run, Ota sticks Baragon's head through the opening for cameraman Murakawa to determine how far it should jut out. Once action is called, Ota pushes her costumed front-half into the tunnel. Above, Tony shakes gravel and stones off a board while another staffer dumps dirt from a large plastic scoop.

Unhappy with the take, Kamiya calls for another. However, the second one doesn't satisfy him either; he calls for another. This one, too, doesn't meet his

approval. No matter how many times it's shot, the director is unhappy with something. Either there's too much falling dirt, or there's not enough. The issue is, like Landmark Tower, this is analog filmmaking. All the various handcrafted elements make it near impossible for things to go exactly as planned. After the fifth take, a still unsatisfied Kamiya reluctantly calls the shot okay.

Shinada and I have lunch together. Although a bit introverted, he's a fun, friendly guy with tons of passion for the work. Like most of the staff, the movies are what drew him into the profession. As we eat, I ask how things are on his end of the production. He tells me he's just about done with the Godzilla water suit and will bring it to the set in a few days.

"However," he says, "when we get back to 9, I'll show you what we just finished. I feel it's the best piece we've made for the film."

Back in S9, Shinada pulls a standalone Godzilla head out of a box. More polished and detailed than the heads on the actual suits, this has the look I think Kaneko was after in the first place. Soon, a dozen-plus staffers gather around. Manipulating cables running into the head, Shinada impresses everyone by demonstrating its incredible facial range. A big "*wow*" rings from the crowd.

Not everyone is pleased. Standing on the side, Yamabe looks on with a sour expression. I inquire what's wrong. "What's with all the hoopla over the close-up head?" he asks. "Are they saying the full-body suits aren't cutting it?" In charge of the main suits, it seems his pride is hurt. I assure him that praise for this doesn't mean condemnation of the other Godzillas. My words don't seem to do anything for him.

The next shot is Baragon peering over a police station. The prep is labor-intensive and time-consuming. With at least an hour to kill, I find a sturdy miniature building off to the side to rest against. In short order, I slide into a half-nap state. Through sagging eyelids, I scan the scene in S9: Producer Tomiyama is talking to Kamiya in that parental way of his; beside them, Junko scribbles notes culled from their conversation; Miike is urgently rushing to and from the set like he's saving babies from a burning building; an overworked Isao catches his breath atop a Toho opera box; Thunder, broom in hand, is vigorously sweeping up dirt scattered during the Baragon tunnel shoot.

In my half-awake state, the cacophony of noises and voices blend into a soothing drone. Call it déjà vu, but I'm overcome by the feeling that I've been here before, like I've arrived from some future moment, here to relive the GMK set. Th, I snap awake.

That was weird…I think, while looking to see if anyone took note of my transcendental escapade.

With still time until the shot, I conduct an interview with Ota. It's my first one of the production. I start with a question on how she got the Baragon gig.

"I heard through the grapevine that Toho was looking for someone between 146 and 150 centimeters," she recalls. "They wanted a man, but it's hard to find guys in this business this height, so I got the role. When they were making the suit, I was regularly called in to try it on. I'd tell the staff where it felt odd and they'd make corrections. In the end, it was snug to the point it felt like a part of me."

I ask her what it's like being a first-timer at this. "It's a learning experience, for sure," she reveals. "I knew there were

pyrotechnics but didn't know how they were done. I was so nervous at first. Remember that scene a couple of weeks back when Godzilla hit me with his ray while I was crawling up the side of the mountain? After action was called I heard a muffled roar from outside the suit, and then my whole body slid down. Looking at the playback monitor I was surprised by the size of the explosion. It was huge! In the end, I've learned that you have to trust the staff 100% otherwise your nerves won't hold up."

Despite playing one of the film's prominent roles, I learn that she's yet to meet Kaneko. At the end of our chat, I see the director walking out of S9. I ask her to wait and run over to grab him.

I lead him to the sofa at the Vi-Shop station. Seeing Kaneko, Ota blushes. "Kaneko, this is Rie Ota," I say. "She's playing Baragon. Ota-san, this is director Kaneko."

Kaneko thanks her for her hard work as Ota thanks him for letting her be involved. "If possible, I'd like you to appear in a live-action scene," Kaneko puts forth. "I think it's important to show the suit actors faces somewhere in the film. The scene I'm thinking of would pair you with Ohashi, the Ghidorah actor." Ota is happy to hear this and thanks him.

After the shot of Baragon is in the can, I go back to Nakao's station to pack my bags and say goodnight. He's nowhere to be found. It's then I realize that Nakao always vanishes after the last shot of the day. I've never seen him walk around like the rest of the staff saying, "*otsukare-sama deshita*" (an all-purpose Japanese expression meaning, "thanks for the effort," "I'm calling it a day," "good night," "see you later").

Me, I like being one of the last to leave. I enjoy watching the studio empty out and seeing the aura of the day reflected in the staff's face. I can't fault Nakao. Perhaps after forty-five years, I'll be eager to get home quickly, too.

Just then, I see Shinada struggling with bags of garbage, mostly excess strips of latex from the various suits. I grab a couple and help him to the dumpster in front of S9 before leaving for home.

Stepping off the train at Shimokita, I notice people on the train waving at me as it pulls out. It's Thunder and Ota. I wave back. *Good people*, I think. *Real good people.*

24 JUNE 2001

The live-action crew is standing bleary-eyed around the fountain. The gray sky and on-and-off drizzle aren't motivating anyone. At 9 a.m. on the dot, the ever-ready Murakami announces it's time to load onto the buses. In no time, we're pulling out of the studio and are on our way to a day of location shooting in Yokohama.

A minute later, our bus pulls past the nearby Tsuburaya Productions. I recall the day Kaneko and I rode bikes there. It seems like ages ago. Then I spot the café I did my interview with Nakajima. That seems even longer ago. As the bus waits for a light change, I see Kaneko step out from a restaurant. He catches my eye and waves.

"*Holy crap!*" I yell, pointing out the window. "We've forgotten the director!" Looking out the bus windows and seeing Kaneko waving, the crew breaks up with laughter.

Forty minutes later, we arrive in Yokohama. Being a Sunday, traffic is light, and the drizzle outside has the business district we pull into looking like a ghost town. Through my window I see the Landmark Tower. Dominating the city, it has a pillow of fog wrapped around its top. The buses unload a few blocks away from the skyscraper.

As the crew drag carts packed with lights, cables, gels, and camera cases from the trucks and into a building, Futami barks out commands. Maybe "commands" is the wrong word; they're more like remarks aimed at the quality of the work. As usual he's mostly just yelling, "*dame, dame, dame!*" at no one in particular. I don't think anyone is even listening.

I tag along with still cameraman Kudo, and we go to the ninth floor to drop off our bags. There, Kishimoto has the film camera out, testing it and the day's lenses. Catching my eye, he beckons me to follow him. Leading me to a small auditorium with a screen behind a line of chairs, he points to a long desk encircled by several curved tables. "We shot a boardroom scene here for *Godzilla vs. Megaguirus.*" This morning's scene takes place in the office of General Tachibana, father of Yuri, Chiharu's character. I've yet to meet Ryudo Uzaki, the actor playing him. Over morning coffee, I ask Kaneko to tell me something about him.

"Uzaki is not a full-time actor," Kaneko confesses. "While he's appeared in movies and TV shows, he's really a musician. I wanted him because he's got a good look, one I feel will overcome any lack of skill. What I like is how he can appear either evil or kind depending on how you shoot him."

With the actors getting into makeup, Kaneko runs through the scene using

ADs as stand-ins. Surrounding the director, the staff stand with scripts open. Kishimoto cups an eye and moves around the office while the ADs read dialogue. Once the scene's general flow is decided, lights and camera equipment are dragged in and set up.

Actor Uzaki comes in and greets the staff. An interesting-looking man, his high cheeks and goatee-mustache combine well with a pair of aviator sunglasses. The first scene is him on the phone with his daughter. To read lines for Uzaki to act off, Chiharu steps in. Her hair is pinned up. She looks like she was summoned during the midst of makeup. All smiles, Chiharu unleashes a loud *"ohayo gozaimasu"* into the room. She stands in the back and reads her lines as Uzaki acts off them for the camera.

The next shot is actors Uzaki, Kobayashi, and Chiharu having a meeting around a coffee table. A climactic moment, Chiharu tries to impart to her father what Godzilla is and why the monster has such negative feelings toward Japan. A prop is brought out—an ancient-looking book. Uzaki picks it up.

"Do I need to be careful with this? It must be very old."

Kaneko laughs. "It was made for the film," he assures the actor. Uzaki lets out an embarrassed snort. "He made the book." Kaneko points to AD Shimizu.

Kishimoto has the camera on a crane; it's angled down at the book held tight in Uzaki's hands. With so many people crammed in the room, it's hard not to get in the way. I find a spot next to some movie lights by the window. With the camera pointing away, I figure this spot is a safe bet.

As the scene plays, Kishimoto slowly swivels the camera from the book to Uzaki. Steadily, the lens turns toward his face, and…toward me! *This can't be good*, I think, as the glass plate covering the lens faces my way. Quickly, I slide to the right and press myself against the lights. I figure these have to be out of the shot no matter what. Kaneko calls for cut.

I'm half expecting someone to yell, "Goddammit! Norman was in the frame! We need to reshoot!" But nothing of the sort is said, and Kaneko calls for the next set up. Just when I think I've gotten off scott-free, a camera assistant comes up to me.

"That was close," he says, squeezing his thumb and pointing finger together. "Be more careful."

I apologize and punctuate it with a bow. "If I am in the shot, maybe I can be CGed out," I add, trying to lighten the moment.

"Maybe so," he says with a cold shrug.

Lunch is called. I grab a *bento* and find a spot with a view of Cosmo Clock 21, a Ferris wheel by the bay. I sit with makeup woman Izumi. Sharp-witted and matter-of-fact about everything, she nearly chokes on her food after I compliment the *bentos* we've been getting from Toho.

"You can't be serious? All of them suck ass!"

Without asking, she holds her *bento* over mine and shovels in what she can't eat, which is nearly everything. She then asks what Japanese food I like. It's a common inquiry. After years of responding to it, I know the drill:

First, I start with sushi. Japanese love to hear about foreigners' love of sushi. Then I move to okonomiyaki. This raises eyebrows. I knock 'em dead by saying I prefer Kansai okonomiyaki to the kind served in Hiroshima. This inevitably leads to questions about monja-yaki, a dish of Tokyo origin that is considered the Kanto region's answer to okonomiyaki. I hate it. I think it looks like a plate of vomit.

However, don't think that by disliking it I'm insulting Japan! Far from it. This serves as the all-important "Japanese dish the foreigner cannot eat." Why? Although Japanese are overjoyed to hear of their culinary offerings that tickle your palate, it makes them feel special to learn that there are still areas foreigners cannot tread.

Kaneko comes in and hands me a cup of coffee. He wants to know what I thought of the previous scene. I do my best to give feedback.

"Chiharu's good," I say. "I like her serious face and how she delivers dialogue with urgency. There's something modern about her too. Kind of liberated yet struggling to be taken seriously in a man's world... But I'm still not sold on that mustard colored shirt." Even though I think my comments are worthless, Kaneko shakes his head as he absorbs them.

"I'm curious about her character's use of the word *kokka*. It's my understanding that this means something like 'homeland,' a word that has, I feel, a nationalistic twang."

"Actually," Kaneko says, "she's explaining that it's not the Japan of the government that the monsters are out to protect, but *Yamato*, the land itself. To the kaiju, Japan the land is what they fight to protect, not Japan the nation." Just as Kaneko embarks on one of his Japanese history lectures, Aida comes to tell him that the shoot is ready to resume.

It's 5:40 p.m. and the production has moved to an area close to the Yokohama waterfront. The staff is setting up around loading docks behind a run of antiquated-looking industrial buildings. Cutting across the lot are trolley tracks that appear unused for decades.

A unit from the Japanese Self-Defense Force rolls in. In quick military fashion, soldiers pitch tents on the area's left-hand side. Under one, they set up a communication center with military-grade radio gear. Other tents are dressed with whiteboards, maps, and folding desks.

A production truck pulls in with a group of young men, the extras for the night. Shimizu leads them to an empty loading dock and passes uniforms and helmets around. For fun, I put a helmet on and rush around the set snapping photos. Tapping my inner child, I imagine I'm a part of the army scenes in *The War of the Gargantuas*. Seeing Kaneko leafing through his script, I run over.

"Private England reporting for duty!" I say as I salute the director. Kaneko laughs.

"I've finally figured out your purpose here," he says. "It's to enjoy the set." I release my salute and return to taking photos.

Poking my head into a tent where real soldiers are making final adjustments to some equipment, I get to talking to one. He tells me he's a military liaison to film productions. "I even worked on *Battle Royale*," he adds with pride.

The final rays of the sun drain from the sky. In the near distance, the lights of the Ferris wheel flicker on. Off to the side, Kaneko works with Kishimoto to keep it out of an establishing shot of the area.

With Kishimoto busy setting up the camera, I talk with Kaneko. "I like directing soldiers," he admits. "It's like the grown-up version of playing with plastic army men."

Out of the makeup chair, Chiharu comes bounding over. She has that white bandage around her head again.

"*Oi! Oi!*" she calls out energetically. "Norman, did I see you running around with an army helmet on?" she asks. "Shouldn't the director be wearing one and barking out commands?" Kaneko lets out a snort.

Finally, the location is ready. Action called, soldiers do soldier stuff: They march into frame; once out of camera view, they circle back for another pass. One soldier salutes no one in particular; another points in the air; others move their arms as if guiding a truck, only there is no truck. Suddenly, music from a neighboring clubhouse fills the night air. Kaneko calls for cut. The staff shares looks of, "Is this going to go on throughout the shoot?" Fortunately, the music ends after a few minutes, and the production resumes without interruption.

The night's focus is on an emotionally charged Chiharu in the back of a jeep. She pleads on a two-way radio for her dad not to take the Satsuma sub into battle against Godzilla. A speaker is set on the road; from it comes actor Uzaki's pre-recorded dialogue. Crawling under the back lip of the jeep, I snap shots of a serious-looking Chiharu. This spot offers such an incredible first-row view that I keep it during the take.

Once cut is called, Chiharu drops her head. She looks drained; her eyes are dead and dark. I grow worried. I want to help her, but how? Chiharu catches my look of concern. In a flash, a smile peels across her face. *Silly me.* She's an actress. This is what she does.

The next shot is Kobayashi finding Chiharu safe. During rehearsal, he pulls up and leaps out of a car. Seeing Chiharu, a goofy look of mushy relief spreads across his face. There's something off about it that strikes me as screwy. I bite my lip to hold back a laugh. I must not be the only one to feel this way because a roar of cackles erupts from the crew.

Not the reaction he was expecting, Kobayashi looks mortified. Kaneko, in his director's chair, drops his head at the unexpected development. Chiharu comes running over.

"Did you *see* that face…?" she asks before launching into a fit of laughter. Finally, Kaneko caves in and starts to chuckle. Bowing this way and that, all Kobayashi can do is keep his mark and apologize.

After order is restored, Kaneko calls for a take. Kobayashi repeats the scene; just when he is to make that look of love-tinged relief, he breaks into laughter. This sets off another chain reaction throughout the crew. Kaneko puts in a few more attempts at the shot, but everyone, including Kobayashi, is too overcome by the giggles. Eventually, Kaneko yells "Okay" through his megaphone.

"Is it really okay?" I ask.

"No, but I'll make it work," he says.

Kobayashi comes running over and apologizes to Kaneko, who assures him it's fine.

After one final shot of military men pointing at the night sky, the day is called a wrap. It's 11:45 p.m. It takes 45 minutes to clean and pack up; once done, we hop onto the location bus.

Midnight snacks are passed around; everyone is buzzing with the excitement of a good day's shoot. However, not five minutes after getting on the road, the crew falls into a deep sleep. The bus is a roar of snores all the way back to Toho.

27 JUNE 2001

Despite being a furnace out, the SFX crew is sweating it around the big pool, working on a shot of Baragon taking a leap through the air. The art staff has erected a mountain ridge matching the one inside S9. Atop it, sticking out of the Baragon suit, is Ota's stand-in, Sasaki. Due to the shot's physicality, it's decided that he should don the suit. Parked close is a large yellow crane with cables attached to Baragon. Action called, Sasaki leaps from the ridge. Held by the cables, he swings far out and lands on a cushioned mat several meters away.

Stupidly, I wore a long sleeve shirt to the set. Seeking cool, I duck into the air-conditioned S8. Here, the army HQ set is complete and shooting is underway. On one end of the set is a raised section for the upper military brass, and on the other is a giant screen that displays military-related information. On the floor in between the two sections are rows of control panels.

A new actress has come to the production. Kaneko tells me her name is Kaho Minami. Usually, I'd have Kaneko introduce us, but as it's her first day, I feel I should give her space. Minami also looks a bit ill at ease, though this might be an attribute of the strait-laced military outfit she's wearing.

On the other hand, Ryudo Uzaki is in a chair off to the side. Feet up, hands behind his head, and softly whistling a tune, he's looking very approachable. Even so, I'm always nervous doing cold introductions in Japanese. However, whatever deficiencies I might have

with the language is often buoyed by the Japanese people being forgiving of foreigners butchering their language.

"Excuse me," I say, clearing my throat. "I wasn't able to introduce myself on the Yokohama set because you were so busy."

Standing with a smile, Uzaki takes my hand and gives it a firm shake. "Nice to meet you," he says. "Have a seat."

Thankfully, Uzaki turns out to be talkative. We spend a couple of minutes chatting about New York, Godzilla, and Japan. Just when the subject of rock and roll comes up, he's called to set.

"*Ah,*" he says. "We gotta pick this up later!"

On today's schedule is a promotional press conference, an open house for newspaper and TV people to get on set and ask questions about the GMK production. With the press meet taking place in S8, the set wraps early, allowing the PR department time to set up chairs. I go back to the big pool where they're readying another shot of Baragon.

Just before a shot is to lens, a loud bang erupts from the scaffolding next to the set. It's a young guy named Tomohiro Matsumoto. He's slipped off the top! Bouncing off the metal poles, he crashes to the pavement with a thud. Knocked unconscious, his face is covered in blood. Kamiya rushes over and, without wasting a moment, yells for someone to call for an ambulance. Acting quickly, the staff brings over blankets and cleans the blood off his face. Taking his hand, Godzilla actor Yoshida holds it throughout the wait.

I'm distraught. Not an hour earlier, Matsumoto and I were talking about the *Biohazard 2* set I was on several years back. I'd lent him a video of the production, and he said he had a ton of questions to ask about George Romero.

We planned to chat after I got back from S8.

Ten minutes later, an ambulance pulls up to the pool, and a still unconscious Matsumoto is taken away. A visibly shaken Kamiya takes a moment to remind everyone of the importance of safety. Despite the incident, the crew moves onto the next shot. Regrettably, a lot of the wind has been knocked out of the crew's enthusiasm. I don't think anyone will feel at ease until we know Matsumoto's condition.

At a little after 11 a.m., the press has gathered in front of S8. What a line! I expected a turnout of ten, like on the first day of shooting, but there are almost a hundred and fifty people! In short order, the reporters are let into S8, where they take chairs facing a display of the GMK poster art in front of four stools: one for Kaneko, Tomiyama, Uzaki, and Chiharu.

The press-greet starts with Tomiyama reading a prepared statement. Covering the Godzilla series basics and how honored Toho is to have the talented Shusuke Kaneko at the helm, his talk comes across a bit too press releasey for my taste. Kaneko livens things up with his vision of Godzilla and what he plans to achieve with the film. However, the real showstopper is Chiharu. With charm set to 11, she laughs and kids around, handling the crowd like a pro.

When it comes time for the photo op, the reporters gather in front. Godzilla (with Yoshida inside) is led in, and the four GMK representatives gather around. After a minute, the reporters ask for shots of just Chiharu and Godzilla. Rather than stand side-by-side her kaiju co-star, Chiharu places her hands on Godzilla's knees, and,

leaning back, snuggles into the large suit like it was a cuddly teddy bear. One of the most risqué poses ever seen in the G-rated Godzilla franchise, it sends the reporters into a photo-snapping feeding frenzy!

Once over and after the reporters have been led out, I say hi to Chiharu. Like some sort of earthbound Venus, she's spot-on lovely today, moreso than usual. Chiharu asks how she did in front of the reporters and gives my arm a hard pinch when I tell her she needs to try harder or else she'll get fired. Off to the side, Kaneko watches us with an amused smirk.

A bit of good news comes in: Matsumoto didn't suffer any severe injuries. He'll be out for a few weeks, but the prognosis is that he'll pull through with no ill effects.

28 JUNE 2001

The last day of command center scenes in S8, it's mostly officers in uniform talking tough and barking out commands while watching monsters duke it out on the large monitor (images to be superimposed later). Kaho Minami is back and Kaneko has gotten nice moments out of her: worried expressions as she follows the progress of the Godzilla/Baragon face off.

About half the personnel in the control room are actresses. I ask Kaneko if he isn't over doing it.

"No, not really," he says. "Most military women in Japan do desk work."

I walk up and down the aisles listening to the extras chitchat. At the front right station, a young woman is staring intently at her monitor. I peek over to find she's playing solitaire, the one standard with

Microsoft Windows. *Ah*, I see…all the monitors are running Win98. As a guy who's spent more time playing this than he cares to admit, I give her pointers. Just then, Kaneko walks over. "This is Mizuki Kanno," he says.

Once the room is emptied for lunch, I explore the S8 set. Some of the console buttons are hysterical. One reads, "Don't push," another says "Karaoke," yet another reads "saké." For fun, I sit in the main military chair and imagine the rush I'd have were I a ten-year-old. Hell, even at 42 it's a rush!

I go to the cafeteria and join Mizuki and her manager for lunch. She tells me she's a gravure idol, which would be what you call a bathing suit model in the US. Later on, during a break in shooting, I bring them into S9 and take a few photos of Mizuki playfully posing against the Godzilla suit.

Outside in front of the big pool, the staff is prepping more shots of Baragon. The art staff has built a wall of dirt and rocks. Ota is back in the suit. She butts her head into the wall, smashing it to bits.

The SFX crew then moves to an approximately 3-meter tall length of Godzilla skin. Erected on the pool's left, it's a 1:1 scale strip of Godzilla hide. The top has been rigged to release water, which washes down during the take.

At the end of the day's shoot, I walk back to the production rooms with Kaneko. He asks about the buzz on the American Godzilla chat boards. I tell him it's a mess, with people praising his choice to make Godzilla fierce, while others feel the best Godzilla is the one you can root for.

"Well," Kaneko asserts, "you can't please everyone."

29 JUNE 2001

Nakao is lounging at his desk reading a magazine; opposite us, the Vi-shop guys are prepping Godzilla. Me? I'm on my computer finishing updates for Kaneko's website and the "Norman Report." Nakao peeks up to give me a dirty "you kids and your damned technology" look. Unlike live-action-set still photographer Kudo, who uses a top-of-the-line Nikon D1 digital camera, Nakao has stuck with analog film.

In front of us at the Vi-shop station, the pyrotechnic guys test explosives on one of the Godzilla suits. The squibs go off with loud, unpleasant "pop" sounds that set a ringing in my ears. The charges send bits of Godzilla flesh everywhere too. I'm hit smack in the forehead, sending Nakao into a fit of snickering.

While at times seemingly off sitting on the moon, Kamiya has been friendlier recently. Taking advantage of this, I call him over to run photos past him that I want to use on Kaneko's website. He pages through them on my computer, not commenting one way or another. Eventually, he stands and says that he has no issue with any of them. However, just when he's a foot away, he pauses and turns back.

"The best shots are the ones you can't see my face. I don't want it to affect my ability to buy porn." I can't tell if he's kidding.

After the squib test on the suit is over, Godzilla actor Yoshida takes a seat next to me for no particular reason. Looking at the English on my computer screen, he jokingly asks if I can read that "stuff."

Yoshida's easygoing manner and unabating smile go far to take the edge off the intensity of S9. In many ways it's the Godzilla suit actor and not the director who determines the set's mood. All the work—the efforts of nearly 100 men and women—revolves around Godzilla. Were Yoshida to be demanding or difficult, the set would undoubtedly fall into disarray. On several occasions, Yoshida's ability to maintain his cool has held the crew together and gotten the production through tight spots. As much as physical strength, stamina, and agility are necessary to play Godzilla, this too is an indispensable quality needed to perform as the King of the Monsters.

Whenever we talk, I try to work out interesting tidbits about playing Godzilla. For example, he tells me now that one needs to have a grasp on the concept of film speeds. Often Kamiya will alter the camera frame rate; it's up to Yoshida to interpret this and adjust his movements accordingly.

Today's schedule calls for shots at the film's end when Godzilla's skin ruptures from the inside. They're simpler than imagined; no miniatures, just a large white sheet stretched behind the suit with the camera set low on a tripod. With Godzilla having just risen from the waters off Yokohama, the staff needs to wet down the suit. Two men spray water from portable pumps while others run rags over Godzilla to ensure the water gets into the suit's deep ridges. After this, the explosion on Godzilla's shoulder is shot four times. Following each attempt, Godzilla is patched and re-squibbed.

After dinner, another set of rushes is up for viewing in the screening room. Filing in with the staff, Junko asks if I plan to sleep through it again. I tell her that there is no way I will…unless they're monotonous, never-ending element inserts, like water pouring over Godzilla skin.

I get a seat and settle in. Junko is behind me reading off notes as Baragon jumps through a forest and, in the next set of clips, is popping his head from a tunnel. Cool as it all looks, sure enough, the chair is comfortable to the point my body feels like it's been lowered into a tub of warm gelatin. I doze off. I must've started snoring because Junko flicks a finger hard against the back of my head!

"Norman! You promised!" she reprimands me. I work myself awake and focus on the screen.

Up now is a seemingly never-ending reel of water pouring over Godzilla skin…

30 JUNE 2001

The art department takes center stage this morning with a shot of a parking lot "erupting" in front of a police station. Having started on it yesterday, they've dressed the space atop several platforms with all the miniature goodness and attention to detail that I've come to admire. The platform is rigged with a row of jagged zigzag cuts; it's to break down the middle in timed sections, moving toward the camera to make it look like Baragon is boring underground.

Miike is in full Miike mode. With an eye glued to the camera's viewfinder, he directs his staff, ordering them where to place miniature cars, bikes, vending machines, and trees. During a break, Miike cites this as one of GMK's better examples of forced perspective. Sure enough, a peek through the lens shows a greater depth of field than when viewed with the naked eye.

None of the other photographers have come today, not even Nakao. When it comes time to run the shot, I take a spot next to the camera without having to vie for a position. I soon understand why.

Kamiya calls for action. Several small charges push the flaps up under the parking lot. It's over in an instant. I review my photos: a couple of dull shots of tabletops with a busted parking lot in the middle.

4 JULY 2001

Another day with me the only one taking stills. The scene up is a large head of Ghidorah bursting through ice. The head (with a bit of neck) is affixed to the end of a dolly and set under a sheet of thick Plexiglass. The "ice"—pre-cut in jagged breakaway patterns—is attached to a rig by hinges. In this way, the ice slabs can move up and down like flaps on a box. It's the same technique used on the parking lot destruction scene a few days ago. The shot is ready at 2:30 p.m. As Ghidorah's head is nudged upward, pushing the "ice" sections up and away, staff members blast fire extinguishers around it for added ambiance.

On slow days such as this, I'll sit with the art staff and shoot the breeze. Today, Inatsuki asks about some of the Godzilla pieces I've written for *Fangoria*. I mention the one I did with suit actors Nakajima and Satsuma.

"The interviews were great fun," I tell him. "Nakajima was pretty normal, but Satsuma was like a mountain man living in a self-styled dojo."

Inatsuki stops work on some miniature trees. "Wait, you mean you *actually* went to Satsuma's dojo? That place is a legend!

The thing is, he built it on unused public land. When local officials discovered it, they made him tear it down."

Now, why doesn't this surprise me...

5 JULY 2001

Baragon is sprawled across a table with his arms slumped over the front and looking very much as if he'd been shot dead. He's slated to crash into a parking lot, now just undressed tables pushed together.

The staff flips the red kaiju over and fits him with wires linked to the ceiling. After determining Baragon's trajectory and point of impact with the table, they hoist him into the air (without Ota inside). Miike and his crew get to work dressing the tables with buses, cars, greenery, etc. It'll take a while, so I head over to S3, where Kaneko's team has started shooting Satsuma sub interiors.

S3 is a medium-sized studio similar to S1 and S2. In its center is a mock-up of the submersible's cockpit that when seen from the back has the appearance of an outhouse. However, a walk around reveals an opening through which switches, dials, levers, and a cool command chair can be seen. It's positioned atop a wide, wood platform that is itself balanced atop a large half-ball soldered together from metal beams. To simulate the sub's underwater movement, staffers hold rails affixed to two sides of the platform and tilt it about on the half-ball bottom.

The first scene features actor Hiroyuki Watanabe. As he says his lines, the crew gently rocks the sub. It adds a nice touch of reality, one better than had the camera been moved around à la *Star Trek*. After it's done, I introduce myself to Watanabe. It turns out he speaks decent English.

"Call me Yuki," he says in a friendly tone. In no time, we're chatting about Jazz, something Kaneko told me is his great passion.

Watanabe is a popular actor in Japan. Handsome and well built, he was featured in all three of Kaneko's Gamera films and the TV show *Ultraman Gaia*. To the average Japanese, however, he's best known for a series of TV commercials for power drink Lipovitan D. In them, he and another strong-looking male find themselves in a dangerous situation (such as a collapsing rope bridge) that requires all-out brawn to overcome. Invariably drenched in sweat, one of them yells out *fighto!* (fight), and the other *ippatsu!* (do it!), before they rectify whatever predicament has befallen them.

Today is Ota's final day to play Baragon. For this reason, I opt to spend the rest of it in S9. First up is the parking lot shot. One row of tiny cars and buses at a time, a whiteboard is placed between them; the camera is run for a minute for each take. Just as the final shot is up, a staffer yells out, "There's a ladder in the way!"

Sure enough, a ladder off to the side has been in every shot so far. A collective gasp passes through the staff. Kamiya, however, starts cracking up. The ladder is pulled away as he reviews the footage. Kamiya decides it's not an issue and they move on.

Finally, it's time for the crash. I get a perfect spot next to the camera. Kamiya calls for action. Baragon is released. Sliding back first down guide wires, he plows into the parking lot, landing with a heavy thud as a series of charges are ignited. The miniatures blast into the air—bits find their way onto my face and into my hair.

Wearing the special top-half Baragon suit, Ota is led to the front of a blue screen. Kneeling on blankets, she preps herself for close-ups of Baragon being vanquished by Godzilla's atomic beam. As I snap photos, I tell her how much she looks like a *rakugo*[14] performer. Holding my camera to a peephole for her to see, she starts laughing.

"You're right! I do!" she exclaims.

Ota is encased in the full suit and hoisted nearly four meters into the air for composite elements of Baragon swatted by Godzilla's tail. From the floor of the studio, staffers keep a check on her.

"You okay up there?" an AD yells.

"I'm fine! Don't worry!" comes her muffled voice through the overhanging suit.

The final shot is Baragon scampering through a forest and coming up to the camera lens where Ota will take a butt-down/face-forward position before letting out a bark-roar. The first time she scampers across the platform, she loses her way and falls off the stage. A strip of white tape is laid down for her to follow. Scuttling across on the next take, she halts right in front of the camera and lets out a muffled yell that seems to emanate from deep within Baragon's belly. It's both ferocious and adorable at the same time.

With that, the Baragon scenes for GMK are complete. As Ota slips out of the suit for the last time, Kamiya walks on stage. He holds out a large bouquet of flowers. In an official tone, an AD announces the completion of her performance. Everyone applauds. Right away, Ota starts crying. The applause increases.

---

14 - *Rakugo* is a form of entertainment begun in the Edo period in which storytellers perform while kneeling on pillows.

It's a special moment. The crew is all smiles, happy over the terrific job she did and glad to see it was a good experience for the actress. Even I find myself tearing up.

After the hoopla dies, I go up to Ota as she gathers her belongings in the Vi-shop area. I thank her for being cool to me throughout the production. Taking my hand, she pumps it and thanks me for being supportive from the get-go. She admits how terrified she was at the start of production but through everyone's kindness, had the time of her life. Shinada is nearby and takes a photo of the two of us together.

6 JULY 2001

I make it to Toho earlier than usual. Even so, Junko, Murakawa, and Kikuchi are already reviewing the day's plan.

"Don't you people ever go home?" I joke.

"Don't you ever wear anything but black?" the sharp-as-a-tack Junko retorts.

"I didn't wear black yesterday," I protest. "In fact, I wore my awesome *Double Trouble* t-shirt!"

Murakawa inquires, and I explain that it was a situation comedy about twin girls from Iowa living in New York City. It's my favorite goofy '80s TV show. I add that the father of the twin actresses was Boris Sagal, director of *The Omega Man*. Murakawa picks up to this and we praise the coolness of Sagal's film. Junko rolls her eyes.

"You guys…" she says. "Too nerdy!"

Over at S3, the Satsuma interiors continue. Once again, Yuki works the sub's controls with the camera square in his face. After finishing his scenes, he asks if I'll join him for lunch. He even

offers to pay! Being as broke as I am, I'm not one to refuse a free meal.

Over in the cafeteria, Yuki tells me about when he lived in LA and his preference for US-style acting, claiming it employs more body language than in Japan, where they rely more on dialogue.

After lunch, I return to S9. The shots are close-ups of a free-floating Godzilla arm clutching the Satsuma sub. Between shots, I try on the Godzilla arm and tell Kamiya that this is what it would look like if I were to exercise only one arm for ten years. Junko adds that the real joke would be if I were to exercise at all. I guess she knows me too well.

Things get more interesting when the Godzilla suit is wired up, lifted in the air, and set before a blue screen. Suspended like this, it's more massive looking than ever. Moreover, it's just weird to see Godzilla seemingly in defiance of the law of gravity. Murakawa rides a crane and does various takes while moving across the suit.

Yuki pays a visit to the SFX set with some friends and family. He asks me to show them around. I lead the group through the various stations in S9, explaining what each one does. Many of the GMK crew worked on the Gamera trilogy and exchange greetings with him.

Before leaving, I introduce Yuki to Yoshida, who breaks into a string of bows. I tell him that Yoshida played the monster Legion in *Gamera 2* and that he should apologize for attacking him so fiercely. The two look puzzled. Kamiya, who's been standing not far off, starts to bellow with laughter. At least *someone* gets my joke.

Starting today, GXM director Tezuka has joined the production to supervise the shooting of SFX B-roll material. The schedule has fallen behind and Tomiyama (I suspect) has asked Tezuka to help put it back on track.

I'm happy to see Tezuka, and we talk a bit about a Loft Plus One event we attended a few days back in Shinjuku. He and Shinji Higuchi were guests because Yuriko, the woman who runs Loft, was afraid that the main guest, golden age Toho cameraman Sadamasa Arikawa, wasn't going to be talkative. Tezuka and I share a laugh over this. It turned out to be just the opposite. Arikawa was a chatty powerhouse that night, recalling his tenure on the Godzilla sets of the Showa series.

Tonight are rushes from the past few days. The parking lot crash looks terrific, as do the final shots of Baragon. When Baragon trips off the stage, the crew breaks into laughter.

After rushes, the just-completed trailer for GMK is shown. Quick cuts, pounding music, good SFX. It looks fantastic! Unfortunately, Toho has decided to run GMK as a double feature, pairing it with an animation film starring Hamtaro, a hamster character popular with the eight-year-old set.

The staff is in tears over how absurd the trailers look side by side. I mean, it's almost beyond belief to see a towering, fierce-looking Godzilla paired with a tiny, dewy-eyed hamster.

Kaneko is here, and when we file out of the theater, no one can look at him without tittering.

Mortified, Kaneko comes up to me. "I have been raped by a hamster," he says with a sigh.

7 JULY 2001

S3 is dark; it takes my eyes time to adjust. As they do, I hear a voice. "It's been a while." I squint at the chair beside the entrance to see Uzaki in uniform signaling me over. Next to him is Kaneko. I sit with them as they review the coming scene.

After Kaneko leaves, Uzaki and me pick up our music talk. I mention I was a rock musician in New York City. Uzaki names some studios he recorded at in New York. I'm impressed. They're all top-notch/top-dollar studios. It turns out that because of my former job in the city, I've been to all of the ones he mentioned, which impresses him.

Chiharu is on-set too. She has one scene with Uzaki as a type of apparition. Feeling like having fun, I bring her over to the sub's interior. "Check this out." I flip open a small lid covering a torpedo release switch. "See this?" I point to a label in English. "I wrote that."

A *wow* look spreads across her face.

"Between us," I continue, "the English translates to 'Hit this switch and Japan will self-destruct.'"

A priceless look of shock spreads across her face, which quickly turns to disbelief. Realizing I was pulling her leg, she laughs loudly, attracting Kaneko's attention.

"Mr. Director," I say. "Please cast Chiharu in all your films. She's the best!"

Chiharu grabs Kaneko's arm and squeezes tight. "Yes, cast me more!"

Kaneko rolls his eyes.

Some of the scenes with Uzaki require the sub to be shaken violently. One of the ADs asks if I wouldn't mind lending a hand. I find a spot under Uzaki and grab hold of a rail. On cue, I shake the sub with five others. At one particularly violent point, we throw our backs into it, managing to lift the whole contraption off the floor! We let it drop with a loud thud. Lights in the sub flare and blow out sparks.

Taki is here today to report on the production. He's off to the side watching as we rock the sub back and forth. Between shots, I mention that no one will mind if he lends a hand. Frankly, things being what they are on Japanese sets, they could use the help. He shifts his eyes back and forth trying to decide. With giddy abandon, he jumps into a spot behind me. Kaneko calls for action.

"Come on, Taki!" I shout over my shoulder. "Put your back into it! Do it for Godzilla! Do it for *Kaneko's* Godzilla!" We fight to hold back the laughter as we shake the sub with everything we've got.

During a breather, I ask Kaneko when it would be a good time to do our official interview for *Fangoria*. He pulls out his schedule book; just as he's pointing to a date, Saito comes running up.

"Director, do you know what kind of lens is being used?"

"How should I know," Kaneko replies.

Feeling this just another of Saito's lame tactics to cut in on my time with the production, I look around to see if anyone else has noticed. Taki is nearby and, completely getting it, cracks up when we make eye contact. Later on, one of the PR guys labels it a shitty move on Saito's part.

Six kids on a school field trip file into S3. Around their necks are clipboards for them to jot down what they see in the studio. Led by their teacher, they go up to Kaneko and ask questions about being a director. I look at one boy. *Ah*, Suzuyuki, Kaneko's son. This explains how the class

got in. Kaneko introduces his son to Chiharu, who squeals over how much he looks like his dad. Suzu turns bright red.

Lunch is called and I ask Uzaki and Chiharu if they'll pose for a few shots outside. I've always been a fan of stills showing actors standing in character around the Toho lot. Looking at those old photos, I've tried to imagine the situation surrounding the productions and what must have been an exciting moment for them and the crew— moments gone forever with only photos left to mark the occasion.

As Uzaki and Chiharu pose, I ask myself if one day anyone will look at these photos and wonder about them in the way I have over those photos from decades past.

8 JULY 2001

A Sunday, the Kaneko crew is a bit low-key this morning. Trying to wake ourselves, we hang around the fountain and munch on junk food and down canned coffee. As unfailing as ever, Murakami yells loudly at 9 a.m. for us to pile into the location bus. We're soon headed to Akasaka for a full day of shooting inside the office of "BS Digital Q," the broadcast station where Yuri Tachibana, Chiharu's character, works.

The location turns out to be an actual office that the production arranged to use during its day off. The place is big with islands of desks collected about. SFX supervisor Matsumoto and I set up in a back corner, mindful because we've invaded someone's real-life workspace. Right away, Matsumoto starts compositing shots on his laptop.

"Can't you just enjoy the shoot?" I ask.

"With the workload I have?" he replies as he dips his head into his monitor.

I go into a side room where Chiharu is being made up.

"Norman, look!" she yells, pointing at her outfit. "You keep complaining I always wear the same thing. Well, today I've got something different on!"

She's right. Rather than the usual mustard and white combo, she's in a yellow pullover and black pants. "And tomorrow I'll be wearing a pink dress with frilly shoulders!"

I look at her shocked…until she breaks into laughter. *Ah*, now she's pulling *my* leg!

In the room is actor Shiro Sano. For GMK, he's been cast as Chiharu's boss. Makeup woman Izumi has fit him with a silly-looking wig with hair that hangs over his shoulders.

"Say, didn't you come to the set of G2000?" Sano asks.

From a bag, Sano pulls out a videocassette of *King Kong vs. Godzilla*. "Brought this for inspiration," he announces as he slips it into a nearby VHS deck. Curious, Chiharu sits beside us. Right away, Sano and I start in on how great the film is, pointing out details that captured our imagination as boys.

A scene with a miniature construction set comes on. Sano explains to Chiharu that whereas most productions would have shot the scene at a real construction site, Tsuburaya chose to recreate it with miniatures. He explains that Tsuburaya's goal was not to simply offer reality, but to create an alternate reality that drew you in through its artistry. Later, when Kong springs spectacularly out of the water after breaking free from his captors aboard a ship, Sano and I jump up and applaud. Chiharu can't help but laugh at the two of us.

Chiharu and Sano are called to set. In the scene, they spar over the intent of her reporting. It takes forever to get right. For one thing, it's a long scene, almost a minute in length. After ten takes or so, Kaneko calls for a break so the actors can regain their wits. During this, I chat with producer Tomiyama.

"This is a very professional crew," Tomiyama remarks. "I like Sano's suit, too. It's very funky."

Also on set is Saito. I'm doing my best to keep my distance, but it's impossible. "Check out these photos I took of Kaho Minami on the day you didn't come," he brags. "You don't have photos of her, right?" I respond with a disinterested "congratulations" to everything he says and shows me. It seems to annoy him.

One thing that bugs me is how he keeps referring to me as *kimi*, an informal version of the word "you," one pretty much used for children and underlings. (It can be argued that it's also used between men who share a close friendship, but there is no way my relationship with Saito could ever be described as close). Things take a turn for the worse when one of the ADs asks me to move out of my chair.

"You're in the shot," he says. "The director feels there won't be any non-Japanese working in a company like this." I'm cool with the reasoning, but not with him replacing me with Saito and sitting him in front of my computer.

I eat lunch with Kaneko, Sano, and Chiharu. We continue watching *King Kong vs. Godzilla*. Sano asks if I've seen the US version of G2000. He heard it has many editing changes. I haven't yet, so can't comment.

I take Chiharu outdoors for a photoshoot. It's utterly fabulous out, unseasonably cool and not at all humid. With us is a man from Toho and Kono, her manager at talent agency Horipro. I'm slightly nervous. To be honest, it's the first time I've ever shot photos in a photographer/model-like setting. Don't photographers always say things to motivate their subjects? I give it a go.

"Chiharu, give me a look like you're about to take on Godzilla!" Rather than look empowered, she breaks into laughter. Oh, well. I tried.

In total, we spend twenty minutes walking around the neighborhood with me snapping photos along the way. I'm an amateur at this, but you'd never know by Chiharu's reaction. When we get back to the set, she can't thank me enough and makes me promise to give her copies.

In the late afternoon, Sano, Chiharu, and Takashi Nishina (an actor playing a member of Chiharu's news team) review a TV playback of the interview they did with actor Amamoto in jail. Sano's character has been chewing on dried squid in every take. Before the umpteenth go, Sano is handed another strip of squid.

"I don't think I'll be able to stomach this again as long as I live," he complains.

Between takes, talking about more Showa Toho fantasy films, I mention to Sano that I lunched with Amamoto a few times at Toho. He's floored. Sano reveals his great admiration for Amamoto, both as an actor and as a human being.

"He's a man of great conviction," insists Sano. "It's a quality sorely lacking in Japan today."

The next shot is Sano and some extras reacting to the news of Chiharu's live-report of the Godzilla/Ghidorah battle. They're overjoyed because her scoop has put their tiny station at the top of the national TV ratings. Upon hearing the news, they raise their arms and yell, *Banzai!* After the take, I walk over to Kaneko.

"Are you sure you want to have these guys yelling that?" He looks puzzled. "I know what it means, but nearly everyone outside of Japan links the word to Japanese war aggression. Given the theme of the film, it might give non-Japanese the wrong idea."

Kaneko goes into deep thought. A moment later, he approaches the actors. "Let's try it again, but this time leave out the *banzai*."

Back at my seat, Matsumoto shows me some clips of the Satsuma sub he's been working on.

"You'll probably think I'm nuts," I say in response, "but when seeing the ship for the first time, I got the same feeling I did when seeing the Proteus for the first time."

I don't even have to mention that the Proteus is the sub from *Fantastic Voyage*. Matsumoto gets misty-eyed and talks about the impact *Fantastic Voyage* had on him as a boy.

As if on cue, Saito butts in. "Did you know that Isaac Asimov wrote the novelization of the film?"

This is just the kind of otaku talk I hate: miscellaneous factoids tossed into the air. Here we are basking in the film's emotional impact, not on who can one-up the other with tidbits of minutiae! And Saito keeps calling me *kimi*!

Finally, I look straight at him. "Can you, you know, stop calling me *kimi*?"

Matsumoto and a female extra standing nearby begin to laugh.

Saito looks at me bewildered.

12 JULY 2001

The morning in S9 starts with Godzilla rounding a Yokohama city corner. A pair of staffers zigzag spotlights across his body. A seemingly simple shot, it has Kamiya frustrated. He's not happy how the beams sweep over Godzilla's body. Getting together with the spotlight operators, he draws Godzilla onto a sheet of paper and maps out how he wants each light to pass over the body. It takes a bit of work, but they finally get something Kamiya is happy with.

I zip over to S3. The recently completed bridge of the battleship Aizu fills the stage. Another fantastic set, it features control panels, consoles that light up in various colors, and one of those standing, opaque navigation boards, the kind sailors plot courses on with a grease pencil.

If you can forgive the pun, there's a boatload of extras on hand today. They strut about in military outfits and take positions behind main actors Uzaki, Yuki, and two actors I'm unfamiliar with. With time to spare, Kaneko introduces me to the new actors. One is a distinguished-looking, middle-aged man named Takeo Nakahara. He gives me a firm handshake. The other is a younger actor named Toshikazu Fukawa. Kaneko tells me he's with Johnny's, a talent agency known for pretty boy groups.

"So, how do we stack up against the American military?" Nakahara asks.

I tell him about the time an Army helicopter landed in my college in an attempt to impress students to enlist. "They let me sit in the pilot's seat, where I proceeded to hit every switch and lever, and even flooded the engine with gas. It was my way of showing them what little regard I have for the military." The actors look at each other in nervous silence.

"Well then," Kaneko says, "I guess we should keep Norman away from the controls." Everyone breaks up laughing.

The larger the set, the more time it takes to light things. With a while until the first shot, Kaneko and I make ourselves coffee. Speaking of which, here's something I gotta rag on: set coffee. There's only ever instant, rarely any sugar, and milk is invariably a powder substitute called "Creap," which the Japanese pronounce as "creep." If that doesn't sound bad enough, the water in the thermos comes from the sink in the toilet closest to whatever stage the crew is working in. Whenever I make myself a cup, I take a couple of sips to get a coffee feeling going and then pour the rest out. Unlike me, Kaneko doesn't seem to mind it.

"I found out that the SFX team has fallen behind schedule," he says as he sips away on his coffee. "I'm trying to get them more time, but Toho isn't budging. I'll probably have to make difficult decisions soon and make cuts to the effects list."

Just then, Kaneko's mother Shizue pays a visit to the set. Kaneko introduces her around. He tells me that she's a skilled *kirie* (a Japanese art involving paper cutting) artist. She watches a few setups before leaving with Jiro.

Back in S9, the PR staff has arranged a photoshoot of Godzilla fighting Mothra for us photographers. The SFX crew puts up a row of buildings and casts spotlights behind them. Once they're done, Nakao takes charge. He positions Godzilla and Mothra tightly together and tells Yoshida where to place Godzilla's arms and how to hold the head. It's now that I really see how skilled he is at photographing giant monsters. Once Nakao has the kaiju how he wants, we start snapping pictures like wildfire. After a measly three minutes, the staff makes us stop so they can get to the next shot on their schedule.

"In the old days, we'd have had at least an hour for something like that, and we'd have had a lot more of the set to work with," Nakao confides after we go back to his station. Surprisingly, he doesn't seem frustrated, more like amused at how things are today.

"By the way," Nakao says. "Do you want my storyboard script? Once shooting is done, you can have it."

The storyboard script is the most secretive document of the film shoot. Each one is numbered and has the name of the staff on the cover. It's unlike the actual script, of which 900 or so were printed.

"Coming from you," I tell him, "it'll be my most prized keepsake from the production."

13 JULY 2001

Before stepping into S9, I stop by the big pool where a full-scale street of demolished buildings is under construction. Facades, the building interiors are just support beams. Men wearing heavy-duty filter masks spray polyurethane around the base of the buildings. Great, more noxious fumes, I think, and head for S9.

The scene up this morning is Mothra flying past Godzilla. Regrettably, the Mothra animatronic isn't playing nice. It's motors keep getting hung up, sending the legs into wild spasms; it would be funny if the schedule weren't so far behind. Watching Mothra glide over Godzilla only to see it flip out in mid-flight makes one realize how much more manageable it is to have a human in a suit.

Kaneko and his team are in S3 shooting the live-action scene with suit actors Akira Ohashi and Rie Ota. Set in an office near a dock, Godzilla's roar is to cause the office windows to blow inward, spraying the actors with (fake) glass. To accomplish this, the office has been fit with four breakaway candy glass panels; aimed at each window is a cylinder of compressed air.

The scene is called to action. The actors move near the windows. At that instant, the windows shatter, showering them with glass. Unfortunately, not all the panels broke. The set is cleaned and the panes are replaced. It's reshot. Again, not all panes break. In total, the scene is filmed four times; each take is no good due to one or two panels not breaking. The shoot ends when all the spare window panels have been used up.

"We're going to have to do this again another day," Kaneko laments.

After dinner, the model of the missile launcher is carried into S9. While one could describe it as "mecha" (a term to describe fantastic machinery in kaiju movies), it's difficult to call it such because it's not fantastic enough. True mecha shoot electric beams or have "fire mirrors," weapons not found in real life. Supervising the shot is Isao. He has the art staff place it in front of a blue screen.

It's filmed several times with the launcher cannon turning and raising up.

The night's final shot is Godzilla falling sideways into a building. At around 9:30 p.m., Chika, Nakao, and I stake out spots beside the film camera. It's just the three of us shooting stills tonight. Chika is cool because she isn't a hog for the best spot and doesn't raise her elbows sideways when shooting like some of the other still photographers. Nakao is cool because, frankly, as this is his last production, he doesn't seem that concerned and is easy going to a fault.

As we wait for the staff to prepare both the set and the Godzilla suit, the three of us share camera settings and just goof around. The staff, too, is in a playful mood. Sometimes at night, like now, when the studio quiets down and the shot at hand isn't too demanding, a calm settles in. People are working, of course, but the pace is leisurely and the pressure nonexistent.

I spot Kamiya up on stage. He's quietly piling rubble along the edges of a building. I've noticed this being done on several of the shots where buildings are razed. Isao explained the why of this several days ago: Buildings that explode or get trampled on are in reality hollow. To compensate for a lack of innards, rock and plaster are laid along spots out of camera view. When explosives are detonated, these bits fly out, making the buildings appear to have meat.

Feeling playful, I call out to Kamiya. "Glad to see you're giving it your best effort." Nakao and Chika laugh at my audacity. Suddenly, a staffer across the way bumps into a film light, causing it to point right into my face, blinding me. "*Ah*, now you have your staff enacting revenge, do you?" Kamiya lets out a booming laugh.

The playfulness of the evening gets me thinking about how bizarre this situation is. Here I am, in a far-off land, sitting with its natives in a movie studio about to film a rubber-made, reptile-like creature falling against a human-sized skyscraper wired to explode. "*Swish! Bang! Blam! Boom! Kerpow!*" I'm knocked back to reality when Kamiya starts directing Yoshida with his collection of action sounds. *Man*, I never want this evening to end!

Later, as I'm leaving, Kamiya asks if I'll be coming tomorrow. I think it's the first time he's expressed an interest in my being on set.

14 JULY 2001

I'm in the PR office, listening in as Kaneko gives a couple of short interviews. To pass the time, I flip through some of the Toho monthly information mags. Once Kaneko is done, it's my turn to gather comments for his homepage. After this, we get coffee.

"What do you think of the production so far?" he asks when we find a quiet corner in the cafeteria. Although I don't feel it's my place to start giving loudmouthed, clueless advice, I manage to come up with a couple of positive remarks. However, the only thing I say that could be thought of as critical is a mention to tone down some of the hammier acting, the kind Japanese films are often bashed for in the west.

"I liked Sano's performance, but I worry it might be a little over the top," he admits. "I'm also worried about Uzaki. He might be coming across as stiff."

Listening to Kaneko open up, it strikes me as the sort of thing every director must worry about during any production. While some directors famously come across as abusive dictators, Kaneko is more the statesman faced with difficult decisions, concerned his choices will be the correct ones for his citizens.

Kaneko shares the bad news that he cut a dozen shots from the SFX schedule. "I respect Kamiya's commitment to quality," he says, "but the film has to come in on schedule. There's no way around it."

Lightening things up, Kaneko apologizes for the day at the office. "I understand how you felt when Saito took your place at the desk. I didn't want to use him, but moving extras around is the responsibility of the ADs, and Shimizu placed him in the shot. I wanted to say something but I couldn't make a scene. I'm truly sorry… And, by all means, keep complaining about Saito! It's hysterical!"

This afternoon in S3, the Mothra and Ghidorah suits are slated to be photographed for publicity material. Mothra is up first. The Vi-shop staff has the animatronic hung from the ceiling when I arrive with Nakao and the other photographers. Rather than a Nikon, Nakao uses a large Mamiya camera. "These shots are for the movie poster. The designers need the highest quality photos I can give them," he explains.

I watch Nakao closely: How he angles the camera to get Mothra's head and body balanced just right in the frame. "Kaiju are like people," he notes. "You must find their best angle."

Without warning, the mechanics in Mothra go haywire, causing the legs and head to wiggle wildly. It's kind of gross—this large cockroach-like moth hanging in midair going through what look to be death throes. After Mothra is brought under control and photographed, Shinada wheels in Ghidorah. We do the same thing for this suit.

Back in S9, the art staff is prepping a miniature building for destruction. They furiously cut break lines throughout its insides and stack small bits of plaster in out of the way spots. It's then turned over to the pyro staff, who tape explosives throughout the building.

During setup, a staffer in the rafters drops something. Hitting the floor, it sends a loud bang throughout S9. This is followed an English "Shit!" Kamiya tilts his head upward. "Is Norman up there?" Everyone laughs. I guess I do curse a lot…

At 5:30, the building is ready for destruction. None of the still cameramen are here, giving me more freedom than usual. Yet, no matter where I stand, it doesn't look right through my lens. The only halfway good spot is next to the movie camera, which is encased in a large wooden box with a square hole in the front for the lens. I snuggle up next to it.

"That might not be the best place to sit," camera assistant Itakura says diplomatically.

"When it blows, it's going to shoot straight out," Isao warns.

"I think you're all being overly cautious, but thanks for the concern," I say. "By the way, should a piece of building kill me, be sure to tell my mom I love her." Murakawa snickers from the camera box at my comment.

Kamiya calls for action. The *shamisen* operator detonates the charges in the building. In a series of high-pitched bangs, the face of the building sail outward. Pieces of building shrapnel pound the wood box protecting the camera. As the daredevil I imagine myself to be, I'm entirely pleased to come out from the blast unscathed. That is until I look at my camera. Something hit its wide-angle converter leaving behind a deep nick.

148

"It's not like you weren't warned," an unsympathetic Isao says as he and the other art staffers begin the job of picking up the mess.

15 JULY 2001

Kaneko and staff are in S1 filming soldiers in front of a gigantic blue screen. Necessary but dull to watch. After losing interest, I wander over to S2, where the Aizu set rests under minimal studio lighting. With no one here, it's quiet as a tomb, a big switch from the insanity of three days ago. Moments like this, where I can walk unimpeded and study set details that the camera only skims over, are some of my favorites. One thing I've grown to love is the smell of S1 and S2. Both stages are nearing 70 years of age and give off an odor similar to that of aged cedar. For fun, I set my camera on a table and take candid shots of myself acting the part of the Aizu crew.

Once the blue screen stuff is complete, I meet Kaneko in his production room. Right away, he starts bitching about a backache. I call him an old lady. Matsumoto is here too and, glancing my way, simply says, "George Pal." It's his way of instigating a discussion on the influential sci-fi producer. Matsumoto says he's on a quest to find an early film of his called *Puppetoons*.

Aida interrupts to ask if I'm willing to do more English label writing. He says there's going to be a close-up of a military drill missile and that they want the English to be correct.

"What do you want me to write?" I ask.

"Anything you like," he says. "Just make it look like something you'd see on a missile and give it to me tomorrow." That's welcome. "Tomorrow" is better than "now."

There's a small scene set for tonight with actresses Ai and Aki Maeda putting in cameos. They'll pay homage to The Peanuts, the sister singing duo who played the tiny Shobijin in *Mothra*, *Mothra vs. Godzilla*, and *Ghidorah, the Three-Headed Monster*.

Piling into location buses, the live-action staff heads to Hachioji, a city on Tokyo's western outskirts. After arriving, I locate Kaneko's bus[15] and find him sitting alone with a Pearl Buck novel. I climb into the seat next to him and start talking about old books. Fans of pre-Soviet Russian literature, we chat about *Peasants* by Anton Chekhov.

After a few minutes, we step out to join the production. "This is weird," Kaneko says looking around. "Where do you think everyone went?"

"Beats me." I point a finger down a shop-lined road. "That's the way to the station. Let's try there."

The correct choice, we find the crew amid set up. They're transforming the local *shotengai* (shopping street) to look like Kagoshima, a city on the island of Kyushu. Banners and posters are hung with words like *Kagoshima* and *Sakurajima* printed on them.

The actresses arrive dressed in matching white outfits and come over to greet Kaneko. I haven't seen Ai since the Gamera set. I remember how much she wanted to learn English.

"So, can you speak English now?" I ask teasingly in English.

15 - The department heads (director, DP, lighting chief, chief AD, etc.) usually travel together in a small van-like vehicle called a Hi-Ace.

"Sure can!" Ai replies without missing a beat.

Whoa! Two years ago, she couldn't put two English words together, now she sounds like a native speaker. "What happened?" I ask disbelievingly.

"I took time off from acting and went to Canada to study," she explains.

"I don't know who taught you," I add, "but they should give him or her an award for excellence in teaching."

Ai introduces me to her sister Aki, whom I recognize from the film *Battle Royale* (*Batoru Rowaiaru*, 2000). "She doesn't speak English, so don't even try," Ai kids. Aki lowers her head and apologizes.

In the center of the *shotengai*, Kishimoto and his crew have set up a large camera crane. With Kaneko in the seat beside him, they ride high into the air. This attracts the attention of passersby, and people gawk and gather around. Some ask the crew for the name of the production. Despite the inquiries, no one is saying "Godzilla." I'm surprised. In New York, crews always share a film's title with onlookers no matter how big the production. It's considered word-of-mouth advertising.

Godzilla actor Yoshida is here putting in a cameo. Kaneko places him and Murakami's wife behind the Maeda sisters. Just before shooting, I take the time to introduce them to Yoshida. "Ladies, allow me to introduce you to… *Godzilla!*" They're delighted to meet the man behind the kaiju. Embarrassed, Yoshida bows relentlessly.

To reproduce the strong wind whipped up by Mothra flying overhead, a large wind machine is turned on the area. The staff throws pieces of paper and leaflets in front of the fan. They fly and whip around the actors and extras. The first shot is going well until a brochure slaps onto the camera lens and sticks, ruining the shot.

A few takes later, Kaneko calls it a wrap. The staff passes out crew t-shirts to the extras, their pay for joining the scene. Some of them get Kaneko and Yoshida to sign them. A group of fans asks if I'm the Norman from Toho website's "Norman Report."

"We think that instead of writing every two weeks, you should write a new report every day," one of them says. I tell them I'd have a nervous breakdown if I had to write that much.

Ai and Aki come over to say farewell. Honestly, Ai's English ability is impressive. While it's easiest to learn a language when young, her progress in two years is still remarkable and shows a sharp mind.

"See you next kaiju," I say as they turn to go. Ai laughs.

"Yeah," she replies. "See you next kaiju!" Aki tugs her arm and asks her to translate. I hear her snickering as they make their way to the makeup trailer.

A few of us hit a local *izakaya* for beer and food. After a toast, we set into the usual chitchat. I learn that Yoshida is also an illustrator and has worked for VFX director Matsumoto; in addition to playing the film's title character, he did rotoscoping for the movie *Zeiram* (*Zeiramu*, 1991). Murakami's wife, a member of the Japanese self-defense force, shares how she met her future husband on the set of *Gamera 2*. Her English is nearly flawless; she says she also speaks Korean.

At 11, we call it a night. Jiro drives Kaneko and me home to Setagaya. I enjoy hanging out with the Kaneko brothers. Of the two, Jiro is more emotional and vocal, whereas Kaneko is more logical and cautious. We talk about the production and how, despite the pressure, wish it would never end.

18 JULY 2001

This is unexpected. I'm in the cafeteria having lunch when out of the blue Kamiya sits with me. He asks if I like what I'm seeing on the set. I offer a few comments, all positive, and then ask how close the rushes will be to the final film. He says they need color correcting and other enhancements, adding that they won't look as crisp as they do now.

Kamiya went to see *Pearl Harbor* and I think this is his motivation to sit with me. He's curious to hear WWII irk points Americans have with Japanese. Instead, I tell him that I personally don't give a crap about war; that I believe my living in the nation that was once the bitter enemy of my home country is a testament to the futility of war. Kamiya shakes his head up and down as he absorbs what I've said. I add that my anti-war opinion is probably a bit extreme. When it comes to Americans, the answer you get depends on who you ask because America—being as diverse as it is—is home to just about every opinion possible. Just then, Matsumoto interrupts us.

"I have been fired by Tomiyama," he announces. We look at him dumbfounded until realizing he's pulling our leg.

"What about me?" asks Kamiya. "Can I be fired too?"

Today's main SFX shot is incoming missiles hitting Godzilla as he stands at the end of a rubble-filled street. First, several platforms are pushed together and laid end-to-end to form a rectangle. The camera is placed on a crane opposite Godzilla. The plan is to have the camera track toward Godzilla as missiles (to be added in post-pro) zoom down the street.

The art staff hauls over prefab buildings. They arrange them on the sides of the platforms, leaving space for a road in the center. As they do, an art staffer draws street lines directly onto the top of the platforms. I think there's no way this will look convincing. Peeking through the camera lens proves me wrong.

Masuda comes over in a panic begging me not to mention to Saito about the Maeda sisters or show him any photos from the day in Hachioji. He admits to not wanting Saito to come and now doesn't want to listen to him complain about not being invited.

In any case, Saito is up to his usual crap, going around showing staffers his shitty photos and boring them with unemotional film facts. Director Tomoo Haraguchi made a surprise visit to the set today. It might sound petty, but I was pleased when Haraguchi came over to Nakao's station to say goodbye to me and ignored Saito.

A group of day-tripper reporters have come to watch. I go to the toilet and on my return find one of them has taken my spot on the ladder I'd set up across from Nakao's position (we'd staked out spots on opposite sides of the set: he on the left, me on the right, with the film camera between us). Mercilessly, I order the reporter to vacate my spot.

After he climbs down, Nakao turns to me. "That's the spirit!" he says from his ladder perch.

The afternoon's first take is a back shot of Godzilla walking down the road with the city aflame before him. Several Styrofoam buildings have fire pots hidden within; others have been dabbed with a chemical that releases thick streams of deep black smoke. The camera tracks behind the Godzilla-suited Yoshida as he pounds across the roadway.

While the scene unfolds, S9 fills with toxic fumes. *Hmm…Maybe I should wear a mask,* I think. *Screw it!* If I'm to die, let it be from Godzilla! Who wouldn't love their tombstone to read "Killed by Godzilla"?

The last shot is Godzilla in the open space at the street's end. Behind Godzilla, the sky is a deep orange, with the surrounding buildings ablaze with flame. All at once, charges on the suit blast outward. Hot white sparks zip about as a cloud of gray smoke envelopes the kaiju king.

Cut called, Kamiya squats before his monitor to review the shot. I pray he calls for a retake. Not only do I want another chance at shooting it, I also just want to watch it again. It's spectacular and one of the best shots to date. And this ladder makes for the perfect box seat.

"Once more!" Kamiya yells out.

Hell yeah! Nakao, who's been watching me, starts to chuckle. He knows exactly what's going on in my mind!

It takes over thirty minutes to reset. Once again: *Bam! Bam! Bam!* Explosions rip across Godzilla. I'm back in hog heaven! Kamiya checks playback. *Please, dear god…*

"Once more!" he yells.

Godzilla is re-rigged and filmed again.

This time it's a keeper. One thing about it that strikes me as odd, however. As one of the most iconic shots of the GMK shoot so far, why are Nakao and me the only still camera guys on hand? Even the day-trippers left hours ago.

At 4:30 p.m., the live-action crew, back from location, filters into the space around the pool. Earlier in the day, the final additions to the Yokohama rubble set were put in place. The area has been transformed into a convincing-looking section of a city following a kaiju attack. In total, there are three demolished buildings, several wrecked cars, and a couple of crushed lampposts, not to mention a mountain's worth of debris and, as a final touch, a fire hydrant that spews water high in the air.

Tonight, too, is the night I'm to do my "official" interview with Chiharu. I proudly show my question list to Masuda.

"What the hell? You have thirty-two questions! You gotta cut it down."

Maybe he's right. I circle the five I like best and he gives me the thumbs up.

Chiharu gets to the set around 8 p.m. She has on her mustard shirt and white pants as well as that bandage around her head. Smudged over with dirt, she's looking disheveled. That's just her character; the real Chiharu is bursting with energy and smiling in the way you'd expect someone would after winning the lottery.

With the set ready, Shusuke walks Chiharu through the scene. In her hand is a compact video camera. The first shot is up. Chiharu stumbles about the burning, smoking set. Kaneko calls cut and gives it his okay.

In between shots, Chiharu turns the video camera on herself and talks directly into the lens. She's even got the side monitor flipped so she can see herself. Catching me snickering at her narcissistic moment, she turns bright red.

Between setups, Chiharu and I sit on a side bench for our interview. Just as I'm to ask my first question, she breaks into her recently on-going routine of fake English. The funny thing is, while nonsensical, it actually does sound like English. Slightly annoyed, I ask her to cut it out, which sets off her adorable cackling laugh.

Once that's out of the way, Chiharu proves to be a great interview. She's one of those actors that can take a question and run with it. In fact, she answers a lot of things I had on my original list. Unfortunately, AD Shimizu steals her away for a shot every five minutes or so. It's fun to see her go from reporter-struggling-with-army-soldiers to bubbly-actress-answering-real-reporter's questions.

In the end, I get a half-hour in with her. Best of all, Masuda looks happy, Chiharu's manager looks happy, and most importantly, Chiharu looks happy. Chiharu even thanks me for asking such interesting questions. Then she turns the tables and asks me something.

"So, when are you going to teach me English?" I'm not exactly sure why, but we both break up laughing.

During the shoot, Kono, Chiharu's manager, asks me to speak English with her. At first I feel it's a lost cause, then I recall Ai Maeda's incredible transformation. So, I try saying things like, "Chiharu, what do you think of this photo?" as I face my camera's back screen to her. Most of the time, Kono has to whisper replies in her ear.

"It...looks... *Yeah!*" she says before giving me a thumbs up.

Later, producer Tomiyama comes up to me. "I just want to say I find it nice to hear you speaking English with the staff and cast," he remarks. I ask why. "It reminds me that Godzilla has international appeal and is not strictly for the domestic market. Your being here helps the crew understand this too." It's kind of him to say this, and I'm rather touched by it.

The shoot will go late, but I have to leave because of the accursed last train. Jiro has his scooter and offers to ride me to the station. I check the timetable and see that the final train leaves at 12:12 a.m. I plan things down to the minute.

Just before midnight, I zip into S9 to gather my things. Jiro and I are surprised to find it completely empty of staff. Thinking it wouldn't be me if I didn't take advantage of the situation, I run around S9 flapping my arms squawking, "Check me out! I'm Rodan!"

19 JULY 2001

Today's first shot is the Satsuma sub miniature in the Aizu battleship hangar. I'm trying to get a photo but the lighting department has set so many black screens to keep flares off the camera lens that it's impossible to get a clear shot.

During the setup, Kamiya and Matsumoto start banging on their bellies like kettledrums. I try to join in, but I'm too thin. "Sorry guys, you're on your own," I say. "I'm just too ripped."

To that, Junko lets out a loud snort in disagreement.

Ghidorah popping up from behind several buildings is readied. When it's about to go before the camera, I look for Nakao. He's not on set. Rushing to his station to alert him, I find him behind the morning paper.

"*That*?" he says. "No reason to photograph it."

I dash back and do my best to find an angle, but nothing looks good. *Screw it!* I plop myself on the floor in front of the set, point my camera up at the buildings, and snap away as Ghidorah's three heads wave about.

"Show me," Nakao says after I return to his desk. He smirks as he hands back my camera. Yeah, they're less than stunning.

Just then, Isao comes over. "Norman, you look bored. Give me a hand." He doesn't even wait for my response.

I follow Isao to the front of the art department, where large boxes hammered together out of plywood are lined up across several platform tops. Painted black, they're laid out to form a cityscape, one reminiscent of the end credits in the '60s *Batman* TV show. Isao has been sawing window squares into them all morning.

"See those colored gels?" He points to a pile on a nearby table. "Cut squares out and tape them over the windows from the back. You Americans can do something as simple as that, right?" Isao's sarcasm aside, yeah, I guess I can do menial work like this.

"What's it for?" I ask.

"We're doing shots of Ghidorah and Godzilla in the pool tomorrow night. We'll put this along the back of the pool as a stand-in for Yokohama."

After a few hours, I reach my window-taping limit and step outside for a break to see what the SFX crew is up to. I find Murakawa on a crane over the pool working out the logistics of a POV of Godzilla. The shot itself is unremarkable;

what is remarkable, is seeing him and the staff against the set of crushed buildings used by the Kaneko crew the other night. Even though they've finished with it, the set has to stand until the rushes come in. Once the crew verifies no re-shoots are needed, it can be dismantled.

Isao has designated a run of the Yokohama backdrop buildings "the Norman section." I work to make it as colorful as possible. As I do, Kamiya passes by. He lets out a snicker. "So, you're finally doing something useful!" he says.

"Mr. Director," I begin with feigned respect. "It may seem like basic grunt work, but far from it. Before any gel can be taped in place, I must ask myself, 'Who is in this room?' 'What is happening in it?' For example, take this one." I point to a yellow gel covered window. "What we have here is your basic family unit sitting down for an evening meal. And this white one over here, it's a high school student studying for his finals."

Kamiya points to a room with pink over the hole. "And this one?"

"Oh, that," I reply. "They're shooting a porn film in there." Kamiya and Isao break into laughter.

I decide to go home when dinner is called. I say good night to Junko.

She looks at me with wide, disbelieving eyes. "What? We're just getting started! I'd better see you here tomorrow at 9 a.m. sharp!"

Bowing, I promise to not be a minute late.

20 JULY 2001

Well, I get to S9 at 9:10 a.m. to find Junko arms folded, glasses on the tip of her nose, looking very much like a fearsome British schoolmarm.

"*Uh*, my alarm didn't go off," I begin. "And, you see, I had to rescue puppies from a burning *izakaya* on the way over." For some reason it doesn't look like she's buying my excuses.

"Isao is looking for you," she says and points over to the art department.

Sure enough, Isao puts me back to work covering the seemingly endless amount of windows on the backdrop.

After lunch, I relax with Nakao. A couple of his friends have dropped by, but they look more like an otaku clan than actual friends. They've come armed with cameras and have descended on a Godzilla suit hanging in a brace a few meters off. Roll after roll, they snap shots of the suit from every imaginable angle. One guy has a detachable flash that he holds out with one hand while shooting photos with the other. After a few minutes, they're sweating heavily. Catching my eye, Nakao just shrugs.

The crew works in front of the pool. They've erected two large blue screens: One covers a platform with the other acting as a back curtain. Placed in the center of the blueness is the large miniature of the Aizu battleship.

Housed atop a crane in a futuristic-looking, multi-directional swivel mount, the camera swings around the ship. Murakawa is operating it by a remote control unit, which seems to be giving him a difficult time. The first few sweeps are no good; in fact, they're so bad they have everyone laughing during playback. Going for another take, Kamiya makes full use of his sound effects arsenal, producing weird whooshing sounds, while Murakawa struggles to maneuver the camera over the model.

Back in the oasis-like cool of S9, I open my computer to work on emails. One of the still cameramen (the pros, not Nakao's otaku buddies) catches sight of my new wallpaper: a shot of Godzilla roaring at the camera from the street scene two days ago.

"What the hell is *that*?" The other cameramen gather around.

"I'm not sure why, but all you guys took off that day," I say. "Pretty cool, no?"

Actually, they don't think it's cool. There must have been miscommunication between them and Toho because they're livid over having missed such a spectacular photo-op. I offer to share my shots but they won't hear of it. They tell me that this isn't the point. In a huff, they storm over to the PR room.

Kaneko stops by S9. Grabbing me, we walk around the set. "You should come to live-action tomorrow," he says. "But I've some bad news." What now, I think, bracing myself. "It's... The thing is… Well...Saito is coming!" Kaneko starts chuckling. *God*, I don't know who's enjoying the developing feud more, Kaneko or Nakao.

I get back to Nakao's station and, lo and behold, Saito is there. "I'll be going to the Chiba location tomorrow," he boasts. "It's going to be Uzaki's final day and the ending scene of the film. Will you go too?"

I flip my wrist up and look at it like I wear a watch, which I don't. "If I have the time," I say, and give Nakao a wink.

"By the way," Saito adds. "Do you know anything about the shoot with the Maeda sisters the other day?"

It's 7:30 and I'm standing next to the pool. A tall black crane stands over the water. From its top, wires are lowered and latched to the Ghidorah suit. Off to the side, Yoshida is preparing to enter

Godzilla. Looking like an Olympic swimmer, he wears swimming goggles and a nose clip.

The cityscape boxes I helped with were brought out earlier in the day. They're lined up between the pool and the back wall. Pyrotechnic guys start placing smoke pots behind them that when ignited will give the effect of a smoldering Yokohama off in the distance.

As the crew prepares Godzilla and Ghidorah, several staffers are curious where the "Norman section" is. For the life of me, I can't pick it out. "Whatever section you think looks coolest!" I brag.

Kamiya is in discussion with Yoshida and Ohashi about the upcoming scene. As he's prone to do, he directs via wild noises to describe their upcoming fight: *whoosh, swish, ka-thoom!*

Although it's hard to put a finger on, there's something otherworldly in the air this evening. First, the sun has just set behind S10, and the hue of the cloudless sky is a gradually deepening blue. There's also no breeze—the air is unnaturally still. Sounds far off seem amplified. A few of the art staff scoop leaves and other debris from the pool's surface. I can hear their scoopers drag through the water as if they were beside me. Reflecting off the pool's waters, the lights of the Yokohama boxes cast long, colorful ripples. Serendipitously, someone begins to whistle the theme to *Close Encounters of the Third Kind.*

Ohashi, locked in Ghidorah, is hoisted into the air. He dangles over the pool as crewmembers guide him along by the feet of the suit. With the monsters' positions decided, lighting director Saito and his crew start focusing gels on the kaiju. A bright, greenish light is aimed at Godzilla's fins, while a yellowish one is shone on Ghidorah to emphasize its golden hue.

Soon, Kamiya deems the set-up ready. He screams for action. Ghidorah is released. He swings over to Godzilla, smacking him in the open mouth. Over and over, Ghidorah is rocked back and forth, bumping his groin awkwardly into Godzilla until Kamiya yells for cut.

The shot is reviewed. Kamiya's not completely satisfied but feels it can be worked out in the edit.

Hearing this, Matsumoto moans. "You mean it's up to me to make it right?" He puts his hands on his head to overstate his worry.

Next, the Ghidorah suit is wired with at least a dozen black squibs. Once again, Ghidorah sails toward Godzilla, wings flapping via several wire pullers. Godzilla opens his mouth (atomic breath to be added in post). A loud bang rings out and Ghidorah lights up like a supernova. Gold scales rain down on the area. The explosion was bright to the point that I'm seeing spots in front of my eyes.

21 JULY 2001

I'm in Makuhari, a town in Chiba the production is using as a stand-in for Yokohama. Today is the film's finale, where actors Chiharu and Kobayashi come running up to meet Uzaki after defeating Godzilla.

First off, it's blistering hot out. Kaneko has on a baseball cap and a bandanna hanging under it to protect his neck. Following suit, I borrow a towel from Izumi and drape it over my head and shoulders. It'll be a miracle if I get out of this without a sunburn.

Chiharu is at supernova energy level,

with the brunt of it focused on Kaneko in failed attempts to make him smile. At best, she's getting shy side-glances out of him. As I watch her work him over, I notice a cell phone on the ground. It seems to not belong to anyone on the crew.

"Maybe it's a cheap way for you to call your mom in America," Uzaki kids. He motions for the phone and calls a number on it. Someone answers and, by luck, is with the owner. In no time, a woman comes running over. She's dumbfounded at the sight of Uzaki in a military suit handing her phone over. He salutes her as she leaves.

Today's scene is on a long stretch of pavement running beside a concrete wall; on the other side is the sea. A crane is set up for a shot of Chiharu and Kobayashi running to meet Uzaki. It's crucial they stop in a specific spot, and Murakami stains the ground with oil to use as a mark. Once the shot is complete, the crew moves in for close-ups.

For the reaction shots of Chiharu saluting Uzaki, I crouch next to still cameraman Kudo to take photos. As tears run down her face, I realize it's my first time to see an actor cry on cue.

Kaneko calls cut, and we gather around his monitor. The scene looks great; Kaneko is satisfied. With that, Chiharu is back bubbling over every little thing around her. Her ability to go from one extreme to the next is cute but baffling.

Uzaki calls me over. "Didn't you want to interview me today?" We walk over to a nearby lot where he has his Benz parked. "Try to make this long," he says. "I don't want to go back into the heat."

"Acting in GMK has been a great experience," Uzaki reveals as he gets the A/C blasting. "I've worked with many

directors. Kaneko is... How can I put it? He's delicate and a bit scholarly."

In contrast to how Shinobu Nakayama described him during our interview in Kyoto, Uzaki paints a different picture.

"His direction is quite detailed. I don't mean to say he's a 'do this and this and this' type of a director. Instead, he'll tell you what he wants you to focus on. He's excellent at conveying his ideas and the emotion he wants to see. There's never been a moment where I couldn't understand what he was after."

Uzaki reveals some difficulty he experienced during shooting. "I had to make a speech in front of military students about Godzilla. It was my longest line in the film. From the moment I got the script, I practiced it every day. Unluckily, it was scheduled for the first day and had to be delivered in front of fifty young extras. I was terrified whether I could do it or not. I don't mean just getting the line out, but also coming across like a military man with decades of experience. I was relieved when Kaneko called the take okay!"

After chatting for the better part of a half-hour, we rejoin the crew. It's time for the staff/cast memorial photo. This is something all productions in Japan do: Near the end of a shoot, everyone gathers and stands behind a signboard inscribed with the production's title, the director's name with the Team (*gumi*) suffix added, and the day's date. The upper staff sits in the front row, with the director in the center flanked by the actors. As the crew arrange themselves, I get up on a knoll where Kudo is readying his camera.

"I wish I could be in the shot," Saito mumbles as he pulls out his pocket camera.

"It's a production-only thing," I remind him. No sooner have I said this than I hear my name called. It's Chiharu. She has a huge smile on her face and is waving.

"Get over here!" she shouts. Everyone on the crew goes silent and looks at the two of us.

"I'd love to," I yell over, "but it's up to the director."

Chiharu turns to Kaneko. With both hands, she pumps up and down on his arm. "*Come on! Come on!*" she pleads.

Slowly, a smile cuts across Kaneko's face. "*Oh*, get over here," he says.

Chiharu's face is beaming as I skip down to join them. She hops from her seat and points to a spot behind her. As I move through the crew, they smile and pat me on the back, doing their best to make me feel welcome. But I'm overcome with worry. My head's been wrapped in a towel all day. My hair must be a total mess!

"Chiharu," I ask, "how's my hair?"

She looks me over, squinting as she assesses the damage. All of a sudden, she's running her fingers through my hair, straightening it out and patting it down. As she does, I can't help but feel this may be a contender for my best moment on any Godzilla set.

After Kudo shoots off a bunch of photos, we disperse. Kaneko comes up to me. "Now you're a part of Team Kaneko."

"And it's a good place to be," I add in response.

22 JULY 2001

My friend Michio has come to visit. As one of my more dependable Osaka pals, I'm taking him to the Godzilla set to thank him for his years of friendship. Walking together down the tree-lined street to Toho, he's more excited than I've ever seen. It'll be fun watching him try to make sense of the insanity of S9.

The first shot is a dynamic one of Mothra stuck on Godzilla's back and flapping its wings before being hurled away. Once done, Mothra is maneuvered over the set; it comes to a halt directly above us. Without warning, the insect kaiju begins to descend. It's so magnificent looking that we can only stare dumbfounded.

"You two!" a staffer yells over. "Move your asses!" Embarrassed, we jump out of the way.

Mothra is lowered to a position a half-meter off the floor. There, men from the suit staff gather around and start working on its internal mechanisms.

I introduce Michio to Nakao. He's awestruck to meet the master photographer. Moreover, I'm happy because Michio engages Nakao in thoughtful conversation, asking about his choice of cameras and other specifics that have helped define his work. You know, the kind of stuff that doesn't make you come off like a slobbering fanboy.

Before we head back to the set, Nakao makes a wry smile. "By the way, I saw your 'lover' yesterday." (This is his new term to tease me about my poor relationship with Saito.) "He couldn't stop complaining about how you got into the staff photo."

Being a Sunday, the set atmosphere is more relaxed than usual, which gives me the chance to kid around with Kamiya. I point to the ECC and NOVA English school signs atop some miniatures.

"Do me a favor," I request. "Could you have Godzilla smash those? They give us foreigners a bad name." Kamiya roars with laughter.

One sign reads "Drug Higuchi." I ask if it's a reference to Shinji Higuchi, the SFX director on the Gamera series.

"Come on, Norman," Kamiya says. "How long have you been in Japan? Drug Higuchi stores are all over Tokyo!" Of course he's right. I only asked because several miniatures make reference to staff and friends of staff. With that, Kamiya rattles off a few from films he's worked on. One mentioned is "Kawakita Loans," a nod to SFX director Koichi Kawakita.

"Yeah, and it went bankrupt," cuts in Junko.

"Thunder!" Kamiya screams. Thunder, who's been busy adding detail to the upcoming shot, pops his head from between two buildings. "Make me a sign that says, 'Norman's School of English!'" Thunder looks at him like he's nuts.

I introduce Michio to Godzilla suit actor Yoshida, and the two spend a half-hour talking at Nakao's station. After learning from their chat that Yoshida studied both Judo and Karate, I ask if he's able to break blocks of ice with his forehead, which causes him to roar with laughter. Ghidorah actor Ohashi joins us and before heading back to the set, I get them to pose for a photo together.

Just when I'm to snap it, Yoshida makes a goofy face. "Ohashi," he says, "from now on, whenever Norman takes our photo, let's make funny faces." I beg them not to but if this photo is any indication, I'm going to have my work cut out getting those all-important "tough suit actor at work" shots.

The art staff has spent the morning prepping a foreground of two buildings that have collapsed away from each other, creating a kind of V shape through which Godzilla and Ghidorah will be seen grappling. Complete with bicycles, a crushed car, telephone poles, vending machines, and other items, the detail is exhausting.

Just before Kamiya yells for action, the pyrotechnic crew dab chemicals in select spots in the foreground. This produces lines of smoke that rise off the miniatures. Near the rear of the set, burning pots are placed out of camera view. The scene is up and the two monsters struggle against each other. Before Kamiya can call cut, however, Ohashi slips from the stage and falls to the floor, causing one of Ghidorah's heads to rip clean off. Shinada and his crew are quick to reattach it.

I decide to skip out on the final shot to have dinner with Michio before he leaves for Osaka on the last Shinkansen.

"Norman, where are you going?" Junko asks after I thank Kamiya for letting me bring a friend to the set. I explain, but she won't accept it.

"Can't you two eat here?" she asks. The sentiment is nice, but the truth is, I'm near collapsing. I hardly slept last night and taking care of my friend has left me feeling beat. Ducking out, we get dinner near the station.

Michio can't thank me enough. He rattles on about Mothra, seeing Godzilla in action with Ghidorah, and his talks with Nakao, Yoshida, and Ohashi. However, one thing puzzles him.

"Is everyone always that laidback? It's like you guys were making non-stop jokes."

"It might seem so," I admit, "but the staff is under intense pressure to deliver the goods. When the crew can afford to, they kid around to balance it out. There are plenty of days where it's so serious you can cut the air with a hatchet. Luckily, today wasn't one of those."

25 JULY 2001

Outside, Isao sets the large model of the missile launcher on a table next to the S9 entrance. After setting whiteboards to lighten the shadows around the wheels, Nakao leads us photographers in a photoshoot. Forming a semi-circle, we snap away, shifting and sharing positions from time to time. Off to the side and leaning against the doors of S9, a bored looking Isao watches us work. When feeling the time is right, he turns the launcher to a different angle—and we repeat the process all over again.

Photos like this—ones showing every angle imaginable of a piece of hardware—are a staple of books and magazines in Japan. Not just kaiju mecha but gear of any kind and in any genre. Japanese love this sort of minutia. I find it interesting to watch the photographers go at it knowing that in less than six months, the otaku base will obsess over their photos.

In the afternoon, while I'm picking Nakao's brain for photography advice, Kaneko walks by. He's on his way to Shinada's station with questions about Mothra. When he's done, I ask if he'll pose for a photo next to the empty Godzilla suit. He's happy to and even loops an arm through one of Godzilla's. Just then, Kamiya pops by to confer with Shinada. I realize that this is my chance to get the two directors together with Godzilla. I can't say Kamiya is enthused, but complying, he stands beside the suit with Kaneko on the other side.

The photo turns out well; however, on closer inspection, something odd stands out: Whereas Kaneko is all smiles, Kamiya is grimacing. Picking up my computer, I walk over to show Junko. Sure enough, she laughs at Kamiya's expression—a laugh fueled further when I dub it the "Jekyll and Hyde" shot. Curious, Kamiya leans in.

"You've got it wrong," he insists. "I'm not showing defiance at having my photo taken. I'm merely imitating Godzilla's aggressive face."

Junko and I look at each other doubtfully.

The evening SFX shots of Godzilla grappling with all three of Ghidorah's heads are the most interesting of the day. Technically, it's difficult because of the wire works involved to make the heads move convincingly. Since it's an action shot, all the still cameramen are on hand, making getting a good spot tough. Iizuka is having the hardest time of all. Late in securing a location, what's available to him reveals the "seams" of the set.

"If you want, you can have my spot," Kamiya says, noticing his plight.

The cameramen laugh. "*Whoa*! You're making the director move!" one exclaims.

"I've been doing this for forty years, and I've never seen this before." Nakao whispers to me.

It's pouring rain outside and a fierce thunderstorm has erupted above the studio. Each roar of thunder shakes S9 to its foundation. Following every booming crack, the crew responds with *ohs* and *ahs*. As SFXs are shot silent, the shoot isn't affected. Quite frankly, the thunder makes the confrontation between Godzilla and Ghidorah all the more intense!

At the end of the night the large doors to S9 are swung open. A pool of water that had collected out front rushes in like a wave. Well, that's one way to clean the place, I think.

26 JULY 2001

While sitting with Nakao this morning, AD Kikuchi comes over to request that he confer with Kamiya. It seems Kamiya is curious about a setup of Mothra from a Showa era film.

"Don't steal my camera while I'm gone," he kids.

The staff is working on Godzilla biting down on Ghidorah's neck as Mothra flies in from behind. At the last moment, Godzilla is to swing his tail and swat Mothra away. The art department has set up the usual complex maze of buildings in the center of S9. From a standing position, the set looks disjointed and incomplete. Some buildings are flush to the stage while others are propped up on opera boxes. Naturally, it all looks correct through the camera lens.

The first shot is a master of all three monsters. Just before action, the pyrotechnic staff sets fire to pans tucked throughout the city wreckage. From them, thick gray smoke billows into the studio air; several crewmembers frantically wave fans about to even out the smoke. Kamiya screams that "*Aye*"-sounding yell of his, which signals the start of the shot.

As Yoshida struggles against the Ghidorah suit, Mothra comes gliding in from behind. I've got to hand it to the crew. It's awe-inspiring. Like the other still cameramen, I go nuts snapping as many photos as the buffer on my camera can hold while also letting the fan in me enjoy this incredible sight.

Yamabe uses a syringe to apply crimson stage blood to the spots where Godzilla is biting down on Ghidorah's neck. I tell him he needs to pump the blood like there's no tomorrow.

"I want to," he admits. "But Kaneko ordered us to keep the gore to a minimum."

The next shot—Godzilla's tail knocking Mothra away—is more complicated. It's the same free-floating tail used for the hospital destruction. This time it's set on a swivel tucked out of view behind Godzilla. A couple of gentle test swings against Mothra are done before the actual take. Action called, the staffer swings the tail up and hits Mothra on the side, sending her spinning wildly away.

Kaneko and crew are in S8 working with blue screens. The first shots employ stunt doubles of Chiharu and Kobayashi. They're wired and hoisted a good three meters off the floor. The Kobayashi stand-in is positioned to lean over the edge of something. What that is, I can't tell because it's completely wrapped in blue screen. Actually, everything is covered in blue except for the actors! For the take, the two fall with wires catching them before they hit the floor. I ask Kaneko how this'll be used in the film.

"These shots are of their fall off the bridge. Matsumoto here has the pleasure of putting all the elements together and making it look good."

I look at Matsumoto but before I can say or ask a thing, he makes a heavy frown.

"I need more time!" he pleads.

Kishimoto has the camera up on a crane and is pointing it over (the real) Kobayashi and down at (the real) Chiharu. Although the finished film will look as if she's suspended high above Yokohama Bay, in reality, she's a mere inch off a blue screen laid across the studio floor.

Speaking of Chiharu, I think I may

161

have made a poor judgment call in my relationship with her. A few days ago I asked her to pose with the Godzilla suit. She got weird and made a wishy-washy excuse not to. After this, she seemed less friendly toward me. Worried, I share my concern with Kaneko.

"This is what you should have done," he explains. "First, you should have talked to the Toho PR department. If it was okay with them, they would have put in a request with her manager. If he felt it was okay, he would have run it past her to see if it was something she would be interested in."

"I see... Do you think I should apologize to Chiharu?"

"Well, you don't have to but I think she'll be happy if you do."

During a break later on, I come clean and tell Chiharu I'm sorry for breaking protocol. She insists it's okay, but I have to wonder. For one thing, I know Japanese. They'll assure you things are cool even when they aren't. I decide there's not much more I can do and file it under "live and learn."

Up to now, my chat time on the live-action set has been spent mostly talking to either Kaneko or Chiharu. Trying to put some distance between Chiharu and me, I shift my attention to actor Kobayashi. Not like I planned it this way, but after an hour of being chummy with him, Chiharu comes bounding over. She holds out her hands with clenched fists facing down.

"Pick one."

I tap a hand and she turns it over to reveal...

"Want a piece of chocolate?" she asks with a smile.

It's just a single, wrapped piece taken from a large bag at the snack table, but it's meaning is clear. She opens the other hand, which also holds a piece of chocolate, and quickly pops it in her mouth.

"Incidentally," I say, "I printed out some set photos. Take any you like."

With a huge Cheshire Cat smile, she flips through the photo album, sliding out prints that catch her eye, which is nearly all of them! After this, Chiharu shows me her newest *shashinshu*[16].

So, here I am, paging through sexy bathing suit photos of Chiharu with her staring at me and gauging my reaction. Honestly, I can't think of anything to say that won't make me look like a total idiot.

It turns out that today is the final day of live-action shooting, something I wasn't aware of.

"Well, officially," Kaneko clarifies. "We still have pick-up shots to do and I want to re-shoot a few things."

Realizing this might be my last chance, I ask Chiharu and Kobayashi if it would be okay to take a personal photo with the two of them. I give Matsumoto my camera, and he snaps a few shots. Best of all, Chiharu is back to her usual sweet self. She even slips an arm through mine for the photos.

27 JULY 2001

I get to S9 and drop my bags at Nakao's station.

"The set's pretty large today," he says, lowering his morning paper. "It's gonna take a while to get going." I glance through Vi-shop's maze of kaiju suits to see the crew busy dressing the set. "Have you been up to the rafters?"

---

16 - *Shashinshu* are photobooks of actors, nearly always actresses/idols, in various settings: on the town, at the beach, in bed, etc. The level of erotica ranges from the sisterly to the overtly suggestive.

Nakao leads me to the right side of S9, through a door, and up a set of stairs. Resting against the stairwell walls are man-sized miniatures of construction cranes, the white and red kind you see around Japanese piers. After reaching the top, Nakao opens a door. The smell of dust and mildew is immediate.

While I've been to the rafters of other stages, the wooden maze above S9 is by far the biggest and most complex. It's also the highest off the ground. An extensive catwalk the length and width of S9, it's suspended from the ceiling by thick ropes, which, while sturdy looking, are dripping with the build up of oily brown gunk. Nakao waves a hand, a signal for me to make myself at home.

"I'll be at my desk. Shout down if you get lost," he says before shutting the door.

I walk onto the plankway carefully. The studio floor is at least five meters below. Nakao told me that staffers have fallen to their death; I've no desire to learn if this is true or not. However, the view is incredible, and offers a unique perspective of S9. From here, looking straight down on the set, it's easy to see the layers of forced perception: A line of distant buildings, a second line of nearer buildings at a slightly larger scale, and finally, the stage itself, which is to scale with the monster suits.

Back on the studio floor, I rejoin the crew. The makeshift pool has been filled with water and on the stage stands an empty Godzilla suit. Nearby, Mothra has been lowered from the rafters and is waist-high to pyrotechnic chief Kume and his staff, who are fitting her with squibs. The art staff is at work building up detail close to the camera; Inatsuki peers through the lens and yells instructions to Yuri, Thunder, and Jimmy.

The set, a rendering of a dock in Yokohama, is dotted about with miniature cars and lifters, as well as those multicolor crates common to waterfronts. Several small boats float in the harbor; there's even a large ship that a guess puts at over two meters in length. Two buildings have the words "Tezuka" and "Suzuki" affixed above their entrances, references to the directors from the two previous Godzilla films.

Following lunch, Masuda calls me into the PR room. There, he and fellow PR staffer Nakayama unroll the film's latest poster. It shows Godzilla in a towering profile with photos of the other kaiju and the actors assembled in a montage on the right-hand side. I get in real close and inspect it. I must have an overly serious look on my face because they start laughing.

"Norman," Masuda says. "You don't have to scrutinize it. Just enjoy it."

Sitting with Nakao back in S9, I mention the poster. "Hold it," he starts. "You're telling me that the PR guys showed *you* the poster based on *my* photos before they showed *me*?"

Uh oh...

Slipping out of S9, I rush to the PR office and tell Nakayama that if he knows what's best, he'll get his ass to 9 with the poster and run it past Nakao.

A half-hour later, with the poster in hand, Nakayama stops by Nakao's desk. Unfortunately, it's a lost cause. Nakao is furious and uses words I don't think my Japanese slang dictionary even carries. All Nakayama can do is apologize and bow umpteen times.

After he leaves, the still fuming Nakao leans over. "And the poster sucks too!"

Nakao cools down when a retired staffer from the Showa Godzilla productions pays a visit. The two reminisce and quickly slip into a "kids today" type conversation: "The lighting back then turned the studio into a furnace—it was murder but we just had to deal with it!" "Nearly everything was done in-camera, none of this fix-it-in-the-mix crap!" "No playback monitors! You either knew it was good or you didn't!"

A few hours later, the set is ready to roll. As I gather with the cameramen, I notice the letter P is visible on my display. For the life of me, I can't figure out what it means. Nakao asks for my camera. He turns it over to find a switch labeled "Panoramic." I must have flipped it somehow. The cameramen around us roar with laughter.

"Don't feel bad," Nakao says. "I did the same thing once on an important shoot. When I got the film developed, everyone's head was cut off." Nakao grabs some tape and puts it over the switch. "There, it won't bother you again."

The shots at the dock are some of the best so far. The set is bathed in a vibrant, orange hue. Several fire pots billow with thick gray smoke. When action is called, a burning Mothra flies over to Godzilla, who stomps toward the waterfront with thuds that echo throughout S9.

28 JULY 2001

The day's main shot is a massive miniature cityscape to which a CG Ghidorah taking a hit from Godzilla's beam will be added in post-production. The staff has set up the most hysterical-looking Ghidorah stand-in: One of its heads on a pole and two large Styrofoam wings stuck on the sides.

To pass the time, I help the art staff move buildings onto the set. As we do, we talk about films currently playing. Thunder went to see *Jurassic Park III*, which he calls a "worthless story with good effects." I start laying into *A.I.*, which I saw recently. Abruptly, Kamiya jumps up and down while grunting and pounding on his chest.

"Don't say another word!" says Matsumoto. "I haven't seen *Planet of the Apes* yet."

For the shot, the camera is outfitted with a wide-angle lens. As it appears on the monitor, Godzilla is on one end with Ghidorah on the other. Due to intense lens distortion, they warp unnaturally at the edges of the frame. I tell Kamiya it's making me seasick; he offers to buy me motion sickness medicine.

On stage, Yoshida is sticking out of the Godzilla suit as he waits for Matsumoto to finish with the tech side of the shot. Hopping up, I photograph the set-up while chatting with Yoshida. I mention how one of my favorite details on the suit is its knuckles. For fun, I take close-ups of Godzilla's hands. Each time I do, Yoshida rattles the suit, ruining the picture. Although I tell him to cut the crap, he snickers and keeps it up.

To exact revenge, I sing *Go! Go! Godzilla* (*Yuke! Yuke! Gojira*), an annoying children's tie-in song from 1972. Yoshida counters with *Pulverize The Smog Monster!* (*Hedora wo yattsukero!*), another Godzilla promotional song, this one from *Godzilla vs. The Smog Monster* (*Gojira tai Hedora*, 1971). Matsumoto—holding a silver orb on a stick, a device used to aid the placement of CG objects—orders us to zip our pants because our otaku is hanging out.

30 JULY 2001

I'm sitting with Chika at Nakao's station when the Godzilla suit built for water scenes is wheeled to the edge of Vi-shop. Though not as intricate as the main suits, it has its interesting points. For starters, since they won't be seen, it's legless. Also—and here's the touch I like best—there's dark tubing dotted with tiny holes strung below the waist.

Shinada explains that air will be pumped through it to form bubbles around Godzilla. "It's a small touch," Shinada says. "But it adds realism."

Chika mentions the suit looks odd because of how its arms stick out to the sides unnaturally. Taking the bait, I climb onto the cart and, getting behind Godzilla, reach around and grab his arms. "I'm king of the world!" I yell out.

"What are you two doing?" someone asks behind us. It's Kaneko.

"Check it out," I say, and do my best *Titanic* for the director. Kaneko lets out a snort of a laugh.

Here with Jiro, Kaneko's come to fetch me. Today is the day of the staff baseball game, which he explains is a tradition at Toho. Outside the studio, we meet up with Nanako and Suzuyuki. Like his dad, Suzu wears a GMK staff t-shirt. After a *ramen* lunch, we head to a baseball field somewhere in the Setagaya ward.

We arrive to find the live-action crew gearing up for a game. Split into three teams, I'm put in team two, with our coach being Saito the soundman (not to be confused with my nemesis Saito, the writer). As I haven't played baseball since I was 13, I strike out my first time at bat. When the next team is up, Saito has me play shortstop between second and third. A hit comes my way. Allowing the ball

to roll under my legs, I put my baseball incompetence on full display. After this, I'm banished to the outfield.

Actor Yuki Watanabe steps up to home plate. He's wearing a tight black shirt that shows off the muscles in his chest and arms. Actor Kobayashi is pitching for one of the teams; it turns out he's got ability. He tells me he used to play ball in school. Surprisingly, Masuda is good too, saying that the only thing he enjoys more than Godzilla is baseball. With all these good players around, I take comfort that the only guy as bad as me is Kaneko.

And lest I forget, Futami is here too. He's walking around in shorts and no shirt. In a hand is a big stick that he waves around to emphasize his two patent phrases: "*dame, dame, dame!*" and "*ii ne.*"

Despite my team sucking, we manage to win, little thanks to me.

At 5 p.m., driving back to Toho, we settle into our distinct personalities. I'm boisterous and work to maintain a high level of group enthusiasm; Kaneko announces he wants to take a nap; Jiro talks about music, in particular The Who, his favorite band. Suzu has found a Godzilla book in the back of the car. Whenever he comes to a photo of Jet Jaguar (an Ultraman-like robot that teamed up with Godzilla in *Godzilla vs. Megalon*), I ask if this is his favorite kaiju. After about the tenth time, he gets fed up. Putting his small hands on my shoulders, he looks me in the eyes and—with complete conviction—says, "Norman... Jet Jaguar sucks."

There's a small party in the building between S1 and S2 tonight for the live-action crew. I walk upstairs to find things in full swing. Leading the activities is soundman Saito, who motions for me to sit next to Kaneko.

"I'd rather sit by the beer," I say, causing the room to break into laughter.

With most of the shoot over, a feeling of accomplishment hangs in the air. This helps make it the most carefree, let-your-hair-down party I've been to at Toho. I spend time talking to Kishimoto, who tells me about starting out at Toho on *The War of the Gargantuas*. Saito yells over, "Don't forget to tell him that I did boom on that one!" I apologize to them for not knowing sooner that I'm shoulder-to-shoulder with Toho superstars.

Suzu starts bugging his dad to take him to S9. He wants to see Godzilla. Kaneko glances my way. "Come on, Suzu," I say.

Along the way, we stop into one of the prop sheds. On a wall is the original buzz saw-like chest blade of giant monster Gigan. I pick him up so he can touch it. He's excited beyond words.

With the SFX crew working by the pool, S9 is empty. Walking inside around a demolished city set, Suzu is the proverbial kid in a candy store. He stomps through it pretending to be Godzilla. I point out the adult-stage suit of King Ghidorah hanging silently above us. Suzu looks at it with the kind of wonderment only possible for a person under ten. After this, I take him to the Vi-Shop station to see the other suits. As we look around, Godzilla actor Yoshida comes by. In his hands is a bull frog.

"Check out what I caught hopping around the pool," he says. He leans down and lets Suzu pet it.

We go outside to where the staff has readied a shot of a burning Mothra flying to attack Godzilla. A chest-high stage stands atop the lot in front of the pool. At the back of the set, Mothra is being wired up. Just then, Tony hands me a package of sparklers. "Why don't you take Kaneko's kid over there and light these up?" Joined by Chika, we start playing with sparklers in front of S8 to pass the time until the shot is ready to lens.

"What the hell do you think you're doing?" It's Kaneko. He's come from the party—and, boy, does he look pissed! "Do you think this is a playground?" he asks me sternly. Fortuitously, some SFX staff by the pool light up sparklers and wave them around.

"See?" I answer back. "The staff gave these to us and told us to light them up here."

Kaneko looks embarrassed. Calming down, he says, "Just don't look like you're having too much fun, okay? This is a movie set after all."

When the shot is ready, I climb on stage with my camera. Mothra, her wings on fire, glides toward Godzilla. The natural night sky's ambiance mixed with the summer night's pleasantness imbues the monsters with a quality different from the one in S9. On the side of the stage, Suzu looks up with eyes the size of saucers.

Kamiya calls for a re-shoot. It seems the wind is whipping the set smoke too strongly. I sit through one more take before heading back to the live-action party.

I get back to find they're at the end of speech-making, a Japanese tradition. Seeing me, Saito stands. "*Ah*, the hero of today's game," he announces sarcastically. "Norman mentioned he expects his next time at bat to be in another thirty years. Let's hope he keeps his promise and stays away from the game." Saito has me make a short speech that is remarkable only by how unremarkable it is. But, this being Japan, it's the effort that counts, and I'm given a loud round of applause.

As we've been drinking since the afternoon, everyone is sloshed. However, no one is as sloshed as Kobayashi. He puts an arm around me and, slurring his words, thanks me for being on set so often.

"Well, it's not like I had anything else planned this summer," I say, kidding. Kobayashi gives me a tight, endless hug, one that generates laughs from the room.

Standing, Murakami leads us in *iponjime*, a Japanese thing in which everyone gives a single, unified clap. Together, we yell *hai* and crash our hands together.

Saito then points at Matsumoto. "The film now rests with Matsumoto! Good luck, Matsumoto!" We toast Matsumoto, who cringes visibly.

Jiro, Kaneko, and I leave at 11 p.m. As we pull out of Toho, I see Kaneko has a colossal smile on his face. I can't recall him looking this happy.

"Today was fun," he says. This, too, is unusual because he seldom voluntarily comes out with descriptions of his emotional state. Abruptly and uncharacteristically, Kaneko makes a fist and throws it out of the car window and up into the air.

"*Yeah!*" he yells as loud as he can.

Jiro and I follow with enthusiastic *yeahs* of our own.

1 AUGUST 2001

I get to Toho late. Even though I spent yesterday at home recovering from the baseball game and endless day of drinking, I still feel like a well-wrung rag. My back feels like I slept on bowling ball and I've got a headache that'll probably stay with me for the rest of the day. Man, I hope the SFX doesn't have any explosions on the schedule today.

The mood in S9 is more pensive than usual, which is probably because of the scale of the—just my unluck—pyrotechnics slated for the first shot. The scene centers on Ghidorah taking a death blast from Godzilla. A wedge of miniature buildings has been pushed together and set around an already half-crushed building, which the pyrotechnic guys wire with explosives.

Once the charges are in place, Ghidorah is carried over. It's hard enough to move suits around, but Ghidorah's three long, unwieldy necks make it trickier to deal with than the other kaiju. Yesterday, the suit staff touched it up, and all three heads were wrapped in foam. It has Ghidorah looking like something out of old-time photos of people with toothaches and handkerchiefs tied around their heads.

Once trial runs are complete, the foam is removed. Kamiya calls for action. A barrage of explosions creates a blinding white fireball in front of Ghidorah, knocking him into the building behind him. As expected, the explosion is like a pickax to my gray matter.

Over in S1, Tezuka and crew are shooting smoke—just smoke—to be used as an insert in front of Godzilla's feet during post-production. Although not the most exciting thing to watch, its lack of drama is made up for by Futami's presence. For whatever reason, he doesn't know anyone's name on Tezuka's crew. When a staffer does something strenuous, Futami yells out,

167

"Hey..." He then turns to someone. "What's that guy's name? ...Hey, *Yamada*, keep up the good work!"

His role as self-anointed quality control set manager reached a new level when I overheard him give pointers to Kaneko a week or so ago on how to direct. "You gotta speak *louder*," he told him. "Directors need *big* voices!" to which Kaneko responded with a simple, "Got it."

Back in S9, I find Tomiyama sitting with Nakao and Saito. I'm happy to report to Tomiyama that I've finished my next piece for the Toho website.

Standing, he shakes my hand. "Thank you," he says. "I find your work to be the most interesting writing on the film."

Saito cringes hearing this.

Nakao got a thank you letter from his friends who visited a few weeks back. They sent prints of the photos they took. We leaf through them. They are, like, a thousand and one shots of the suit: full-body, medium, close-up, extreme close-up, ones from all sorts of weird "artistic" angles, etc. Nakao mentions that one of the men is an English teacher.

"Why didn't he speak to me in English when he was here?" I ask.

Nakao can only shrug.

I spend a chunk of the day in the cafeteria working on Kaneko's website. It being after lunch, the place is empty. One of the women here chats me up for a bit and then gives me free coffee when her co-workers in the kitchen aren't looking.

For Kaneko's site, I put together a silly photo section of various women posing with the Godzilla suit. I don't know if it's sexist or not, but monsters & women have a long film history. It's fun to carry on the tradition. I've gotten photos of nearly all

the women staffers standing next to the Godzilla suit. They've all enjoyed posing with the King of the Monsters.

2 AUGUST 2001

At 3:30 p.m., the Toho PR staff leads a gang of reporters into S9. I don't like this because it makes taking photos more difficult; the staff doesn't like it because it interferes with their work, especially now with everything under the gun. Making matters worse, Masuda asks AD Okamoto if it'd be okay to do a photo session of the monsters fighting for the reporters. Okamoto flat-out refuses. Masuda pleads and, finally, Okamoto relents.

Working quickly, the staff gather buildings for the kaiju to stand in front of. Nakayama comes from the suit area with Mothra. Carrying it with the grace one takes out the morning trash, he nearly knocks over a light with a wing. Frantically following him is one of the Vi-shop guys.

Nakao does his best to make something of the slipshod setup. He gets the staff to burn smoke pots in the background and has Nakayama hold up Mothra behind the buildings. As Godzilla and Ghidorah put on a mock fight for the reporters, he bobs Mothra up and down. Worse, his hands are clearly visible. When it's over, I mention to Nakao how poor I thought the whole thing looked. He doesn't share my worry.

"It's no big deal," he insists. "The photos will be tiny in newspapers and look fine."

Back at Nakao's table, our afternoon chat is interrupted when Saito comes around. From his bag, he pulls out two clear plastic *gachapon* "eggs," the kind dispensed by vending machines. Being kaiju themed, they contain monster figures. One is Anguirus, a monster from the Godzilla universe that resembles an ankylosaurus. The other is a bird creature. Saito is unimpressed that I know Anguirus's name. He holds up the bird and challenges me to name it. I shrug my shoulders.

"Of course you don't know," he scoffs. "That's because this is the heart and soul of *Japanese* kaiju!"

I look to Nakao for support but he's glancing up at the rafters struggling to suppress his laughter.

I'm trying to figure out Saito's point. It seems he's suggesting that my not being Japanese means I can't comprehend the "heart and soul" of kaiju…if something like that even exists.

For argument's sake, I put it into cultural context. I mean, I can't help but wonder how dumb I'd appear if I were to wave a CZ-3 figure in front of a non-American and proudly assert that they couldn't possibly understand the deeper meaning of *Star Wars* because of not being able to identify one of a thousand background droids by name.

When Saito steps away to use the john, Nakao gives me a look. We jump on the bird. As it's made of soft, stick-together pieces, it's easy to re-arrange. We take the wings and place them where the legs should be. I even manage to get Anguirus's head to stick out of the bird's tail hole.

Saito returns. Seeing our Frankenstein monster-like creation, he picks it up and, dumbfounded, turns it slowly around. The look of violation on his face is the kind I'd expect had I called Japan every derogatory name in the book. Nakao and I look about innocently until a burst of snickering gets the best of us.

Saito attempts another go at it with more of his nationalist-bordering spiel: "So, are American miniatures as detailed as the ones on the GMK set?"

"You've seen *Close Encounters*, *Blade Runner*, and *Independence Day*. You know the answer to that as well as I do."

Ignoring me, he then tells me that those egg toys I so flippantly made fun of are a big part of Japanese culture and are only found in Japan.

"I guess this means I was hallucinating when I bought similar junk items out of the same type of vending machines in America when a kid," I reply.

Without acknowledging what I'd said, Saito takes out fuzzy photos he took on set. "Check out this rare expression I caught of director Kamiya." I look at it, but the photo was taken from so far away that Kamiya's face isn't much larger than the nail on my pinkie.

For the life of me, I can't understand what he wants from me. Talks like this— ones that pit one culture against another— always deteriorate into shouting matches. It's a game I won't play. At least Nakao is enjoying it. He really gets a kick seeing me suffer through these pointless exchanges.

Things are back to normal now that the reporters have left. The next shot up is a low-angle one of Godzilla on a bare stage roaring into the sky. The camera is set on the floor and placed in front of a large wood panel. This creates an empty chasm between the camera and Godzilla.

Deciding to have fun, I take a spot on the floor between the wood panel and the camera. From here, I've got a clear view looking straight up at Godzilla. As Yoshida moves about, I hear all kinds of suit squeaks and noises I'd never noticed. Best of all, when action is called, I can remain here because, despite being right in the middle of the shot, I'm in the way of neither the camera nor Godzilla. From this position, it's as if Godzilla is truly a living, giant creature. I couldn't imagine the actual thing appearing much different.

3 AUGUST 2001

Looking a bit worse for wear, Matsumoto tells me he's only got a bit over two months to get the film ready for its premiere at the Tokyo International Film Festival this December. I suggest for unfinished shots he put up clips that read "Scene Missing."

"I've a better idea," he counters. "I'll run a clip of me bowing in shame." He pauses. "Or, maybe I'll just call in a bomb threat and get the screening canceled."

With everything behind schedule, things are grim on the SFX set. The second unit is doing its best to pick up the slack. Today, under the guidance of Tezuka, they're at work around the big pool. When I check on them, Tomiyama is talking with Tezuka, Kikuchi, and Kenichi Eguchi, a cinematographer who worked on several previous Toho productions, including *Godzilla vs. Biollante* and *Orochi, the Eight-Headed Dragon* (*Yamato Takeru*, 1994). The glum look on Tomiyama's face is enough to tell me to keep my distance. I return to S9.

Curious, I ask Nakao if he's seen a second unit on a Godzilla film before.

"Never," he says. "I'd have thought they'd asked Suzuki to handle the B unit. From what I hear, Tezuka requested the position."

After lunch, the crew is summoned in front of S9, where we form a large circle.

Once everyone has gathered, the floor is turned over to Tomiyama. With him is Morichi, the Toho executive I met a year back in Osaka. He stands with his hip cocked to the side and a cigarette dangling from his lips. Morichi starts talking, but his voice is low; it's hard to catch his words. When he finishes, Tomiyama speaks. Now *he*, I can hear.

Tomiyama explains how next Wednesday is "crank up," the final day of shooting, and that it will be impossible to finish on time at the current pace. For this reason, he's calling for Sunday, a scheduled day off, to be a workday. Having said his piece, Tomiyama motions to Kamiya to add a few words. Despite being the director, Kamiya reacts with a "who me?" look. When realizing he has to say something, he comes out with a near meaningless *"yoroshiku onegaishimasu."*

The staff is pissed. Some fuss how they couldn't understand what was going on because of "fuzzy" Japanese. Isao is miffed because he planned to go to Wonderfest, a bi-annual toy/model kit event, on Sunday. Thunder is upset too, but for a different reason. He tells me that he wouldn't mind a longer shoot at the same level of pay in exchange for a more leisurely schedule.

"I just want to make my rent and make a good film," he laments.

I go to S1, where Isao is supervising the filming of fire to be used as a superimposition element. Rancid-looking plastic burns wild in metal pots. Jet-black smoke pours so thick I figure it'd take a thousand burning plastic army men to produce the same consistency. And the smell! I make a beeline for the confection cart the moment I get a whiff of it. I grab a surgical mask and quickly slip it on. Everyone is wearing one…

except for Isao. I tell him that surely this must be where he draws the line.

"Sorry," he says unapologetically. "I never wear masks. This is my life. It's what I do."

Later at the big pool, I mention to Tezuka what Isao said.

"Well, you do know Isao is a bit nuts," he kids. "Seriously, he's going to pay for it later in life."

Tomorrow, Godzilla will be blasted into the waters of Yokohama Bay; it's the shoot's last big effect. Half of the art staff has been working around the clock on constructing a dock running from the pool's right side to its middle. Careful not to bump into any buildings resting atop, I walk out onto the dock. Miike is in the water wearing waist-high rubber fishing pants. He's fitting tiny tetrapods along the dock's edge that he mentions are leftovers from the G2000 production.

Back at Nakao's station, I sit down to rest my feet. Abruptly, a longtime staffer, a guy who has been on the Godzilla crew since *Godzilla vs. Mothra* ('92), asks if he can sit with me. Right away, he goes into a rant against Kamiya.

"I can't figure the guy out," he complains. "When it was Kawakita, we always knew who the boss was. He didn't tell you what he wanted, he ordered you. Suzuki was a different breed of director. He was always smiling and trying to be everyone's buddy. Still, he told you exactly what he wanted. Kamiya is the *onegaishimasu* director. That is, he doesn't order, he requests.

"And I've never worked at such a slow pace," he continues. "I get the feeling that Kamiya is doing things like it's a hobby, not work. There's no point in shooting the same thing fifteen times or more.

Kawakita would call a shot okay even if it was just good enough. He'd never re-shoot something because of a tiny detail that only an otaku would notice."

I'm shocked hearing this and don't know if it's my place to agree or disagree, not having the experience to judge. All I can do is try to understand his opinion. However, I do feel he's being too hard on Kamiya. I put forth that the days of a Japanese director bossing and literally beating staff members are over, adding that I think this is a good thing.

"This is Kamiya's first time up as an SFX director," I posit. "He's worked side-by-side with you guys as a regular staffer and might feel uncomfortable to now find himself the guy calling the shots."

After mulling on what I said, he leans in close.

"Don't get me wrong," he says. "I want the film to succeed. The truth is, if things work in the way Kamiya is aiming, it's gonna be special."

Art staffers not on the dock are in the center of S9 building a *shotengai* shopping street. Unlike other shots with maybe one or two buildings made to break apart, the entire run of stores has been constructed from plaster. A material common in both Japan and Hollywood for miniatures marked for detonation, plaster shatters into chunks that are believable fill-ins for masonry and concrete. As the art staff paints shop fronts and adds the insane detail the Toho art staff is renowned for, the pyrotechnic team wires squibs throughout the interiors. Additionally, a tremendous amount of time has been given to the tedious job of cutting break lines into the shops. Before covering them with paint, the vein-like lines in the walls have them looking like the aftermath of a large earthquake.

I spend time taking photos around the *shotengai*. The detail level reminds me of the home destroyed by Godzilla's foot at the top of production. There are even those illuminated *denshoku kanban* stands that Japanese shops and restaurants place beside their front doors. An after-hours bar sports the name "Yurippe," the nickname of art staffer Yuri.

"So this is how you wind up later in life," I say teasingly as she places tiny potted plants into a shop's window. "A mama-san at a crummy bar for low-level, married businessmen over fifty."

Yuri looks up from her work. "I'm sure you'll be my best customer, Norman."

Ah, touché! Thunder and Jimmy laugh at her quick comeback. Another snack bar is called "Maki," named after art staffer Maki Kobayashi[17]. Having learned my lesson, I don't dare come out with another wisecrack.

Mothra has been flipped upside down and locked onto a metal plate attached to steel tracks. Using a handle on the plate, one of the staff will pull Mothra down the track and smash her into the *shotengai*. Timed together with the *shamisen* detonator's metal-tipped pen, explosive charges hidden throughout the miniatures will level the set.

Once the art staff calls it quits, I talk to Thunder, who looks pleased as punch. "I'm happy we get to do this one," he says with pride. "There was talk of cutting it because of the schedule."

For the take, I climb up a lighting rig and settle next to a large movie light shining down on the set. It's a perfect bird's eye view. The crew goes through several dry runs.

The concern is the timing between Mothra and the detonations. They have to match perfectly when Mothra hits the buildings.

When the crew feels ready, Kamiya screams for a take. Mothra sails down the tracking. The moment the insect kaiju touches the shops, the explosives detonate. Dried clay and unidentifiable bits of material fly high into the air as grating, high-pitched *pop, pop, pops* reverberate throughout S9. As usual, I'm bathed in pieces of clay and miniature "poo."

It's 10:30 p.m. and the clean up begins. The art staff is filling garbage bags with the remains of the shopping street. The Vi-shop people pull Mothra out of the rubble and assess the damage. She will have to go through major repairs. Okamoto yells out that the shoot is officially over for the day and the time when everyone is expected tomorrow morning.

I go to say good night to Nakao, but as usual, he's already gone.

4 AUGUST 2001

An underwater section of wreckage from the Yokohama Bay Bridge has been laid across the studio floor; at its end lies the beating heart of Godzilla!

Okay, it's not really underwater and it's not really Godzilla's heart; it's an open-air set that Matsumoto says will have water effects and CGI fish added during post-production. *Oh*, and the beating heart is a blue, heart-shaped sculpt by Sagae that will be replaced in post by CGI. Cameraman Murakawa does a couple of test crane runs over it before committing it to film.

17 - Maki's father, Tomoki Kobayashi, was Toho's last in-house suit maker before the studio began outsourcing the work.

Outside, with construction of the dock nearly complete, I stroll across it with my camera. The art staff is nearing the end of their work and has turned things over to the pyrotechnic guys. They're wiring the hollow interiors of the miniatures with the myriad of explosives needed to destroy a set of this size. The amount of cable required to link the charges together and run them to the *shamisen* is intense; this is in addition to the cables needed to power the lights strung throughout the various warehouses and buildings. Trying to walk across without tripping brings back memories of that tire obstacle course game from elementary school.

I get a call from Ayako Fujitani. I'd invited her to tonight's explosion but she's unsure if she can make it on time. I ask Kamiya when he thinks they're going to shoot. "7:30," he guesses. Ayako says she'll get there around 8:30 or 9. I tell her to move her butt.

Kaneko offers to buy Jiro and me dinner if we drive to the KFC by the station and pick something up. Once back, the three of us sit on folding chairs in an out-of-the-way corner of the pool with boxes of chicken on our laps.

"To be honest," Kaneko says as he eats, "I'm worried about the film. I was happier at this point during the first Gamera. There's still too much up in the air for me to relax."

"Look what's going on now," I say, waving a greasy finger in the air. "We've got front row seats to a giant explosion in a Godzilla film. You must be doing something right." A smile appears on his face, and we finish our meal without any more complaints.

Friday night, and with working hours over, staffers from the Toho offices gather in front of the pool. Word leaked about tonight's explosion and they've come to see the fireworks. All the while, Ayako keeps calling to see if the dock's been blown or not. As is typical, with issues cropping up at the last moment, the explosion keeps getting pushed back. Still, I tell her that no one's going to wait for her.

Earlier in the day, Nakao drew a map of the pool area and plotted the best spot to shoot stills from. The verdict: the wall by the wave makers. However, when we get there, TV reporters have claimed the area and are setting up large video cameras. Thinking quickly, we decide on a spot to the left-center of the pool. Grabbing a couple of tall ladders, we set them a meter apart, climb to the tops, and take seats. We have a perfect, unobstructed view of the dock. Now, we just have to wait for Kamiya and company to get their act together. It's already 8:30 p.m., an hour past when the director said the detonation would go off.

The pyrotechnic guys have finished their work and now Saito and his lighting team are going at it as fast as they can. Complicating matters is that most of the surrounding lights sit atop scaffolding in the water; to make adjustments, someone has to wade over just to get access.

"Have I got a story for you," Nakao says from his perch on the ladder. "Remember I said I'd give you my storyboard script at the end of the shot?"

How could I forget? It's a keepsake I'm looking forward to receiving.

"Well, your 'lover' asked for it. When I told him I'd promised it to you, he got a long face and asked, 'Do you think you could rip it in half and split it between us?'"

Through my laughter, I ask which directions Saito wants it sliced, across the middle or top to bottom.

Just then, the TV reporters who'd set up by the wave makers start to move their cameras; the staff needs the spot. Taking their place, a crane is driven over and a Godzilla suit is fit to its cables.

"Guess we got lucky," Nakao says, tapping the tip of his baseball cap. "We'd never have been able to finagle the spot we have now this late in the game."

Kamiya calls for a dry run. The plan is for an empty Godzilla suit (not one made specifically for this production but a refit of an event suit) to be blown off the dock and thrown into the sea. Godzilla, by means of the crane, will sail to the left of the set in time with the explosions.

The first test is up. Kamiya yells, *"Bam! Bam! Bam!"* to show when he wants the explosions to detonate and when the Godzilla suit should be yanked away. As the staff resets things for a second test, Godzilla is swung back to his position a bit too forcefully. The suit smacks into a side of the dock and nearly takes out a model ship. The sixty or so onlookers let out a collective *"Ahhh!"*

My ladder is right above Kamiya's station, making it easy to spy on him and his staff. I overhear talk about difficulty with the timing. It's the wind machines; they're making it hard to hear his commands. Kamiya is handed a megaphone, which they feel will cut over the racket.

For the hell of it, I ask Nakao to compare now to the Godzilla sets of the '60s, '70s, and '80s. "Pretty much the same," he says matter-of-factly. "Same

kind of men and women. No, not much has changed."

I'm not sure why, but I'm happy to hear this.

Finally, Kamiya decides the shot is ready. The wind machines start up; the din is intense. Staffers on the dock spread smoke around before scurrying off to rejoin the staff at the pool's edge. Kamiya yells through his megaphone for the cameras, four in total, to roll. One at a time, the operators respond with "speed!" Kamiya screams for action.

With that, the entire dock lights up. Fire bursts from every window of every building. The blasts build and converge into a tremendous fireball that not only erupts upwards but spreads sideways across the water. As Godzilla catapults backward, bits of dock shoot everywhere. The explosion produces an intense wave of heat that washes over the area. It's so scorching that after it passes over me I check my eyebrows to make sure they're still intact.

"*Whoa!* That was *hot!*" Nakao exclaims. He's touching his face too to feel if it's still there.

I watch as Kamiya reviews the take on his monitor. "Okay!" he yells. It's not like he has a choice—the dock is now smoldering ash. A reshoot would be impossible.

I climb down and join the crowd. Everyone is excitedly talking about the intensity of the explosion. I find Jiro. He's pissed. An office guy, freaked out by its force, ran off and plowed right into him.

My phone rings. It's Ayako. She's arrived. I go to the side gate and meet her and Yuriko from Loft Plus One. When we get to the pool, Junko sees Ayako and reprimands her.

"You're late!" she scolds.

Ayako's presence has the staff elated; some even ask for her autograph. While she talks to Kamiya, Shu Kageyama, the man shooting the behind the scenes video, starts filming them. The fanfare reaches the point I feel sorry for getting her involved—and she didn't even get the compensation of seeing the explosion!

I take Ayako and Yuriko into S9 to show them around. I do my usual bit of having guests touch Godzilla's chest, lower jaw, and finally, the upper lip. The material on the body is what you'd expect: hard and cold. But the face is spongy...creepily so. As soft as a baby's behind, it's not what you'd expect from physical contact with the King of the Monsters. Both women let out a "*yuck!*" when touching it.

Back outside, we step onto the dock to survey the damage. For fun, we pose for photos like fighting monsters beside a still half-standing building. Pretending to be kaiju, Yuriko and Aya pick up miniature cars blackened from the blast and hold them in the air. After this, Yuriko takes photos of me with my hands around Aya's neck.

"I'm the Brown Gargantua and you're the Green one!" I cry as Ayako does her best to figure out what I'm talking about and when I'll stop choking her.

We head over to the editing suites in search of Kaneko. While waiting in the lobby, I poke fun at a Japanese drama on the lounge's continually running TV.

"Japanese dramas have it all!" I say in a deep, announcer-like voice. "*Action!*" On the TV, a man hits another man. "*Adventure!*" As if on cue, he rushes into the arms of a woman. "*Romance!*" They kiss. The timing is so freaking perfect that Aya and Yuriko are rolling with laughing.

Kaneko joins us. We decide to get dinner and head to Soshigaya-Okura Station in Jiro's car. In a local restaurant, we order beer and proceed to get flat-out drunk. It must be the beer because the normally reserved Kaneko is entirely outgoing. He reminisces about the Gamera production, bringing up stories he thinks will embarrass Aya, who continually asks him to cut it out.

At 2 a.m., we call it quits. Outside the restaurant, Kaneko puts his arms around Ayako and hugs her.

"My god!" she exclaims. "This is the first time he's ever shown me any affection!"

Jiro drives Ayako and me to Shimokitazawa. We crank The Clash all the way home.

5 AUGUST 2001

I stumble hung-over into S9. Junko takes one look at me and chuckles.

"You're not going to blow up anything today, are you?" I ask Kamiya. "I don't think my head can handle it."

Junko makes a gesture to indicate I've been hitting the bottle.

"I'll be sure the staff is considerate of the obvious health issues you're experiencing," Kamiya replies.

I drop my bag at Nakao's station; he peeks up from his morning paper. Without warning, Yamabe pushes a Godzilla suit smack against Nakao's desk. "Mind if I park this here?" he asks without bothering for a reply.

This is one for the books: Godzilla is flush against Nakao's desk, towering over us with heated, angry white eyes. Nakao and I turn to each other. After a bewildered pause, we break into heavy laughter.

In the center of S9, the art staff has erected another stretch of Yokohama waterfront. Behind a makeshift pool stands a run of prefab buildings. In on itself cool, the real attraction is found around the water's edge and a collection of half a dozen docked model boats. My favorite touch is a small walking path off to the side that's been detailed with mooring bollards, those steel knobby things boats tie themselves to.

The youngling version of Ghidorah is hauled to stage right and Ohashi is helped into the suit. Being the one that requires him to operate the outer heads, he works his arms into the necks. I can't imagine it being very comfortable. But, as it goes with Japanese suit actors, you'd never know by his all-or-nothing attitude.

The mood on the set has evolved over the past few days. I might be wrong, but things seem to be entering panic mode. Many crucial shots remain with not enough time to get to all of them. As a grim reminder, a wood board was placed at the entrance of S9 this morning. Taped on it are the remaining storyboards. When a shot is complete, the illustration is cut out with a razor and tossed in the trash.

The way Nakao explains it to me is that it wasn't unusual to go over a deadline in the recent past because Toho EB, a subsidiary of Toho Co, produced the SFX. Now that Toho EB has been absorbed into Toho proper, the front office won't budge on the wrap date. "What's going to happen is anyone's guess," he says.

Kaneko comes around Kamiya's desk with a videotape of the film's ending. It's fast-paced, with scenes quickly trading off between different locations. Soon, crewmembers gather for a peek, more and more, until the production comes to a standstill.

"I wonder why everyone is watching the film here when the film is going on over there and there is still so much to do," Kamiya says loudly. It's his roundabout way of telling everyone to get back to work.

The art staff has started cleaning S9. They toss out miniature buildings and other small items built for the film that are no longer needed. 4th AD Taguchi picks up a garbage bag and places pieces from the junk pile into it.

"I'm working on a low-budget kaiju film of my own," he says. "These will come in handy."

I look at the pile and see neat pieces, like lampposts and furniture. I grab a few as souvenirs. One looks like a ramp. Thunder tells me Yuri made it. She blushes when I thank her.

6 AUGUST 2001

Arriving at Toho, I find Tezuka and the B-unit on the pool's right-hand side. They have the camera pointed at a large five-meter-high scaffold with a water tank braced to its top and a black sheet dangling down its front. When tipped, the tank drops water over the sheet. Tezuka tells me the water will be used as a composite element when Godzilla comes out of the sea. I watch a test spill before heading into S9.

The art staff has crafted a strip of city rubble in front of the camera. It's a tangled mass of street lamps, signs, and vending machines. As they work, pyrotechnic head Kume and his staff prep Mothra. When action is called, Mothra, its wings aflame, rises from behind the rubble. For the shot, I huddle with the usual gang of photographers.

"That was spectacular," Iizuka says to Kamiya after the fire on Mothra has been extinguished. "Was this your idea of giving us a nice send-off on our last day?"

I'm surprised. I didn't know it was the final day for the photographers. I guess it's just Nakao and me from here on out.

Today features one of the most insane shots I've seen so far. The staff has brought over a long, black steel pipe; wide on both ends and narrow in the middle, it resembles a dumbbell. They place it on a table, hook a tank of propane to it, and point it at another platform a meter away.

A test is called. An enormous *whoosh* blares from one end. Although sounding like a fire extinguisher, it doesn't eject white mist—the thing spews out a huge, mean-ass fireball! Following this, the Godzilla suit is set atop a length of tracking on the platform opposite the pipe.

I decide to take photos from atop a ladder. From here, I can effortlessly scan the entire studio floor. In addition to the pipe shot, other upcoming ones are being prepped: On one side of S9, the art staff is readying the large missile launcher model for its explosive demise later tonight. Further over, Shinada stands on a stepladder and is peering into a portable water tank, preparing it for a close up of Godzilla's neck wound. Finished with the water shoot outdoors, Tezuka and his crew are staking out a spot on the studio floor for a shot they're in charge of tomorrow.

I attempt a head count. I lose my place around one hundred. And who among them most stands out? Futami. One can

clearly hear him over the din yelling, "*dame, dame, dame!*"

I presumed an empty Godzilla suit would be used for the pipe shot, so I'm open-mouthed when Yoshida climbs inside. Before being locked in, he dons a pair of goggles with the lenses painted black. After a few dry runs, Kamiya calls for action. The Godzilla suit is rolled down the tracking. When it reaches the halfway point, a ball of blinding white flame shoots out of the pipe. It completely envelops the front of Godzilla. Even from the ladder, I can feel the furnace-like heat it gives off.

When done, a smiling Yoshida is pulled from the suit. He walks over to me. "Wanna do our interview now?"

For a guy who looked like he'd just been blasted by the exhaust of a jet engine with nothing but a raincoat for protection, he's pretty nonchalant about it.

The interview goes very well. Yoshida talks a lot, which is what you hope for from your subject. Better yet, his answers are wonderfully specific. Sure, Nakajima and Satsuma are legends in the field, and the interviews I did with them were informative. However, they revolved more around their attitude toward the art of suit acting. They didn't offer much hard information on what it takes to operate the Godzilla suit. On the other hand, Yoshida gets into specifics, explaining how the suit behaves during operation, where it moves oddly, how he deals with its idiosyncrasies, how the materials have shifted and adjusted themselves throughout the shoot, the different repairs done to it during filming, and what this all means in terms of playing the King of the Monsters. Still, when talking to suit actors, it all comes back to Nakajima and Satsuma, and Yoshida makes sure I understand that these two are the undisputed "gods" of the field.

"I wanted to come up with a new style of Godzilla," Yoshida explains, "but it was too difficult coming out of the gate. Instead, I started out by being faithful to the basics: I made Satsuma's Godzilla my foundation. When Godzilla battles other kaiju, I tapped Nakajima's Godzilla because he fought a lot of kaiju hand-to-hand.

"It was hard at first because of the weight of the suit," he continues. "So, I focused on keeping my arms close to my body and acting with my fingertips in keeping with the Satsuma method. He's a master at *Jigen-ryu*, you know, and in that, you minimize the space between your arms and body. However, due to the way the suit was built, even though I tried my damnedest, it was difficult to keep that pose. I suppose if Satsuma sees my performance he'll say, "That's not Godzilla!""

After an hour, we call it quits and return to the studio floor. "Good timing," Yoshida says pointing to the missile launcher model.

Walking up to the launcher, Inatsuki tells me that the scale directly around it is 1/10th, while buildings further back are 1/25th. I like 1/10th because the level of detail is high. Sure enough, the stores closest to the model sport all sorts of neat items. There's a furniture shop called "Y Furniture." In its front window is a tiny sofa, behind which are chairs, plants, and in the very back, a staircase. The predominant shop is "Omocha no Osama—King of Toys." In its window are rows of toys that include several versions of Hamtaro and a tiny Betty Boop doll.

The explosion looks like it's going to be heavy duty. Many staffers huddle behind solid wood boards or position themselves far across the studio floor. Wanting to get a photo of the fireworks, I've little choice but to stand in the open. However, I step back a few meters and zoom in with my camera.

Once the film camera hits speed, Kamiya yells for action. The launcher flies apart in a massive ball of orange flame. Bits and pieces sail out. A few pieces strike my face and chest. I hardly notice anymore; getting pounded by set shrapnel is just life in S9.

As for the launcher, all that's left is a lump of burning debris. Men with fire extinguishers rush over to douse the residual flames. While it went up in a beautiful display of in-studio pyrotechnic skill, I'm saddened. It was my favorite piece of hardware in the film. I'll miss it.

7 AUGUST 2001

It's hard to believe, but only two days remain. For this reason, I get to the studio early. Even so, the crew is already at work when I arrive at 8:30 a.m. The first shot up is Ghidorah wire works. Across the way, Mothra is being readied for one immediately following. In another spot, angling a drill missile tip into a stand-alone patch of Godzilla hide, is Tezuka's team.

Seeing three effects happening simultaneously illustrates how the shoot has evolved. For a long time it was like a trek up a steep mountain. Now, it's like a wild ride down the side of Mount Fuji. It's gotten to the point that I'm enlisted to move miniature buildings around and do other small tasks to help speed things along. After helping clear an area for an upcoming shot, Junko comes over to ask if I plan to be here for the last day of the shoot tomorrow.

"Wouldn't miss it for the world," I say.

"That's good," she answers. "I'm going to be busy. Forgive me if I don't find the time to talk to you."

This is what I like about Junko. I've never seen her come unhinged. Even now, when I know she's under pressure, she still manages a smile and some kind words. Wish I could say the same for other staff members who can be rude even when the pressure isn't on.

With this fresh on my mind, I sit with Nakao and bring up the subject of ill-disposed staffers, the ones who wouldn't bother to say, "Look out, a stage light is about to fall on your head!" I speculate it might be related to work stress.

"No," Nakao says. "It's not the job. It's just their deficiencies as human beings." Leave it to Nakao to lighten things up and make me smile.

The adult version of Ghidorah hangs in front of a large blue screen across from Nakao and me. The crew furiously tugs wires to make Ghidorah's wings flap and heads bob. Even so, Kamiya prods them further.

"Come on, guys!" he yells. "Flap those wings! Harder! *Harder!*"

Nakao chuckles. "Some things never change," he mutters.

For fun, I ask Nakao which Godzilla film was the hardest to work on.

"This one," he responds without hesitation. "In the old days it was what-you-see-is-what-you-get. You didn't see results until the rushes because there were no playback monitors. If it looked acceptable when shooting, then it was done with. Nowadays, with so much optical work, it's hard to know what's truly going on. It's been this way for the past few films, but none have been this ambitious. Never thought I'd live to see three crews working side-by-side."

The drill bursting through Godzilla's shoulder is ready. "Time to get to work," Nakao says. Picking up a plastic garbage bag, he cuts holes in it and slips it over his head. Working it around his torso, he wears it like a pullover sweater.

Out of laziness, I position myself behind Nakao. Using him as a protective wall, I set my camera on his shoulder and snuggle up behind him.

Oddly, at the exact moment Tezuka yells "action" for the drill shot, Kamiya yells "action" for a shot of Mothra. Tezuka shouts out a polite, "After you," to which Kamiya replies with an equally polite, "No, after you." I facepalm myself as I watch them sink into a Japanese routine of you firsts.

Finally, Tezuka insists. "Come on, we're B and you're the A-unit. You first." This does the trick. Kamiya takes the lead and calls for action.

When it's our turn at bat, the drill is driven right through the Godzilla skin. Wet, sticky pink gunk shoots out. Thanks to Nakao, I emerge without a spot. Nakao, however, got splattered.

"See," he says as he tears the slimed garbage bag off his body. "Nakao knows best."

Kaneko stops by. We walk over to the board with the remaining storyboard shots. He searches through them for things to cut. I point to one of Godzilla's foot smashing through a rooftop.

"That's important," he says.

"They're all important," I add.

Kaneko shakes his head in agreement.

I get to S9 at 9 a.m. I thought I was late, but today's call was pushed to 9:30, meaning I'm early for once. Nakao must have cleaned his space out last night as I find my computer and other things stacked neatly on a chair. Double-checking my gear for the long, last day of SFX shooting ahead, I hear AD Taguchi yell, *"Kaeshimasu!"* (a call for the staff to resume work used at the start of the day or when returning from meal breaks) for the last time. With my camera over my shoulder, I pop by the Vi-shop area to say good morning to Shinada. He's tossing out Ghidorah scales.

"Want a few souvenirs?" Who am I to refuse pieces of Ghidorah DNA?

Tomiyama arrives with Morichi. Both are long-faced as they silently scan the storyboards at S9's entrance. There still remain a mammoth amount of shots to get in the can. After they step into S9, Yamabe and I look the storyboards over.

"It's incredible, isn't it?" he says, pointing to them. "Today may turn out to be the longest day of my life."

Though not yet 10 a.m., S9 is operating at full steam. There isn't any other choice. Shots must be completed. If not, they're cut, which would be detrimental to the integrity of the film.

Probably the staffer most concerned with the situation is Isao. I ask him to explain how a few less SFX shots will affect the film.

"Imagine special effects as a meal." he begins. "In the West, you get large portions of a few items. In film terms, this means a few big money shots. In Japan, we view effect films like our multicourse meals called *kaiseki-ryōri*. Rather than your large slab of steak with a mountain of mashed potatoes beside it, we satisfy our audience's visual palette with a variety of smaller dishes. This translates to various kaiju, mecha, the destruction of buildings, bridges, and towers, etc.

"Sometimes our individual effect shots don't have the work put into them needed to pull them off properly, but that's not the point. Like a small dish that the audience doesn't like in a large meal, they can discard it and, because of the variety we offer them, still feel full at the film's end.

"For example, the upcoming one of Godzilla's foot smashing through the rooftop. Is it necessary to the story? No. But it is if it's to satisfy what the audience expects from a Godzilla film."

Coincidently, Tezuka and his crew are crafting this very shot. The large foot prop used at the start of the shoot has been secured above a specially prepared miniature of a warehouse with a breakaway rooftop. Art staffer Jimmy begins jamming pieces of rock and plaster into hidden spots within and around the area where Godzilla's foot will crash in.

Saito is here and is a thorn in my side. For one thing, he seems keen on my understanding of how "tough" the Japanese staff is; how the Japanese get through the rigors of shooting without complaint; how profoundly hardworking the Japanese are; and, well, just how "unique" the Japanese are. After this, I'm informed that there is no way American crews could possibly work at the level of Japanese crews.

Of course, I admire the Toho staff and love the work they do, but I've also heard enough grumbling to counter claims of "without complaint." I've also seen enough ass whooping to make me believe that some motivation is not out of dedication but out of fear. For Japanese Godzilla fans like Saito, however, there's an eagerness to believe that the Toho staff is the hardest working crew on planet Earth.

I feel these fans are confusing work ethic with working conditions. The most notable difference between US and Japanese crews is that Japan has no unions to prevent studios from exploiting workers. As admirable as it is to see everyone giving it all they've got, it's nothing to celebrate. And a film going over schedule? Any studio worth its salt knows to prepare for this. Besides, this is Godzilla. These films have long shelf lives that justify giving the crew the few extra days they need to get the job done correctly.

"Whatever floats your boat," I respond, not bothering to share my thoughts because I know it'll lead nowhere. Of course he takes my reticence as a concession that American crews don't stack up against those in Japan. If not for Nakao smirking off to the side, I'd probably have just told him to go to hell.

As the crew films Ghidorah in flight, Saito observes that its tails are not moving correctly.

"And if they aren't, is that important?" I ask.

"Well, the fans will complain if they don't move in just the right way," he insists. "For the fans, however, most important is how Godzilla's tail moves."

After this, Saito pulls out his cassette player and turns on a crackly recording of Kamiya yelling commands by the pool. Why would anyone play a recording when the real thing is happening less than ten meters away?

Saito then lays out some beef about how he asked to visit VFX supervisor Matsumoto's studio during post-production and got "no reaction." He asks if I'm going to visit him. I don't have the heart to tell him that I already

have, several times.

Finally, Saito wanders off. With him gone, Nakao slips me the storyboard script and brings back up Saito's bizarre request to tear it in half. Nakao then asks if I'll be coming back next year. To be honest, with the way I feel now—worn out and exhausted—I can't imagine going through this again.

"Well, if you're not coming back, then neither am I." He knows I already know his secret—that this is his last production, but it's flattering to hear him put it this way. It's always a little hard to gauge how far one can push the emotional thing in Japan, but I tell him how truly honored I am to have been able to watch him work.

"Hey," he says. "Let's take a photo together with Godzilla!"

We walk over to Vi-shop, where Shinada kindly snaps a picture of us with the film's star. As we stand in front of Godzilla, Nakao invites me to his home. "I'm not just saying this," he says. "I want you to meet my wife."

Chika joins me for lunch in the cafeteria. She finished work on GMK last week but seeing it's the final day of the shoot, I "ordered" her to stop by. Before heading back to S9, I treat her to ice cream. I've a thing going with one of the women working at the cafeteria. On sale in the cooler are chocolate éclairs with the image of a dinosaur from *Jurassic Park III* on the package. It's usually the first ice cream to sell out. Before lunch, if I give the woman a signal, she saves one for me. Today, even though I didn't motion to her, she's held two, one for Chika and one for me. We open them in front of the big pool to find they're flat; it's like they'd melted and been refrozen.

"It's the thought that counts," I tell Chika as we bite into them.

The doors to S8 are wide open. Curious, we step in. A music video shoot is going on featuring one of the guys from SMAP, Japan's top (and most insufferable) male idol group. It's a follow-up to his (cringe-inducing) novelty song, "Shingo Mama." We finish our ice creams while watching SMAP's Shingo Katori in housewife garb make weird, muggy faces at the camera. I ask Chika which would be worse, working on this or on Godzilla.

"To tell you the truth," she admits, "it's all the same to me." I give her a light, teasing bonk on the head.

Today is Isao's birthday. Chika and I picked up chocolates earlier and in front of S9 we write messages on the bag. I put a bunch of hearts next to my name. We find Isao working on the foot effect and, in an attempt to embarrass him, loudly sing *Happy Birthday*. As hoped, he turns bright red. Despite his protests, I can tell he's happy that we remembered.

After seeing Chika off, I go over to Shinada and propose that he let me climb into the Godzilla suit. I tell him I want to use the experience for future articles. Of course I'll do this, but I also just want to wear it. It's safe to say that this is the foremost dream of any kaiju fan. Luckily, he's cool with the idea. Still, he feels I need to check with someone on the Toho side of the production.

Together, we walk over to the offices in front of S1. It's my first time in this building. If not for the movie posters on the wall, it would look like any other Japanese office. We talk to Takahiro Kawada, one of GMK's production mangers. I explain my reasons for wanting to wear the suit and, smiling, he assures me it's fine with Toho as long as it's fine with Shinada.

"How about this Friday?" Shinada asks. "Be warned. It's heavy. I bet you don't get more than two meters in it."

Back in S9, Yamabe mixes a concoction of Godzilla blood. Knowing I write for *Fangoria*, he asks if I'm into Italian zombie flicks. Does Ghidorah have three heads? To our delight, we learn we're both fans of Fabio Frizzi, the man who wrote soundtracks for many Lucio Fulci films. Together, we hum the theme to *Zombie*. This opens the floodgates; the suit staff starts asking what it's like writing for *Fangoria*, what makeup guys I admire, and what horror films I recommend. It strikes me as somewhat Japanese that they've waited until the very last day to ask this of me.

At 2 p.m., Tezuka and Eguchi are ready to shoot the foot smashing scene. Once the camera hits speed, Tezuka calls for action. The Godzilla foot drops through the roof with a bang. Dust billows around. Too much in fact; it's hard to make out what came through the roof.

Eguchi frowns and shakes his head in disappointment. As much as they'd like to do a reshoot, there isn't time. It'll just have to do. They wrap and move onto blue screen shots of the Battleship Aizu.

It's the last shot of Ghidorah; for it, Ohashi is inside the suit in front of a blue screen. He screams wildly as he performs. Kamiya is yelling too, directing the scene with his stock of grunts and barks. The crew vigorously pulls wires that yank the heads about, causing them to bounce off one another to comical effect.

Once done, Ohashi is helped out of the suit for the last time. All work in S9 stops as Okamoto announces Ohashi has completed his performance as Ghidorah. Applause erupts from every corner of the sound stage. Kamiya walks over with a bouquet of flowers.

"Why am I giving flowers to a guy?" he jokes as he passes them to Ohashi.

I've seen some unusual things in S9, but this one is up there: Six extras dressed as cheerleaders from the *Shingo Mama* video have invaded S9. A Godzilla staffer brought them over as a prank. All in identical blue and white outfits, the women shriek in peppy, squeaky shrills when seeing Godzilla on stage.

"*Oh*, it's Godzilla!" "*Wow*! It really is Godzilla!" "He's *so* cute!!" In a flash, they have cameras out and are snapping photos.

Activity in S9 crashes to a halt as the staff roars over the bubbly cheerleaders. Kamiya too. I can't recall ever hearing him laugh this hard. The cheerleaders clamor together and ask someone to take their picture with Godzilla. I snap a shot for one of the women and Tezuka takes a shot for another.

Deciding enough is enough, the ever-serious Okamoto claps his hands together loudly and orders them to leave. They comply and chatter incessantly as they're escorted out of S9.

Godzilla is standing on a blue screen laid across a long platform with another blue screen draped behind him. Getting the heavy suit cleanly atop the blue screen (to minimize wrinkles and dirt) was a chore.

First, the staff had to hoist the suit into the air via ceiling cables. Once secured, the feet and tail were covered in plastic. After this, wood planks wrapped in blue screen were laid across the stage. Finally, Godzilla was lowered gently down. In total, it took over an hour just to get things this far. For the shot, Godzilla

walks across the platform as pots near his feet blast debris into the air.

Around midnight, I spot Tomiyama in an intense talk with Kamiya. Once over, Tomiyama calls the entire staff to the center of S9. We form a circle. Kageyama, the behind the scenes video guy, starts filming. Tomiyama glares at him and does that "X" thing with his arms. Kageyama lowers his camera.

Once everyone has gathered, Tomiyama explains that it's impossible to finish in the time remaining. Today's plan (if you can call it today because it's already tomorrow) is to complete all the Godzilla shots using the A-unit; the B-unit will handle the non-Godzilla ones. This will still leave a few minor shots, insert elements that can be taken over the next week.

"If we can finish all the kaiju shots, I feel this will constitute *crank-up*," Tomiyama announces.

A break is called at 3 a.m. We're given a midnight snack of sushi and a half-hour to rest. Staffers scurry for chairs and sections of stage where they quickly eat before napping. I lie across Nakao's bench and start to doze off. Sensing something above me, I open my eyes to find I'm looking right into the lens of a camera. It's Isao!

"I'm taking photos of everyone asleep," he says. "Hope you don't mind." He shows me a few photos, but I'm having a hard time focusing on the tiny screen of his digital camera.

At 3:30 a.m., the loud clap of an AD signals it's time to resume the shoot. I pull myself up but quickly fall back onto the bench. I'm beyond tired and have a weird, hollow feeling going on in my chest. I debate whether to go home. However, looking around, I decide against it. Of everyone here, I probably have it the cushiest. Besides, I wouldn't want to be a so-called lazy American and prove Saito right!

One of the teams is working with a miniature helicopter, an insert for when Baragon falls from the sky. Set before a blue screen, the helicopter blows up with a loud, irritating pop. Plastic flies everywhere. Once the smoke clears, I look at my watch: 4:10 a.m.

It's around this time that a surreal fog engulfs S9. Without question, everyone is hard at work, but things feel off. Camera assistant Itakura's eyes float in pools of grease; they look like they could be effortlessly popped out of her skull. Cameraman Murakawa isn't much better. He lifts his head from the cup of the camera's viewfinder to reveal a deep, circular imprint around an eye. Matsumoto is passed out in front of his laptop. His forehead is resting on a white towel laid in front of his computer. Just about everyone seems to be in some sort of personal hell. Honestly, I think if I were to look in a mirror, I'd probably look just as bad.

The B-unit is at work on a shot of the missile wound to Godzilla's shoulder. Earlier in the day, a close-up section of Godzilla's hide with an injury reminiscent of the cell walls in *Fantastic Voyage* was placed inside a large, portable water tank. At 4:30 a.m., it's given a test run. Blood oozes from the wound and dissipates into the water. Both Tezuka and Eguchi agree the effect looks solid and order it to go before the camera. Shinada prepares to drain and refill the tank; it's a process that will take hours.

At 4:45 a.m., I step outside for fresh air. Though the sun is still below the horizon, blue has begun to seep into the sky. Bats dart over the big pool, skimming its surface in the hope of catching water striders. Occasionally the waking burp of a cicada crackles from one of the trees beside the pool's backdrop wall. Most striking is how stages 8, 9, and 10 are shrouded in morning mist.

Takayuki Nakashima, a PR guy who started at Toho this year, joins me for a walk through the pool area. In his early twenties, he talks about how exciting it's been to be a part of such an incredible filmmaking event. Because of how unnaturally silent it is out, we speak in whispers.

At 6:30 a.m., the Godzilla wound effect is shot. Unfortunately, Eguchi is unhappy with the result and orders it redone. "I understand," responds Shinada, stone-faced. He begins the task of draining the tank and resetting the effect.

At around 7 a.m., something in Godzilla's neck breaks. An *oh crap* look passes across the faces of the Vi-shop crew. A worn-looking Kamiya says nothing; it's not like he has to say anything; the Vi-shop guys know it's their responsibility. Like automatons, Yamabe and Shinada get to work repairing the damage. The look on Shinada's face is nothing short of heartbreaking. I put a hand on his shoulder to remind him it'll be over shortly. Abruptly, he puts his arms around me and hugs tightly. It takes them almost two hours to repair Godzilla.

At around 9 a.m., breakfast is brought in: chirashi sushi (strips of sushi over a bowl of rice). I look at it. *Raw fish?* Although hungry, I can't bring myself to take a bite. I think it's just me but Tony feels the same: "I'd rather die than eat sushi now."

The second go at the Godzilla wound is attempted. Luck is on Shinada's side. The wound glows and just the right amount of blood seeps from its edges. Tezuka labels the take as "in the can."

At 10:20 a.m., Godzilla is put atop a circular board with wheels. Staffers out of camera's way spin him like a record on a turntable. Next—the second to last shot of the day—is Godzilla gearing up to shoot his beam. Working the remote, Yamabe pulls out the stops, getting Godzilla's eyebrows to flair and his lips to reveal fangs.

After checking it on the monitor playback, Junko comments, "That was one of the best head shots of Godzilla yet—and at the very last moment!" Yamabe smiles proudly. Given the pressure these last few hours, that he pulled it off so well is testimony to his skill.

Finally, at 11:30 a.m., Godzilla's last shot is up. It's a complicated one of Mothra struggling on Godzilla's back. Likewise, the B-unit is on their final shot. Nakao and I take bets on which team will finish first. I put my faith in Kamiya, with Nakao on Tezuka. I mention the bet to Junko. She finds it funny enough to tell Kamiya.

"What are the stakes?" Kamiya asks.

"The loser has to clean up for the other."

Kamiya frowns. "And you bet on me to finish first? I hope you're prepared to scrub Nakao's floor!"

It seems for a while that Kamiya's group is going to finish first. However, Tezuka's last shot goes off without a hitch—their work is done for the day.

"I'll show you where the mop is," Nakao says with a wink.

Godzilla and Mothra are filmed against a green screen. One of the crew is up on scaffolding and manipulates wires attached to Mothra's back. Its colorful wings flap about as Godzilla tries to swat the insect kaiju away. Standing at the lip of the stage, I take in Yoshida's muffled yells one last time and soak in the final moments of the GMK Godzilla.

Unfortunately, Kamiya calls the shot okay the first time around. I was hoping he'd do at least one more. After Yoshida is helped out of the suit, Kamiya passes him a bouquet of flowers. The crew applauds as Yoshida bows around the room. With that, the day is wrapped.

A row of tables has been covered with snacks: Pocky chocolate sticks, potato chips, strips of dried squid, beef jerky, and, in a bucket, lots and lots of cold beer. Everyone dives for the beer. Tomiyama has us make another circle, where he thanks everyone for the tremendous effort over the past day-plus. We crack open our beers and make a toast.

People mill about, share production tales, and clink beers together while saying that *otsukare-sama* phrase. Suddenly, a commotion erupts at the snack table. Kamiya has picked up a PA and is dunking him head first in the tub of ice housing the beer. Following suit, staffers pop open beers and pour them over PAs and other lower rung crewmembers. Inatsuki tells me this is a signal for the traditional big pool dunking to commence. I go to gather my things and say goodbye to Nakao, but he's gone. Before leaving, I seek out Kamiya and thank him for putting up with me throughout the production.

"Well, it's hardly over," he says. "Please come by during editing any time you like."

It's 1 p.m. and the sun is hanging high over Toho. One by one, staffers are thrown into the muck of the pool. I try to slip away when Thunder yells out. "Look! It's Norman! Throw him in!"

I'm bum-rushed, but with my computer and camera in hand, I beg them to give me a break. Bowing to the crew, I walk off, thankful to leave without a mouthful of algae. At the entrance, I say goodbye to the guards. They tell me to show my face anytime I want to visit.

I walk up the small hill behind Toho. From here, a part of the studio is visible below, including the top edge of S9. With my equipment feeling twice as heavy as usual, I put it down and take in the view. Checking the time, I see I've been up for over thirty hours.

GODZILLA, MOTHRA AND KING GHIDORAH: GIANT MONSTERS ALL-OUT ATTACK
Post-Production

I'm trying to get my mind back into operating in the ordinary world. However, after months of near-daily Godzilla set activity, to go kaiju cold turkey isn't easy. Under the flimsy guise of following up on wearing the Godzilla suit, I head over to Toho after breakfast.

I learn that Shinada is not in today. I wander over to S9 to see if anyone is around. Not only is it devoid of human activity but it's empty—wall-to-wall empty: No benches, no tables, no miniatures, no nothin'! After a quarter-year of brimming with staff, equipment, and monster paraphernalia, to find it barren is nothing less than a shock. If it weren't for the remaining back wall painting of the Hakone landscape, I might think I'd imagined the whole production.

I walk over to the staff rooms and poke my head into the art department office. Will this be empty too? Happily, it isn't. I say hello to Miike, and he asks me to join the staff at the screening room for a reel of SFX rushes.

We walk over to the on-lot theater. Just about everyone has turned out. Eguchi gives me a friendly hello while Junko looks at me in disbelief.

"You're really going to sit through the entire screening?" I don't understand. "It's *all* the SFX footage combined. Over four hours long!"

"*Yikes!*" a surprised Eguchi says, cutting into our conversation. Junko tells him it will take at least two hours to reach the scenes he shot. With a smile, he excuses himself and departs.

Just then, Kamiya steps in; despite his friendliness on the last day, he looks me over coolly.

"Maybe I should go," I say to Junko.

She insists I stay. I leave anyway. It's not like I need to watch raw takes the film-length equivalent of *War And Peace*.

I wander over to Kaneko's production room to find AD Makoto Kumazawa filing papers. I tell him how grueling the last day of SFX shooting was and, jokingly, mention how much more comfortable the live-action crew has it.

Big mistake.

Kumazawa launches into a long bitch session, complaining how everyone says this when the truth is the live-action shooting is just as difficult with similarly long hours and…

Ugh, why didn't I just stay home?

17 AUGUST 2001

Tonight is GMK's wrap party. By chance, I bump into live-action cameraman Kishimoto on the train. Sitting together, we get to talking about—what else?—movies. Kishimoto goes into his envy of American cinema's ability to retain a personal voice even with big budgets and large crews.

"Big budgeted films in Japan," he laments, "look like committee efforts as they try to appease an unwieldy number of backers and producers. For example…" Kishimoto goes blank. Tapping the shoulder of a businessman reading a newspaper next to him, he explains the plot of the film he's trying to remember. Without looking up from his paper, the man replies, "*Alien*." Jumping back into our conversation, he cites *Alien* as an example of an American big-budget film with a strong sense of director. What he's telling me is interesting, but I'm more fascinated by the brazen way he pulled the information out of the guy next to us. If this were New York it wouldn't register; for Japan, it's radical.

At the hotel, I follow "Godzilla" signs to the second floor, wondering how the hotel patrons must be reacting to them. Before stepping into the party, I enter my name in a registry book. Kido hands me an envelope. Inside is the staff photo taken on the waterfront in Chiba. *Wow!* There I am right behind Chiharu with my hair a complete and utter mess!

Inside are two dozen circular tables each topped with a collection of amber-colored beer bottles. In the center are two rows of buffet foods, a podium on one side, and against the back wall, a gold *kin byobu* screen. The room fills quickly with staffers, actors, and office folk. It's odd to see the filmmakers out of the studio, especially the SFX staff. It's my first time to see Yuri in clothes that aren't stained and a face minus grimy smudges.

I take a seat in the back and Rie Ota asks to sit with me. Looking well, she says she's been doing a live hero show for kids since her stint as Baragon. To her question about how the shoot went after she left, I tell her it was all downhill from there. She breaks into a wide smile.

A staffer takes to the podium and signals us to hit the drinks. I grab a glass of beer and decide my order of business is to get drunk and have a blast. However, almost immediately, it's time for the obligatory speeches. Getting drunk will have to wait.

Producer Tomiyama steps up and introduces Shusuke Kaneko. In private and on the job, Kaneko is soft-spoken. That is, he's never loud or boisterous; what comes from his mouth comes from a well-contemplated place. On stage, he's different. There, he transforms into something more spirited.

When talking to groups, Kaneko controls his energy in a curious way.

Most people making speeches find a level and maintain it; Kaneko's fluctuates as he punctuates his words with energized bursts that he zaps out when wanting to emphasize a point. I'm not sure why, but when talking in front of an audience, he reminds me of a person who was once intensely shy but found the means to overcome it.

Kaneko talks about having directed Gamera and how he worried it would prevent getting the job to direct Godzilla. He scores his biggest laugh when saying that after learning GMK would be paired with a Hamtaro movie, his goal was not to let Godzilla lose to a hamster.

Producer Tomiyama calls up Kamiya, but he's nowhere to be found. After he is, he reluctantly takes the stage. Standing beside Kaneko, Kamiya thanks everyone for their effort throughout the shoot. Then, rejoined by Tomiyama, they lead the room in that *iponjime* handclap the Japanese like to do. After smashing our hands together in a collective, thundering smack, the party is finally on!

Someone calls my name. It's Chiharu. She gives me a hug and a beaming smile. Wearing a pink kimono, she spins in place. "What do you think? My mom made it!" I ask about the string of pearls around her waist. "That's my touch. The shoes too." She sticks her feet out to reveal cheap sandals studded with plastic jewelry. She thanks me for the set photos and says she shared them with her family. Suddenly, Chiharu is called onto the stage. The speeches have resumed.

In front of the *byobu*, Chiharu is energetic and giggly. After each talking point, she looks my way and smiles, embarrassing the hell out of me. When done, she bounces back and gives me two whacks in the tummy. "Let's pig out!" she commands.

At the buffet, Chiharu loads my dish with more food than I eat in a week. Once she feels I've enough, we go to where Uzaki and Kaneko are talking. With beers, the four of us toast the real star of the movie: Godzilla!

I share my latest scheme with Uzaki. "We should all start a band. I'll play guitar, and Chiharu will sing."

"Okay, what do I do?" he asks.

"I'm working on that."

Kaneko, Chiharu, and Uzaki break up with laughter. After all, Uzaki is a high-profile and successful musician. Unexpectedly, he says he'd be happy if I play on one of his recordings. His manager hands me his card and asks me to contact him.

One thing I notice is how the party has divided itself. On one side of the room is the live-action crew and on the other is the SFX staff. Even though I'd spent most of my time with the SFX people, I find the live-action crew a bit more accessible and, if this makes sense, "brighter." This isn't to say the SFX staff is the Dark Side, but there is an irrefutable Eloi/Morlock vibe going on between the crews.

Still, I make sure to spend time on the SFX side. However, when heading back to the live-action people, Thunder bitches. "You suck," he says. "You're the only one walking between the two crews." I'm a little unsure what to make of his observation.

For reasons I don't fully understand, parties of this type in Japan end after a scant two hours. After this, things move to a *nijikai* (second party.) With a group this big, there are going to be many splintered second parties. Invited to a few, I'm undecided on which to attend. However, when the time comes to vacate the hall, I find myself thrust into Kamiya's group. He and two of his staffers get the bright idea of walking down the hotel's up escalator.

As they struggle to reach the bottom, one of the SFX crewmembers, a guy who was dickish to me throughout shooting, approaches.

"I've decided on your nickname," he announces snidely. "It's 'Always-With-Chiharu Norman.'" His remark forces me to recall Nakao's comment about crewmembers' human deficiencies.

On the way to the station, this same staffer peels off an ad for a soap club (prostitute establishments operating in gray areas of Japanese law) and sticks it on Kamiya's backpack. Kamiya peels it off and hands it to me.

"Wow," I say in my most sarcastic tone, "I finally got something from you: Porn!"

My phone goes off. It's Kaneko asking me to join his group. I go hoping Chiharu will be there. She isn't. In fact, there are no women at all. Just middle-aged Godzilla crew guys. I mention this to Kaneko.

"Norman," Kaneko says, "we're all aware of this—don't rub it in!"

I sit beside soundman Saito. He talks about American actors Nick Adams and Russ Tamblyn and says that he groups me in with them as foreigners prominently involved with Toho SFX films. It's something I'd never given thought to before. While I'm not sure I agree, it's a nice thing to be told.

I mention how Tamblyn badmouthed the experience of working in Japan in a letter to American writer Henry Miller[18].

"I don't blame him," Saito says. "I was an assistant soundman on *The War of the Gargantuas*. Tamblyn was a Hollywood star and was used to a certain style of filmmaking. He demanded a stand-in and didn't want to rehearse. I think he thought he was slumming, which he probably was."

Two hours later, Kaneko and I catch the train and head back to Setagaya. As we converse, a drunken businessman asks to join our talk. It's not like he's giving us a choice. He wants in. Whenever I say something to Kaneko in English, the businessman translates it into Japanese. Kaneko doesn't speak great English, but he certainly doesn't need this guy's help.

"Where are you from and why are you in Japan?" the inebriated man eventually asks me.

"I'm from Germany," I reply. "I figure since Japan and Germany were such good pals in the war, it would be an easy place to live."

Kaneko turns his head to hide his grin.

Now it's my turn. "Mind if I ask a question?" The businessman is wide-eyed and shakes his head up and down. "If you had the choice, would you rather watch a Hamtaro movie or a Godzilla movie?"

"*Huh*?" he responds.

I ask again.

"Godzilla is an anti-war film..." he stutters in response. At least he's sober enough to recall that.

We arrive in Shimokita. I get off, leaving Kaneko alone with the guy still talking to him in broken English. What a way for a Godzilla director to end his own wrap party.

24 AUGUST 2001

Immigration has ordered me to find a guarantor, someone who will assume

18 - *Letters from HENRY MILLER to Hoki Tokuda Miller*, Hale, 1990

responsibility for my actions in Japan. Kaneko has agreed and I go to Toho to hand him the paperwork. Expressionless, he looks over the instructions.

"They want me to disclose my finances," he points out.

"*Oh*, just do it!" I tell him.

He looks at me hesitantly before relenting. "Sure, no problem. I'll get the information to you in a few days."

We're in the editing room for GMK. It's on the second floor in "Toho Sound Studio," a two-story building (the same building as the screening room) across from the back guard booth. Editing GMK is Isao Tomita, a cheerful, enthusiastic man whom Kaneko insists is one of Japan's finest film editors. I first met Tomita during the wrap party for Kaneko's *Crossfire*, where he excitedly ran up saying, "You're the guy in the restaurant scene! I recognize the red sunglasses!"

Sadly, Tomita is suffering from cancer, and his hair has fallen out from chemotherapy. Despite an uncertain future, he's working hard to a point I'd call inspirational. Tomita plays us a rough edit of the scene where Godzilla fights Ghidorah. As the film runs across the small screen of his Moviola, the three of us make monster sounds whenever the kaiju appear. It's a fun, slightly silly moment, just the sort of thing to take the edge off post-production stress.

Kaneko mentions that today is the last day of SFX filming. Tearing myself away, I dash over to S1 where I find Inatsuki, Isao, and Kasuga next to the vending machines in front of the PR department.

"*Ah*, if it isn't Goro-chan," Isao says, dragging out his nickname for me.

"So, you've come to see 'marine snow,'" Inatsuki says.

Marine snow?

Before stepping into S1 they both put on masks. For Isao to wear one, I figure it must be pretty hairy inside. Sure enough, the studio is awash with floating white particles. This, I find out, is "marine snow," the name given to all the gunk you see clouding up water: plankton, dirt, fish shit, etc. The crew is shooting it as a composite element for the underwater scenes.

Surprisingly, I'm given a warm "good morning" from Kamiya. However, after taking one look at me, Junko snickers.

"Norman, as usual, you're decked out in black. Be warned, you're going to look like a dandruff victim."

Yuri hands me both a mask and goggles. It's the first time I've been given eye protection.

It's great being back and seeing the familiar faces of the Godzilla set. Since the wrap, I've been having dreams near-nightly of the production. Now feels like one of them—There's Kamiya yelling out in his deep, booming voice. Next to him, in one of her many Bon Jovi t-shirts, is Junko scribbling notes. The art staff sits, lined in a row, across the edge of a platform. Except for Thunder. He stands with arms akimbo, eager to show he's ready at a moment's notice. Things wouldn't be complete without Futami—and there he is off to the side pounding a stick on the concrete floor, yelling "*dame, dame, dame!*" even when nothing is particularly wrong.

For the first time ever Futami says good morning to me. I wouldn't call it the most respectful good morning; his head never faces mine. But, I'm happy just the same.

It's time for a take. Tony drops white powder in front of an industrial, high-powered fan. The powder blows into a space between the camera and a large black screen. Like the crew operating it, the camera is wrapped in plastic sheets.

"This is nothing compared to *White Out*," he scoffs, referencing a Toho action film from last year that was set on a snow-covered mountain in Japan. "We had so much of this in the air that you couldn't see your hand in front of your face."

A few takes later and I'm ready to pack it in.

"Where do you think you're going, Norman?" booms Thunder. "This is the *real* final day of shooting. How can you even think of leaving?"

Thunder promises things will be done in an hour. Reluctantly, I stay, taking a seat with Inatsuki on the edge of the platform.

To illustrate how monotonous it is, Inatsuki shapes a piece of clay into a heart. When done, he hands it to me.

"Giving me your heart, Inatsuki-*kun*?" I ask. The art staff breaks up with laughter.

Well, an hour rolls around. By the look of it, the crew is nowhere near finished. Another hour later, at 6:30 p.m., they break for dinner. With everyone at the nearby convenience store, I slip out and head home.

27 AUGUST 2001

With my Godzilla suit-wearing arrangements finalized, I'm at Toho bright and early. I step into Kaneko's always-unlocked production room to find it empty. With nothing going on here, I zip over to S9. Toho has struck a deal with Wonda Coffee to shoot a commercial featuring Godzilla, and Shinada is readying one of the suits for the upcoming one-day production. His

hand is still bandaged, and the doctor told him it needs another six months to heal. Despite this, he's using it as if it were uninjured. I suggest to him that at this rate it won't heal for a year or more. In any case, Shinada says he needs a couple of hours before he can fit me into the Godzilla suit.

To pass the time, I go to the sound mix building. In the lobby leafing through newspapers are Kido and Kaneko's three ADs. Pseudo news rules, and the top story concerns four girls joining the idol group Morning Musume. Sharing the headline is a scandal involving corporate boy band SMAP. One of its members was involved in a parking violation. He's on all the front pages, head dipped in shame, throwing himself on the mercy of the public to a point you'd think he'd defecated on an image of the Emperor himself.

Kaneko arrives and we head into Toho's recording room. There, in front of a mixing console, soundmen Saito and Taira are checking levels as they prepare for the day's looping session. Continuity person Miho Iizuka runs over notes with Kaneko as I help myself to the pot of coffee next to the couch behind the console.

The first actor up is Takashi Matsuo, the policeman in the scene where Baragon frees Amamoto from jail. He matches various grunts to footage playing on a screen. After this, Masahiro Kobayashi comes in for his overdubbing. As a lead in the film, his recording will take up much of the day.

During a break, Kobayashi and I sit down for an impromptu interview. We grab lunch and go up to the second floor, where we find a sunny, unused room.

Surprisingly, unlike many Japanese guys his age, Kobayashi isn't up on his kaiju lore. "I was born in '71," he begins. "Probably the first movie I saw in the theater was *King Kong* (1976). I told everyone about the film in kindergarten the next day. After that, I didn't feel the need to watch any more giant monster films. I guess I'd had my fill. I knew about Godzilla, of course, and I had a couple of toys, but I never watched any of the films.

"Likewise, I usually don't watch movies by the directors of films I get hired to, but I watched Kaneko's *Gamera*. If it's okay to say this, I always thought kaiju movies were like Ultraman TV shows, but his *Gamera* was *a lot* different. I was like, *whoa!*"

In GMK, Kobayashi plays Teruaki Takeda, a science writer, and cites his uncle as a source of inspiration. "I don't know much about science, and when it comes to writing, I've only ever dabbled in poetry. I have an uncle who is an architect. In his spare time, he's a UFO researcher. He goes to the mountains near his home to take photos of UFOs and aliens. He showed me some of them. On their margins, he wrote notes in a language he created so that no one can read them. I figured if I were into science, I'd be passionate about it like him."

With the shoot now over, I ask him what scene stands out most in his mind. "The most memorable scene for me was when I took Chiharu home drunk," he says after some thought. "I know it's got nothing to do with Godzilla, but the way Uzaki, her father, answered the door very soldierly was impressive. I enjoyed doing that scene very much."

After finishing, I thank Kobayashi and speed over to S9 to see if Shinada is ready for my Godzilla suit wearing adventure. Me, I'm all set to take it for a spin. More

than "all set," I'm raring to go! The ultimate for any Godzilla fan, I think of ways to equate it: Like pasting on Spock ears during the production of *Star Trek*? Like walking around the set of *Star Wars* in Darth Vader's helmet? Like cracking Indiana Jones's whip during the shooting of *Raiders*? Well, whatever it may be likened to, it's something I never thought I'd do in my lifetime.

I get to S9 to find Shinada by the entrance. "Where'd you like to do it?" he asks. "Inside or outside?"
Outside, of course!
Shinada, Yamabe, and Daisuke Sato, a member of their crew, push the cart housing the Godzilla suit across the studio floor, parking it between the open front doors of S9. I've chosen to wear the action suit. I picked this one because Yoshida said it moves the best, although he did add that it was also the heaviest.

As the three men look over the suit, I have second thoughts. What if I hurt myself, like pull a muscle, or worse, do irreparable damage to my body? After all, at 70kg (154 pounds), the suit weighs more than I do. It's not as if I'm putting on a Don Post Halloween mask!

Yamabe reaches into the suit's back and flips out several straps that he lays over Godzilla's shoulders. He instructs me to take off my sneakers. I place them next to the cart. Stepping up and getting behind the suit, I put a foot on each side of Godzilla's tail. I then grab the cart's top metal beam and hoist myself into the air. Hanging like a monkey, I look down into the suit's dark interior. Taking a deep breath, I drop my feet into the black holes of the legs.

My feet go in and down, but somewhere around the knees they abruptly stop. Though I try, I can't work myself in any further. I ask Yamabe what to do.

"Push," he responds unsympathetically.

So, I push.

And I push...

And I push...

I push to the point I think my feet are going to break. All at once they slip through and drop into the bottom half of Godzilla's legs. With my feet secured, I'm a bit more relaxed. However, before sticking my head in, I assess the space before me: The neck is riddled with various-sized pinholes. Obviously how the actor sees out, my face goes in front of them. I aim for the holes. As I move in, my head scrapes against a fiberglass helmet located around the top of Godzilla's neck. I fit the top of my head snug against it.

Shinada jokingly asks if the inside smells like Yoshida. I remind him that I'm not intimate enough with Yoshida to know. If anything, the suit emits a strong odor of rubber and glue.

Next, come the arms. Not as tough as working my legs in, still, they're an ordeal. I vigorously wiggle my hands past the wrists, which are skin-thin with no padding. After they're in, I use one hand on the other to wedge my fingers in place. Two of the fingers—pinkie and ring—are a single unit. At last, it's time to get sealed inside!

The guys start fiddling behind me, and I abruptly feel straps pulling hard against my back. One strap yanks tight around my groin. This is followed by the sound of plastic locks clicking together. Shinada wants to know if I want to wear the fins. I insist since it wouldn't really be Godzilla without them. As they come into place, everything around me grows dark—black-ink dark.

Floating about six centimeters in front of my face is the mesh of neck holes. While I can see out of them reasonably well, my sight is limited to what's directly before me. Just then, Shinada walks past. That is, I guess it's Shinada; I can't see above his shoulders. He asks how I'm doing.

"Never better," I reply.

"Good," he says. "Because here's where the fun begins."

Yamabe tells me to brace myself. With that, the suit is released from the overhead bar. An incredible mass, like being jumped by a wild bear, slams down against my back. As I adjust myself to the weight, Shinada beckons me forward. I move away from the cart and onto the asphalt. I take a few heavy steps forward. Around me, the suit shifts and moves as it settles into place.

For fun, I paw the air. However, when my hands come into view through the peepholes, I'm thrown for a loop. These aren't my hands! They're gray and lumpy with claws the color of dull ivory! Like that, the feeling of self vanishes. No longer am I plain Norman England. *I am Godzilla*!

By surprise, Shinada grabs my hands and begins grappling with me. In my altered-identity state, I fight back, watching through pinholes as my reptilian-like hands repel an attacking enemy. It's not until I grasp the extent to which I'm fighting back against Shinada that I snap back to reality. Deciding not to get too carried away, I shift my focus to the reason for being in the suit in the first place: to experience the challenges Godzilla suit actors face.

I find if I move my head in a small circle while looking through the neck holes I get a better idea of the area in front of me. Spotting the path leading to the big pool, I make for it. Each step is a chore. It feels like bricks are strapped to my feet. As I trod forward, I recall Nakajima telling me about testing the first Godzilla suit and how he passed out after several meters. Considering this, I think it best not to let my zeal get the better of me. Stopping where the road slants up, I turn the suit at the waist and look back to see Shinada and Yamabe smiling wildly; I think they find the idea of me in the suit a bit absurd. I notice that passersby have gathered. I ham it up by scratching at the air and rolling my body around like I've seen Yoshida do.

Yamabe steps forward to tell me that my stance is wrong. "Spread your legs wider," he says. "From outside it looks like they're sewn together."

Obeying, I spread them apart. It must not be wide enough because he starts kicking at the inside of my legs. I spread them so far out that it feels as if I'm splitting down the middle. I finally reach a point he says looks right.

Unexpectedly, Shinada announces that he's going to open me up. They crack the fins off and unstrap me. I pop out until I'm half-in and half-out of the suit. Assistant Sato takes a padded rest piece and fits it under my crotch. I squat down. Relief pours over my body as the weight of the suit disappears. Shinada asks if I want to come out.

"*Hell no!*" I protest.

Strapped back in, I pace about the area in front of S9. I try a few maneuvers, like bending down to pick up an imaginary boulder that I throw at an imaginary Ebirah. I snap my butt around thinking I'm whipping the tail, but without assistance from a wire, it doesn't budge. In a brisk move, I thrust my hands to the side and lean slightly forward, pretending I'm shooting Godzilla's atomic beam. Gradually, it becomes more and more trying to move in the suit. After a few more minutes, I feel I've reached my limit of endurance.

I signal the guys that I'm done and head back to the cart. When I get to it, Shinada tells me to turn the suit around, that I can't just step up onto it. One tiny step at a time, I work the suit around. Then, while the men hold up the tail, I back my feet up onto the cart. When I'm in place, they clip the suit to the overhead bar. The fins come off and light shines in around me. I pull my head out and work my hands from the suit. The final step is freeing my legs, a task that turns out to be more difficult than getting them in.

Once again, I'm stuck around the knees. No matter how hard I try, I can't get free. In desperation, I grab the overhanging bar and pull with all my might. It's no good; my feet remain trapped. I try shaking them forcefully. This does nothing. It seems the only option is to cut me free. I tell Yamabe to get a knife, but he simply orders me to try harder. Mustering my remaining strength, I pull at the bar; I tug so hard that I lift the entire suit off the ground! Suddenly, my feet pop out. I'm free!

Back on the ground with the weight of the suit gone, I feel as light as a feather. I'm experiencing a weird tingling sensation throughout my body. It's as if every cell in my being has been stabbed with a sharpened pencil. After catching my breath, I ask Shinada how my performance as Godzilla was.

"If we ever need a sick Godzilla, I know who to call."

I thank Shinada and bow to him and the others umpteen times. I speed off to find Kaneko, who is in the cafeteria having coffee. I excitedly describe my Godzilla suit-wearing experience. He's both captivated and amused.

Later that night, I can hardly stay awake. I'm so completely drained that

I fall asleep at 9:30 p.m. and sleep until noon the next day. How do those suit actors do this day in and day out?

29 AUGUST 2001

Today is the Wonda Coffee commercial shoot. I get to S9 to find the crew already at work. Or, I should say, a skeleton crew. While several art staffers are on-set, people like Miike and Jimmy are nowhere to be found. The camera crew is different too. Oddly, several of the live-action team are here, such as Aida, Kaneko's AD. The rest of the staff are outsiders brought in by the client.

A stack of storyboards rests on a table next to S9's entrance. I help myself to one. The commercial centers on Yoshida and how drinking Wonda Coffee energizes him to meet the demands of playing the King of the Monsters. What makes this different from the regular shoot is that the crew will be visible in shots. As the storyboards reveal, the commercial is not about Godzilla, but about Yoshida and his work environment.

The one crewmember noticeably absent is Kamiya. Playing the part of director is stunt coordinator Abe. He tells me he's basing his actions on his observations of Kamiya. The only criticism I can offer is that he's smoking. Kamiya doesn't smoke.

It takes an hour for the camera to roll. A money shot, the first take is Godzilla walking between burning buildings. At one point, blasts go off on the suit. While the Godzilla suit is being re-squibbed, I notice the pyrotechnic crew is the same as on GMK. As a specialized job, "can safely set explosives off on monsters

suits" is likely not something you'll find on many resumes.

When it comes to productions, Japanese commercials have all the money. This shows in the excellent lunch we're provided. As I eat, Yuri and Yoshida join me. It's my first time seeing Yoshida since wearing the Godzilla suit.

"I bet it stunk after a summer of me sweating in it!" he says as he pops the top of his *bento* off. He and Yuri are all ears as I tell them about my time in the Godzilla outfit.

Although the shot of Godzilla walking through a burning cityscape is standard fare, the one of Yoshida out of the suit and walking through the set minus the suit is new. The idea is to segue from Godzilla to the man within the suit. It's fascinating to watch Yoshida in his gym shorts making his way across the set. However, I find the shot in which Yoshida is removed from the suit a bit silly. Covered in fake sweat, he makes a pained expression. Nothing could be further from the truth. Thinking back, I can't remember Yoshida ever emerging from the suit without that ear-to-ear grin of his. Even after taking a spill off stage, he always came up looking hit-the-lottery happy.

I leave in the late afternoon and stop in at the editing rooms. Kaneko isn't around. I pop into Kamiya's editing suite to say hello. As usual, Junko is hunched over a thick notebook. For reasons not apparent, Kamiya is lying flat across the bare floor. From this odd position, he has me tell him what I saw on the TV commercial set. He roars with laughter when he hears that Abe was tapping his director's spirit.

Kaneko calls to say he's at Soshigaya-Okura Station with editor Tomita and his

196

wife Nobuko. They want me to join them for dinner. I bid farewell to still-on-the-floor Kamiya and zip off to the station.

After I arrive, we go to a nearby restaurant for dinner. Tomita is ecstatic. He's gotten news that his cancer is in remission and may have been arrested altogether. We're all overjoyed by the news.

During dinner, Tomita and I talk about editing. I mention making Super-8 films as a boy and how my favorite step was editing. He gets a kick hearing me brag about my skill at scraping film emulsion and making wet splices that would pass through projectors without a hiccup. In return, Tomita shares his childhood love of Godzilla and how it led to him becoming a film editor, adding that editing GMK is the culmination of a lifelong dream.

Saying he's had a breakthrough by making a few sections come together in editing, Kaneko is happier than usual. However, he does admit to still having trouble with the underwater battle between Godzilla and Ghidorah. He doesn't feel the photography looks real enough. He wants to trim it, whereas Kamiya wants to lengthen it. For example, after Godzilla shoots his ray, he feels the shot should end quickly; Kamiya wants it to hold on Godzilla until he takes a step forward. Kaneko adds that he went through similar issues with Higuchi during the Gamera series. Although he's complaining, Kaneko is highly animated.

"It seems to me," I say, "making Godzilla films is a thrill."

Kaneko smiles. "It sure is," he admits.

7 SEPTEMBER 2001

I'm hanging with Tomita. Rather than edit, he's double-checking scenes at his bench before tomorrow's *all-rush* screening[19]. I pull up a chair and sit beside him. He runs a scene of Godzilla blasting Baragon to death.

"Did you see that?" Tomita asks excitedly. "Godzilla's fins moved!" I tell him how the suit was built this way and mention being there when the scene was shot.

"You were there? That's fantastic!!" As the film plays silently, Tomita goes into his charming routine of barking out sound effects.

Tomita and I head out to meet the staff for a screening of VFX shots Matsumoto has prepared. We find Kaneko, Kamiya, Junko, and Matsumoto killing time in the lobby. Tomita looks them over.

"Norman," he asks loudly, "why do you think it is that SFX staffers are all fat?"

After a deep gasp, everyone starts laughing. Although Kamiya and Matsumoto are heavyset, I wouldn't call them fat. Though my take on their size might have something to do with my being from America, a place where people grow to massive sizes. However, not wanting to miss an opportunity to get a dig in, I join in on the fun.

"Tomita," I posit, "it's probably because they have so much spare time on their hands."

To this, Kamiya roars with laughter, while Matsumoto shakes his head in self-pity.

In the theater, we review footage of a teacher and her students looking out of a classroom window at a mushroom cloud

---

19 - *All-rush* is *wasei-eigo* for footage edited together but lacking music, sound FXs, and some SFX shots. In English it would be close to "rough cut."

rising in the distance. Another shot shows Baragon digging into the ground. Altogether, the reel runs less than four minutes and is shown twice. After this, Matsumoto asks us to go to the staff room where he'll preview VFX shots not yet rendered to film.

Outside, I catch Kamiya getting on his bicycle. I feel this is my chance to ask about doing an interview for *Fangoria*.

"Why not interview Kaneko?" he suggests. I tell him I have, umpteen times. Kamiya points at Matsumoto. "How about him?"

"*Come on…*" I say, frustrated.

Kamiya pushes down on the peddle of his bike before letting out a simple, "No."

In the staff room, Matsumoto has his Mac open and is playing several new effects shots. One is a scene of army missiles lifting off and hitting Godzilla. Rather than explode on contact, they attach themselves by metallic claws. Kamiya points out how they aren't emerging quickly enough. The bomb hits, pauses, and then the legs fold out. Kamiya wants them to fold out without hesitation.

After this, the staff piles over to a Chinese restaurant down the road from Toho. Since we're eating Chinese, Kaneko feels the need to tell me about Chinese history. For some reason, I mention that Kamiya didn't attend GMK's Shinto *oharai* ceremony. Overhearing my remark, Kamiya tells me about a Czech filmmaker who refused to partake in rituals like this because they're religious-based and have nothing to do with filmmaking. I have to say, not only do I agree with him on this, but admire his decision to buck the system.

8 SEPTEMBER 2001

Today is the *all-rush* screening of GMK. Gathered in the lobby, Kaneko's three ADs, Tomita and Nobuko, Kamiya, Junko, and Kaneko and his brother Jiro hang around drinking coffee. At a little after 1, we pile into the theater. I take a seat with the Kaneko brothers.

The film begins. It has temporary titles and a sound mix that's all over the place: background audio is either eerily silent or overblown with ambient sounds. There are heavy splices now and then, and some of the VFX work is simply drawn onto the picture. It's my first time to see a film in such an unpolished state; frankly, it's jarring and difficult to watch. As such, I can't form an opinion of any kind. Is the movie good? Bad? I really don't know. Afterward, the staff returns to the lobby to pass around ideas.

Everyone sits in silence with eyes focused far off. Eventually, someone comes out with an *ummm* sound. Attention drawn, they start talking—slowly at first—as they form their thoughts. Once they've had their say, heads in the room bob up and down as the words are digested. Gradually, other comments and opinions are shared. Taking the plunge, I make a suggestion about the scene with the Maeda sisters and Mothra.

As it stands, you see them walking toward the camera with people scurrying about. They look up to see Mothra overhead. I speculate putting a shot of Mothra at the top to let you know right away that Mothra is causing the wind. Kaneko tells me there will be wind sounds added during the sound mix, which will be enough of a clue for the audience. As I figured, given my unfamiliarity with the filmmaking process, I should keep my mouth shut.

However, the more everyone talks about GMK, the happier they seem with it. Soon, the once stoic faces become animated. Although there is much work left, the consensus is that the movie is in a good place.

I did spot one thing unfortunate—my elbow! It's in the scene in Tachinaba's office from the day in Yokohama. I thought I'd escaped the camera, but you can just see my arm pulling out from the first shot. The kicker is, I shouldn't have moved at all! You wouldn't think it to be anything more than the edge of something on the windowsill. When we walk out of the theater, I try to tell Kaneko but stumble on my words.

"Are you making a confession?" he asks. I am and get my explanation out on the second try. He laughs it off. "I didn't notice. I'm sure it's okay."

Well, I hope so...

23 SEPTEMBER 2001

Although claiming I'll probably find it boring, Kaneko called last night to invite me to today's looping session. Boring or not, I'm making the walk down the long, tree-lined street to Toho. It's a stunning morning, and I'm basking in the touch of autumn, letting it conjure boyhood memories of falls in New York...

New York...

These two words have been foremost on my mind for the past week and a half, a week and a half best described as "fucked." I can't go anywhere without someone bringing up the World Trade Center attack. It's the only thing on TV, in the newspapers, and on people's lips. More than the constant reminder, it's the general sense of panic, like the world has taken an abrupt, unexpected turn—destination unknown—that gnaws at my insides. I heard from my mom that my brother was pulling people from the wreckage and is in the hospital from smoke inhalation. I've tried but still haven't been able to reach him.

I get to the Toho Sound Studio building at 10 a.m. In the lobby, the ADs read the morning paper. *Great.* More photos of jets crashing into the Twin Towers and plumes of billowing white smoke. It's difficult to accept what's happened, the loss of life and the scarring of the New York City skyline.

In my hometown of Rockland County was a spot atop a tall, quiet hill. I'd go there now and then with friends on weekend nights to listen to 8-track tapes. Far off, the Towers shimmered over the treetops, a reminder that the greatest city in the world was within our grasp. Years later, after moving to New York City, I'd often sit on a bench in Washington Square Park that offered an arresting view of the Towers. The bench faced LaGuardia Place, a straight-as-an-arrow road with street lamps that converged to a point from where they rose kaiju-like. Guess it'll have to live in my memory...

The scene up for dubbing is a teacher and students watching an atomic bomb-like mushroom cloud from their classroom window. Ten children led by their moms file into the sound studio. Kaneko asks me to sit in the control room with him and Saito and Taira, but I opt to watch from the studio floor. I go in through heavy, soundproof doors and find a seat across from the children, who stand in two rows. Aida is here running things. He passes out scripts with various phrases for the kids to say.

The whole thing turns out to be a bigger ordeal than anticipated. First, Kaneko asks the kids to make basic classroom noises. He calls for action. Dead silence. Aida is nice enough about it and manages to win a bit of enthusiasm through kindness. They try again and Kaneko finds the take lacking but usable. For the shot where their desks rattle about, they try recording the kids yelling in panic and, *boy*, is that unconvincing. Several more takes later and they still have nothing usable.

As Aida pleads with the kids, I slip back into the control room. Kaneko has his head tilted back and is staring at the ceiling. Another take is attempted. Kaneko flips himself forward and leans into a mike, "Once more." From the control room speakers, we hear Aida bark, "Hear that? That's the director! Now get your act together and yell!" We laugh at Aida's newfound tough-love approach. In the end, it takes about two hours and no one is satisfied with the result.

Taking a break, we go to the lobby. There, Taira asks about the Twin Towers and the situation back home. He shows me his t-shirt. Across the chest is the John Lennon phrase, "War Is Over." Concerned about the situation, he asks my thoughts on where things might lead, especially military conflict. I didn't know this, but Taira is a staunch pacifist opposed to military intervention of any kind.

As we talk about the uncertainty that lies ahead, Taira begins to cry. Make no mistake, they're not a sign of solidarity with the US government. Instead, they represent sympathy for my pain, sadness at the destruction to my home and its loss of life, compassion for what my friends and family are going through, and concern for the doubtless conflict and killing that will come when America unleashes its wrath. Taira wraps his arms around me and gives a deep hug. I hug him back and thank him for opening up.

Once the day's recording is done, Shusuke, Aida, Shimizu, Iizuka, and I stroll over to a run of model homes in the area behind the big pool. In the center square, someone in a Godzilla event suit walks around and keeps the children of prospective homebuyers entertained. For fun, we look through a couple of houses. Many are impressive three and four-story structures with luxurious interiors. A few even sport elevators. The home prices are out of this world, which prompts Iizuka to comment, "Looks like I gotta marry rich."

On the way back, after taking a group photo in front of a hedge cut in the shape of Godzilla, I tell the gang about my experience wearing the Godzilla suit.

Shimizu is amazed. "I always wanted to do that," he admits. "It's not just something anyone can do, you know."

Kaneko and I go for a bite to eat at a nearby ramen shop to talk about the progress of GMK and the situation in New York, which Kaneko worries might have a negative impact on GMK.

"I don't mean to sound insensitive," he insists. "But it could turn people off from seeing a film with scenes of city destruction." I agree, but remind him that it's out of his hands. I also mention that, at its heart, Godzilla is an anti-war statement and is just the message needed now.

"You're right," he says, "Still, it might affect the film's promotion. It's similar to when my first Gamera film came out. That was released soon after the Kobe earthquake. We had to tone down destruction shots during advertising."

24 SEPTEMBER 2001

Today is the Foley session for GMK. This is when sounds such as footsteps, doors opening and closing, cups being placed on tables, chairs squeaking, and all the odd noises we take for granted are recorded. Kaneko thinks I'll enjoy being in the studio with the Foley artists rather than in the control room. He interrupts the session in-progress to let them know I'll be stepping in. After apologizing for the interruption, I find a spot in an out of the way corner.

Three guys do Foley for when teen punks see Mothra speed towards them from the ocean. Standing in a large rectangle of dirt in front of a projection screen, they match their steps to those of the actors. They also ruffle shirts tied around their waists to mimic the noise of the actors' clothing.

The next scene is Chiharu coming home drunk. One guy does her footsteps, another does those of Kobayashi's. The scene following this—Chiharu getting up in the morning and having breakfast with her father—is more complicated. It takes all three men just to get her sounds: the dishes, the plates, her clothes, and, of course, her footsteps.

It's eye-opening seeing an aspect of filmmaking that gets little attention. In fact, it makes me sensitive to the sounds I make in the course of everyday moments. For instance, as I jot this down in my GMK journal, I become aware of the sound of the pen against paper and the shuffling of the pages in my notebook.

For lunch, together with Kaneko, his ADs, and Iizuka, we pile into a Toho van and drive to a nearby Royal Host restaurant. Typically, Japanese menus are like food photonovels with pictures to help you select your meal; instead, the menu has drawings. It's baffling why they would do this and makes it a hassle to order. When the waitress comes, Kaneko coolly tells her to inform her bosses that menus like this are probably not a bright idea.

As we eat, we talk about the situation in the US. Kaneko ponders aloud what would happen if the Japanese send in troops to aid the US in their inevitable Twin Tower counterattacks. He tells us he'll block the airstrips with his body if they do. Like many Japanese born in the shadow of WWII, Kaneko is fine with Japan keeping their military at a barebones domestic protection level.

In better news, Kaneko mentions that he spoke to Tomiyama about letting me look over the English subtitles. A few months back, Kaneko asked if I wanted the job of writing them. I declined because I didn't feel qualified. However, I do think I can give them a "native check," the term in Japan for giving subtitles a double-check by a native speaker. On the spot, Kaneko calls up Tomiyama. Getting off the phone, he said Tomiyama will be emailing me a copy of the subs.

25 SEPTEMBER 2001

I get to Toho for a morning screening of an updated edit of GMK. The lights go down and the Toho logo comes up. Oddly, although the picture looks fine, the audio is a mess. The opening temp music crackles like it's being broadcast through a Radio Shack walkie-talkie. After thirty seconds, the film stops. Two minutes later, it starts up again— this time, when General Tachibana speaks, instead of dialogue, a horrid hiss screams out.

A few more tries go by but the sound only worsens. It's so grating that I plug my ears. Finally, the lights go up and the thirty or so of us in attendance wander into the lobby, leaving the projectionist to sort out the trouble. Soon we're told that the sound playback device is busted. Pulling outside speakers into the theater, a workaround is found. On with the show…

While there are still plenty of dummy shots in place, the newly completed SFX work looks terrific. There's a neat one from an observation spot in Hakone of people pointing at Baragon in the valley below. Another completed shot is Baragon busting through the forest. CG birds flapping out from trees have been added. It's a pleasing touch. Less impressive is the CG fish added to the Satsuma sub's first underwater shot. "What the hell are those supposed to be?" someone yells, sending the staff into a fit of laughter.

4 OCTOBER 2001

I head straight for the Sound Studio building this morning, where the staff is working on the film's pre-music sound design. It's my first time in the large Studio A. To the left of the entrance, a couple of guys are working with Pro Tools and the assortment of sound effects and kaiju roars they've created for the movie. At a long mixing console are Saito and Taira. Seeing me, Taira rushes over to show me a videocassette he received from a friend of a benefit concert given in NYC for the WTC deceased and their families.

In front of the console facing a movie screen is a couch that Kaneko shares with Shimizu, Aida, and Iizuka. Kaneko sits with his hands folded behind his head, half his shirt out, and his unshoed feet stretched before him.

"Why don't 'cha make yerself at home," I say in jest.

Kaneko gives me an English "Hey!" and signals for me to sit next to him. The lights dim and a section of the film plays. A hospital scene, background sounds now include murmuring, moaning, a distant siren, a ringing phone, etc. It's played multiple times; after each viewing, Kaneko offers comments on their balance and what needs to be added or nixed. I mention I find the siren sound odd; it just goes on and on without ever arriving at the hospital. Kaneko turns to the sound guys and gives them a "make it so" signal.

Kaneko's wife Nanako has plans to see a movie with her friends and drops off Suzu and Yurina. Slightly embarrassed to play dad while in director mode, Kaneko begrudgingly leads them to the couch and has them sit in front of him. I like these life touches. It's a reminder that movies are made by real people with ordinary life issues.

When Chiharu's character comes on screen, Kaneko leans close to Yurina. "Her name is *Yuri*." (The name is a reference to his daughter.) Yurina doesn't take well to this. From then on, whenever Chiharu shows up on screen, she announces loudly, "I'm calling her Yumi. Her name is Yumi. *Yu-mi!*"

Kaneko rolls his eyes. "She's just embarrassed," he whispers.

One reason the kids are here is for their weekly English lesson. We watch the film until Yurina gets bored and then move to the lobby, where we go over vocabulary and do ABC writing. I can't say it's the best spot to have a lesson. Toho execs and staff are constantly walking past. At best,

I'm given bewildered looks; at worst, people chuckle.

Junko passes by and I invite her to join us. "I think this level is just right for you," I say with a wink. "Besides, as part of Toho's *eikaiwa* division, I can swing you an employee discount."

Junko sits and tries her hand at English. She's not bad, and I'm happy to learn she can hold a conversation. I wish I'd found this out earlier. She then shares the story of entering a contest when the film *City Slickers* opened in Japan. She and a friend won an all-expenses paid trip to the American West.

After dinner, the kids take to jumping from sofa to sofa in the lobby. Yurina starts waving her arms and making invisible "barriers" I have to fight my way through. They eventually run into the screening room. Kaneko, done with the day's mixing session, and I chase after them. Opening the door to the darkened theater, He makes ghostly sounds. I hide in the projection booth. When the kids emerge, I jump out and scare them. They laugh gleefully and speed into the lobby.

After the kids have gone home with their mother, we return to the editing suite upstairs. Here, Tomita reviews scenes with Kaneko and Kamiya, letting the two directors talk in detail over editing choices and pacing.

5 OCTOBER 2001

I'm out getting breakfast when Kaneko calls. "This...is...Shusuke..."

I don't know why he always says this. It's not as if names don't pop up on phone screens. In any case, he tells me the schedule has changed and that monster yells will be added to the audio *before*

mixing in the music.

"You should come to the studio now," he insists.

I zip home, grab my camera, and hightail it over to Toho. I arrive during the Baragon battle. The sound designers are dropping in various grunts, growls, and yells and running them past Kaneko.

After saying hello to Shimizu and Iizuka, I sit next to the director and kick back to watch the intricate and fascinating process of monster roar insertion.

A break comes and some of us go into the lobby for coffee and a change of scenery. The TV runs footage of the just-launched US attack on Afghanistan. I mention how it reminds me of Vietnam coverage from my childhood, only less graphic, and my worry that, although the US is saying this will be wrapped up in no time, it's going to last a lot longer than they're letting on—again, like Vietnam.

Kamiya cuts in with an off-the-cuff remark about the Twin Towers. "I wish we could have seen them go down before shooting the Landmark Tower destruction. It might have helped us make it look more real."

As you can imagine, this pisses me off. Not only does he know I'm American, but he also knows I'm a New Yorker. Even if one were to argue that the US government bears responsibility due to its long-time, finger-in-the-pie involvement with politics in the Middle East, I find his remark insensitive. I mean, despite it being fifty-six years after the fact, I wouldn't tell someone from Hiroshima how photos of atomic bomb victims make for good special makeup effect reference material or that Japanese kaiju fans should be grateful for the nuclear bombings of Hiroshima and Nagasaki since they inspired the first Godzilla film and, for that matter, the whole kaiju genre. No, that would be tasteless.

Kaneko steps outside to take a phone call. Shimizu and Iizuka use the chance to ask what I thought of Kaneko when first meeting him.

"Didn't you find him scary?" Iizuka asks.

"Well, I was intimidated at first," I reflect, "but that was because of the preconceived notion everyone has of directors. After I came to know and understand him—how he thinks, what he likes, and how he approaches his work—I realized we have much in common and that 'director' is just a title. So, any feeling of intimidation I had was replaced by respect for him as a person and feelings of friendship. To be honest, I think what people find scary about him—his aloof nature—is what makes him a good director. He's contemplative and is always weighing things against each other as he searches for the correct answer or the best course of action. It might make him seem gloomy or distant, but far from it. He's probably the most fair-minded person I've ever met."

My answer seems to surprise them.

Soon it's time to screen new VFX sequences. In the theater, Okamoto calls out shot numbers as they appear on the screen. The staff has the opportunity to comment or forever hold their peace. If there is no objection, Kaneko signs off on the shot.

Like in the editing room, Tomita accompanies the silent footage with vocal noises. Either he's enhancing shots with sound effects or saying things to no one in particular, like, "Hey, what's the deal with this shot?" Or statements such as, "I see! The cars have been zapped out from the front of the tunnel!" That he does this doesn't astonish me; what does is how totally unconcerned he is with the racket he's making. I'm beginning to think that Tomita's passion and zeal might be the most memorable thing about GMK's post-production.

Afterward, a jubilant Tomita thanks me for running his photos on Kaneko's website. He tells me that friends worried about his health are relieved to see him looking fine (despite the hair loss) and working on a major motion picture.[20]

Tomita leads a group of us to his work suite to get new edits approved by Kaneko and Kamiya. As always, Tomita's unabashed excitement is on full display, and he proudly shows them the re-worked underwater battle scene.

When a D-03 missile comes on screen, Tomita yells out, "Here it comes! One of Norman's phenomenal labels!"

Just then, Aida pops in to tell us that idol group Morning Musume is making a TV commercial in S2.

"Now's your chance," he says to me. "Go and tell 'em just what you think of Japanese idols!" Iizuka and Junko egg me on, too, suggesting I "put my money where my mouth is."

When I look at Kaneko for support, I see he's making far-off eyes. He's trying to come up with a reason to get on their set because, well, he just wants to meet them.

7 OCTOBER 2001

Today is the recording session of the GMK soundtrack. I arrive at Ichigaya Station and walk over to the Nihon TV building a few minutes away. In a studio on the

---

20 - Sadly, Tomita passed away from cancer on 18 October 2002. His last editing job was to make trims for the TV version of GMK. His wife Nobuko, also a film editor, passed away 29 October 2012.

6th floor, I find composer Kow Otani at a desk behind a console and Kaneko on a sofa behind him. Other staffers are here: Iizuka, Aida, Shimizu, and PR man Masuda. Seated beside Otani is Kyoko Kitahara, a music producer at Toho. On the other side of the console window, a 20-or-so-piece orchestra warms up.

With a pile of sheet music spread before him, Otani appears well prepared for the long day of recording to come. Before starting, he stands to address us.

"Today, we're recording the music for Godzilla. Not Gamera! And there will be NO Ifukube themes!" Everyone breaks up laughing.

First up is the film's main theme. Otani prepared a synthesizer track in his home studio. He signals the engineer to play it over the studio speakers. As the prerecording runs, the orchestra performs in time with it. Blended together, the sound is incredible. As he takes the music in for the very first time, a big grin spreads across Kaneko's face.

For the next several hours, the orchestra works its way through the score. Otani spends his time either following the orchestra on sheet music or sitting at the console with the engineer to check levels. While all the music is wonderful, for me, the standout piece is a military march. It's forceful and dramatic with an easily discernible melody. When its recording is done, I lean over to Otani. "Play that again," I beg. He smiles.

The musicians are released once the orchestra portion of the recording is complete. We have quite a long break—nearly three hours—until the next phase of recording.

In the interim, Kaneko goes to a nearby bookstore. He returns with two books: one on world history and another titled *Morning Musume Bible*. A history book and a book on Japanese female pop stars? I think there's no better way to describe his interests than these two publications.

After leafing through the Morning Musume book at Kaneko's request, I hand it back with a scoffing, "*Uh…thanks.*" The timing of my delivery leaves the room in stitches. It's my way of teasing Kaneko about something I find an incongruous aspect of his personality.

Kaneko, Otani, and I step into the empty studio. In a corner is a Yamaha grand piano. With Kaneko seated beside him and me leaning over the piano's top edge, Otani serenades us with several GMK themes. Kaneko closes his eyes; he appears to be in a trance. Me? I stare at Otani and savor the moment. Not only is Otani a fantastic composer, but he's also a superb pianist. His fingers move over the keys with a fluid, effortlessly touch.

After he finishes, I ask Otani to play the themes in different musical styles.

"How about the main theme as a marching band?" I request. Sure enough, he bangs it out as if it were written for a Sunday parade.

"Let's say we're in the lobby of an airport?" I posit. Otani plays a bit of GMK music in a sickly sweet lounge style.

"The military theme…reggae style?" Without further adieu, he renders the theme in a form suitable for Toots and the Maytals. Once Otani is done, I take a turn at the piano. While in no way as accomplished, I manage to tinkle out a few originals I'd written in New York in the '80s. Both Kaneko and Otani seem impressed…that, or they're just humoring me.

Following dinner, I go out for coffee. On the way back, I bump into Hiroko, Otani's daughter. A music student, she's come with other students from her university to perform the chorus for the Mothra and Ghidorah themes. Just before 9, the rest of the singers arrive. One of the women calls out. "Norman, what are you doing here?" It's "Maru-chan," a young woman who works at my local Starbucks. A friend of Hiroko's, she's a music student at the same university.

"Is there anyone you *don't* know?" Kaneko asks as he slaps his head.

I step into the studio with Otani and the singers. For the session, nine men will sing the Ghidorah chorus.

"I know you wanted to play guitar on some of the tracks," Otani says apologetically, "but I couldn't find a spot in the music. If you like, why not join the Ghidorah singers?"

"That's kind of you," I say. "But you *really* don't want to hear me sing." Otani shakes his head to show he understands. "However," I add, "if you need someone to yell out 'Oh baby!' with perfect English intonation, I'm your man!" The singers and Otani get a laugh out of this.

Gathered around a pair of U-87 microphones, the male singers perform. The sound from the studio speakers, where it's mixed with Otani's prerecorded track, is rich and booming. Everyone in the control room grins broadly; there's a strong feeling we're witness to something incredible.

For the Mothra tracks, the women, ten in all, go in to record their parts. I join them in the studio. As they sing to sheet music propped before them, I listen from the bench of the piano. Like the male singers, their voices are lush and, in the best Mothra sense, enchanting.

This phase of the recording is different from the one earlier as most people unconnected to the actual recording left hours earlier, including my foe Saito. Here for much of the session, he managed to be the sole pain in what is otherwise a great experience.

For example, I was in the middle of a conversation with Masuda when *flash from the past* Saito cut in with a question having nothing to do with what we were discussing. Another time he turned to me for all to hear. "So, Norman, now that GMK is over, are you back teaching English to children?" What I do to make rent is no business of his. Besides, I do my job well, and, as far as jobs go, it's decent work. Seriously, I wonder if he's asked the non-A level actors in the film if they'll be back waiting tables now that the production is over.

The recording session ends at 11 p.m. I thank Otani for allowing me to hang out, and we shake hands before parting. Aida is kind enough to give Kaneko and me a ride to our homes in his Mustang.

12 OCTOBER 2001

Now that the music has been delivered and the background audio and dialogue balanced, the final sound mix for GMK has begun. Back in the Toho Sound Studio, I'm on the couch with Kaneko on my right and Tomita on my left. We'd been watching the same raw footage repeatedly and it'd gone a bit stale. Now, Otani's score is breathing new life into the film and has everyone re-energized.

Off on the studio's right-hand side and taped to a wood board is a long sheet of paper with six days marked off in descending blocks. Each block is labeled with a section of film to be mixed. Kaneko tells me that between fifteen to twenty minutes of the film will be mixed a day and in chronological order. Once a day is complete, its block on the board is oranged out.

Today is actually the second day of mixing. Starting at the police station scene in Yamanashi, today's portion runs to when Godzilla first comes ashore. After this is screened, Kaneko leans over the couch and offers feedback to Saito. As he speaks, Shimizu jots down the director's comments. To make sure nothing is missed, Shimizu sits with Saito; they run down the list together as Saito implements the adjustments. Kaneko doesn't bother to follow their progress. He's said what he has to say. Once done, the section is run again, and again, and again, and...

As exciting as it is to see the film with music, after a few hours of watching the same section ad infinitum, I'm ready to rip my hair out. Kaneko notices my flustered state.

"If you want to know about filmmaking, this is the heart of it. Here, you're forced to watch the film so many times that any emotional attachment you had is effectively killed. It was like this with me for *Gamera 3*. I lost all feeling for the movie during the sound mix."

For lunch, Kaneko, Iizuka, the three ADs, and I go to a restaurant near Toho's back entrance. As we eat, Kaneko mentions that the Toho PR department has him booked on *Time Shock*.

"It's part of the GMK promotion," he explains. "It's a TV quiz show co-hosted by Chiharu." Kaneko says he'll be asked several questions and given a minute and a half to answer. I ask what the topics will be.

"That's the thing," he says. "It can be anything: Japanese or world history, art, sports, popular culture, politics..." As expected, Kaneko starts to worry about how he'll do.

Back with the mix, I make a few suggestions. For example, in a scene where Chiharu and Kobayashi have lunch, Kobayashi's first two lines are distant and tinny; they sound like they were recorded at the bottom of a swimming pool. Kaneko agrees. He has Saito and his guys tweak and match the ambiance to the following dialogue.

As they work, producer Tomiyama steps in. Seeing me next to Kaneko, he lets out a laugh. "You certainly are taking this as far as you can," he observes.

With Saito and his team busy with technical points, Kaneko turns his attention to a book of world facts. It's part of his preparation for *Time Shock*. I tell him he's nuts and that he should just *Zen* it out.

"Do you know the 1950's TV show *The Honeymooners*?"

"Is it something I should know for the quiz?" Kaneko asks in a worried-sounding response.

"That's not what I mean... In one episode, the main character is a guest on a *Name That Tune* type of show. He prepares day and night, yet a warm-up song his friend kept playing on the piano—the name of which he finds he doesn't know when asked on the quiz show—is what does him in."

Iizuka jumps in. "How many films have you directed?" Kaneko thinks about it. He can't recall.

"Something like 24 or 25," he answers.

"I think Norman's right," she says. "You can't anticipate what they'll ask."

Even so, Kaneko won't be steered from his drive to memorize as many factoids as possible. He's even asking me the answer to American trivia: "Which is stronger, The American or National League?" "Why is a Teddy Bear called a Teddy Bear?" "What was the last state to join America?" The questioning is interrupted only when we watch Godzilla footage at near, earsplitting volumes. If this isn't the oddest thing I've been through in my life, I don't know what is.

14 OCTOBER 2001

I know I've said this before, but today really is my final day on GMK. The sound mix is almost done and my company has been bugging me to resume a regular work schedule. I guess it's time to return to the real world...

On the way to Toho, I buy a couple of boxes of Mr. Donuts. In the studio, I place them on a table by the entrance. Right away, the staff forms a line and picks out their favorite donut. I also brought Kamiya a gift. I'd been telling him about the fantastically chintzy yet ultra-fun Empire Pictures movie called *The Eliminators*. After hearing me rave about it, he expressed interest in checking it out. As luck would have it, I found a used videotape for five hundred yen in Shinjuku the other day.

I've arrived for the Baragon battle; Kaneko laments how he wished Baragon were handled differently.

"Baragon is too big," he grumbles. "Perhaps he could have been made smaller through a CGI process like the hobbits in the trailer for the upcoming *The Lord of the Rings* movie."

I insist it looks fine and that the point of Godzilla being a bully comes across. Unfortunately, this doesn't reassure him. Trying to take his mind off it, I mention that between the two monster battles, my favorite is the one in Hakone.

"This is because it's easier to keep track of," he points out. "It takes very little work to follow the camera's positioning. If you were in the Hakone forest, it would appear as it does in the film. By contrast, the camera angles in the city battle are unreal. If you were in Yokohama, it would be impossible to see the conflict as it appears in the film."

Considering his answers, I figure it's best not to try and cheer him up. Even innocuous compliments spark worry or overly detailed explanations.

Lunch is called and I take my food out to the pool. The area is just how I'd hoped, silent and people-less. The sun beats hard against the water, causing reflections to sparkle hypnotic-like off the surface. In a spot under a patch of shade, I snap open my *bento*. As I eat, I recall the G2000 shoot. I don't think I'll ever forget the excitement of seeing the pool for the first time. Even in the rain and with Godzilla wrapped in plastic, it was an incredible sight. Now, too—just the pool and me—is mind-blowing.

One common question Japanese people ask foreigners is to name their favorite place in Japan. The standard (and expected) answer is Kyoto (or Nara if you really want to get on their good side). From now on, I'm telling everyone mine is the big pool![21]

Done with lunch, I walk to the pool's edge. The water is filthy. Huge clumps of green mold dot the surface. Something glints off the bottom. It's a Ghidorah scale! There must be hundreds of them.

21- The big pool was razed in 2004 to make way for new studios.

Finding the right mix for the Godzilla/Baragon battle has turned out to be hell. This morning, the scene had wall-to-wall music. Then Kaneko tried it with music coming in and out at various spots. Each time the scene looked and felt different. The infuriating thing is, each way has its positive and negative points; no single way seems better than the other. I can see it weighs heavy on Kaneko. He's carrying so much in his mind that I'm afraid he's going to recreate the exploding head from *Scanners*.

After the umpteenth run-through, we go over the good and bad points of the last mix. Suddenly, a thought comes to the director. "You know… There's never been a kaiju battle without music backing it up…"

Turning to the sound crew, he asks them to try it with no music up until the moment Baragon bursts from the ground. The scene is run this way.

"That's it! I think we're good," Kaneko says, relieved. "The sound effects and visuals are strong enough to carry it without music. It also sets it apart from the ending battle. Besides, it's always been a wish of kaiju fans to see a monster fight in its pure, raw form."

I find Kaneko's logic sound. For what it's worth, I give his decision the thumbs up. The crew reruns the scene and Kaneko approves it.

After dinner, there is a meeting in the staffroom. With twenty of us here, it's cramped. Matsumoto has the lights lowered and shows new VFX clips on his computer, including a preview of the opening title sequence. Following this, the schedule for the last phase of production is covered and discussed.

At 11:30 p.m., the final touches to the day's audio mix are being tweaked. I say goodbye to everyone, particularly Iizuka, Aida, and Shimizu, who've been nothing but kind to me throughout the production. I don't say goodbye to Kaneko. Instead, I give him a "See you later." He tips his head.

I walk out into the cool autumn night and up the hill leading back to the station. From the spot overlooking the studio, Toho sits tranquil below; the lights around the various stages afford it a sleepy town look. It's hard to believe the end has come. Well, there are still PR events, the premiere at the Tokyo International Film Festival, and the opening in December to wean me off the production. Nevertheless, each step towards Seijo Station puts me one step further from what has been my most interesting experience in Japan, perhaps my life.

21 OCTOBER 2001

I'm sitting outside Starbucks having coffee with Otani. He's keen to hear my thoughts on how the mix went at Toho. One musical section I especially liked was Chiharu in the back of a jeep talking to her dad on a radio. I tell him it fits in perfectly with the on-screen moment. Otani is relieved to hear this.

"I worked hardest on that one," he confesses. "Between us, I cried five times while writing it!"

As promised, I received a copy of the GMK subtitles and gave them a look over. I plan to pass my suggestions on to Masuda when I see him at today's taping of *Time Shock*. I hope I didn't go overboard but I must have changed a third of them. I'm not a professional subtitler—and by no means do I want to disrespect the work of the person(s) who did them—but I felt some of the writing could have been stronger.

For example, when TV manager Shiro Sano sees Amamoto on the playback of Chiharu's video, the subtitles use the words "old man" to refer to Amamoto. I suggested "geezer," which I think is more in-line with his eccentric character. So, the original went: "Yuri, do you believe this old man?" I changed it to, "Yuri, you actually believe this geezer?"

In my opinion, Amamoto's lines from the jail interrogation room lacked foreboding and failed to reach the level of criticism I felt his character was leveling at Japan. I changed them to read:

230: Because people have forgotten...
231: Forgotten the agony of those killed in the war.
232: Forgotten the pain and sacrifice.
232a: Forgotten at the expense of their souls!

The *Time Shock* production is on the other side of Tokyo at the Terebi Asahi studio near Toyocho Station. At the back entrance, guards point me to the main floor, where I find PR guys Nakayama, Masuda, and Nakashima standing around a Godzilla event suit. It's decided that low-man-on-the-Totem-pole Nakashima will wear it for the show.

Looking for Kaneko, I take an elevator upstairs. Stepping off, I bump into Chiharu and her manager Kono. Chiharu lets out an ear-piercing, "Norman! How are you?"

The commotion pulls Kaneko from a side room. He gives me a low-toned "*Uh*, hello" greeting. He looks worried. Listening to him, I think the excessive prep work only served to muddle his brain.

On the other hand, Chiharu is most definitely up. She's yelling *Oi!* every chance she gets and is beaming a smile so powerful were it a laser it could slice clean through steel. Having just stepped from wardrobe, she's been fitted for the show: a pink and black shoulder-less dress with a red belt that drops under her breasts and travels around her hips. She's also wearing black, knee-high boots with red patches on the sides and toes.

"What do you think?" she asks as she twirls around. "Do I look like an alien, or what?"

I hold out my pointing finger and slowly move it toward her. Catching on, she does the same. When our fingers touch, we say, "Phone home!" in unison.

"Name that movie!" I query, spinning towards Kaneko.

A staffer leads us into the studio proper. It's spacious with the stage is decorated in that absurd, tacky style Japanese game shows are noted for worldwide. Although Kaneko is the main contestant, he's not alone. Like him, the other guests are part of the Japanese entertainment world. I recognize one as a member of the popular *body-con* idol group Shape Up Girls.

The contestants are introduced before their turn in the *Time Shock* seat. For this, the main attraction, they're strapped to a chair and lifted into a large oval contraption. Questions are asked as lights move clockwise around them. Their time is up once the lights complete the oval. Get less than six questions correct, and the seat spins in the most vomit-inducing way.

After Kaneko is interviewed, the Godzilla suit stomps out spewing white smoke around the set. As Godzilla growls and claws the air, Chiharu and her male co-host quake in fear. The emcee asks Kaneko how he controls Godzilla on-set when he goes wild like this. Kaneko looks at Godzilla and, holding a hand out, yells, "Cut!" Instantly, Godzilla turns docile. Everyone, including the off-stage production staff, howls with laughter.

Of the contestants, Kaneko is last in the *Time Shock* seat. He's strapped in and raised up. Kaneko starts off great, getting the first three questions correct. Things then turn to an area he knows nothing about, and he misses everything until the ninth question. Having failed, he's spun and covered in stage smoke. To add to the humility, Godzilla blasts smoke over him the moment he steps from the chair.

Later in the dressing room, I remind a mortified Kaneko that, despite the loss, he's still my favorite person in Japan, which elicits the desired chuckle out of him.

28 OCTOBER 2001

I get to Chofu Station in the early evening and meet up with model and prop maker Sagae. We plan to eat before the *zero-go* (proof print) screening of GMK at Tokyo Genzosho (Togen for short), a film lab in the area Toho partially owns. We settle on yakiniku and, as we eat, share memories of the GMK production. Not having seen the film yet, Sagae is excited to see how it's turned out.

Sagae is one of the most understanding guys I know. Even when I get overbearing with my opinion, which is almost all the time, he doesn't hold it against me. I'm also learning from him how to look at this as work even if you're also a fan. I mention giving the subtitles for GMK a rewrite.

"Did they pay you?"

"Well…you know…" I reply.

He lets out a snort and tells me of an experience he had early on in his career when he was asked to build a maquette for a Toho film and got an autograph from SFX director Kawakita in place of payment.

"Don't let anyone tell you you're going to get rich in this business," he warns. "Seriously, don't let them take advantage of you. Toho has the money but they'll get cheap if they smell fan boy on you." He asks if they've paid me for the "Norman Report."

"What do *you* think?" I respond.

Togen is a ten-minute walk from the station and is located past a couple of heavily tree-lined streets. Being autumn, the roads are thick with yellow ginkgo leaves that give off a pleasant, decaying odor. We arrive just as a taxi pulls up. Out steps Kamiya. I say hello; rather than respond, he's back to giving me unemotional head nods. In an attempt to make small talk, I ask if he came to the screening for the Toho bigwigs yesterday. Kamiya then embarks on a detailed account of his movements over the past twenty-four hours. I look at Sagae, who just shrugs.

We're directed to the second floor, where the GMK staff has gathered. A kind of production reunion, I exchange hellos with as many staffers as I can.

Tomiyama thanks me for giving the subtitles a look over. He says they've incorporated about half of my suggestions. I assure him it was my pleasure. Seeing this, Sagae shakes his head in disapproval.

At 8 p.m., we enter the screening room. I'm uncertain where to sit but seeing Kaneko in the theater's middle, I turn to Sagae. "*Screw it*, I'm sitting with the director!" I don't know if it's Japanese film etiquette but Kaneko has an entire row to himself.

Every time I see the film I feel differently. Sometimes I think: *Wow!* If this isn't the greatest Godzilla film of all time! Other times I think: Is this really working? However, while I start the screening undecided, by the end I'm totally into it. The film moves! It rocks! It's kaiju in the best sense of the word!

Once over, the theater goes dead quiet. Kaneko looks at me. I give him the thumbs up. As if on cue, the theater breaks into loud applause. In the lobby, everyone is smiling and congratulating each other enthusiastically. I find Jiro. He's beaming and labels the film "fantastic!"

Kaneko offers to take Jiro and me out for dinner. I climb into the back seat of Jiro's car with Kaneko riding shotgun. Before pulling out, Tomiyama comes over. He's wearing a spiffy trench coat over his suit and looking very much like a sharply dressed studio exec. He thanks Kaneko for making such a wonderful film.

"I didn't think so much could be achieved in a single movie." Then he gives the director a heartfelt "*arigatou gozaimasu.*"

As we drive away, I tell Kaneko that their exchange had a big fat neon sign over it reading, 'Maverick film director meets by-the-numbers studio producer and together make a great film.' This, the crew's positive reaction to the film, and Tomiyama's comment has him in a good mood.

Over dinner, we discuss GMK in detail. Kaneko mentions that there are still a few changes to be made, mostly in the music. Otani said that some cues were laid in wrong and need adjusting. This leads to Jiro proclaiming Otani's score the first rock and roll soundtrack of the Godzilla series. I'm not sure I'd go that far, but it is kick ass for sure.

GODZILLA, MOTHRA AND KING GHIDORAH: GIANT MONSTERS ALL-OUT ATTACK
Release

The day of the GMK premiere at the Tokyo International Film Festival, I get to Shibuya at noon. A Saturday, it's awash with tourists, teenagers, and parasitical street hucksters. Making my way through the crowd, I head up to Orchard Hall in the Bunkamura complex. When I get there, I find a long line extending from the front door. Bypassing it, I sign in at the press table, where Masuda tells me the seating situation.

"The thing is," he explains, "there are no more tickets. So, go in with the press. When they leave, pick any seat you like."

After I thank him, Kaneko's ADs—Aida, Shimizu, and Kumazawa—step from the hall. They're decked out in black suits and ties. "Toho elected us to help with the screening," Aida explains. "The suits are mandatory; we had no choice!" I assure him they look sharp.

Near the head of the line are friends who've flown in from the US. They're ecstatic to learn that today's screening will have subtitles. As we talk, a group of Japanese men rushes up to ask for my autograph. In short order, I'm signing Godzilla books, scraps of paper, and whatnots while fielding questions about the GMK production. I'm not sure I deserve the attention but it's flattering.

I spot SFX director Kenji Suzuki and suit maker Shinichi Wakasa by the entrance. As always, Suzuki is personable and easy-going. On the other hand, Wakasa seems irritated. "So, you have a nifty time on the GMK set this year?" His tone is patronizing.

A commotion erupts around the street in front of Orchard Hall. From a taxi step producer Tomiyama and actor Amamoto. Like a Hollywood red carpet premiere, camera flashes blaze around them. Although Tomiyama is a bigwig in the Godzilla community, the commotion is over the legendary Amamoto.

I see Amamoto's duded-up for the night. By this, I mean he's got on a brand new knitted skullcap. Ignoring the crowd, he walks straight up to me. Taking my hand, he shakes it passionately. "How are you?" he asks. *Gosh*. I'm flattered he remembers.

Inside, as usual, I gather with a large group of press wedged between the stage and front row. For some reason, a PR person I'm unfamiliar with lectures me on how there won't be seats available and that I'll have to vacate following the opening ceremony.

After he walks off, Masuda comes running over. "I got you a ticket!"

I thank him and throw my bag on the center, front row seat—and not a moment too soon! The doors opened, the scamper for seats has begun. In no time, the auditorium fills up.

After a few commercials on the screen, the same pair of emcees from the past two years takes the stage. They run through some introductory comments and then call out select members of the GMK staff and cast: Tomiyama, Kaneko, Chiharu, Uzaki, and Nobuaki Kakuda, a well-known K-1 fighter who appears as a soldier in the film.

As expected, Tomiyama is in a suit. Kaneko, however, has a kind of leather jacket/pants thing going. It's probably the most fashionable thing I've seen him in. And Chiharu… *Ah, Chiharu*. I love you, but you have the strangest taste in clothing: She's in a black dress with purple tire tracks running across a side of her chest. On closer inspection, I see it's a print of the Leaning Tower of Pisa.

The Godzilla suit steps onto stage. White smoke erupts from his mouth, sending the audience into rounds of cheers and applause. Following an introduction by the emcees, each guest gives a brief, impassioned speech about the film. After the mandatory press photo session, it's movie time!

By now I've seen the film umpteen times. However, rather than bored, I'm electrified. It's a new experience seeing it with English subtitles; I'm thrilled to spot ones I had a hand in writing. Yet, the real kick comes from seeing it with a regular crowd. The ordinarily docile Japanese audience is vocal and enthusiastic throughout, gasping and cheering from time to time. Once over, the movie receives a robust and prolonged ovation.

I call Nakao on my cell phone. We meet in the lobby, where I ask for his reaction. "It was good enough," he says in a lackluster tone. After working on these films for so long, especially during the genre's height in the '60s, a little indifference is understandable.

Some western friends join us. The consensus from the foreign contingent is that GMK is a winner. Tom and Diane Dougherty, who run Clawmark Toys, an online kaiju toy outlet, call it the first high-quality Godzilla film in longer than they can remember. Also in agreement is Richard Pusateri, an occasional writer on kaiju cinema. He boasts about meeting Amamoto before the show, only to have the actor lose interest when learning he isn't from Spain.

The biggest compliment comes from Katsuhito Ito, the editor of *Hobby Japan* magazine. He feels it's the second greatest kaiju movie following the original *Gojira*. Knowing I was on set for most of the production, he proposes I write a massive article for their upcoming *Hobby Japan Extra*[22].

I finally reach Kaneko on his cell phone. He says he's doing interviews on the fifth floor. I wander into the backstage corridors of Orchard Hall to look for him when a woman wearing a TIFF badge stops me.

"Where are you going?" she demands to know. I explain, but she's paying little heed, having no doubt decided that a guy like me has no business being backstage. Not really caring, I move around her. Freaking out, she points at me as if this were the end of *Invasion of the Body Snatchers* and shouts to a pair of guards down the hall, "We have a *foreigner* loose back here!"

Giving them the slip, I work my way upstairs, where I find Chiharu in the middle of a TV interview. Off to the side is Kono, her manager. I ask what I should do about photos I took of Chiharu during the production that I wish to run in upcoming articles.

"Use what you like. We've seen your work and trust your judgment."

Wow, that's one of the best compliments you can get in this business, especially from an agency known to micro-manage all aspects of their talents' PR.

Her interview over, Chiharu runs over, erupting in a bubbly wail of *Oi's!* We step out to look for Kaneko. Instead, Uzaki comes walking by. On his way to leave, we escort him to a nearby elevator. As the doors slide to close, he yells out in English, "Chiharu! I love you!"

The actress turns bright red.

From a door, Kaneko pokes his head out. "Let's get dinner," he says. "How about that Italian restaurant upstairs?"

"You mean, the place we go after *every* TIFF screening?" I answer back.

Following dinner, Kaneko returns home with his wife and kids. Jiro and I join a party given by Godzilla super fan couple Hico and Shizue. They hold annual after-TIFF Godzilla parties and, as usual, it's a mix of fans and pros. There are close to forty people in attendance: thirty-eight men and two women.

"This is a pretty accurate representation of the ratio of men to women in kaiju fandom," Jiro notes.

"Are you sure?" I ask. "I mean, that would make it one female per twenty males. I'd say the ratio is more like a thousand to one."

A mike is passed around and introductions are made. I like SFX director Suzuki's best: "Hello, my name is Kenji Suzuki, and I had nothing to do with GMK."

When it's my turn, I describe myself as a fan from the US and leave it at that. Hico orders me not to be so humble. He tells me that everyone here has been reading my set reports on the Toho webpage.

"*Oh*, and that too," I add, eliciting laughs from the room.

Later, when everyone is sufficiently drunk, several guys corner me and demand I choose sides.

"So, which do you like better, the Wakasa or the Shinada Godzilla?" "Kaneko or Tezuka?" "GXM or GMK?" Most annoying is that, puffing on a cigarette not a meter off, Wakasa is waiting to hear how I answer. Ultimately, I choose not to.

As if this isn't enough, Hico lectures me on how he prefers Wakasa's Godzilla due to its adherence to suitmation philosophy and tradition. He argues that the GMK suit has too many mechanisms trying to make it look real.

"Fans of suit acting prefer stiff suits.

---

22 - *Hobby Japan Extra*, 2 February 2002, pg 24~35.

The quality of a kaiju performance is not based on how emotive a suit's face is but in how the actor moves it." I'm not sure I agree, but it's a valid point, and I thank him for sharing it with me.

By 10:30 p.m., I'm ready to split. The room is filled with cigarette smoke and, with non-GMK staffers like Suzuki and Wakasa here, I'm not digging the GMK negativity. I sign a few autographs and leave with Jiro. It's pouring outside and I've no umbrella. I'm thoroughly soaked by the time I reach Shibuya Station.

12 NOVEMBER 2001

I meet Kaneko at the Shimokita Starbucks this afternoon. By chance, Maru-chan, one of the "Mothra singers," is working. I introduce her to Kaneko, which sends her into a fit of bows. The Starbucks manager says he saw a TV report about Baragon actress Ota and noticed me in the background. I didn't even know a show like this was on-air.

"I taped it," Kaneko says. "I'll give you a copy."

It's a nice day, and we window shop through the area. We talk about this and that, trying hard to avoid mentioning Godzilla. It's not easy. We (him more than me) have been consumed by it for the past year-plus.

A few hours later, we stop in a local *izakaya* for dinner. As if to make sure we stay trapped in the world of GMK, taped to a wall is a poster for the movie. It turns out that actor Nishina, who played Maruo, an AD at "Digital Q," lives nearby.

"Sometimes actors bring posters of films they're in to hang at their local restaurants," Kaneko explains.

We're looking through the menu when

a young woman holding out a cell phone comes over. Puzzled, I put it to my ear.

"Hello…?" I ask.

"Hi, it's Aya," says the voice on the other end. Ten minutes later, Ayako Fujitani joins us. The phone woman turns out to be her roommate.

"What're you doing today?" she asks Kaneko. He looks at me. "*Ah*, a Norman day."

"Aya," I boast, "everyone needs a Norman day now and then."

13 NOVEMBER 2001

I go to the immigration office in Otemachi to pick up my visa. *The fools!* They gave me just one year, meaning I'll have to go through this crap again in another ten months. At least they've raised my status to that of permanent resident, which should bring me a modicum of peace of mind.

Since I'm close to Yurakucho, I call Masuda to ask if I can stop by the Toho office. When I get there, he's smoothing out a GMK poster to hang in the screening room. Toho has begun press screenings.

At his desk, he lets me thumb through GMK slides and pick the ones I like. I'll scan them at home and return them later. When done, I call Kaneko. By chance, he's on the 7th floor giving interviews. I wait for him to finish.

Arriving on our floor, Kaneko greets me with a "Let's get a power lunch!" I ask who taught him this ridiculous English phrase. He points at me.

With a few Toho PR people, we go for Chinese food. Stepping outside, Kaneko dons a pair of dark sunglasses.

"Why the specs?" I ask.

"*Time Shock…*" he says. "The show was on-air a few days back. I don't want to be recognized."

"Aren't you taking this a bit too far?" I ask.

Ignoring me, he pushes them tight against the bridge of his nose. I don't think I've ever seen the PR gang laugh as hard as they do now.

24 NOVEMBER 2001

I meet Otani in the early morning and climb into his sporty red Alfa Romeo. Like a rocket launch in a '50s sci-fi film, the acceleration pins my head deep into the headrest.

A few weeks back I asked Otani for an interview about his work on GMK. I'd have been satisfied to sit in Starbucks and talk for an hour. This trip is his idea. Don't get me wrong, I'm totally thrilled for the chance to get out of Tokyo and drive around the countryside with my favorite composer in Japan.

Three hours after leaving Tokyo, we pull into the out-of-town holiday home of Taihei Shimoi, an architect we know from Shimokitazawa. He invited us to spend the night. His place is modern, spacious, and enjoys a splendid view of a distant, snow-capped Mt. Fuji.

After settling into a snazzy tatami matted guest room with a high glass ceiling, his wife carries in a tray of cut fruit and saké. We eat, drink, and chat. It turns out that our friend knew original Godzilla composer Akira Ifukube. He shows us dishes made by Reiko, the composer's daughter, he received as a present.

An hour or so later, we drive to a nearby café/art space located in a heavily wooded area. While looking over local art, I ask about the area. I'm told that many people from Tokyo keep their *bessho* (second home) here. *Ah, rich folk's town.*

After finishing our coffee, we go back to Otani's car. With that, Shimoi leans into the window on Otani's side.

"Well, thanks for coming. Have a good drive back." He walks back into the café. Otani and I shift our eyes at each other.

"Weren't we staying the night?"

"That's odd…" Otani murmurs. Neither of us is up for the long drive back to Tokyo.

"I've an idea!" Otani exclaims.

We drive along through winding mountains for an hour, eventually arriving at a resort hotel nestled deep within a forest close to Sagami Bay.

"I know the guy who runs the place," he explains. "It's off-season and there are plenty of rooms available."

The hotel, hand-built from trees in the area, is beautiful. The sizable lobby appears to have been constructed from a collection of tree trunks fastened together by rope, with the ceiling a weave of powerful-looking branches. The owners, a couple in their 40s, are thrilled to see Otani. With no bookings, we get the best room in the place. After dropping off our bags, we hit the lobby for drinks and a game of pool.

"You know where we are?" Otani asks as he sinks the six ball in a side pocket. "Not too far from where Baragon fought Godzilla in GMK."

At midnight, we go to the hotel's outdoor *onsen* for a dip. The stars shine down bright and the sliver of moon is just enough to illuminate the top edge of the surrounding forest. Although cold out, the water is warm and steamy. It's a wonderful, calm moment, and we spend an hour chatting.

Every now and then, creepy noises from deep within the woods reverberate around us. It's a reminder that not all of Japan is an endless run of train stations and shoebox-shaped buildings.

The next morning the area is covered in a heavy mist. We hang out in an alcove in our room that sits on the edge of an apple grove and talk about music, spirituality, and man's never-ending source of befuddlement: the opposite sex. Somewhere within this, we find the time to get to GMK. One thing that comes up, and a thing we both agree on is that while we love Kaneko as a person and respect him as a director, he has the worst taste in music. Otani labels his choice in music as "otaku-driven."

On the way back, we listen to his Godzilla soundtrack. When we get to my favorite piece, *Mirai wo mamoru ketsui* (*Determined To Protect the Future*), I mention that it bears a resemblance to the Ifukube melody from the main title theme in *Gojira* '54. Otani grows quiet and listens closely.

"You're right! I hadn't noticed. I must have done it subconsciously."

I tell him it's not obvious and, ultimately, creates a subtle connection to past Godzilla films. He's relieved to hear this.

As it's nearby, we pull over to take in Mt. Fuji. The view is spectacular. There isn't a cloud in the sky and cruise ships laze about Lake Ashi. Seeing Fuji picture-perfect this way has been a long-held dream. I thank Otani before we hit the final leg of the drive back to Tokyo.

2 DECEMBER 2001

Kaneko invited me to a GMK "talk event" at the HMV in Shibuya. Getting there at 4 p.m., I find a mob gathered on the street out front. In the crowd is writer Taki, who is as surprised as me by the large turnout.

A commotion erupts down the street. It's Rie Ota. She's walking hand in hand with a Godzilla event suit. People on the street squeeze close and snap photos; a TV crew records the moment. Aided by the Toho PR guys, Godzilla is helped up the steps to HMV. Stopping in the middle, Ota and Godzilla turn to pose for photos.

A few floors up, displays and CD racks have been pushed to the side to make way for a stage. Behind this, a projection screen displaying GMK's trailer runs on a loop. Off to the right is the main Godzilla suit from the production. It might sound odd, but during filming, even when Yoshida wasn't inside, Godzilla felt alive and conscious. In contrast, standing like a stuffed animal in a natural history museum, Godzilla comes across as soulless...dead. Weirder yet is on the ground next to him is the head of Baragon...just the head.

The event is attended by Kaneko, Tomiyama, and actors Uzaki, Hotaru, Ota, and Shingo Katsurayama. Leading the talk show is Shinsuke Kasai, a popular TV newscaster who's had cameos in several Godzilla films. The turnout is fantastic. The aisles are crammed with onlookers. Oddly, nearly everyone in attendance is female.[23]

As talk shows go, this one covers the basics: the actors tell of the shoot's

---

23 - Kaneko later tells me that many were here to see Katsurayama, a handsome actor from the *Kamen Rider Kuuga* TV show. Even though *tokusatsu* and *henshin* programs are made for kids, they've become popular with the housewife set who watch for the pretty boy stars.

challenges, Kaneko shares what Godzilla means to him, and Tomiyama expresses the company's position on the Godzilla franchise. At the end, a raffle is held and Godzilla toys are given to the winners.

As the crowd disperses some women approach me. "Are you Norman from Toho's 'Norman Report'"?

For whatever reason, they make a big deal out of this and ask for my autograph. A line forms and the HMV staff brings over a desk and chair for me to sign from. I'd like to say I'm thrilled, but this is precisely what I do at the end of English teaching. As a guest teacher visiting schools around the Tokyo area, classes finish with me signing the students' attendance book. *Great*, I finally get people lined up for my autograph and the novelty is blown because of my freaking job.

Over dinner, I complain to Kaneko about this but all he can do is shake his head and call me ridiculous.

14 DECEMBER 2001

I meet an altogether somber Kaneko at the Shimokita Starbucks. With the premiere tomorrow, I'm guessing he's suffering from pre-GMK-opening jitters. As he's not one to come out and announce what's on his mind I have to ask.

"Just worrying about tomorrow's opening," he mumbles.

We go to a nearby okonomiyaki restaurant for dinner and warm ourselves around the table's large hot plate. After this, I take him to a bar I know on Shimokita's south side. Small, it's little more than a 3 or 4-meter rectangle with a bartender on one side and seven chairs on the other. It's so tight you have to shift your chair forward when someone wants to get past you. I order beers.

"Know what tonight is?" I ask as I hold my glass his way. Kaneko shakes his head. "It's GMK eve!" Kaneko thinks for a moment then reacts with a smile. He raises his glass to mine. We toast to GMK.

As we drink, we recall the production. Rather than the usual "wasn't it great when…" we go over mishaps, funny incidents, and who annoyed us during production. Kaneko asks if I've any new Saito stories. Unfortunately, he's heard them all. Still, I treat him to a Saito's Greatest Hits, like the time Nakao and I messed with his *gachapon* and his ridiculous request to rip the script in half. Kaneko is in stitches.

It's a special moment for me. Not for having opened the bolted doors of a Godzilla production or because I now share a prime seat with one of the greatest kaiju directors of all time. No, it's because I've found a friend in Kaneko. A sentimentalist, I grow misty-eyed and order tequila. As I slide a shot his way, I thank him for a remarkable year.

"Thank you too," Kaneko replies in a rare moment of openness. We knock our glasses together and down the shots. I turn to a woman seated next to us and ask if she wouldn't mind snapping our photo. Considering how cross-eyed drunk she is, I'm impressed she's able to aim the camera at our faces…

When she hands it back, I ask if she's a Godzilla fan.

"What?" she responds, bewildered. I ask again. "Are you drunk?" she questions in return.

Maybe I am… Maybe I am…

15 DECEMBER 2001

When I was ten, my family rode an ocean liner from Germany to New York. It marked the end of a six-month trip traveling throughout Europe. Although the voyage took ten days to reach America, it felt like ten years. Each day was packed with new friends, new sights, and new adventures; every day was a near lifetime. Even so, time did pass and our ship did reach the Hudson River shoreline. Sitting at Starbucks this morning, a similar feeling passes through me: The long voyage on the good ship GMK has reached port; like it or not, with GMK opening nationwide today, it's time to disembark.

After a quick morning coffee, I zip over to Nichigeki, Toho's flagship theater in Yurakucho, where the director and cast will be doing stage greets throughout the day. I meet Jiro at 11 a.m. in front of the Godzilla statue. He tells me that some roses were placed in Godzilla's hand, but five minutes earlier an old lady swiped the batch. Chuckling over this, we walk to the theater. There's a line of ticket buyers stretched around the block. Traveling to the 8th floor, we locate Masuda, who kindly gives us staff passes.

The movie is already playing when Jiro and I step in. We stand against the back wall. Kamiya and Matsumoto are here too gauging audience reaction to the film. We exchange silent head tip greetings. Masuda taps me on the shoulder just when the Baragon battle kicks in.

"The director is calling for you," he says.

Jiro laughs. "The master calls, Norman!"

Masuda and I walk down a hall beside the lobby and into a room behind the stage. Kaneko is pacing back and forth. He appears ill at ease.

"Remember last night when you said you were totally fine about today?" I remind him. "Recapture that feeling." To distract him further, I mention how hungover I am.

"It's because, unlike me, you are a weak drinker," he jokes.

"I hate to break it to you, but you're just as weak a drinker as me!" This seems to get him in a better mood.

A theater staff member enters. With arms firm against her sides, she bows formally. "Chiharu Niiyama has entered the building!" From behind her, Chiharu pokes her head into the room.

"*Oi!* Norman's here!" Not sure why I'm singled out, but it's flattering.

I respond with an English, "*Wow*! It's Chiharu Niiyama, star of GMK!"

Also present is Kaneko's son, Suzuyuki. Chiharu gives him a pat on the head. She asks about school. Nervous, he can only mumble and stare at his feet. After this, Ryudo Uzaki steps in. The team for the day's stage greet is complete.

Back in the lobby, my name is called. It's Taki…and he's with Saito! It's good to see Taki, and, in a weird way, Saito too. That is until he starts in on me again.

"So you're staff now?" he questions as he thumps the sticker on my chest.

"Yeah, Saito," I say bluntly. "I *am* staff."

Saito mumbles something about how this is only because I'm friends with the director and… Ignoring him, I turn my attention to Taki. Really, no law says I gotta listen to misplaced fanboy prattle.

Also here are Americans I know from on-line. One is Robert Troch, a fellow New Yorker, and the other is Sean Linkenback, a prominent movie poster collector. It's always nice to be able to shift cyber-friends into real world friends.

Soon, it's showtime. Kaneko, Uzaki, and Chiharu are called to the stage. The audience goes wild. Guys in the crowd yell out *kawaii*! (cute) when Chiharu struts out.

Their speeches are typical fare: how hard they worked/how great the production was/what an honor it is to be in a Godzilla movie/what a wonderful director Kaneko is, etc. After a few minutes, they're ushered off stage and the next screening of GMK begins.

On their way to the lobby for PR photos, the stars are led across metal grating to a row of elevators. Stories up, the view down to the first floor is dizzying. Worse, Chiharu's heels keep getting stuck in the spaces between the grates. Her manager has no choice but to carry her to the other side. Chiharu laughs all the way.

Down on the first floor, Kaneko, Chiharu, and Uzaki pose for photos in front of several large Hamtaro costumes. Once over, Kaneko invites me to join them for lunch. While I'd like to go, the truth is, I don't want to overstay my welcome.

"I'll go back in and watch the movie with Suzu and Jiro," I tell him. But first, I turn to Chiharu. "Could you please translate my English for Kaneko?" On cue, she goes into her English gibberish routine, letting us all share in one final laugh. I thank Chiharu and Uzaki and wish them the best of luck. I walk a few feet and turn back.

"And the band!" I shout. "Don't forget about the band!" Uzaki breaks up laughing and Chiharu gives me one last beaming smile. For me, it's the perfect capper to my GMK voyage.

I sit through one more stage greet with Suzu. Both Kaneko and Chiharu give us little hand waves from stage, which sends Suzu into a tizzy. "That's my dad! That's my dad!" he says pulling on my arm. They walk off stage, and I watch GMK once more in its entirety.

Later, after a home-cooked dinner, I draw a hot bath. It's not like I feel dirty. I just want to snuggle in its soothing embrace and bask in the mountain of memories I've gathered over the past year. While it's hard to believe it's over, I'm not sad, far from it. More than anything, I'm grateful and surprised—surprised at how things worked out and how, despite the odds, I came to understand the deep-rooted humanity of a Godzilla production.

"Well, one thing's for certain, I'll never get to do *that* again!" I think as I swirl the bathwater around. "*Hmm…* Didn't Toho just announce they're making another Godzilla film next year?"

I make a mental note to call Masuda in the morning.

The End…?

EPILOGUE

This year marks GMK's twentieth anniversary and thus twenty years since the stories in this book took place. As noted in the introduction, I originally wanted to release this right away. However, I'm glad I didn't. Had I, I think it would have turned out much differently and been much more about the mechanics of the set rather than the experience of the set. (Not like that would have been a bad thing.) By this, I mean, as the book stands now, I feel it's as much about giant monsters as it is about Japan, its culture, and its people.

Another reason I didn't get to work on this following the release of GMK is that I was still actively pursuing the experience. Although my involvement with Godzilla peaked with GMK, I stayed with Godzilla until 2004 when the Millennium Series ended. The Godzilla production was also just one of many film sets I was involved with at the time.

Twenty years on, my relationship with the Japanese film industry has changed considerably. Reading the text in this book today, I'm almost embarrassed by how brazen I was. Take the infamous "*bento* incident" on the set of *Gamera 3*. In retrospect, I should have spoken to Kobayashi first and explained the situation. Instead, I went over his head and took it up with the director. Since then, Kobayashi has become a film producer at Kadokawa Pictures (a company that bought Daiei in 2002). I've worked on a few Kadokawa films over the years and bump into him from time to time. We still get a laugh over that night in Kyoto Station; since then, Kobayashi has said on numerous occasions, "I gave Norman his first lesson about the Japanese movie set."

Over the years, I shifted careers, and today I make a living from Japanese cinema. The move occurred slowly and came about through the people I met while reporting on Japanese cinema. These days, my income mainly comes from subtitling Japanese films into English. This gig began with the movie *Vampire Girl vs. Frankenstein Girl*, a wacky, gore-fest released in 2009 that I covered for *Fangoria*. Its director phoned me during post-production to say (more like demand), "Subtitle my movie!" Since then, I've subbed over one hundred Japanese films.

The Japanese movie business being what it is, I take work wherever I can find it. To date, here are the jobs I've done to "pay the rent": director, scriptwriter, still cameraman, actor, PR creator (press books & catchphrases), English and Japanese on-set dialect coach, voice-over performer, sound and boom operator, behind the scenes cameraman/director/editor, and a few others that slip my mind. I also write about cinema, which includes a monthly column for movie mag *Eiga Hiho*, various books on cinema, and liner notes for Blu-rays. On occasion, I go so far as to design entire booklets for Blu-rays. All in all, I enjoy the diversity of the work, and if there's one thing I'm grateful to Japan for, it's giving me a career in film, my first true love.

I've also made three films I feel a certain level of pride over. The first one was *The iDol*. Shot in 2005, this came about when I decided to see if I could handle the rigors of a production. I called in a bunch of favors and cranked out a 52-minute movie that I can watch today without feeling embarrassed. One thing I'm not is a good promoter. Although it played several film festivals at the time, including premiering at the Fantasia Film Festival in Montreal in 2006, I became disillusioned by the festival scene and the business end of movie making for reasons

I won't get into. But, all's well that ends well, and *The iDol* was released in 2020 by distributor SRS Cinema LLC—fourteen years after I finished it!

Another movie I'm proud of directing is the documentary *Bringing Godzilla Down to Size*, which I made with writers/producers Ed Godziszewski and Steve Ryfle. It was released in 2008 by Classic Media on the double-disc set of Toho kaiju films *The War of the Gargantuas* and *Rodan*. Shooting the film was a blast and creatively satisfying. Unfortunately, its rights have been tangled up by Toho, who claimed ownership of it for the better part of ten years, yet when pressed to allow its inclusion in the 2019 Criterion release of Godzilla Showa films couldn't state definitively if they possessed them or not. (Insert eye roll here.)

The last movie I shot was *New Neighbor*, a darkish movie about a sexually repressed woman. The film was given a wonderful release by German distributor Midori Impuls in 2017. Unlike the two films mentioned previously, this one was a difficult production spread out over a year. The film played for a week at the Shibuya art house theater Uplink. In Japan, art house theaters are expected to feature stage greets with the filmmakers; I hosted shows nightly with different guests, including a memorable evening in which lead actresses Ayano and Asami recreated the film's climactic ending in Asami's sex den. *New Neighbor* also played Fantasia in 2013.

Getting back to this book, readers are probably asking, "He keeps talking about set photos. Where are they?" Yeah, where are they? The truth is, Godzilla copyright holder Toho Co., Ltd. was uncooperative and pulled the typical Japanese business practice of being glacially slow to respond, hoping I'd eventually just give up, which I finally did. On the other hand, I spoke to Kadokawa Pictures about my set photos for G3 and within a day they permitted me their use. I assembled a selection of photos but in the end felt that with the text so heavily Godzilla-centric, not to have photos of Godzilla drew attention to their lack of Godzilla. Maybe one day, if Toho sees the error of its ways, I can release this in a big, color photo-filled edition.

If I do have a regret for sitting on the text for as long as I have, it's that some of the people herein have passed away. In particular, Takashi Nakao and Junko Kawashima, two people who showed me great kindness during the production of GMK.

As he'd promised, Nakao retired after the GMK production—and I did visit his home and did meet his wife. We had a stupendous yakiniku meal; he also invited eccentric Godzilla actor Satsuma along just to make it all the more memorable.

Junko Kawashima stayed on with the Godzilla productions and always had my back. Her untimely death in 2018 came as a blow to everyone who knew her. I hope the book's text gives readers a sense of this hardworking woman who never let the pressure affect her ability to be a real sweetheart.

Morihiko Saito, my "nemesis" in the text, passed away. In the years after GMK, I bumped into him on occasion. He never let up on giving me a hard time over something trivial. When I was in the (so-far-failed) process of releasing this text in Japanese, my editor at *Eiga Hiho*, who was good friends with Saito, contacted him to see if it was okay to use him as the foil in the story. Saito said he had no issue with it.

As odd as it might sound given our history, I attended a wake in his honor in 2018. I might have had my issues with the man, but he passed away too soon (like Junko, he was in his mid-50s) and I was saddened to learn of his passing.

Another particularly painful loss was that of Hiroshi Sagae, one of the finest artists I've ever known and one of the most loyal friends too. He was a guy who either loved you or hated you. (I like to think he loved me.) He had a good sense of humor and always looked positively to the future. Even when seeing him the last time in the hospital at the end of 2019, he spoke eagerly of a kaiju film based on an idea of his that he wanted to create. I volunteered to do set stills and English subtitles. (I hope someone in Japan carries on with this project.)

Respected by all, on the days he came to the Godzilla set, the art staff treated him like royalty, always referring to him as sensei. After the release of *Gamera 3*, he made a set of small figures of the film's human characters for a layout in *Hobby Japan*. It was my honor that he gifted me the Ayana one. Today, it sits on my desk right in front of where I'm now typing this out.

In this way, I wish that I had been a bit quicker in writing this so that I could have shown these special people how I took what they gave me and made something out of it.

As a final thanks, I'd like to thank you, the readers, for allowing me to share with you my snapshot of an era in Japanese cinema that has passed into history. I hope it's given you an understanding of the ins and outs, the seemingly endless days, and the general sense of controlled madness that defined the Godzilla production. It's an experience I'll always cherish, and I'm equally grateful for the opportunity to have shared it with you.

Otsukare-sama deshita and thanks for letting me peel back the kaiju curtain!

www.ingramcontent.com/pod-product-compliance
Lightning Source LLC
Chambersburg PA
CBHW080234270326

41926CB00020B/4239